A New World of Law?

BY THE SAME AUTHOR

The Common Law of Mankind (1958)
The World Beyond the Charter (1968)
Law, Freedom and Welfare (1963)
Law in the World Community (1967)
The Law of International Institutions
  The Prospects of International Adjudication (1964)
  International Immunities (1961)
  The Proper Law of International Organisations (1962)
The Headquarters of International Institutions (1945)
Human Rights and International Labour Standards (1960)
The International Protection of Trade Union Freedom (1957)
Space Law (1965)

A New World of Law?

A study of the creative imagination in international law

C. Wilfred Jenks,
LL.D.(Cantab.), Hon.LL.D.(Edinburgh),
of Gray's Inn, Barrister-at-Law.

Member of the Institute of International Law,
Member of the International Academy of Comparative Law,
Corresponding Member of the International Academy of Astronautics
Principal Deputy Director-General of the International Labour Office

'International law ought not to be considered as belonging to specialists',

John Westlake, Inaugural Lecture as Whewell Professor, 17 October 1888,
Collected Papers on Public International Law, Cambridge, 1914, p. 412.

Longmans

Longmans, Green & Co Ltd
London and Harlow
Associated companies, branches and representatives
throughout the world

First published 1969

SBN 582·50815·0

Set in 'Monotype' Times New Roman 10 on 12 pt.
and printed by The Camelot Press Ltd.,
London and Southampton

For Jane

Contents

Preface xi

I Law and human destiny

1 The vocation of our age 3
2 The world is one 5
3 The challenge to legal scholarship 13
4 The creative spirit 21

II The goals of creative effort

5 Peace with justice 27

1 The threat or use of force 28
2 Self-defence 29
3 Internal war and escalation 30
4 Mercenaries 31
5 Armament 32
6 Peacekeeping forces 36
7 Collective security and alignment 39
8 Settlement of disputes 42

6 The dignity of man 43

1 Political freedom 46
2 Civil liberties 47
3 Social justice 53
4 Freedom of the mind 54
5 Fullness of opportunity 56

7 Economic stability and growth 58

1 Monetary policy 58
2 Trade 62
3 Commodity policy 67
4 Restrictive business practices 68
5 Investment 70

6 Development aid 75
7 Know-how 78
8 Industrial development 79
9 Shipping 79
10 Insurance 81
11 Rural development, agriculture, and food production and distribution 82
12 Migration, refugees, and travel 84
13 Population 87
14 Wealth and welfare 90

8 Science and technological progress 92

1 Nuclear energy 93
2 Space 95
3 The ocean depths 98
4 The polar regions 101
5 The centre of the earth 102
6 Environmental changes 103
7 Pollution 104
8 Noise and sonic boom 106
9 Electronics and cybernetics 108
10 Molecular biology and mind control? 111
11 Common standards and common services 112
12 Science in the service of man 113

III The law in motion

9 The living law 123

1 The concept of law 124
2 Sovereignty 130
3 Custom 137
4 General principles of law 148
5 Equity 153
6 International public policy 155
7 The judicial process 156
8 Codification 162

10 Towards the parliament of man 166

1 Legislation as a creative force 166
2 The law of treaties 168
Invalidity of treaties procured by the threat or use of force 169
Jus cogens 169

Treaties and other rules of international law 170
Agreements with subjects of international law other than states 171
Treaties adopted within international organisations 171
Conclusion of treaties 172
Reservations 173
Amendment and modification of treaties 173
Invalidity, termination and suspension of the operation of treaties 173
3 Law-making treaties 175
Concept and development of the law-making treaty 175
Defective technique of law-making treaties 176
Termination of law-making treaties 179
Modification of law-making treaties 181
An international legislative drafting bureau? 184
4 Quasi-legislation: functional 186
I.L.O. 186
F.A.O. 189
UNESCO 190
W.H.O. 190
I.C.A.O. 192
I.M.C.O. 194
U.P.U., I.T.U. and W.M.O. 195
Fund 196
World Bank Group 197
I.A.E.A. 198
GATT 200
5 Quasi-legislation: the General Assembly 200
Matters within the authority of the General Assembly 201
Agencies established by the General Assembly 202
Recommendations with legislative effect 203
Declarations of the General Assembly 203
Legislation by consensus 205
6 The Security Council 211
Peace and security 211
Vested rights 213
7 The interparliamentary approach 214
8 The ultimate problem 217

11 The architecture of the world community 219

1 The universal community 221

2 The community as an organism 226
3 The implied powers of the community 231
4 The whole and the parts 233
5 Universal and regional action 239
6 Due process and orderly procedure 244
7 The processes of community decision 247
8 The public service of mankind 249
9 The sinews of peace 251
10 The legal régime of world services 258
11 The effectiveness of community decisions 264
12 Law and institutional development 265

IV Creative scholarship and the law

12 Orthodoxy and vision 271

13 Law and other studies 273

14 Logic, experience and intuition 282

1 Logic and experience 282
2 Intuition and public policy 284
3 Precedent and inventiveness 285

15 Doubt, chance and mutability 287

1 Uncertainty in the new jurisprudence 287
2 Uncertainty in the law of nations 288

16 Reason and morality 291

1 Magnanimity and generosity 292
2 The basic elements of world political morality 292
The unity of mankind 293
The immorality of arbitrary force 294
Sovereignty limited by law 295
Third-party judgment 295
Good faith 296
Fair play 296
Mutual aid 297
Human dignity 298
3 The ultimate values of international jurisprudence 299

Bibliography 301

Index 327

Preface

This volume is an attempt to express the frame of mind which I believe must inspire and guide those who seek to make international law more effective to do the world's work by achieving in our time a breakthrough towards the creation of a new world of law comparable to the successive scientific and technological breakthroughs which have so completely transformed the everyday life of society.

This frame of mind is primarily the outcome of thirty-seven years of practical experience as an international civil servant in attempting so to develop international law and international organisation that they reinforce each other in meeting human need in a world of dynamic growth and constant change.

The challenge to reduce to writing what would otherwise have remained an instinctive but largely unavowed philosophy of practical action I owe to the invitation of the Yale Law School to deliver the Storrs Lectures on Jurisprudence for 1965. The present volume has grown out of those lectures as delivered on 12, 13, 14 and 15 October 1965, but elaborates in much greater detail an approach which I then sketched only in the broadest outline.

For the stimulus afforded by the invitation to deliver the Storrs Lectures I owe a special debt of gratitude to Professor Eugene Rostow who, as Dean of the Yale Law School at the time, extended the original invitation, Dean Louis Pollak, Dean when the lectures were delivered, and Professor Myres McDougal, whose personal friendship I have enjoyed and valued for a quarter of a century. I can only hope that what has now grown out of their invitation may assist in strengthening the indispensable bridge between scholarship and action without which we cannot hope to resolve the problems which beset us. Whether we or those who follow us succeed in establishing a new world of law will depend on many factors, not all of them within the control of the wisest statesmanship or the subtlest scholarship, but will be significantly affected by the measure in which we allow the creative imagination to be the shaping spirit of the common law of mankind.

C. Wilfred Jenks

23 April 1968

part I

Law and human destiny

1

The vocation of our age

We are living in a wholly new world, a newer world than any of our conflicting ideologies has sufficiently appreciated; a world in which politics, strategy, economics, science and technology, and not least the range and intensity of human aspirations, have been transformed within our lifetimes; a world in which change at an ever-accelerating rate has become the status quo. In this new world man must refind his true vocation.

The vocation of man in our age is to secure a mastery of his own destiny comparable to the mastery which he has secured over the world of nature. He can secure it only in the same manner, by learning and respecting the laws which govern the life of society no less than the world of nature. If we fulfil this vocation, the prospects before mankind are infinite. If we fail to fulfil it, civilisation as we have known it has run its course. In political terms, the essence of this vocation is to develop a world community in which men of varied races, cultures and ideologies can live together in peace and freedom on a shrinking planet. We must develop the 'laws' which are the natural order of society into a 'law' which is the accepted basis of its orderly government.

Human freedom in political society presupposes law. The development of a world community therefore poses acutely the question of the role of law in world affairs. Can law play a part in promoting the unity, freedom and welfare of mankind in the nuclear age comparable to that which it plays in securing freedom and good government within a well-ordered state? How effective a contribution can law make to securing peace with justice, protecting the dignity of man, promoting economic stability and growth, and ensuring that scientific and technological progress serves the common interest and does not enslave mankind? Is law in the service of mankind or is it one of the inherited inhibitions from which he is seeking to win his freedom? If the law fails us in these high matters, can there be a world community of peace and freedom? The answer to this last question is clearly no. Without a new world of law there can be no world community.

The consequences are far-reaching. They involve a fundamental revaluation of the place and status of international law in political and social studies and action. The future of international law has become much too big an issue to remain the exclusive concern of international lawyers or even of the legal profession at large. The development of an effective common law of mankind has become a challenge to every thinking citizen concerned with the future of freedom in the world community. It involves the whole future of man.

How much the law can contribute to the growth of world community depends partly on how much statesmen and diplomats, politicians and peoples, expect from it and will allow it to contribute, partly on how the legal mind itself responds to the task. The goals which statesmanship should set for creative effort and the spirit in which legal scholarship should seek to attain these goals are not separate questions which statesmen and scholars should deal with separately. The challenge to statesmanship poses the largest questions of contemporary international policy; the challenge to scholarship poses fundamental questions for the general theory of international law and the science of jurisprudence in general; these questions affect each other decisively and arise in a context and with an urgency which is wholly new.

2

The world is one

During the last century there have been fundamental changes in the sociological foundations of international law. Only in the last twenty years has the full impact of these changes begun to be apparent. There has not yet been time for inherited modes of thought to readjust themselves to the new conditions. If we wish to make a reasonable estimate of the current problems and prospects of international law, we must first attempt to grasp and measure the significance of these fundamental changes in the sociological foundations of the law.

The world has become one. This may be the most controversial but it is also the fundamental point, and most of the controversy arises from a misunderstanding of what is meant when it is said that the world has become one.

This one world no longer accepts the supremacy of any of its parts over the whole or any other part.

In this one world, any war or threat of war has become an immediate danger of overwhelming catastrophe for the whole world.

In this one world, respect for the dignity and worth of the human person has come to be widely accepted as the foundation of fundamental and inalienable human rights.

This one world recognises a common responsibility for the common welfare, among as within nations.

This one world needs a common discipline to ensure that advanced science and technology serve man and do not destroy him.

This one world is in process of organising itself by conscious effort as a world community.

The implications of these changes are not accepted in the same measure everywhere or recognised in full anywhere, but the perspective in which international lawyers must approach their task has wholly changed during the brief span of years since the Second World War.

All of these points require some fuller elaboration.

The world has become one in a sense in which it has never been so before. This oneness of the world does not presuppose or imply any unity of purpose, ideology or interest, or any proved capacity for common action among the conflicting forces which are struggling for mastery or self-assertion. It consists essentially of the immediate sensitivity at all times of all the leading centres of power and decision in the world to happenings in all its parts. In brief, the world has become a unit by reason of the growing intensity of the struggles which divide it no less than the growing intimacy of the bonds which unite it. If I may use Harold Lasswell's terminology, the world, without having become one as a 'sentimental area', or having yet become one as an 'organisation area', has become irrevocably 'one inclusive activity area'.[1]

The interplay of political and military rivalry and cultural and commercial intercourse between different civilisations and continents can be traced through most of recorded history, but this interplay remained intermittent until the maritime discoveries of the fifteenth and sixteenth centuries inaugurated the age of western supremacy. Only with the industrial revolutions of the eighteenth and nineteenth centuries did the economic interdependence of nations begin to foreshadow its contemporary importance. World politics remained until the dawn of the twentieth century essentially a projection over a wider area of the interplay of the interests and policies of the major European powers. Only in our own time have the first world wars, and the first world economic depression, brought 'untold sorrow to mankind' on a global scale. The whole process has been immensely accelerated in recent years. Aviation (especially since the coming of the jet and the imminence of supersonic transport), telecommunication (especially with the new volume and dependability of communication made possible by satellites), and mass communications have knit the world together for good and ill in a manner previously inconceivable. To know within minutes what is happening at the ends of earth has lost the magic of a miracle and come to be taken as a matter of course. To travel regularly in every continent without ever being out of touch with one's home for more than a few hours has become a common pattern of life for twentieth-century man.

The pattern affects every phase of modern life. Political forces interact upon each other throughout the world. Ideological conflict overleaps all frontiers. Strategy has become global. In industry and commerce, transport and finance, the organisational structure of economic life has become international to the point at which it eludes any possibility of effective national control. Science, though constricted by security controls, owns no instinctive allegiance to anything but the freedom of the mind.

In this one world, the power structure on which international relations

---

[1] *World Politics and Personal Insecurity*, pp. 8 and 9.

have rested for centuries has collapsed. In these circumstances, international law can no longer remain the law of a loosely-knit society regulating the peripheral contacts with each other of sovereign states. It has not in fact done so. Society has become too closely knit for the law to be effective on such a basis. The paradoxical result is that the law has become simultaneously far less and far more effective. The traditional authority of the law has been weakened and its restraining influence upon power has become more precarious at precisely the time when it is rapidly evolving into the common law of mankind.

This one world no longer accepts the supremacy of any of its parts over the whole or any other part. The change is more fundamental than any particular redistribution among countries or continents of political power or influence. The dissolution of the Hapsburg and Ottoman empires in 1918, the subsequent collapse of the European balance of power, the failure of the Axis and the Greater East Asia Co-Prosperity Sphere, the revolt against European supremacy of the non-European world, the brief unchallenged heyday enjoyed by the U.S.A. and the U.S.S.R. during the immediately postwar period, have all been but passing phases in a process of fundamental change, the persistent tendency of which is a wider distribution rather than a greater centralisation of political authority. The military predominance of the nuclear powers has obscured the significance of this tendency. The tendency is nevertheless persistent and fundamental. As the nuclear powers have neutralised each other by the balance of terror and have tended to be paralysed by the impossibility of measuring or circumscribing the consequences of any unrestrained recourse to their unprecedented overkill capacity, their military strength has been discounted in the assessment of authority and influence in everyday international relations. How far there will be in the future great powers, middle powers and lesser powers, who they will be and what their mutual relations will be, and how the structure of world organisation can be accommodated to the nature of their relations to each other remain unpredictable, but it is unlikely that the political structure of the world will ever again be built around the mutual relations of a small number of great powers. A pattern which has run through much of history since the rivalries of Assyria and Egypt is being superseded by the relentless pressures of a world in which the Wilsonian call for self-determination has echoed through half a century to the ends of the earth. No one who has travelled widely in recent years in Europe, Asia, Africa and Latin America can doubt this. Self-determination will outlive any and every grand alliance. Woodrow Wilson's vision of the basis of world community will ultimately survive that of Franklin Roosevelt.

In this one world any war or threat of war has become not merely, in the language of the Covenant of the League of Nations, 'a matter of concern to the whole League' but a danger so imminent and with potential consequences so catastrophic that it not only justifies but requires the immediate intervention of the community to restrain the freedom of action of the individual state. The threat to the future of society represented by war has not merely grown in scale; it has changed in nature. Throughout history war has distorted, disrupted and destroyed civilisations; but civilisation has survived. The progress of man has been interrupted and deflected, but it has continued. Nuclear weapons and long-range delivery systems have created a wholly new situation. A single nuclear submarine can deliver from an unknown point beneath the sea to any target in the world missiles with greater destructive power than all the armament of both sides in both world wars. Time has become the essence of military operations and preparedness to an extent which eliminates any real element of reflection from the strategy and tactics of self-defence and counter-attack. Second-strike capability in nuclear war presupposes existing and not merely latent military strength; it depends primarily on the dispersion of forces available for immediate retaliation and can no longer be provided by the gradual mobilisation during years of endurance of previously untapped civilian resources. The dangers of escalation have become formidable. The distinction between internal and international conflict has become imperceptible. Civil strife may be as fraught with danger to the world as a whole as overt aggression. The role of mercenaries in certain developing countries has become reminiscent of the anarchy of the least settled centuries of the past.

In this one world respect for the dignity and worth of the human person has come to be widely accepted as the foundation of fundamental and inalienable human rights. The promotion and protection of these rights is now acknowledged to transcend the domestic jurisdiction of States. The Charter of the United Nations embodies a pledge by all members to take joint and separate action in cooperation with the Organisation to promote universal respect for, and observance of, human rights and fundamental freedoms for all without distinction as to race, sex, language or religion.[1] The Universal Declaration of Human Rights proclaims a comprehensive series of principles as a common standard for all peoples and all nations. The United Nations Covenants on Civil and Political Rights and on Economic, Social and Cultural Rights will, as they are ratified, have the effect of transforming these

---

[1] Articles 55 and 56.

principles from a standard of conduct into firm treaty obligations. The Charter, the Universal Declaration and the Covenants change fundamentally the status of human rights in international law. The concept of an international obligation to respect human rights is admittedly not a novelty. Among its early champions was Francisco de Vittoria. We can detect an anticipation of it in the religious settlement of the Peace of Westphalia. It owes much to Wilberforce and the English anti-slavery movement. It was a major element in the 'eastern question' which preoccupied nineteenth-century European diplomacy. Gladstone, protesting against the Armenian massacres, made it the leading issue of an election campaign. Towards the end of the century it was a significant influence upon the Congo Basin Treaties. In the League of Nations it found expression in the mandates system and the minorities treaties. The International Labour Organisation gave a new scope and vitality to the concept from 1919 onwards. But until the Second World War international action to promote and protect human rights was regarded as an exceptional measure to be invoked only in the most unusual circumstances. 'In principle' such matters were within the 'reserved domain' of matters 'exclusively within the domestic jurisdiction' of states. Nor was this regarded as one of the crucial weaknesses of the international legal system. The idea of progress had increasingly dominated political thought from the seventeenth century until the catastrophe of 1914. From the eighteenth century onwards it had become closely associated with the ideas of the rights of man and the perfectability of human society.[1] The assumption was that the ordinary course of human progress would increasingly establish and guarantee the rights of man. This illusion was shattered by the inter-war period and the events culminating in the Second World War. The reaction against Nazi barbarism gave altogether new breadth and vigour to the movement for the international protection of the rights of man. While much of the original impetus to more effective action was lost without achieving more than a fraction of what had been hoped from it, enough was achieved to set a new course for future effort. The doubling of the membership of the international community in recent years has given a new emphasis and urgency to the problem. In many of the new States the future of civil liberties and of human rights generally is far from assured, and the existence of international obligations and standards in the matter may be of decisive importance. This is sufficiently widely recognised to have created a degree of international concern with the promotion and protection of human rights previously inconceivable.

---

[1] Bury, J. B., *The Idea of Progress*.

Ignorance and hunger, disease and want, are no longer accepted as the inevitable lot of the vast majority of mankind. The change of outlook which has occurred goes beyond a change of economic and social philosophy. It has crystallised into broad and far-reaching legal obligations embodied in the Charter of the United Nations and spelled out in greater detail in innumerable other international instruments. All the members of the United Nations have pledged themselves to take joint and separate action in cooperation with the Organisation to promote higher standards of living, full employment and conditions of economic and social progress and development. This implies as revolutionary a change in the scope and content of international law as the concept of the welfare state has implied in municipal legal systems. Nor are these obligations nominal. In retrospect, lend-lease and the broader policies of mutual aid into which it developed were a turning-point in the history of the world. There had been many earlier cases in which, from generosity or policy, one State came to the succour of another; but only since the Second World War has mutual aid to bridge the gap between affluence and lack of opportunity become an accepted commonplace of international policy. Originating as mutual aid in bearing the burdens and repairing the ravages of war, it has developed into a new philosophy of international economic life comparable to the responsibility for the promotion of the general welfare vested in the federal government by the Constitution of the United States. The Charter formulates the obligation in the language of 1945; as interpreted with general consent at the United Nations Trade and Development Conference of 1964, its implications in respect of currency, trade, commodity policy, investment, industrial development, shipping, insurance, transfer of know-how, and other matters are considerably more far-reaching than the draftsmen of the Charter would have envisaged. However true it may be that the gap between affluence and want is continuing to grow, a wholly new philosophy of a common responsibility for the common welfare has won general acceptance; the outstanding questions, which are grave and many, concern the application, not the validity, of this philosophy.

This one world needs a common discipline to ensure that advanced science and technology serve man and do not destroy him. When man can exploit for good or ill the energies released by fundamental changes in the constitution of matter and can telecommand scientific apparatus at a distance of 300 million miles from the earth, the problem of controlling scientific and technological development in the public interest assumes a world-wide character. Nothing on a smaller scale can hope to be effective. The Charter was signed six weeks before Hiroshima and did not anticipate the new problems of the nuclear and space age. Since that time they have pressed ever more insistently upon us. The underlying concept of the Acheson–Lilienthal–Baruch plan of 1946 that 'the development and use of atomic energy are not essentially matters of domestic concern of the individual nations, but rather have predominantly international implications and repercussions' did not meet with general acceptance at that time, but subsequent international action relating to atomic energy has been a process of groping towards the fuller acceptance of this principle. In respect of outer space we have made a more promising start. The Declaration of Legal Principles Governing the Activities of States in the Exploration and Use of Outer Space, adopted by the General Assembly of the United Nations on 13 December 1963, recognises 'the common interest of all mankind in the progress of the exploration and use of space for peaceful purposes' and deduces from this common interest the basic principles which should guide States in their space activities. The Treaty on Principles Governing the Activities of States in the Exploration and Use of Outer Space, including the Moon and Other Celestial Bodies, of 27 January 1967, elaborates and expands these principles and gives them the force of treaty obligations. In both fields it remains to translate principles into solid political realities. Nuclear energy and space are the most dramatic illustrations of the need to deal with the impact of science and technology on human destiny on a world-wide basis; but the problem is a much broader one and includes all the manifold ramifications, over the whole range of current scientific and technological development, of the determination of the role of law in man's control of, and adaptation to, his changing natural environment.

The concept of 'one world' has inspired the attempt to give institutional form to a nascent world community. We are still groping and stumbling in the matter. The League of Nations remained a league, too readily if unfairly regarded as an alliance of the haves against the have-nots, and this was a major element in its failure. The United Nations remains disunited, with a quarter of mankind still excluded as a matter of policy from its effective membership. Until we accept, and give effective institutional expression to, the concept of a world community universal in its membership, with no exclusion, expulsion or withdrawal of members, we will be unable to grapple effectively with the most pressing of the major problems which confront us – the problem of peace, the problem of armament, the problem of the impact of science and technology. Until we so organise the world community that it is an effective instrument for the responsible pursuit of the common welfare, the have and have-not business in the much graver form which it has now assumed will continue to bedevil us. Successive crises in the United

Nations have thrown into dramatically sharp relief the problem of giving lasting institutional form to the oneness and indivisibility of the world and the mutual interdependence of all mankind for peace, freedom and welfare.

3

The challenge to legal scholarship

The magnitude of the changes which have transformed world society has had a complex impact on international law. There has been more growth and change in international law during the last half-century than at any previous time in history; the transformation of society has begun to be reflected in the transformation of the law. The gap between life and the law has nevertheless widened; the scale and rate of growth and change in world society have far outrun the adaptation of the law to the changes in society. Both the widened gap between life and the law and the rate of change in the law itself have created a widespread *malaise* in the law. 'Law is happiest when dealing with a static environment and for that reason is apt to assume that the environment is static.'[1] When any such assumption is clearly untenable the law loses the self-assurance which contributes so much to its authority. Legal scholarship finds itself confronted with a challenge which involves the fundamentals of its art. The challenge to legal scholarship of this post-capitalist, post-Marxist, post-colonialist – but not yet, alas, post-nationalist or even post-militarist – world involves fundamental questions concerning the nature of law in the world community, the relevance of law to the major concerns of the world community, and the capacity of the law to grow and change with the growth and needs of the community.

We have been told that 'the law of nations is but private law "writ large" '. The phrase comes not from Lauterpacht[2] but from Holland,[3] who also told us that international law is the 'vanishing-point of jurisprudence'.[4] The life of the law in international relations has been a constant battle-ground between these two conceptions, the one holding that the relations of states are subject to the same moral and legal principles as those of individuals, the other that the normal rules of law and

---

[1] McIver, R. M., *The Modern State*, p. 261.

[2] Who quotes it on the title page of *Private Law Sources and Analogies of International Law*, of which the concept expressed by the phrase is the theme.

[3] Holland, T. E. *Studies in International Law*, p. 152.

[4] Holland, T. E., *The Elements of Jurisprudence*, p. 392.

morality cannot be invoked against the higher interests of the state. The controversy runs back through the ages, and has never been more vigorous than today. It constitutes a major challenge to present-day scholarship in international law. The controversy merges into the debate regarding the relevance of law to the major concerns of the world community, in which one school of thought denies that the vital interests of peoples can be governed by the rule of law while the other contends that only by the rule of law can they be protected and preserved. Both of these questions resolve themselves into that of the capacity of the law to grow and change with the growth and needs of the community.

The capacity of the law for growth and change depends on three main factors, the vitality of the law as a body of living principle responsive to changing need, the adequacy of international legislative procedures and techniques, and the extent to which developments in the law are matched by adequate institutional arrangements. The vitality of the law, vigour in legislative action, and vision in institutional development all presuppose a high degree of creative imagination guided by enlightened statesmanship and disciplined by practical wisdom and skill. What is the scope for creative imagination in a normative discipline such as the law? An authority no less gifted than Maitland with creative insight into the processes of legal and institutional development warned us with his habitual wisdom that 'a lawyer must be orthodox, otherwise he is no lawyer'.[1] Orthodoxy in the law is more than a mantle of respectability. It is the discipline of consistency without which law ceases to be a dependable rule of conduct and loses the fundamental quality of binding obligation. How then are we to reconcile the obligation of orthodoxy without which law becomes politics with the creative purpose and creative vision necessary to bring politics within the rule of law?

That we should live in a cynical age despite unparalleled opportunities for creative action is the most startling paradox, and may yet be the final tragedy, of our time. Cynicism and sophistry are as great a danger to society today as they were in the time of Socrates and Plato, but on a wholly new scale. The stake is no longer the future of Athens but the future of man.

A generation ago the literature of international law was preponderantly a literature of hope. William Edward Hall had written in 1889: 'I therefore look forward with much misgiving to the manner in which the next great war will be waged, but with no misgiving at all to the character of the rules which will be acknowledged ten years after its termination, by comparison with the rules now considered to exist'.[2] In the

---

[1] *Collected Papers*, Vol. I, p. 491.

[2] *International Law*, Preface.

1920s Hall's view was seen in retrospect as a triumphant prophecy. The outstanding figures of those days, men of the stamp of Max Huber, Nicolas Politis, Georges Scelle, Hans Kelsen, Charles De Visscher, Henri Rolin, Hans Wehberg, Cornelius van Vollenhoven, Sir John Fischer Williams, J. L. Brierly, Arnold McNair, Manley O. Hudson, Edwin Dickinson, Philip Jessup, Hersch Lauterpacht, held divergent views on many questions, but they shared a common faith in a new world of law. Their views on the interplay of law and politics, the scope of justiciability and similar matters, covered a wide spectrum; their temperamental preferences for pragmatism or principle, caution or boldness, varied widely; they drew in different degrees on the analytical, historical and sociological schools of legal thought: but they were bred in a common tradition and spoke with a common voice on fundamentals; they had evolved a new orthodoxy of creative purpose and vision which acknowledged the overriding obligation of the present to the future rather than the past.

We live today in a more complex world, in which the combined impact of the Fascist reaction, the Nazi terror and Stalinism, the Second World War, social revolution and cultural change in varying degrees almost everywhere, the cold war, decolonisation, and conflict and uncertainty in South-east Asia, the Middle East and Africa, have tended to shatter established intellectual values.

Among the most responsible scholars we continue to find a firm insistence that while 'a realistic study of law must . . . see law in relation to its institutional support'[1] the international community is going through a period of crisis in which 'the task of international lawyers and statesmen alike is to weed, to prune, to create – not to cling to outmoded solutions of another era and bemoan the passing of international law as they do so';[2] the quotation is from a recent work by two joint authors, one of whom has since served as Attorney-General and Under-Secretary of State of the United States. There have been notable pleas for an international law of human dignity[3] and for a recognition of the potential contribution to the avoidance of major war of law and morality, 'our two strongest cultural traditions of restraint';[4] 'stable patterns of restraint', it has been wisely said, 'depend upon the consistent relevance of restraining norms of law and morality'[5] and 'the moral foundations

[1] Kaplan, Morton A. and Katzenbach, Nicholas de B., *The Political Foundations of International Law*, p. 6.

[2] Ibid., p. 29.

[3] McDougal, Myres S. and Associates, *Studies in World Public Order*.

[4] Falk, Richard A., *Law Morality and War in the Contemporary World*, p. viii.

[5] Ibid., p. 12.

of international law' have an important place among our resources for resisting totalitarianism and reducing the prospect of nuclear war.[1] We have been invited to agree that 'the normative structure of the United Nations – in particular as expressed in the principles and purposes of the Charter – constitutes a significant element in the decisions of its political organs and in the achievement of its main objectives'.[2] We are assured that 'the changing structure of contemporary international relations is reflected in a more diversified pattern of modern international law' which is 'becoming a more and more complex and many-sided subject' the scope of which 'is bound to expand as the organisation of mankind, on a universal or regional basis, increases'.[3] We are told that 'the prime task of the international lawyer today in a world community undergoing continuing revolution' is 'one of building a new system of world public order with an ideological basis broad enough to derive support from, and to encompass, all the main competing social and economic systems of the present day' and 'of developing, in the international arena, that necessary symbiosis between positive law and social change that we regard as axiomatic for our own national law system in our own national society'.[4] We are summoned to play our part in meeting the demand for 'an international law that will promote the welfare of all' in an international community which 'is not merely one of peace' but 'a welfare community concerned with the welfare of every one of its members'.[5] These are restrained and balanced views, conscious of the barriers to progress and the dangers which confront us, but sustained by a continued faith in the future of man. Acknowledging that ' "realists" who do not recognise the uses and the force of the law are not realistic' and that ' "idealists" who do not recognise the law's limitations are largely irrelevant in the world that is', this general approach sees progress towards a welfare society as depending on 'maintaining the order we have, through the law there is' and on 'nations paying more, not less, attention to law, extending its domain, and sacrificing some, often superficial, immediate interest for law's longer, deeper promises'.[6]

There nevertheless continues to be a persistent denigration of the present effectiveness and potentialities of international law by writers

---

[1] Ibid., p. 48.

[2] Schachter, Oscar, 'The Relation of Law, Politics and Action in the United Nations', *Recueil des Cours de l'Académie de Droit international*, pp. 169–252.

[3] Friedmann, Wolfgang, *The Changing Structure of International Law*, pp. 367–368.

[4] McWhinney, Edward, *International Law and World Revolution*, pp. 11–12.

[5] Röling, B. V. A., *International Law in an Expanded World*, p. 83.

[6] Henkin, Louis, *How Nations Behave: Law and Foreign Policy*, pp. 269–270.

who, while sometimes wrapping themselves in the mantle of the law, claim an outstanding measure of intellectual integrity and political foresight as they proclaim any belief that law and morality can be major factors in world affairs to be a snare and a delusion. We are advised that the Charter of the United Nations rejects 'the principle hitherto accepted in Western Europe, and most clearly expressed in the Constitution of the United States, that the function of law is to control the exercise of power'[1] and is based on the totalitarian concept 'that law is merely the instrument or agency through which those who hold the supreme power make known their will'.[2] For others this is the chief virtue of the Charter. We are invited to find the chief hope for the future in the recognition by the Great Powers of the lesson of history that they have 'a common responsibility for an international order' to which they all belong,[3] but the invitation is accompanied by an intimation that we should take little stock in attempts to institutionalise this notion; we are assured on historical grounds, with no indication that the proposition has been rejected as a proposition of law by the International Court, that 'obligations deriving from a State's consent do not impair its sovereignty' since 'what a sovereign State has conceded a sovereign State can, if it wishes, revoke';[4] the 'United Nations would therefore be wise to recognise that its only practicable role – both when disagreements between the Great Powers have diminished and while the Great Powers remain seriously divided – is that of an accessory to their diplomacy, a moral check upon its excesses and a physical and procedural assistant in its processes'.[5] It is urged upon us that 'the mark of a genuine concern for the observation of the legal principle in the affairs of nations is a recognition of the realistic limits beyond which the principle cannot be pressed'.[6] 'The phrase "world community" ', we are informed, 'is political and cultural nonsense.'[7] We are warned that 'programmes for establishment of the rule of law among nations can offer little relief to remove fears of war' and that they may 'do very real disservice to the cause of conflict management'.[8] We are told that 'the international sphere, not being one where any over-all constitutional authority reigns, is not in principle a realm of law';[9] that the law of nations, before and after Grotius, 'was less a code of rules for observation than a supply of materials from

---

[1] Smith, H. A., *The Crisis in the Law of Nations*, p. 88.

[2] Ibid., p. 101. [3] Hinsley, F. H., *Power and the Pursuit of Peace*, p. 9.

[4] Ibid., p. 329. [5] Ibid., p. 345.

[6] Kennan, George, *Realities of American Foreign Policy*, p. 39.

[7] Shklar, Judith, *Legalism*, p. 189. [8] Stone, Julius, *Quest for Survival*, p. 8.

[9] Corbett, Percy E., *Law in Diplomacy*, p. viii.

which a clothing of legitimacy could be fashioned for state claim's;[1] that 'in so far as law operates among states, it is a law of excessive flexibility . . . at the service of the subjectively defined interest of each state';[2] and that 'the lawyer's craft can never supply the wanting social and political basis for an effective legal system'.[3] These illustrations of injunctions to circumscribe and distrust the rule of law come not from thinkers bred in the Prussian tradition, the Marxist dialectic, or the antipathy to legal restraint of revolutionary movements in developing countries, but from widely-respected British, American, Australian and Canadian writers who seek to mould the minds of coming generations and to influence the policies of governments. The immediate issue which they raise is not whether there can be a common law of mankind in a divided world[4] but whether there still remains within the common law tradition the moral and intellectual vitality and political and juridical validity without which that tradition cannot continue to play a major part in evolving a wider synthesis in a world with new problems and a new distribution and balance of political and intellectual forces. A survey of the current literature of international law in other languages would show, in degrees varying for different languages and cultures, similar conflicts of view posing similar dilemmas, but the common lawyer will do well to consider first whether he is discharging adequately his own intellectual responsibilities. These counsels of despair represent a challenge which contemporary international lawyers bred in the common law tradition must accept and rout if they are to play their part in ensuring that the hopes of a new world of law held forth by responsible statesmen become a reality. Hugo Grotius was confronted with a similar challenge.

The protagonists of these views claim, of course, that only by dismissing what they regard as current illusions can real progress be made. Their fundamental mistake is to overestimate the possibility and prospects of a wholly new approach which nothing less than some unspeakable catastrophe seems likely to make practicable, and to underestimate what resolution and patience can achieve by what Secretary of State Dean Rusk has called 'the dramatic progress that shapes and is being shaped by expanding international law'.[5] Seeking to destroy illusions in order that we may build more solidly, they in fact destroy the

---

[1] Ibid., p. 9. [2] Ibid., pp. 271–272. [3] Ibid., p. 273.

[4] Jenks, C. Wilfred, *The Common Law of Mankind*; and see the discussion of objections to the basic thesis of *The Common Law of Mankind* in Larson, Jenks and Others, *Sovereignty Within the Law*, pp. 8–28.

[5] 'The Control of Force in International Relations', *The Department of State Bulletin*, Vol. LII, No. 1350 (1965), 699.

only momentum with which we can hope to build. The processes of growth and change in the law by evolutionary methods are gradual but relentless; as Cardozo expressed it 'they have behind them the power and the pressure of the moving glacier'.[1]

It is a curious paradox that the contemporary arraignment of alleged naïve day-dreaming by international lawyers comes primarily from the academic world. With rare exceptions, the most vigorous spokesmen of this school of thought are writers with little or no practical experience of world affairs or refugees from the great world to a more cloistered life. A substantial part of their work illustrates the danger pointed out by Philip Jessup[2] that our thinking may become frozen by conceptual limitations of the potentialities of international law which are of our own creation; such, for instance, 'are the theories which pronounce, for example, that international law cannot confer rights or impose duties directly on an individual because, says Theory, the individual is not a subject but an object of international law'.[3] Among practical men, even those who, like Abram Chayes, hold that 'most great disputes between States, even when they involve important legal elements, are not justiciable',[4] concede that since nothing important can be done in the international sphere 'without the fairly willing co-operation of many of the nations with whom we inhabit the world' and such cooperation depends on 'political assent to our action', 'the strength of the legal position will be an element in mobilising international assent'[5] and an appeal to law is therefore 'almost always an element of an appeal for political vindication of action'.[6] As Jean Monnet has said, 'it is only by accepting international codes of behaviour to settle their common problems as they arise that the nations will progressively discover their common interests and outgrow their differences'.[7] International law 'is widely heeded because its breach would incur a reciprocal response'[8] and 'there is a hard core of adherence to international law which continues day in and day out'.[9] Practical men, whether they be statesmen, politicians, diplomats, soldiers, scientists, businessmen, labour leaders, or international

---

[1] *The Nature of the Judicial Process*, p. 13.

[2] *Transnational Law*. [3] Ibid., p. 7.

[4] 'A Common Lawyer Looks at International Law', *Harvard Law Review*, *78* (May 1965, No. 7), p. 1409.

[5] Ibid., p. 1410. [6] Ibid., p. 1413.

[7] Carnegie Endowment for International Peace, *Perspectives on Peace, 1910–1960*, p. 97.

[8] Higgins, Rosalyn, *The Development of International Law Through the Political Organs of the United Nations*, p. 8.

[9] Ibid., p. 7.

officials, are all too conscious that we are confronted with new problems for which no solution can be found in old nostrums. It is among the men of affairs that there is the widest recognition that 'our survival and welfare depends upon the capacities of nations and governing groups to have the courage and imagination to transform the world into a different kind of political structure'.[1] Coupled with this recognition of the need is a widespread faith by those in the closest touch with our unparalleled opportunities and resources that the admitted difficulties of the task are not insuperable.

Whether the response of international lawyers to the calls of statesmanship plays any significant part in fulfilling the vocation of our age in the service of mankind will depend primarily on the vitality of the creative imagination which they bring to this task. The newness of a world in which political, social and technological change interact constantly upon each other, which has so clearly become one world, which no longer accepts the supremacy of any of its parts, in which any war or threat of war has become an immediate danger of overwhelming catastrophe for the whole world, which acknowledges that respect for the rights of man has become a matter of concern to the whole world, which recognises a common responsibility for the common welfare, which accepts the inevitability and desirability of social change, which needs a common discipline to ensure that advanced science and technology serve man and do not destroy him, which is in process of organising itself by conscious effort as a world community and is developing as the law of that community a common law of mankind, constitutes an unprecedented challenge to the creative imagination of international lawyers. It calls for a clarification of fundamental mental attitudes. It presents unparalleled opportunities for giving legal and institutional expression to the political, economic and social aspirations and values of a dynamic society seeking the freedom and welfare of the common man on a global basis. It requires a bold revaluation of the general concept of international law and the traditional techniques and sources of the law. It is in this perspective that we must visualise the goals of creative effort and assess the extent to which the aspirations and priorities of our society find effective expression in the law.

---

[1] Falk, Richard A., *Law, Morality and War in the Contemporary World*, p. 40.

4

The creative spirit

We cannot hope to recast the law to the extent which these fundamental changes which have transformed society require unless we approach the task with three qualities: freshness of mind, earthiness, and a sturdy idealism.

We need a re-adolescence of the mind, inhibited by nothing, convinced that the ultimate is within its grasp, but endowed with the resilience to survive the hard shocks of reality, mellow its vision of the possible, and come to terms with the practicalities of human experience. Recalling that Lord Coke was criticised for 'extravagant and exorbitant opinions' and ordered to expunge 'novelties and errors and offensive conceits' from his reports[1] and that Lord Mansfield was accused of introducing into the law his own 'unsettled notions of equity and substantial justice',[2] we must not be unduly disconcerted by any similar reproaches.

We need the right mix of scholarship and shrewdness, of detachment and experience. 'The pursuit of the legal profession', wrote Mr. Justice Brandeis, 'involves a happy combination of the intellectual with the practical life,' the intellectual tending to 'breadth of view' and the practical to 'that realisation of limitations which are essential to the wise conduct of life'.[3] It must never be said of international law that 'All those who actually live the mysteries of life haven't the time to write, and all those who have the time don't live them.'[4] That has never been the tradition of international lawyers and, if it were to become so, worthwhile scholarship in the field of international law would cease to be possible. In international law the practical touch is the hallmark of creative scholarship. The creative imagination must be no less at home in bricklaying than in grand design.

---

[1] Bowen, Catherine Drinker, *The Lion and the Throne: The Life and Times of Sir Edward Coke*, p. 379.

[2] Fifoot, C. H. S., *Lord Mansfield*, p. 183.

[3] 'The Living Law', reproduced in *The Curse of Bigness*, p. 324.

[4] Kazantzakis, Nikos, *Zorba the Greek*, p. 226.

We need a sturdy idealism. The health and growth of every legal system depends on the vitality of the ideals which sustain it. The practical value of such ideals depends on the extent to which they can be, and are, translated into reality. But without such ideals no rules of law can maintain the coherence and unity of a legal system when subjected to the constant erosion of practical contingencies. Roscoe Pound has stated the essence of the matter with simple cogency:

> A perennial problem of the legal order is to reconcile the need of stability with the inevitableness of change. In practice, this reconciliation is achieved by means of ideals, to which lawmaking and interpretation and judicial application and doctrinal development tend to conform. These ideals give direction to change. They lead to change, but they guide it and, as they are applied to authoritative legal materials shaped by the past, and as the ideals are of necessity largely ideal conceptions of the society and institutions and legal precepts with which lawmaker or judge or jurist is familiar, they tend to maintain stability during change.[1]

Pound was writing of the formative era of American law; his analysis is equally applicable to the present formative era of international law.

The partnership of faith and revolt, reason and passion, patience and enthusiasm implied in these mental attitudes has been throughout history the most dynamic catalyst of social change in human experience. To such partnerships we owe the dominant cultural influences which have inspired and shaped the progress of society, the higher religions, the greater philosophies, the ideals and institutions of political freedom, the principal legal systems, the concept of economic growth, the quest for social justice, the spirit of scientific discovery, the habit of technological change.

Approaching the task of recasting the law in this spirit, what are the goals to which our creative energies should be directed and how are we to imbue with creative purpose the traditional techniques of the law?

The goals of creative effort are defined by the fundamental changes which have occurred in the sociological foundations of the law. The objective is an organised world community dedicated to the freedom and welfare of the common man. The immediate priorities are to secure

---

[1] *The Formative Era of American Law*, p. 13.

peace with justice, to protect human rights, to promote economic stability and growth, and to ensure that the progress of advanced science and technology serves the common interest of mankind. The first task of the creative imagination is to restate these goals in terms which provide a satisfactory framework for the future development of the law in a manner which contributes to achieving them.

Custom, general principles of law, international adjudication, multi-partisan review of policies and claims, the law-making treaty, and institutional development in many forms are all among the potential elements of future growth. The second task of the creative imagination is to maximise the contribution of all these potential elements of growth to the future of freedom under law in the world community. This task calls for a blend of deductive and inductive habits of thought in which principle and practice illuminate and correct each other; this fruitful blend nurtures the intuitive imagination without which the human mind can neither evolve a common understanding with cultures and ideologies alien to its own upbringing nor encompass the great leaps forward in moral judgment, intellectual grasp, and technical proficiency which constitute the progress of civilisation and the distinctive greatness of mankind.

If the creative imagination is to play the decisive part which we have envisaged for it in shaping the future development of the common law of mankind and building the legal structure of the world community, the sources of its fertility and vitality become of crucial importance. How are we to be assured that boldness of intellectual initiative is a creative and not a disruptive force? How are we to satisfy not merely ourselves but the world that bold innovations reflect the real needs and true aspirations of mankind? How are we to give bold innovations the breadth and depth of appeal necessary to ensure their acceptability, their solidity and their permanence? What are the respective roles in creative scholarship of legal and interdisciplinary studies, of logic, experience and intuitions of public policy, of precedent and inventiveness, of reason and morality? The third task of the creative imagination is to provide satisfactory answers to these fundamental questions. As Philip Jessup has said, the contemporary international lawyer has no more pressing duty than the obligation to 'respond to the derogations of the common law practitioner and the political realist and reassure the scientist anxious to have new forces of destruction brought under control'.[1] Let us, in response to this duty, endeavour to explore these

---

[1] *The Use of International Law*, p. 2.

pregnant questions. The spirit of the adventure, for such it is, has been well expressed by Charles E. Wyzanski:

> The law is the instrument by which we keep the avenues open to the adventurous ideas that lie ahead. . . . It is the constant teacher of the importance of giving form and style to ideas of right.[1]

---

[1] Wyzanski, Charles E., Jr., *Whereas – A Judge's Premises*, p. 8.

part II

The goals of creative effort

'The law', Morris Raphael Cohen aptly said, 'is not a homeless wandering ghost. It is a phase of human life located in time and space.'[1] We judge it not by its intellectual perfection or consistency, but by the extent to which it meets our moral standards and practical needs. How effective is the present contribution of the law to peace and justice, the protection of human rights, the promotion of economic stability and growth, and the application of advanced science and technology to the common good? In what degree can the creative imagination of international lawyers, guided by enlightened statesmanship and disciplined by practical wisdom and skill, increase the effectiveness of the law in these vital fields, where the interplay of politics, economics, social policy, science and military strategy is so complex and continuous? Is any hope of playing a useful part in relation to these matters an extravagant fancy remote from the practicalities of world affairs? Or is playing such a part the normal task of the international lawyer in the present-day world, a task in which he can find the fulfilment of his moral nature as well as of his professional skill?

For a synoptic view of this broad ground we must specialise in generalisation and refrain from any attempt to explore so broad an area in depth. In the words of Eugene Rostow, discussing the economic order as a problem of law, while 'a large canvas is always a risk' there are 'advantages in trying to achieve perspective from time to time, even at the expense of detail.'[2]

---

[1] *Reason and Law*, p. 4.

[2] Rostow, Eugene V., *Planning for Freedom*, p. 5.

5

Peace with justice

The supreme challenge to the creative genius of the law is the imperative call to 'save succeeding generations from the scourge of war'.

Fifty years ago every State had an unquestioned sovereign right of resort to war whenever it considered that its honour, interests or policy so required. Men had endeavoured since medieval times to formulate criteria of the justice or injustice of war.[1] There were precedents for concerted political action to avert war and for the settlement of international disputes by arbitration and other peaceful means. There was a limited network of qualified obligations to arbitrate. But the right to resort to war in one's discretion was the acknowledged prerogative of sovereignty. Thus Westlake, the most liberal international lawyer of his time, who described war as 'a piece of savage nature partially reclaimed',[2] conceded as a matter of course that 'for the redress of wrongs or the prosecution of claims, States may appeal to force either by war or by certain measures – reprisals, embargo or pacific blockade – not inconsistent with peace'.[3]

Three giant steps, the Covenant of the League of Nations,[4] the General Treaty for the Renunciation of War,[5] and the Charter of the United Nations,[6] have revolutionised the position. It is now settled law that all states shall refrain in their international relations from the threat or use of force against the territorial integrity or political independence of any state, or in any other manner inconsistent with the purposes of the United Nations. The principle is set forth in the Charter, which

---

[1] Vanderpol, A., *La doctrine scolastique du droit de la guerre*; Wright, Quincy, *A Study of War.*

[2] *International Law,* Part II, p. 3. [3] Ibid., p. 1.

[4] Pollock, Sir Frederick, *The League of Nations*; Fischer Williams, Sir John, *Some Aspects of the Covenant of the League of Nations.*

[5] Miller, David Hunter, *The Peace Pact of Paris*; Shotwell, James T., *War as an Instrument of National Policy*; International Law Association, *Briand Kellogg Pact of Paris: Articles of Interpretation as adopted by the Budapest Conference 1934.*

[6] Goodrich, Leland M. and Hambro, Edvard, *Charter of the United Nations: Commentary and Documents*; Kelsen, Hans, *The Law of the United Nations.*

requires all Members to act in accordance with it, and provides that the Organisation shall ensure that States which are not members also do so. The basic principle which underlay the whole of the law of war and neutrality has thereby been fundamentally changed.

If this boldest of all imaginative innovations in the law is to be materialised from creative vision into tested reality we must resolve a whole series of related problems: the scope of the obligation to refrain from the threat or use of force, the delimitation of the right of self-defence, the avoidance of escalation into war, the legal regulation of armament, the provision of peace-keeping forces appropriate for the varied types of emergency with which they may have to cope, the problem of mutual aid for the maintenance of peace and security conveniently known as collective security, and the problem of the peaceful settlement of disputes.

1. The threat or use of force

Whereas the Covenant had prohibited resort to war in breach of the Covenant, the Charter prohibits the threat or use of force.[1] War is a legal condition and the existence of a state of war which involved questions of intention as well as of fact could, as League experience showed, be debatable. The existence of a threat or use of force is a question of fact. An *animus aggressionis* is no longer required. We could indeed well dispense with the concept of aggression[2] if so many of those who have criticised the concept did not appear to be chiefly concerned to defend and maintain the degree of freedom of action by States which it was designed to condemn. The Charter prohibition of the threat or use of force is qualified, however, by certain words of limitation. It enjoins States to refrain 'in their international relations' from the threat or use of force 'against the territorial integrity or political independence of any State' or 'in any other manner inconsistent with the purposes of the United Nations'. The expression 'in their international relations' was intended to exclude from the prohibition the threat or use of force in the exercise of the authority of a State in territory subject to its jurisdiction; such threat or use may nevertheless create a situation likely to endanger the maintenance of international peace and security which any Member of the United Nations may bring to the attention of the Security Council or the General Assembly. The reference to 'territorial integrity or

---

[1] For a comprehensive study of the whole matter see Brownlie, Ian, *International Law and the Use of Force by States.*

[2] Stone, Julius, *Aggression and World Order.*

political independence' can be so construed as to introduce an element of ambiguity into the obligation but not reasonably so as to substitute a subjective test of intention for the objective test of the nature and effect of the action taken. The only limitation upon the prohibition which can be deduced from the purposes of the United Nations as stated in the Charter results from the fact that one of those purposes is 'to take effective collective measures for the prevention and removal of threats to the peace, and for the suppression of acts of aggression or other breaches of the peace'.[1] There remains an important role for the law to play in preserving the effectiveness of the prohibition against any extensive or unilateral interpretation of this qualifying language.

No less important is the role of the law in determining the consequences of violation of the prohibition. Any threat or use of force in violation of the Charter is an international wrong. It destroys the case of the State seeking by illegal means redress for what might otherwise be a justified grievance. It creates a delictual obligation involving an obligation of reparation. It may involve the criminal responsibility of those participating in the decision for a crime against peace as defined in the Charters of the International Military Tribunals at Nuremburg and Tokyo. All of these matters require further clarification in which the creative imagination must play its part.

2. Self-defence

The creative imagination is no less necessary in the analysis and delimitation of the right of self-defence;[2] it must be equally sensitive to the political, sociological and moral inevitability of self-defence and to the importance of avoiding erosion of the prohibition of the threat or use of force. The general principles governing the right of self-defence admit of little debate. The right, or more properly speaking the privilege, lies against conduct in breach of a duty recognised by international law. It exists only in the absence of alternative means of protection. It can be invoked only against a danger which is serious and actual or imminent. The measures taken must be reasonable, limited to the necessity of protection, and proportionate to the danger. These, which may be regarded as general principles of law, are elements in the position which are conceptually clear, however difficult the questions of judgment involved in their application to particular cases may be. The scope of the right poses larger questions. It clearly includes self-defence for the protection of territorial integrity and political independence; so much

---

[1] Article 1 (1). [2] Bowett, D. W., *Self-Defence in International Law.*

results directly from the terms in which the Charter prohibits the threat or use of force. But political independence is a less well-defined concept, and in particular a more relative concept, than territorial integrity. The extent to which the right of self-defence includes a right of protection over nationals abroad, measures of protection against subversive activities, or measures of retaliation against economic pressure, has been, and in a lesser degree remains, the subject of acute controversy. Whether, and if so in what circumstances, anticipatory self-defence can be justified is a matter of exceptional difficulty. The creative imagination can make a significant contribution to the solution of these problems by distinguishing and elaborating three guiding principles.

The first of these principles is that the right of self-defence is not co-extensive with the wide range of cases in which no effective community action is available to give prompt and reasonable protection of the interests of States. Self-help is not justifiable by a plea of self-defence. There is an overriding public interest in avoiding breaches of the peace in the light of which self-help involves intolerable risks. Injustice, subjectively determined, does not justify the threat or use of force to protect or enforce rights which the community has not yet evolved adequate means of securing.

The second principle is that the world community must recognise the need, and assume the responsibility, for external intervention in cases not covered by the right of self-defence as so defined in which a world interest or the conscience of mankind is involved. The world community cannot tolerate acts of savagery on the ground that its civilised members have renounced the threat and use of force in their international relations. Wherever practicable any such intervention should be undertaken by or on behalf of the United Nations, or through the appropriate regional organisation; whenever any State or group of States is called upon to undertake rescue operations in an emergency it should simultaneously report fully to the United Nations the circumstances and action taken and offer to place the operations under United Nations control.

The third principle is that every act of self-defence, or of emergency intervention on behalf of the world community, is subject to review by the community. The final word rests not with the State acting in self-defence but with the community.

3. Internal war and escalation

The renunciation and restraint of force and collective review of self-defence are further complicated by the erosion of the distinction between international and internal war[1] and the danger of escalation.[2] Internal war has become 'the most prevalent and threatening form of international violence, involving both the principal pathway of aggression and a dangerous breeding-ground for a provocative initiation of an escalatory spiral that has a thermonuclear catastrophe as its upper limit'.[3] The classical rules concerning civil war,[4] based on the principle of non-intervention, have as a practical matter ceased to be an effective protection against external involvement in civil strife. In many quarters the principle itself is now questioned. The way of progress appears to be in a fuller recognition that international law cannot regard its concern with internal war as limited to the recognition of insurgency and belligerency and the definition of their consequences with a view to maintaining in an orderly manner the interests of third States. We are witnessing the emergence of a recognised community responsibility for circumscribing by organised action, including when necessary community intervention, the consequences of civil strife, especially when the scale and nature of the conflict involve, or create the possibility of, interventionary participation by great powers or other major States.[5] The nature and implications of this responsibility, and the techniques whereby it can be made effective, are one of the gravest problems confronting contemporary statesmanship. Rethinking the legal principles involved may be a significant element in its solution.

4. Mercenaries

The crumbling of public order in so many of the new States has given a renewed importance, especially in Africa, to the problem which is currently described as that of mercenaries. Is it permissible for a government, or a political movement seeking to challenge its authority, to engage in its service for military operations foreigners in pursuit of undisciplined adventure or private gain? Is it permissible for an advanced State to allow its citizens to perpetuate anarchy in developing countries by entering into military service there for undisciplined adventure or private gain, whether at the instance of the established

---

[1] Rosenau, James N., *International Aspects of Civil Strife.*

[2] Kahn, Herman, *On Escalation.*

[3] Falk, Richard A., 'The International Law of Internal War' in Rosenau, *International Aspects of Civil Strife* at p. 224.

[4] Castrén, Erik, *Civil War.*

[5] Pinto, Roger, 'Les règles du droit international concernant la guerre civile' in *Recueil de l'Académie de Droit international*, Vol. 114, (1965 (I)), pp. 455–553; Falk, Richard A., *The Vietnam War and International Law.*

government or at that of some movement seeking to challenge its authority? The employment of mercenaries is almost as old as the art of war and is not prohibited by any traditional rule of the law of war; the history of mercenaries includes chapters as varied as the Swiss Guards of the Papacy, the *condottieri* of late Medieval and Renaissance Italy, the Hessians of the American War of Independence, the sepoys of the East India Company and the French Foreign Legion; but the whole question assumes a new complexion in a world in which the threat or use of force is prohibited by the Charter and the instability of settled government in developing areas is one of the gravest threats to the peace. The development of the law of war during the first half of the twentieth century involved an increasing abridgment of the rights of neutral commerce; the development of the law of peace during the second half of the century may well involve a comparable abridgment of the right to engage and serve as mercenaries. The Organisation of African Unity has condemned such practices, but do we not need a more generally recognised law on the subject? A State which has practised or condoned the use of mercenaries must of course treat its own ex-mercenaries with justice and humanity, and other people's mercenaries in accordance with the laws of war; retroactive criminality is no less objectionable in respect of mercenaries than in respect of other adventurers condemned by a more enlightened law; but should there not, for the future, be a general international convention making it a crime against the common peace to seek adventure or gain at the expense of other people's peace and in particular the peace of newly emerging nations? Are not the mercenaries of today the successors of the pirates and slave-runners of yesterday? Should they not, subject to an amnesty for the past such as the Organization of African Unity has envisaged for the Congo mercenaries, be treated in future in the same manner as *hostes humani generis*, liable to severe punishment in any jurisdiction where they may be found? May not some such measure be necessary to avoid the danger that the passing of the empires may be followed, in areas of the world where the nation has not yet displaced the tribe as the effective unit of political organisation, by a degree of chaos comparable to that which followed the fall of the Roman Empire?

5. Armament

The prohibition of force and recognition that the right of self-defence is subject to collective review will inevitably remain precarious in an armed world. 'In proportion as the armaments of each Power increase, so do they less and less attain the object aimed at by the governments. . . . If this state of affairs be prolonged, it will inevitably lead to the very cataclysm which it is designed to avert, and the impending horrors of which are fearful to every human thought.' In the effective control of armament 'lies the supreme duty today resting upon all States'.[1] These are not the words of any unilateral nuclear disarmer. They come from the note proposing the First Hague Peace Conference circulated to the powers on 12 August 1898 on behalf of His Imperial Majesty Nicholas II, Tsar of All the Russias.

The regulation of armament is not to be dismissed as a question unfit for lawyers. Within the State the law plays a significant part in limiting the indiscriminate keeping, carrying and use of weapons. In the world community it must play a similar part in regulating the possession, testing and use of arms.

Prohibitions and limitations of the use of arms are as old as international law itself. The prohibition of poisoned weapons, explosive bullets, dum-dum bullets, submarine attack without warning, gas and bacteriological warfare and aerial bombardment of non-military objectives are so many successive chapters in the long story of efforts to 'humanise' the destruction and suffering caused by new weapons and methods of war.[2] The current debate on the legality of nuclear warfare is a further chapter in this story.[3] To this debate legal argument can make but little contribution.

The prohibition of testing is a recent accretion to the law, exemplified by the partial nuclear test ban embodied in the Moscow Treaty of 5 August 1963.[4] In this sector lawyers have thus far contributed little and may at this stage have little to contribute. Their criticism might have given us a better test ban treaty but it might also have imperilled the compromise which made the treaty possible. Statesmanship must sometimes take risks, and accept makeshifts, from which the prudent lawyer will shrink.

The crux of the problem is neither the use nor the testing but the possession of arms. The problem has been continuously before the world and before international lawyers since the First Hague Peace Conference. There were virtually continuous disarmament negotiations from

---

[1] Scott, J. B. (editor), *Reports to The Hague Conferences of 1899 and 1907*, p. 2.

[2] Higgins, A. Pearce, *The Hague Peace Conferences*; Moore, John Bassett, *International Law and Some Current Illusions*; Garner, J. W., *Recent Developments in International Law*; Greenspan, Morris, *The Modern Law of Land Warfare*; Lauterpacht, Sir Hersch, *The Law of War on Land*, being Part III of the War Office Manual of Military Law; Tucker, Robert W., *The Law of War and Neutrality at Sea*, Naval War College, International War Studies.

[3] Singh, Nagendra, *Nuclear Weapons and International Law*.

[4] Jacobson, Harold Karan and Stein, Eric, *Diplomats, Scientists and Politicians*.

1919 to 1934,[1] and such negotiations have been proceeding in the United Nations since 1946.[2] The record of success is meagre,[3] consisting chiefly of the elimination of naval rivalry between Great Britain and the United States during the inter-war period and the integration of German re-armament in a West European system during the nineteen fifties.

The responsibility for successive failures and delays cannot be imputed directly to the inadequacies of the law but is nevertheless a reflection of the inadequacy of the whole international legal order. The fundamentals of the matter have not changed since Salvador de Madariaga analysed them in 1929 as being 'that in the absence of an alternative system of policy – which can be no other than cooperative international running of the world – armaments are indispensable as instruments of power, and that therefore all disarmament discussions are bound to transform themselves into armament discussions'.[4] The creation of such an alternative system of policy is the essence of the challenge which the call for peace with justice presents to the creative genius of the law.

The lawyer can also play a constructive part in the regulation of armament by applying legal techniques, experience and skills to the concrete problems which arise in the actual process of disarmament.[5] The areas within which he can profitably hope to do so are defined by the Joint Statement of Agreed Principles for Disarmament Negotiations issued by the United States and the U.S.S.R. on 20 September 1961. The Statement envisages 'strict and effective international control' through an International Disarmament Organisation to be created within the framework of the United Nations. The Disarmament Organisation would 'be assured unrestricted access without veto to all places as necessary for the purpose of effective verification'. Progress in disarmament should be accompanied 'by measures to strengthen institutions for maintaining peace and the settlement of international disputes by peaceful means'. These measures would include 'the obligation of States to place at the disposal of the United Nations agreed manpower necessary for an international peace force to be equipped with agreed types of armaments'. The arrangements for the use of this force should ensure 'that the United Nations can effectively deter or suppress any

---

[1] Noel-Baker, Philip J., *Disarmament*; Chaput, Roland Aimée, *Disarmament in British Foreign Policy*; Temperley, A. C., *The Whispering Gallery of Europe*.

[2] Bechhoefer, B. G., *Post-War Negotiations for Arms Control*; United Nations Office of Public Information, *The United Nations and Disarmament, 1945–1965*.

[3] Noel-Baker, Philip J., *The Arms Race*.

[4] *Disarmament*, p. 211.

[5] See, for instance, Gotlieb, Allan, *Disarmament and International Law*; Martin, Andrew, *The Legal Aspects of Disarmament*.

threat or use of arms in violation of the purposes and principles of the United Nations'.

This basis of negotiation defined the problems at issue without reconciling the persistent divergences of view concerning the extent of the action necessary to resolve them.

The problem of verification[1] involves a wide range of issues: the composition and structure of a verification organisation, the manner in which it can take and implement decisions, the powers and position of its inspectors, the relationship of arms control and inspection to national legal systems.[2] All these aspects of the problem arise in novel forms, and in order to resolve them statesmen, diplomats and soldiers will need the aid of legal skill of a high order. The solution may be to combine a maximum of automation of the inspection process with a minimum of intrusion into national affairs in a manner which ensures, within a framework which represents a mix of impartial and adversary elements, an unimpeded flow of reliable information without any corresponding certainty of political decision.[3]

The effect of violation of disarmament obligations, and possible methods of restoring compliance therewith following any breach, call for consideration as an exceptionally vital aspect of the problem of securing respect for treaty obligations and defining the consequences of any failure to fulfil them. The key to any satisfactory solution of the problem of violation is that 'States must give up self-reliant postures to attain security through community procedures'.[4]

The problem of how justice is to be secured in a disarmed world raises important issues. In this connection it is encouraging that Korovin should have written that 'the disappearance of the possibility of settling disputes by force will inevitably enhance the importance of all kinds of peaceful legal procedures', that 'instead of being optional many of them will become compulsory and instead of casual, habitual'.[5] To evolve and secure the acceptance of such procedures is among the largest of our responsibilities. The questions at issue include that of how national interests may be protected and advanced in a disarmed world and that

---

[1] Wright, Sir Michael, *Disarm and Verify*.

[2] Henkin, Louis, *Arms Control and Inspection in American Law*.

[3] Falk, Richard A. and Barnet, Richard J. (editors), *Security in Disarmament*, especially Hans A. Linde at pp. 80–106 and Lincoln P. Blomfield at pp. 123–38.

[4] Falk, Richard A. and Barnet, Richard J., *Security in Disarmament*, Richard A. Falk at p. 208.

[5] Larson, Arthur (editor), *A Warless World*, p. 182, reproducing a symposium from *International Affairs*, Moscow.

of the relationship between a world community with adequate power to enforce disarmament and such power as may still be reserved to national States. Some fundamental thinking concerning the degree of authority which the more advanced nations should entrust to the community as a whole in a disarmed world may well be necessary.[1]

6. Peacekeeping forces

International forces may be of many different types.[2] They may be internationally controlled or organised as a unified command by a State or States acting under an international mandate. They may consist of national contingents or be individually recruited. They may be the agents of the United Nations, or of a regional organisation such as NATO, or of some international body with essentially local responsibilities like the former Shanghai Municipal Council, or of some temporary alliance. There are precedents, of very varying degrees of importance, for forces of all these types.

The possible purposes of such forces cover a wide range. Their purpose may be to repel aggression; to enforce a decision of the Security Council for the maintenance or restoration of peace or security; to police a cease-fire, truce, or armistice; to undertake frontier control; to maintain public order where national arrangements for the purpose have collapsed; to ensure the defence and security of an internationally administered zone; to guarantee the freedom of a plebiscite; or to verify and enforce the application of a disarmament treaty.

Such forces may be engaged in active hostilities, as in Korea, or, as in Cyprus, in operations in which they are allowed to use arms only in self-defence, to preserve their freedom of movement, or to discharge specific responsibilities.

The problems involved in the organisation and operation of international forces inevitably vary with the nature and purpose of the force and the circumstances in which it is called upon to discharge its functions. There are nevertheless a number of elements which constantly recur. These include the authority for creating and maintaining the force, the political control and command structure of the force, and its composition, financing and logistic support. The relationship of the force to the 'host State' may vary, but the question of how far the consent of a

---

[1] Chamberlain, Neil W., *The West in a World Without War.*

[2] Bowett, D. W., *United Nations Forces*; Frye, William R., *A United Nations Peace Force*; Rosner, Gabriella, *The United Nations Emergency Force*; Seyersted, Finn, *United Nations Forces in the Law of Peace and War*; James, A., *United Nations Security Forces.*

State is required for the presence of a United Nations force upon its territory or the transit of such a force, and that of the legal status of such forces and their bases, will always arise in some form. Whenever a force becomes involved in hostilities, the extent and manner of the application to its operations of the laws of war will be an important question.

There is a growing body of law on the whole subject. It includes the relevant provisions of the Charter; the opinions of the International Court in the *Reparation for Injuries Suffered in the Service of the United Nations*[1] and *Certain Expenses of the United Nations Cases*;[2] the decisions of the Security Council and the General Assembly establishing forces; the agreements between the United Nations and participating States for the provision of forces; logistical support and movement arrangements with member States; basic and 'status of forces' agreements with 'host States'; Secretary-General's Regulations for each force governing its organisation and operation; directives given to each force by the Secretary-General and by its commander; and the substantial body of practice which has developed.

What contribution has the creative imagination made to these developments and what further contribution is it now called upon to make?

The steady determination and sustained ingenuity of successive Secretaries-General and their advisers overcame for a number of years the innumerable difficulties inherent in the task but the circumstances and consequences of the withdrawal of the United Nations Emergency Force from the Middle East in 1967[3] emphasise the essential precariousness of the whole experiment. What has been achieved has been the solution of particular crises rather than of persistent problems. No long-term pattern has yet been evolved, and the problems of the political control and financing of such forces have precipitated a major constitutional crisis in the United Nations, not yet resolved. There is now a major challenge to the creative genius of statesmen and the creative imagination of international lawyers. The time has come when, if peace-keeping forces are to remain a significant instrument of United Nations action, it is necessary to evolve more permanent arrangements for the constitution and financing of such forces, at least for the more common and less controversial of the functions entrusted to them.

It is difficult to formulate as broad principles the considerations which must be taken into account in devising such arrangements, but certain points are both reasonably clear and fundamental.

---

[1] 1949, I.C.J., 181. [2] 1962, I.C.J., 151.

[3] For the documents concerning the withdrawal see *International Legal Materials*, Vol. VI, No. 3, pp. 557–642.

D

The crucial problems are those of political control and finance. These problems cannot be solved on either a basis which stultifies all action unless agreement is reached in the particular case in the Security Council or a basis which purports to place positive political, military or financial obligations upon members of the Security Council which dissent from the action taken in the particular case. A compromise must be found which permits of prompt and effective action by less than unanimous agreement, but achieves some practical reconciliation between the capacity of the United Nations to take such action and the unwillingness of powerful States to share in the political, military and financial responsibility for action undertaken without their consent.

In relation to this primary issue the other problems which arise are secondary, but they represent an important proportion of the questions of law calling for consideration.

An international force must enjoy in relation to the host State the status, immunities, privileges and facilities necessary to give it complete independence of action in the discharge of the responsibilities entrusted to it; the test of what is necessary is functional, but in view of the nature of the responsibilities, should be generously applied; what is functionally necessary may be increased by circumstances, especially in situations of acute disorder.

The authority of an international force and the operations which it is appropriate for it to undertake are limited by the nature of the responsibilities entrusted to it. A peacekeeping force is designed as an instrument of peace, not of war; its functions must be limited by the degree of agreement which exists concerning its purpose; its operations will inevitably and properly be influenced by their impact on the public image of the United Nations.

Withdrawal of any consent on the basis of which an international force operates must be regarded as involving at least a potential threat to the peace calling for immediate consideration by the Security Council; it is reasonable to imply an obligation to give sufficient notice of any such withdrawal of consent to afford the Security Council an adequate opportunity to consider the changed position created thereby; failing such an obligation, uncertainty concerning the continued effectiveness of an international force may be a factor of aggravation rather than stability in a crisis.

When international forces become involved in armed hostilities they are bound by the laws of war relating to armed combat, the protection of non-combatants, prisoners of war, and suchlike matters. The basis of this obligation is not any presumed equality of right between belligerents during hostilities, irrespective of the legality or illegality of their recourse to force, or the difference of function between national forces and international forces acting on behalf of the community as a whole, but the principle that any recourse to force, whether legal or illegal, whether in defiance of or to vindicate law and order, remains subject to the restrictions of the law of war on overriding grounds of policy and humanity.[1] But much of the law of war consists of conventions binding on States on a basis of reciprocity. How are we to determine the provisions applicable to international forces and how are they to be enforced? The conventions do not in terms bind the United Nations as such and the States contributing national contingents may be parties to them to varying extents. Their enforcement involves disciplinary measures within national contingents or by the exercise of some new form of disciplinary authority by the United Nations itself. Certain of the standards for which they provide are based on national treatment. All of these problems are soluble without any complete recasting of the law of war by the formulation of principles, standards and arrangements approved in some appropriate manner by the General Assembly which would henceforth be embodied in agreements between the United Nations and participating States for the provision of forces.

A number of different methods might be adopted for the creation of peacekeeping forces; a decision of the Security Council, a recommendation of the General Assembly, an amendment to the Charter, a treaty ancillary to or separate from a disarmament treaty. Each method presents some clear advantages and characteristic practical disadvantages. Perhaps the least unsatisfactory would be the creation of such a force by a treaty entrusting to the United Nations functions relating to the force defined by the treaty and accepted by the organ of the United Nations called upon to discharge the functions in question.

The law relating to peacekeeping forces clearly represents one of the major challenges of the coming years. As it develops, the precedents of the Middle-east, the Congo and Cyprus will fall into perspective as stages in the development of the law rather than a satisfactory solution of the long-term problems involved.

7. Collective security and alignment

United Nations action by means of international peacekeeping forces may reduce the occasions for, but can never eliminate the need for, the

---

[1] Jenks, C. Wilfred, 'Hersch Lauterpacht – The Scholar as Prophet', 1960 *British Year Book of International Law*, pp. 83–86.

mutual aid for the maintenance of peace and security which is the heart of the Charter of the United Nations as it was the heart of the Covenant of the League of Nations. The maintenance of international peace and security is, by the terms of the Charter, the first and foremost of the purposes of the United Nations; the 'effective collective measures for the prevention and removal of threats to the peace and for the suppression of acts of aggression or other breaches of the peace' which are envisaged by the Charter for the purpose, remain an essential element in the general strategy of peace with justice.

The effectiveness of collective measures presupposes generality of support for them; collective action is always liable to be thwarted by the political or private interests of necessary participants in such measures or powerful economic interests affected by them.[1] These political difficulties the law as such cannot overcome, but it can at least throw its weight behind the legality of collective action, recognise the overriding nature of legal measures designed to implement such action, and decline to give an intangible character to contractual and other legal rights and interests which are invoked as an objection to such measures or tend to reduce their effectiveness.[2] The law has always recognised that a state of war justifies extensive interference by a belligerent with private property, contracts, rights of action and other legal rights and interests; it cannot, consistently with the general obligations and purport of the Charter, concede less to 'collective measures for the prevention and removal of threats to the peace and for the suppression of acts of aggression or other breaches of the peace';[3] these must be regarded as having legal effects no less far-reaching. Nor can the law fail to condemn the wholly immoral conduct of States which deliberately seek political or commercial advantage by flouting collective decisions with a view to exploiting another State's legal participation in collective measures; the United Nations should clearly give the fullest publicity to such outrageous conduct, but to make such condemnation effective we should also explore the practicability of treating certain transactions as void and withholding certain facilities, concessions and privileges from

---

[1] Royal Institute of International Affairs, *International Sanctions*, remains invaluable as a study of the problem as distinguished from its current political context.

[2] McNair, Lord and Watts, A. D., *The Legal Effects of War*, 4th ed.

[3] The measures adopted by the League of Nations in 1935, of which the text is conveniently reproduced in *International Sanctions*, pp. 233–238, remain interesting; concerning the measures relating to Rhodesia adopted by the United Nations in 1965–1966 see the Security Council Resolutions reproduced in *International Legal Materials*, Vol. V, No. 1, pp. 167–168, No. 3, pp. 534, Vol. VI, No. 1, pp. 141–143.

offending States; the whole matter calls for a fresh, bold and vigorous approach.

In recent years the relationship between the principle of mutual aid for the maintenance of peace and security and the policy of non-alignment has become an issue of primary importance, complicated by a confusion of thought arising from failure to appreciate that the two concepts operate on different planes of thought and action and are relevant at different stages in the handling of international conflict. 'The policy of non-alignment is a legitimate refusal to pledge support in advance to either party to a potential international conflict; it does not imply continued neutrality in the event of aggression in violation of the Charter of the United Nations; it neither debars the non-aligned country from supporting the victim of such aggression nor precludes it if itself the victim from accepting or seeking the support of aligned countries. Conversely, alignment is a legitimate exercise of the right of collective self-defence acknowledged by the Charter; it seeks to minimise the danger of conflict by making clear the degree of resistance which will be offered to aggression, but does not imply any continued obligation of support for any of the co-aligned countries itself committing aggression in violation of the Charter; any such act of aggression repudiates the purpose and destroys the foundation of the alignment.'[1]

The reconciliation of these concepts must be sought in principles which are essentially canons of broad statesmanship to which the creative imagination must give effective expression in the law.

'The first principle is that aggression in violation of the Charter invariably creates a new situation in which the restraint of such aggression assumes an overriding immediate importance and the common interest in the maintenance of peace and security takes precedence over all other considerations. The second principle is that aid or comfort to an aggressor is a hostile act inconsistent with the Charter which cannot be justified by any arrangements for collective self-defence in virtue of which such aid or comfort is claimed or given. The third principle is that aid or comfort towards a victim of aggression is not a hostile act towards any Member of the United Nations and does not constitute an act of alignment or a renunciation of the policy of non-alignment. The fourth principle is that the receipt of aid or comfort by a victim of aggression does not constitute an act of alignment with the source of such aid or comfort.'[2]

The prospect of translating these principles into practice and

---

[1] Jenks, C. Wilfred, *Law in the World Community*, p. 68.

[2] Jenks, op. cit., p. 69, where I have discussed the matter more fully at pp. 68–71.

developing the collective discipline necessary to make them workable will depend in large measure on the effectiveness of the complementary action taken in related spheres.

8. Settlement of disputes

No aspect of peace with justice has inspired so copious a literature as the peaceful settlement of disputes. The upshot of almost a century of continuous debate on the problem of justiciability is a widespread recognition by scholars that all disputes are technically justiciable[1] but not necessarily soluble by a judicial decision. The keynote of some seventy years of repeated negotiations concerning arbitration treaties and jurisdictional clauses has been a persistent reluctance by governments to abandon the position that jurisdiction is in principle voluntary.[2] If the world community is to be effectively organised as a new world of law there must at some stage be a clear break with the principle of the voluntary basis of jurisdiction. Such a happy consummation lies well beyond our present reach. The immediate task of the creative imagination is to provide the intellectual climate for the necessary process of transition beyond the voluntary principle, leaving it to statesmanship to grasp and create opportunities for practical action. Four master concepts call for special emphasis. The first is that in a world community in which States have renounced the right to use or threaten force, recourse to international adjudication is a normal means of settling international disputes and cannot be regarded as an act unfriendly towards any State. The second is that the rule of law is worth the certain risk and possible danger of losing a particular case. The third is that comprehensive arrangements for peaceful settlement must include effective procedures for the readjustment of vested rights by due process. The fourth is that objectivity can be a reality, even in a divided world, and that its reality can be tested gradually until it commands wider confidence and acceptance. The further elaboration of some of these principles we can discuss further when we pass from stating goals to reviewing methods, and come to consider international adjudication as one of the processes for the growth and development of the law.

---

[1] Lauterpacht, H., *The Function of Law in the International Community.*

[2] Jenks, C. Wilfred, *The Prospects of International Adjudication*, pp. 13–118.

6

The dignity of man

In the Preamble to the Charter of the United Nations, the reaffirmation of faith in the dignity and worth of the human person follows immediately after the expression of the determination to save succeeding generations from the scourge of war, among the objectives sought by the peoples of the United Nations. This is no accident of diplomacy or draftsmanship, but the considered estimate of statesmanship.[1]

At the level of principle the response to this second major challenge to the creative genius of the law has been breathtaking. The Universal Declaration of Human Rights and United Nations Covenants on Civil and Political Rights and Economic, Social and Cultural Rights are among the most imaginative of legal innovations, the equivalent as regards human rights of the General Treaty for the Renunciation of War and the provisions of the Charter itself as regards the supreme issue of the outlawry of war. The analogy is far from superficial. The fundamental basis of the law has been changed, but the new vision has still to be made a reality. There was indeed, prior to the adoption of the Covenants in 1966, a tragic failure to fulfil by effective procedural guarantees the hope held out by the Charter that the United Nations would make a reality of the international protection of human rights; and it remains to be seen how far the procedures provided for in the Covenants, which are open to serious criticism, will be effective in practice.[2]

The Universal Declaration and United Nations Covenants spell out the inalienable rights of all members of the human family. There run through their provisions six leading themes: the equality of man; due process of law; freedom of thought and expression; freedom of peaceful assembly and association; the will of the people as the basis of the authority of government; and the right to share in the fruits of economic

[1] Lauterpacht, Hersch, *International Law and Human Rights.*

[2] Cf. Jenks, C. Wilfred, 'The United Nations Covenants Come to Life', in *Recucil d'études de Droit international en hommage à Paul Guggenheim.*

and social progress.[1] Clearly we are far from having achieved these high purposes; nowhere have we achieved them all and over much of the world even their acceptance as the basis of policy is precarious; no less clearly, these purposes now have an altogether new status in the law.

The Universal Declaration was adopted by the General Assembly on 10 December 1948. At that time there were 58 Members of the United Nations. Forty-eight votes were cast for and none against the Declaration.[2] Though the precise legal nature and validity of the Declaration were left somewhat indeterminate at the time and have been much discussed by legal writers, its political and moral authority have grown with the years to an extent which has given it a measure of legal authority not originally intended by its authors who were thinking in terms of the early adoption of binding covenants;[3] even those who show little respect for the provisions of the Declaration in practice rarely question its authority in principle; but there are no effective arrangements for ensuring the practical application of its provisions.

The United Nations Covenants, which restate with modifications the provisions of the Declaration as obligations binding for States ratifying or acceding, were adopted unanimously by the General Assembly on 16 December 1966; at the time of their adoption there were one hundred and twenty-two Members of the United Nations; there were 106 affirmative votes for the Covenant on Civil and Political Rights and 105 affirmative votes for the Covenant on Economic, Social and Cultural Rights, with no expressed dissent or abstention in either vote; each Covenant will enter into force three months after the deposit of the thirty-fifth instrument of ratification or accession. The Covenant on Civil and Political Rights deals with the full range of civil liberties, including the right to life, freedom from slavery, servitude and forced labour, freedom from arbitrary arrest or detention, fair trial, freedom of movement, freedom from retroactive legislation or penalties, freedom of thought, conscience and religion, freedom of assembly and association, and freedom from discrimination; it was adopted with the concurrence of the Members of the United Nations which have not in the past afforded effective protection of civil liberties. The Covenant on Economic, Social and Cultural Rights is equally comprehensive in charac-

---

[1] I have discussed more fully the manner in which the Declaration elaborates these themes in *Law and the World Community*, pp. 123–126.

[2] There were eight abstentions, namely, Byelorussia, Czechoslovakia, Poland, Saudi Arabia, Ukraine, Union of South Africa, U.S.S.R. and Yugoslavia, and two absentees, namely Honduras and Yemen.

[3] The details are summarised in Schwelb, Egon, *Human Rights and the International Community*, pp. 50–53.

ter; the subjects with which it deals include the right to work, the right to just and favourable conditions of work, trade union rights, the right to social security, the right of family protection, the right to an adequate standard of living, the right to health, the right to education, and the right to share in cultural and scientific progress; it was adopted with the concurrence of Members of the United Nations which have traditionally regarded many of these questions as matters for private or local initiative rather than for national action. The formulation of these provisions in instruments submitted to States for ratification as legally binding obligations is in itself an epoch-making advance, but the real political value and practical effectiveness of the Covenants will depend on the extent to which they are ratified without eviscerating reservations and on the effectiveness of the measures of implementation adopted by each party and arrangements for international supervision by means of which the effectiveness of the measures adopted by each party is assessed. These are matters of the utmost difficulty, presenting different problems in respect of political freedom, civil liberties, social justice and the freedom of the mind, and throwing into sharp relief the wide differences of cultural tradition and maturity which the oneness of the world has not eliminated.

Meanwhile the Universal Declaration and United Nations Covenants are supplemented in Western Europe by the European Convention for the Protection of Human Rights and Fundamental Freedoms of 4 November 1950, negotiated under the auspices of the Council of Europe and in force for all the member States of the Council of Europe except France. It embodies, in a more precise and somewhat more limited form, binding obligations relating to the civil liberties provided for in the Universal Declaration. The European Convention establishes a European Commission of Human Rights the members of which are independent persons serving in their personal capacities; the Commission may examine allegations of a breach of the Convention made by a contracting party and, in relation to States having agreed to such a procedure, petitions from persons or organisations claiming to be victims of the violation of a right set forth in the Convention; there is provision for an appeal in certain circumstances by a party to the Convention or the European Commission of Human Rights to a European Court of Human Rights; and responsibility for taking appropriate steps to secure compliance is vested in the Committee of Ministers of the Council of Europe. The European Commission has dealt with a large number of both inter-State and individual applications, and the European Court has given judgment in its first three cases. The European Charter of Social Rights, negotiated by the Council of Europe with the cooperation of the International Labour Organisation, is a counterpart to the European Convention in the social field.[1]

The European Convention, Commission and Court have served as the prototype for proposals for similar action by the Organization of American States and the Organization of African Unity. Whether such regional approaches are desirable depends on the present and potential vitality of the tradition of respect for human rights in the region concerned at the particular time. Such arrangements could operate in either of two ways: as the seedbed of a regional conscience which gives new vigour to the concept of human dignity and procedures for the protection of human rights in the region, or as a mask for regional tolerance of standards so equivocal that they permit breaches of human rights in which an independent international body would not acquiesce. The wisdom of a regional approach depends essentially on the extent to which respect for human rights is in the marrow of the traditions of the region.

1. Political freedom

Political freedom is the element of human dignity most difficult to express in a legal principle or obligation. The United Nations Covenants provide that 'all peoples have the right of self-determination' by virtue whereof 'they freely determine their political status and freely pursue their economic, social and cultural development', but the practical application of these provisions involves three difficulties. 'People' is a collective plural of indeterminate content; whether a particular group of persons constitute a 'people' is a question of judgment concerning which views and interests may differ. Secondly, self-determination can mean only the wishes of the people concerned, which may differ from the political interests or ideological preconceptions of those who claim to be their champions. Thirdly, the right cannot be exercised by legal process; it presupposes political decisions and political action. These are not reasons for which States which have granted the right of self-determination to more than half the present membership of the United Nations should decline to accept these provisions, but they imply that political freedom is a right entirely different in legal nature from the civil liberties and the economic and social rights. The right of self-determination without a recognised procedure for its exercise, by plebiscite or otherwise, tends to be a political manifesto rather than a legal right, and the international plebiscite, which at one time appeared to

---

[1] For both the Convention and the Charter see Robertson, A. H., *Human Rights in Europe*.

be becoming increasingly common,[1] now appears to be becoming rare and is not infrequently rejected by professed champions of self-determination.

The United Nations Covenant on Civil and Political Rights also provides for political freedom within the State in the form of the right to take part in the conduct of public affairs, to vote and be elected, and to have access to public service. Little precise thought has yet been given to the practicability of international action to secure such freedom as an international policy of continuous and general application, and still less to the exact form which such action might take; there is little or no encouraging precedent on which to draw in the matter. There is no great difficulty about making arrangements to ensure that the facts are determined with reasonable accuracy and widely known but this does not take us very far. The problem is generally that the government concerned is insensitive to opinion. There is no political operation more difficult than that of inducing change in the internal political dispositions of a State by external pressure falling short of war, the threat of war or total boycott; such measures presuppose wide international agreement that they should be adopted, do not guarantee either immediate or enduring success, and may have unpredictable and unmanageable wider implications; they cannot be institutionalised into a legal procedure in any manner at present foreseeable. In the long run the problem of political freedom within the State will prove to be a far graver, more general and more permanent problem than that of self-determination; it will be particularly acute when aggravated by problems of racial discrimination or minority protection. The main contribution of international law in the matter may well be a by-product of the international protection of civil liberties.

2. Civil liberties

During the eighteen years which elapsed between the proclamation of the Universal Declaration by the General Assembly of the United Nations as 'a common standard of achievement for all peoples and all nations' and the adoption by the General Assembly of the United Nations Covenants, there were no effective United Nations arrangements for translating the principles of the Declaration into rights and freedoms enforceable by due process of law.[2] The United Nations

---

[1] Wambaugh, Sarah, *A Monograph on Plebiscites; Plebiscites Since the World War*; 2 vols.

[2] Cf. Luard, Evan (ed.), *The International Protection of Human Rights.*

Covenant on Civil and Political Rights now affords an opportunity, but not yet any guarantee, of giving the civil liberties a measure of international enforceability. Assuming the Covenant to secure the ratifications necessary to bring it reasonably widely into force, its effectiveness will require a complex interplay of national and international action; the test of its value will be the extent to which it precipitates and crystallises far-reaching changes of policy and significant innovations of procedure on the national and international planes.

On the plane of national action the Covenant has two major weaknesses. While the language used in the Covenant appears to be reasonably clear and unequivocal, the potential parties have traditionally had a wide range of varying and in some cases conflicting concepts concerning civil liberties, and it remains to be seen how far we have achieved a clarity of language and community of outlook and interest which constitute a reasonably uniform international standard. Secondly, the effectiveness of civil liberties depends on the effectiveness of the procedures available for their enforcement; the Covenant does not embody any detailed prescriptions or standard of effectiveness by which the adequacy of such procedures can be judged. Each party undertakes to ensure that any person whose rights or freedoms are violated shall have an effective remedy notwithstanding that the violation has been committed by a person acting in a public capacity, that any person claiming such a remedy shall have his right thereto determined by a competent authority provided for by the legal system of the State, and that the competent authorities shall enforce such remedies when granted. While the obligation is to provide an effective remedy, and 'effective' cannot be construed to mean less than it says, there is nothing in the Covenant to ensure the independence and dependability necessary to make the remedy effective.

On the international plane much will depend on the independence, impartiality and thoroughness of the Human Rights Committee for which the Covenant provides. The members of the Committee are to be elected and to serve in their personal capacities, and therefore have the formal status necessary to enable a committee of sufficient calibre to discharge its duties with full independence and impartiality. The powers of the Committee are, however, limited; its primary function is to study reports by the parties concerning the measures which they have taken to give effect to the Covenant and to transmit comments on these reports to the parties and the Economic and Social Council; only as between parties making a special declaration can the Committee consider claims by one party that another party is not fulfilling its obligations, and the most that it can do in such cases is to appoint with the consent of the parties an Ad Hoc Conciliation Commission; only if the party concerned has accepted an Optional Protocol can the Committee consider communications from individuals and all that it is entitled to do on the basis of such a communication is to forward its views to the party and individual concerned. These powers fall well short of those of the European Commission of Human Rights under the European Convention.

The widest possible acceptance of the Covenant on Civil and Political Rights must remain the first priority for more effective international action for the protection of human rights, but it would be a mistake either to underestimate the difficulty or to overestimate the value of securing general acceptance of the Covenant. An approach which involves facing so many of the difficulties of the task simultaneously inevitably compounds them and even when the Covenant has been widely ratified, the difficulties of securing its full implementation will remain formidable. It argues no spirit of defeatism concerning the long-term importance and value of the Covenant to take the view that, without prejudice to its operation or the continued validity of such regional arrangements as the European Convention, we should also explore other means of making more effective the international protection of civil liberties.

One possibility which might be envisaged would be the negotiation of a series of simple conventions formulating in separate instruments, with a minimum of procedural or other detail, some of the basic civil liberties enunciated by the Universal Declaration and the Covenant on Civil and Political Rights. The United Nations has had recourse to this method of special conventions of limited scope for dealing with such matters as genocide, racial discrimination and religious intolerance, but has not hitherto attempted to apply it to civil liberties. Why should not such an attempt be made? It would be wise to start any such experiment in so difficult a field with the matters in respect of which one can reasonably hope for the widest measure of agreement. As a first stage we might envisage the negotiation of three simple conventions, each to be concluded as a separate instrument so that any State prevented by some unanticipated difficulty from becoming a party to one would not be debarred from ratifying the others. The first would establish the presumption of innocence until proof of guilt. The second would preclude guilt by association. The third would prohibit retroactive criminality. There would be a reasonable chance that such a group of conventions would be widely ratified. In the light of the experience acquired with them, consideration could be given subsequently to the possibility of further progress on the same lines in respect of more difficult matters.

There might, for instance, be a second stage consisting of a group of conventions relating to freedom from arbitrary arrest or detention, provision for prompt trial, and freedom from arbitrary or unusual punishment, and at each successive stage the progress made and possibility of further progress could be reviewed. In the first instance the arrangements for the implementation of these conventions might be confined to arrangements for ascertaining the facts in the event of any allegation of non-compliance by another party to the convention, but as the method of approach became established and confidence in its operation grew, it might be feasible to develop more effective arrangements for the implementation of such conventions than would be acceptable in respect of instruments of wider scope. In this connection it is of interest that the United Nations Convention on Racial Discrimination gives the Committee on the Elimination of Racial Discrimination established thereby, powers more far-reaching than those entrusted to the Human Rights Committee by the Covenant on Civil and Political Rights.[1]

In the light of the experience gained, fuller consideration could be given, when the time appears ripe and circumstances propitious, to more ambitious proposals. Some of these are of considerable interest and have deservedly attracted attention.

The most dramatic among them is the proposal, commended to our examination by Roscoe Pound, for a world writ of habeas corpus.[2] The proposal has been put forward in different ways and forms. One is the filing of a petition to the United Nations that the General Assembly should issue a United Nations writ of habeas corpus requiring a respondent government to show cause why the General Assembly should not direct the respondent to set the prisoner at liberty; variants of the proposal in this form contemplate such an application to the International Court of Justice or to the Commission on Human Rights of the Economic and Social Council. In another form the proposal envisages a treaty conferring authority to issue such a writ upon the General Assembly, the International Court of Justice, or a specially constituted International Court of Habeas Corpus. Despite the endorsement of leading authorities, responsible opinion has hardly taken the proposal seriously. Should it be dismissed so lightly? The proposal has clearly no future if it is conceived and advocated as a measure of political warfare. We are more likely to make progress if it is rethought as a common

---

[1] Complaints by one party against another are receivable without any special declaration and communications from individuals when a special declaration has been made.

[2] Kutner, Luis, *World Habeas Corpus*.

advance to a fuller and more enduring freedom. The fundamental difficulty is to make it procedurally effective. The effectiveness of a habeas corpus procedure depends not on the existence of a writ or some equivalent procedure but on the certainty of its issue resulting in a prompt and fair trial. As my almost namesake Jenkes, whom Hallam describes as 'a citizen of London on the popular or factious side',[1] learned to his cost in 1676,[2] when he was committed to custody by the King in Council for uttering an allegedly mutinous speech in Guildhall and making arrangements for presenting a petition for a new parliament to remedy 'the mischiefs and grievances of the people', and his friends cited the authority of Lord Coke in vain to Lord Nottingham in a plea of habeas corpus, the principle of habeas corpus is of little avail in the absence of an effective procedural remedy. The significance of the great Habeas Corpus Act of 1679 was the creation of such a remedy. Its effect, now attested by nearly three centuries of practical experience, is well stated by my more recent namesake, Edward Jenks, redoubtable among legal historians and acknowledged champions of the rule of law: 'It gives every citizen an absolute right to have the validity of his imprisonment speedily raised and discussed by a superior Court in his presence, whether in term time or vacation' and 'imposes a heavy penuniary penalty on any judge refusing the application for the writ'.[3] Can we devise any international equivalent for these procedural elements in the effectiveness of the remedy? There might be an advantage in a procedure which made it possible to get an authoritative international determination that no good cause had been shown for the detention of a prisoner, even in the absence of any arrangements ensuring that such a determination will be effective in practice. It would at least focus and intensify the moral pressures which are always the ultimate sanction of freedom. In exploring the possibilities of such a development, special attention might well be given to ways in which it could have the effect of reinforcing national guarantees of personal freedom and procedures designed to make them effective.

A United Nations Ombudsman has also been suggested. The Ombudsman, or citizen's defender, is an officer appointed by the legislature to receive and investigate complaints from citizens against unjust administrative action. The device is a Swedish contribution to the protection of the citizen against bureaucracy, since introduced in varied forms in Finland, Denmark, Norway and New Zealand, and most recently in the United Kingdom.[4] A United Nations Ombudsman, with

---

[1] *The Constitutional History of England*, Chapter XIII.

[2] *State Trials*, vi, 1189.

[3] *A Short History of English Law*, p. 343.

[4] Rowat, Donald C., *The Ombudsman.*

access to all relevant information, entitled to find the facts and make recommendations, might afford a useful protection against any arbitrary exercise of executive powers over persons or property which may, as the world community develops, be entrusted to any of its organs or agencies. Such an officer would be complementary to the existing international administrative tribunals, or any more comprehensive system of administrative jurisdiction which may develop therefrom, in ensuring compliance with the principle that 'every international organisation has the duty to respect the law and to ensure that the law be respected by its agents and officials'.[1] A United Nations Ombudsman with a general or broad mandate to investigate complaints against national authorities would be a wholly different proposition. There would be wide and strong opposition to such a proposal as an encroachment upon primarily national responsibilities, and the practical difficulties of the task conceived on such a scale would be immense. The existing Ombudsman systems are primarily the creation of small countries; their success in larger countries is still a hope, not yet an achievement. It appears preferable to concentrate international action upon the more effective protection of the basic civil liberties which make it possible for the citizen to make adequate national provision for his protection against bureaucracy rather than to disperse it, ineffectively, over so broad a field. It does not, however, follow from this clear need for caution that no United Nations action in the matter is feasible or desirable. There may well be an increasing disposition to experiment with national Ombudsman systems. United Nations recommendations or studies might serve as the basis of such action and United Nations assistance in the development of such systems may sometimes be welcome. How far any further international contribution can be made to such a process of development requires much thought and careful exploration. Can we conceive that a United Nations Ombudsman might be available to assist a national Ombudsman, thus reinforcing his stature, authority and independence, at his request? Can we conceive that a United Nations Ombudsman might, on the initiative of the Security Council, the General Assembly, the Economic and Social Council, or some other appropriate body, investigate allegations which have become a matter of widespread international concern?

The General Assembly of the United Nations has under consideration a proposal for the appointment of a High Commissioner of Human Rights. If any such office should be created, the High Commissioner might usefully examine these various possibilities.

---

[1] Resolution of the Institute of International Law, *Annuaire de l'Institut de Droit international*, 47 (ii) (1957), p. 488.

3. Social justice

In municipal law the civil liberties, which are largely the heritage of the English revolutions of the seventeenth century and the American and French revolutions of the eighteenth century, have a much longer history than the economic, social and cultural rights, which came to be given legal form as the result of the Mexican and Russian revolutions of 1917 and the German revolution of 1918. On the international plane the process of historical development has been reversed and the Constitution of the International Labour Organisation, which proclaimed social justice an objective of international policy and established permanent machinery for pursuing it, anticipated by almost thirty years the Universal Declaration of Human Rights. We owe to the I.L.O. a *corpus juris* of social justice,[1] comprising 128 international conventions which have now received a total of 3,443 ratifications distributed over 118 States, and a wide range of varied procedures designed to promote its effective implementation.[2] The relative success of these procedures is attributable to a complex of factors: they are based on recognised international standards embodied in conventions, recommendations, and other I.L.O. standards; they operate within the framework of the constitutional obligations of the members of the I.L.O.; they bear the impress of a tripartite organisation in which the representatives of employers and workers play a distinctive role; they include solid guarantees of the complete independence of persons serving in quasi-judicial capacities who are responsible to their consciences alone; they are reinforced by first-class staff work. Much of the I.L.O. experience may ultimately prove to have a much wider application.

The I.L.O. experience may be particularly valuable in connection with many of the problems which will be presented by the application of the United Nations Covenant on Economic, Social and Cultural Rights. This Covenant is primarily a recognition of rights which by their nature are not self-executory or enforceable as such by legal process but materialise into enforceable rights only as they are implemented by means of policies, legislation and administrative action; the nature

---

[1] Cf. Jenks, C. Wilfred, 'The *Corpus Juris* of Social Justice', in *Law, Freedom and Welfare*, pp. 101–136.

[2] Concerning which see Jenks, C. Wilfred, 'Human Rights, Social Justice and Peace', in Nobel Symposium VII: *The International Protection of Human Rights, Proceedings of the Seventh Nobel Symposium*, Oslo, September 1967, edited by August Schou and Asbjörn Eide, pp. 227–260; *The International Protection of Trade Union Freedom*; *Human Rights and International Labour Standards*; and 'The International Protection of Trade Union Rights', in Luard, Evan (ed.), *The International Protection of Human Rights*, pp. 210–246.

of these rights implies, moreover, that their implementation will necessarily be progressive and on this point the terms of the Covenant itself are quite explicit. The Covenant provides for a general appraisal, by the examination of reports submitted by the parties, of the progress made in the implementation of its provisions, but in terms which appear to be designed to exclude any review of the fulfilment by individual parties of their obligations; the reports are to be considered by the Economic and Social Council or the appropriate specialised agency, and the Council may submit recommendations of a general nature to the General Assembly. The effect of these provisions is that the specialised agencies, and in particular the I.L.O., by reason of the number and importance of the economic and social rights falling within its field, are the executing agencies of the Covenant with a major share of the responsibility for its effective implementation.[1] The inevitably general character of the economic, social and cultural rights recognised by the Covenant implies that, to give them a more definable content, more detailed conventions and recommendations providing the common core of uniform or at least comparable legislation and administrative action are necessary; these will normally be adopted and administered by the specialised agencies concerned in their respective fields. The entry into force of the Covenant on Economic, Social and Cultural Rights will therefore put to the test a wholly new series of arrangements for cooperation between the United Nations and the specialised agencies in the implementation of its provisions. The outcome of this test will determine the extent to which the law of nations as a whole, as distinguished from the *corpus juris* administered by the I.L.O., reflects the contemporary insistence on social justice.

4. Freedom of the mind

The freedom of the mind is the source of all freedom; civil liberties make it possible for it to find expression but cannot create or guarantee it; educational opportunity tends to foster and invigorate it; mass communications may stimulate, but are more liable to discipline and inhibit, it. The Universal Declaration and Covenant on Civil and Political Rights proclaim the rights to freedom of thought, of opinion and of expression. The Covenant on Economic, Social and Cultural Rights proclaims the right of everyone to education. Can the law do anything

---

[1] Jenks, C. Wilfred, 'Human Rights, Social Justice and Peace', in Nobel Symposium VII: *The International Protection of Human Rights, Proceedings of the Seventh Nobel Symposium*, Oslo, September 1967, edited by August Schou and Asbjörn Eide, pp. 227–260.

more to give reality to these freedoms? The future of the law itself depends upon their vitality. A new world of law presupposes them. An imaginative approach to the growth of the law in a changing world is conceivable only where the mind is free to challenge accepted authority and established routine. Has the law any contribution to make to creating the fundamental cultural condition for its own acceptance as the basis of civilised life?

The Constitution of Unesco proclaims that 'the wide diffusion of culture, and the education of humanity for justice and liberty and peace are indispensable to the dignity of man and constitute a social duty which all the nations must fulfil in a spirit of mutual assistance and concern'; that peace must be founded 'upon the intellectual and moral solidarity of mankind'; and that the Members of Unesco 'believing in full and equal opportunities for education for all, in the unrestricted pursuit of objective truth, and in the full exchange of ideas and knowledge, are agreed and determined to develop and to increase the means of communication between their peoples and to employ these means for the purpose of mutual understanding and a truer and more perfect knowledge of each other's lives'. The effect of these affirmations, as a statement of policy and charter for promotional action and technical cooperation in the educational, scientific and cultural fields may have been significant and in some contexts dramatic, but their impact on the law has as yet been slight. The Universal Copyright Convention and the limited measures which have been taken to promote the full flow of information[1] cannot be regarded as more than a first step towards the implementation of what are potentially far-reaching obligations.

What can the law, or international action undertaken on some recognised legal basis, contribute to facilitating the free flow of information across ideological frontiers, developing the conception that media of mass communication are a public trust, and restraining or discrediting hostile propaganda designed to perpetuate or create wars 'in the minds of men'? The problem is so vast and complex, so highly political, and in some of its aspects so new, that any approach to it must needs be tentative, but there are a number of possibilities worthy of exploration. Can we conceive of a treaty obligation, which though it would not be universally accepted might nevertheless set a useful international standard, that no restriction of any kind should be placed by any government on the circulation of any publication or document issued by the United Nations or other authorised international body? Can we conceive of a

---

[1] These are summarised in Laves, Walter H. C. and Thomson, Charles A., *Unesco – Purpose – Progress – Prospects*, pp. 133–136.

code of ethics for mass information media, spelling out the implications of the concept that they should be operated as a public trust with a procedure for investigating alleged violations of the code? Can we develop further the right of correction and reply provided for in a little-ratified United Nations Convention of 1949? What action can be taken to restrain malicious propaganda? The principal difficulty in dealing with such propaganda is not the lack of substantive law but the absence of effective remedies[1] and of the political will to create such remedies. There is a substantial body of international law and precedent governing war-mongering propaganda by a State (exemplified by the Nuremburg judgment),[2] subversive propaganda by a State (the prohibition of which is as old as Vattel[3] and remains good law), and defamatory propaganda by a State (the law relating to which corresponds to the municipal law of defamation).[4] The law governing State responsibility for private propaganda is much less certain. The better view, and the only one consistent with the general principle of freedom of expression, is that as a general rule the State is not responsible for private propaganda, but the general rule admits of exceptions and it may well be that States are, as they certainly should be, bound by international law to ensure that their territory is not used for the emission of radio signals which constitute war-mongering, subversive or defamatory propaganda.[5] What scope may there be for a fact-finding procedure, whereby any State can refer for impartial examination allegations concerning it which it believes or knows to be false? Enlisting the law in the promotion of respect for truth would be a significant contribution to improving international relations on the basis of the intellectual integrity and moral dignity of man. Once such tentative steps have been taken, what part can the law play in the broader task of making intellectual freedom a reality which knows no frontiers?

5. Fullness of opportunity

Political freedom, civil liberties, social justice and freedom of the mind are all essential constituents of the good life in political society. They find their fruition in fullness of opportunity. How far has this funda-

---

[1] Whitton, John B. and Larson, Arthur, *Propaganda.*

[2] *International Military Trials, Nürnberg, Nazi Conspiracy and Aggression, Opinion and Judgment*, pp. 11–12.

[3] Vattel, *Le Droit des Gens ou Principes de la Loi Naturelle*, Titre II, Ch. 1, Sec. 18, *Classics of International Law.*

[4] Whitton and Larson, *Propaganda*, pp. 104–132.

[5] Whitton and Larson, pp. 159–164.

mental proposition of political philosophy, the origin of which we can trace back to Plato and Aristotle, find adequate expression in the law of nations? It is now expressed in the Charter of the United Nations, the Universal Declaration of Human Rights, the United Nations Covenants on Human Rights, the Constitution of the International Labour Organisation and innumerable other instruments, but perhaps most clearly and decisively in the Declaration of Philadelphia of 1944, now accepted as an integral part of the Constitution of the International Labour Organisation by 119 States: 'All human beings, irrespective of race, creed or sex, have the right to pursue both their material well-being and their spiritual development in conditions of freedom and dignity, of economic security and equal opportunity; the attainment of the conditions in which this shall be possible must constitute the central aim of national and international policy; all national and international policies and measures, in particular those of an economic and financial character, should be judged in this light and accepted only in so far as they may be held to promote and not to hinder the attainment of this fundamental objective.' This fundamental principle has now permeated policy to the point at which it is decisively reshaping the law of nations; without it we could not have a law of nations responsive to contemporary need. The implications of this development are far-reaching and we cannot yet assess them in full. Social change is one of the imperatives of orderly progress in a wide range of developing countries; without such change we cannot achieve the freedom from fear, freedom from want, and freedom from contempt which are the essence of human dignity. In the nature of the case international law can neither require nor regiment social change, but it can be responsive to the need for it and international society can formulate standards to stimulate it and mobilise financial and technical resources to facilitate it. In the Declaration of Punta del Este and the Alliance for Progress we have an example of peaceful social change, including fundamental agrarian and fiscal reforms, being adopted, in principle if not yet in practice, as the political philosophy of a continent. In the 1967 Protocol of Amendment to the Charter of the Organization of American States the member States pledge themselves 'to a united effort to ensure social justice in the Hemisphere and dynamic and balanced economic development for their peoples' and set forth a wide range of basic goals to be pursued for this purpose.[1] How much more far-reaching in its implications may the principle of fullness of opportunity prove to be?

---

[1] *International Legal Materials*, Vol. VI, No. 2, pp. 4–13.

7

Economic stability and growth

Neither peace nor freedom can resist disruptive forces if the economy fails to provide for the general welfare. Economic stability and growth must therefore have a leading place among the goals of creative effort. What can the law contribute to the future of international economic policy? Let us consider the matter in relation to monetary policy, trade, commodity policy, restrictive business practices, investment, development aid, know-how, industrial development, shipping, insurance, food and agriculture, and population. In each of these fields except the last we shall find that new concepts, reflecting new preoccupations of statesmen and economists, have been developed imaginatively in recent years as the basis of the law, and that new legal devices have been evolved or adapted to international use to make the concepts effective. In all of them we shall find immense scope for further creative work. The guiding principle in all these new developments has been the growing recognition that, for prosperity as for peace and for freedom, the world is one. The I.L.O. set the keynote for the new approach which is now the accepted basis of international economic policy by asserting in the Declaration of Philadelphia that 'poverty anywhere constitutes a danger to prosperity everywhere'. This is the modern equivalent, restated in world terms and transposed into economic language, of the ancient truth that no society can endure permanently half-slave and half-free.

1. Monetary policy

Fifty years ago every State had an unquestioned sovereign right to do as it liked in matters of monetary policy. The Permanent Court of International Justice said as late as 1929 that it is 'a generally accepted principle that a State is entitled to regulate its own currency'.[1] Devaluation, convertibility and exchange control, inflation and deflation were all within the national discretion. They were widely used as weapons of economic warfare. Despite the work of the Financial Organisation of

[1] *Serbian Loans Case*, 1929, P.C.I.J., Series A, Nos. 20/21, p. 44.

the League of Nations[1] and the creation of the Bank for International Settlements in 1930[2] to facilitate cooperation among central banks, there was no basic change in the position during the inter-war period. International law concerned itself with monetary policy only in such special contexts as the effect of gold clauses in loan contracts and special international arrangements for the rehabilitation of particular currencies.

The creation of the International Monetary Fund brought monetary policy within the realm of law. The essence of the Fund is the obligation to maintain orderly exchange arrangements based on par values and convertibility, the right to draw upon a common fund to relieve temporary pressure on the exchanges, and the substitution of consultation for unilateral action as the normal mode of revaluing a currency.[3] There have gradually been added to the Fund system new devices for increasing the volume and liquidity of international monetary reserves. There was a long initial period during which the Fund Agreement was of limited practical application, especially in regard to convertibility, and there was much disappointment and debate concerning the whole system, but that phase has now passed. It has become apparent how fundamental a change was the recognition at Bretton Woods that international monetary relationships are a collective responsibility and require a common discipline.

To this principle there is gradually being added the further principle that domestic monetary policy, in its bearing on inflation and deflation, is likewise, by reason of its international repercussions, a matter of international concern. The Fund, the General Agreement on Tariffs and Trade and the Organization for Economic Co-operation and Development are all increasingly concerned with the relationship between inflationary and deflationary pressures and general economic policy.

The technicalities of international monetary cooperation have involved the development of a wide range of legal devices, new to international law, such as quotas in the Fund, drawing rights and standby arrangements.

The challenge of monetary policy to the creative genius of the law has

---

1 Hill, Martin, *The Economic and Financial Organisation of the League of Nations.*

2 Auboin, Roger, *The Bank for International Settlements, 1930–1955.*

3 Fawcett, J. E. S., 'The International Monetary Fund and International Law', 40 *British Year Book of International Law*, 1964, pp. 32–76; Aufricht, Hans, *The International Monetary Fund: Legal Bases, Structure, Functions*; Gold, Joseph, *The Fund Agreement in the Courts*, and *The International Monetary Fund and Private Business Transactions*; Horie, Shigeo, *The International Monetary Fund*; Scammell, W. M., *International Monetary Policy*, 2nd ed.

thus arisen, and to some extent been met, on two levels: that of general principle in the concepts of collective responsibility and common discipline, and that of technical inventiveness in the development of legal devices new to international law to make these concepts effective.

Further developments of a more far-reaching character now appear to be in prospect. Keynes' view of international monetary cooperation as an instrument for expanding, not merely stabilising, the world economy[1] proved to be in advance of its time in 1943;[2] barely twenty years later it became the keynote of extensive and intensive discussions of further advance. There is now a general preoccupation with the shortage of international reserves and need for increased liquidity in relation to the present scale and rate of growth of world trade.[3] A wide range of remedies, involving varying degrees of innovation, have been canvassed. One approach, not yet adopted but still much discussed, contemplates flexible exchange rates within an institutional framework designed to facilitate economic growth policies without paralysing inhibitions about their effect on the balance of payments.[4] Another suggestion proposes the creation of additional reserve assets by group action, including both a primary asset in the form of a Fund Unit Account administered by the International Monetary Fund and consisting of a mixture of currencies (this account being in the nature of an 'issue department' designed to supplement the existing 'banking department' of the International Monetary Fund) and a secondary asset which might take a number of forms (that of special non-marketable medium-term bonds, that of consolidated loans, and that of a long-term loan of reserve funds for monetary purposes).[5] More ambitious proposals envisaged the internationalisation of foreign exchange reserves under the aegis of the International Monetary Fund.[6] Governments and central bankers have been considering these and other proposals and reviewing the whole position for some time, notably through the Group of Ten countries participating in the General Arrangements to Borrow of the International Monetary Fund.[7] The Fund has now approved amendments to

---

[1] *Proposals for an International Clearing Union.*

[2] Harrod, R. F., *The Life of John Maynard Keynes.*

[3] International Monetary Fund, 'The Adequacy of Monetary Reserves', in *Staff Papers*, Vol. III, No. 2 (October 1953), pp. 181–227, and *International Reserves and Liquidity*.

[4] Meade, James, 'A Plea for Flexible Exchange Rates', *The Guardian*, 3 January 1961.

[5] Roosa, Robert V., *Monetary Reform for the World Economy.*

[6] Triffin, Robert, *Gold and Dollar Crisis.*

[7] Group of Ten, *Report of the Study Group on the Creation of Reserve Assets, Report to the Deputies of the Group of Ten*, 31 May 1965.

its Articles of Agreement which have been submitted to its Members for acceptance.[1] While these amendments are not yet in force, we are clearly in process of opening a new chapter in international monetary cooperation. The amendments are based on the principle of a collective responsibility for international monetary policy which is the essence of the Fund Agreement; they involve the creation of new types of reserve asset and new obligations and procedural arrangements. Mr. Pierre-Paul Schweitzer, the Managing Director of the Fund has described them as being 'based on the principle that the evolution of reserves should reflect a collective judgment as to the needs of the world economy, rather than emerge as the by-product of forces such as fluctuation in the supply and private absorption of gold, the external payments position of reserve currency centres, the incidence of balance of payments assistance to particular countries, or the decisions of particular countries concerning the composition of the reserves'.[2] The new facility is related to 'the long run trend need for economic growth'; it is not designed to influence short-term fluctuations in general business activity which can not be effectively and satisfactorily influenced through such a mechanism. The reserve asset takes the form of special drawing rights, available on a non-discriminatory basis, and allocated according to an objective criterion of economic size; these rights are to be administered in a Special Drawing Account to which participants are to provide currency in return for the drawing rights. The detailed elaboration of these arrangements has provided, and their subsequent interpretation and application will continue to present, a considerable challenge to the creative ingenuity of the law. The multilateral institutional approach represented by the proposals permits of balanced consideration of the varying interests of different countries in their international monetary relationships with a view to their reconciliation in a global context; it forms a startling contrast to the monetary sovereignty of the past.

Certain other elements of international monetary cooperation have remained a matter of banking practice rather than of law. These have included the further development of inter-central bank cooperation through the Bank for International Settlements and the maintenance of the stability of the price of gold through the London gold pool. Nor has

---

[1] *International Legal Materials*, Vol. VI, No. 5, September 1967, pp. 1058–1061 and Vol. VIII, No. 3, May 1968, pp. 473–546; Gold, Joseph, 'The Next Stage in the Development of International Monetary Law: The Deliberate Control of Liquidity', in *American Journal of International Law*, Vol. 62, No. 2, April 1968, pp. 365–402.

[2] International Monetary Fund, *International Financial News Survey*, Vol. XIX, No. 45, 17 November 1967, p. 375.

the role of the reserve currencies been defined, nor the problem of their future resolved,[1] in legal terms.

Conflicts of national policy and interest have been no more eliminated by the Articles of Agreement of the International Monetary Fund than by the Charter of the United Nations and are sometimes dramatically expressed, but, in monetary matters as in respect of recourse to force, though the new legal order may be precarious, the change of fundamental principle has been unequivocal. There will inevitably be a continuing tendency to question the new principle, and to envisage the possibility of reverting to unilateral measures[2] if the further development of the system fails to keep pace with the needs of economic growth, but we must not, in analysing or undertaking what still remains necessary, lose sight of or sacrifice what has already been achieved.

2. Trade

Fifty years ago monetary policy and trade were regarded as being, with migration, the classical examples of matters which are by international law solely within the domestic jurisdiction of each State. The principal exception in respect of trade was the obligation of most-favoured nation treatment widely accepted by treaty. Trade, like monetary policy, is now governed by comprehensive international obligations based on the broad concept of mutual aid.[3]

The General Agreement on Tariffs and Trade is still the firmest expression of these obligations; its provisions deal with most-favoured nation treatment, tariff concessions and negotiations, national treatment in respect of internal taxation and regulation, non-discrimination, subsidies, state enterprises and other aspects of commercial policy; it provides in the broadest possible terms that each contracting party shall accord sympathetic consideration to, and shall afford adequate opportunity for consultation regarding, such representations as may be made by another contracting party with respect to any matter affecting the operation of the Agreement; the decisions of the contracting parties resulting from these consultations now constitute an elaborate jurisprudence.[4]

---

[1] Harrod, Roy, *The Dollar*; Aubrey, Henry G., *The Dollar in World Affairs*; Conan, A. R., *The Problem of Sterling*.

[2] See, for instance, Eshag, Eprime, *Present System of Trade and Payments versus Full Employment and Welfare State*.

[3] Muhammad, V. A. Seyid, *The Legal Framework of World Trade*; and see also Hawkins, C. H., *Commercial Treaties and Agreements: Principles and Practice*; Wilcox, Clair, *A Charter for World Trade*.

[4] General Agreement on Tariffs and Trade, *Basic Agreement and Selected Documents*, with subsequent annual supplements.

The Kennedy Round of trade negotiations, completed in 1967 through the procedures established by the General Agreement, achieved a far-reaching reduction of tariff barriers embodied in schedules of tariff concessions and separate agreements on grain, chemical products and anti-dumping policies. A new Future Work Programme, relating chiefly to non-tariff and para-tariff barriers affecting international trade, agricultural products, and the trade of developing countries, has since been adopted by the contracting parties as a further stage in the development of their long-term Programme for Expansion of International Trade.

GATT in its earlier years was primarily concerned with the trading relationships of the developed free economies and it came to be regarded in some quarters as a rich man's club, but the Agreement was amended in 1964 to give greater weight to the problems and needs of the developing countries.[1] The General Agreement in its new form recognises 'that individual and joint action is essential to further the development of the economies of less-developed contracting parties and to bring about a rapid advance in the standards of living in these countries'; it restates the objectives of GATT as including 'a rapid and sustained expansion of the export earnings of the less-developed contracting parties', 'positive efforts designed to ensure that less-developed contracting parties secure a share in the growth in international trade commensurate with their needs for economic development', and the diversification of economic structures to this end; it waives the expectation of reciprocity for commitments made in favour of the trade of less-developed contracting parties; and it provides that the adoption of measures to give effect to the principles and objectives set forth therein 'shall be a matter of conscious and purposeful effort on the part of the contracting parties both individually and jointly'. The Agreement contains specific commitments by the developed contracting parties for the reduction and elimination, to the fullest extent possible, of tariffs and other barriers to imports from developing countries and an undertaking to give active consideration to the adoption of other measures designed to provide greater scope for the development of such imports; the normal procedures of consultation provided for in the Agreement are applicable to all questions which may arise in connection with the implementation of these commitments. The Agreement also embodies, in guarded but nevertheless far-reaching terms, obligations to take appropriate types of joint action to promote improved and acceptable conditions of access to world markets for primary products of particular interest to less-developed contracting

---

[1] *International Legal Materials*, Vol. IV, No. 1, pp. 121–135.

parties, the stabilisation and improvement of conditions of world markets, the development of the industrial export potential and rate of growth of the less-developed contracting parties, and the expansion of trade for the purpose of economic development. These provisions are not a general expression of benevolence, binding no one and unaccompanied by any procedural arrangements to make them practically effective. They are an integral part of the basic ground rules now governing international trade.

The United Nations Conference on Trade and Development of 1964 has opened a further chapter in the story. The action recommended by the Conference, so diverse and far-reaching in character that it cannot be recapitulated as a brief statement of principles, will greatly enlarge the role of the United Nations in the field of international trade and add to the broad concepts of negotiation and conciliation inherent in the Charter new conciliation procedures which are essential to carry out decisions whose ultimate purpose is to change the existing international division of labour. Mutual aid in large scale readjustments of economic policy has never previously been envisaged in such dramatic and comprehensive terms. As the new policies in process of development crystallise, they may be expected to find expression in legal obligations, but thus far the United Nations Conference on Trade and Development, far-reaching as its political significance and effect on economic thought and policy have been, has not resulted in comprehensive treaty obligations with an immediate impact on the law, comparable to that of the Articles of Agreement of the International Monetary Fund or GATT. UNCTAD has, however, already made a distinctive contribution to international procedures. At the 1964 Conference the cleavage between majority and minority views became so pronounced that the desirability of institutional arrangements to facilitate a wider consensus in the future became one of the leading themes of the Conference. In this respect great progress has been made and the General Assembly has unanimously approved a plan[1] whereby proposals of a specific nature for action substantially affecting the economic or financial interests of particular countries can, before they are submitted for a vote by the United Nations Trade and Development Conference or Board, be referred to a special process of conciliation. The procedure involves negotiation in a specially composed Conciliation Committee whose function is to endeavour to reach agreement. It has a twofold purpose; to facilitate a wider consensus and to distinguish clearly between recommendations which rest upon a general consensus and those which do not, with a

---

[1] *International Legal Materials*, Vol. IV, No. 1, pp. 55–71.

view to ensuring that the support of a majority, not including vitally interested parties, does not give a recommendation a spurious appearance of being authoritative.

Within this general pattern of a recognised common responsibility in matters of trade and development three questions are increasingly attracting special attention, the establishment of common markets and free trade areas by the formation of regional economic groups, the growing importance of trade relations among countries with different economic and social systems, and proposals for the preferential or free entry of exports of manufactures and semi-manufactures of developing countries to developed countries.

Mass production by highly sophisticated, specialised and expensive equipment with a high rate of obsolescence is uneconomical without a market larger than can be provided by any but the largest and richest States. The liberalisation of trade restrictions by general international action is only a part of the answer as its effect may be to give the industries developed in the large markets of the strongest economies an excessive grip elsewhere. The solution of a common market with a highly institutionalised legal framework or a free trade area which reduces trade barriers without a comparable uniformity and institutionalisation in other respects, evolved in Western Europe in the early and mid-fifties, has become by the late sixties the shape of things to come over large areas of the world. In Europe we have the European Communities and European Free Trade Association. In the Americas we have the Central American Common Market[1] and the Latin American Free Trade Association,[2] designed to be merged in the Latin American Common Market,[3] and the Caribbean Free Trade Association.[4] In Africa we have the East African Community and Common Market,[5] the Economic Community of Eastern Africa[6] (designed to cover a wider area), the Economic Community of West Africa,[7] and the Central African Economic and Customs Union. In the Middle East we have the Arab Common Market.[8] These plans are in different stages of realisation and have different degrees of reality; they envisage different degrees of

---

[1] Inter-American Institute of International Legal Studies, *The Inter-American Legal System*, pp. 470–479.

[2] Ibid., pp. 485–503.

[3] *International Legal Materials*, Vol. VI, No. 3, May–June 1967, pp. 535–544.

[4] Agreement signed in Antigua, 30 April 1968.

[5] Ibid., Vol. VI, No. 5, September 1967, pp. 932–1057.

[6] Ibid., Vol. V, No. 4, July 1966, pp. 633–635.

[7] Ibid., Vol. VI, No. 4, July 1967, pp. 776–781.

[8] Macdonald, Robert W., *The League of Arab States*, pp. 209–220.

economic integration, legal uniformity and institutional development, but they represent a common and widespread trend. These developments pose large questions concerning judicial control in regional economic communities,[1] the unification of legal systems within such communities,[2] the creation and control of community corporate entities,[3] and the status of such communities in international law[4] and international organisations.[5] Both the comparative law and the international law of regional communities will call for increasing attention.

The problems presented by trade relations between countries with different economic and social systems are primarily political and economic, but the legal problems which they present include the definition of the respective obligations of the parties to such transactions from different systems and the applicability and execution in respect of such transactions of trade arbitration agreements and awards.[6]

The question of preferential or free entry of manufactures and semi-manufactures from developing countries is almost wholly political and economic, but involves reconsideration of one of the oldest and most widely used devices employed in commercial treaties, the most-favoured nation clause.

The International Trade Law Commission recently established by the United Nations is now available to supplement the work of GATT and UNCTAD in developing the law of international trade, supplementing new legal approaches to substantive economic problems by a concerted approach to the codification of the law of international trade as such.

In the field of trade the challenge of a new world to the creative genius of the law has been met by imaginative concepts which are gradually finding expression in new legal devices. We are increasingly recognising with Brandeis that 'equal opportunity for all peoples as well as for all individuals' is 'the essential of international as well as of national justice upon which a peace which is to be permanent must rest'.[7] The

---

[1] Bebr, Gerhard, *Judicial Control of the European Communities.*

[2] Constantinides-Megret, C., *Le Droit de la Communauté Economique Européenne et l'Ordre juridique des Etats Membres.*

[3] Commission des Communautés Européennes, *Etudes – Serie Concurrence*, 1967(6), *Projet d'un Statut des Societés Anonymes Européennes.*

[4] Pescatore, Pierre, 'Les Relations Extérieures des Communautés Européennes', *Recueil des Cours de l'Académie de Droit international*, Vol. 103, (1961 (II)), pp. 9–203.

[5] Jenks, C. Wilfred, *The World Beyond the Charter*, pp. 140–142.

[6] See, for instance, Domke, Martin (ed.), *International Trade Arbitration*, especially at pp. 93–113.

[7] 'An Essential of Lasting Peace', reproduced in *The Curse of Bigness*, p. 269.

process has barely begun, but wholly new vistas have been opened before us.

3. Commodity policy

Fifty years ago commodity schemes were empirical arrangements not governed by any general principles and frequently regarded as a temporary device to deal with some emergency arising from war or economic depression; for improvisations of this nature, a body of settled law was neither necessary nor possible. Today commodity agreements have become a recognised feature of long-term commercial policy. The free play of market forces is tending to be superseded by negotiated agreements between producers and consumers designed to secure greater stability in production and prices on an equitable basis. The course of development has varied with different commodities, but certain general trends have emerged.[1] We owe to the General Agreement on Tariffs and Trade an internationally agreed procedure for the establishment of commodity agreements and agreed principles to which agreements must conform. The agreed procedure includes the right of any member State to ask the United Nations to appoint a study group for any commodity in the case of which a 'burdensome surplus' or widespread unemployment or underemployment cannot be avoided or prevented by normal market forces; all member States substantially interested in the production, consumption or trade in the commodity may send a representative to the study group; the United Nations then convenes an intergovernmental conference which can establish a scheme. The agreed principles to which control schemes must conform include the principle that all members substantially interested in the production, consumption or trade in the commodity shall be invited to participate, the inclusion of consumers as well as producers with equal voting power for exporters and importers in a Commodity Council, full publicity of the terms of the agreement, the provision of adequate supplies at reasonable prices, a limited term for each agreement or renewal, and official investigation by the United Nations of the working of each agreement at intervals not exceeding three years. The approach is clearly an expansionist philosophy in sharp contrast to the restriction schemes of the inter-war period. The outstanding innovation is the equal representation of consumers and producers. The system has hardly fulfilled the hopes placed in it in the early post-war years; it has been applied thus far to only a limited number of commodities, and all of the industries concerned

---

[1] Rowe, J. W. F., *Primary Commodities in International Trade.*

continue to have acute recurrent problems; but it has played and can continue to play a useful part in stabilising the prices of primary products. How useful a part it can play, and with what measure of agreement, will depend in substantial measure on how clearly and generally it is appreciated that commodity control schemes are a device for stabilising fluctuating foreign earnings, not a device for increasing inadequate foreign earnings; their contribution to increasing foreign earnings is important but indirect.[1] Commodity control has moved far from its origins, and is still in an experimental phase with an uncertain future. Commodity policy is increasingly thought of in broader terms as including, in addition to control schemes as such, the operation and financing of buffer stocks, the role and financing of programmes for the diversification of developing economies, and principles and guidelines for pricing policy designed to increase the receipts from the export of primary commodities. The part which the law plays in the future of commodity policy will depend on the extent to which the international lawyer understands the issues of policy involved and brings an imaginative approach to developing institutional arrangements, and legal instruments, procedures and devices, which facilitate their solution. Without the contribution of the law to the development of bills of exchange, bills of lading and marine insurance, international trade in commodities as we know it would have been impossible; can the law make any comparable contribution to the future of commodity policy?

4. Restrictive business practices

Fifty years ago restrictive business practices were uninhibited by the law of nations and a much less considerable preoccupation of municipal lawyers than they have since become. While conspiracy in restraint of trade was an ancient offence under the common law, statutory regulation of restrictive practices was unusual outside the United States where the federal anti-trust legislation, which is regarded as the constitutional charter of the free enterprise system, dates back to the Sherman Act of 1890.[2]

International concern with the matter was first brought clearly into focus at the League of Nations World Economic Conference of 1927, which 'did not recommend an international juridical régime for the protection of abuse'[3] but urged that the League of Nations, with the

---

[1] See Rowe, J. W. F., *Primary Commodities in International Trade*, pp. 213–18.

[2] For a historical sketch see Timberg, Sigmund, in Friedmann, Wolfgang (ed.), *Anti-Trust Laws*, pp. 403–466.

[3] Salter, Sir Arthur, *Recovery – The Second Effort*, p. 203.

assistance of governments, should watch the development of cartels and publish reports as to their effects upon technical progress, conditions of labour and prices; 'careful, adequate, courageous publicity by a central international body, equipped with the necessary resources and impartial as between countries and classes'[1] was preferred to legal regulation. This suggested alternative approach did not become effective, and in retrospect it was an illusion to suppose that it could become effective in the absence of any legal obligation, procedure or sanction.

The political impact of the 'thirties was to create a greatly increased sense of urgency concerning the desirability of some form of international action as a protection against international cartels and other restrictive business practices. The ever-growing conviction that restrictionist policies had contributed to the great depression and the close link in the public mind between international cartels and Nazi rearmament and economic penetration placed the whole problem in a new perspective.[2] The outcome was the inclusion in the Havana Charter for an International Trade Organization of 1948 of a substantial chapter relating to restrictive business practices. The Havana Charter provided that each Member of the International Trade Organization which it was to have established should take appropriate measures and cooperate with the Organization to prevent restrictive business practices affecting international trade and having harmful effects on the expansion of production or trade and the achievement of the objectives of the Organization; it envisaged a consultation procedure concerning practices which a Member considered objectionable, an investigation procedure for complaints, and cooperation among Members in remedial measures.[3] The Havana Charter was not ratified by the United States and did not come into force.

The General Agreement on Tariffs and Trade which then replaced the Havana Charter as the current code governing international commercial policy omitted the chapter of the Charter (Chapter V) concerning restrictive business practices. The Economic and Social Council therefore initiated, after an interval, a fresh approach to the matter and a committee approved by it drafted articles of agreement the general effect of which would have been to create a new agency to implement provisions which were substantially Chapter V of the Havana Charter;[4] this

---

[1] Salter, op. cit., p. 203.

[2] Hexner, Ervin, *International Cartels*.

[3] Wilcox, Clair, *A Charter for World Trade*, pp. 103–113 and 281–287.

[4] United Nations, *Restrictive Business Practices: Report of the Ad Hoc Committee on Restrictive Business Practices, Economic and Social Council, Official Records, Sixteenth Session, Supplement No. 11.*

approach also was not pursued. The upshot is that there are still no general international obligations or procedures concerning restrictive business practices. Within the European Economic Community and the European Coal and Steel Community there is now an elaborate body of law on the subject, based on the treaties establishing the Communities and the regulations adopted for the implementation of their provisions,[1] but there is nothing comparable of a general international character. The far-reaching developments which have taken place in the municipal law of many countries relating to restrictive business practices[2] have not yet been reflected in any corresponding development in the law of nations. Must we assume that the stalemate will be of long duration or can we conceive of some new line of development?

5. Investment

Fifty years ago the concern of international law with investment was essentially a concern for the investor; it reflected an individualist philosophy of society transposed to international relations.[3] Today the concern of international law with investment is primarily a concern for economic growth; it reflects the new economic and social philosophies which, in widely varied forms and different degrees, have been accepted throughout the world.

The continued growth of the world economy, the measures of economic integration necessary for higher levels of prosperity, the hope of bridging the north–south gap between affluence and underdevelopment, all presuppose the maintenance of a high level of international investment. Only if the volume of such investment continues to grow can the basic economic and social objectives of a world community dedicated to freedom and welfare be attained. The function of the law, in this context as in other matters, is to serve the general good of society by maintaining a reasonable equilibrium between conflicting interests expressed as conflicting considerations of public policy. This function of the law cannot be fulfilled if we allow its mission to be misconstrued either by those who would have it protect in all circumstances the intangible rights of the investor and the sanctity of private property or by those who would have it acknowledge and protect the sovereign right of

---

[1] See, for instance, Campbell, Alan and Thompson, Dennis, *Common Market Law*, pp. 165–173 and 246–250.

[2] Friedmann, Wolfgang, *Anti-Trust Laws*.

[3] E.g. Borchard, Edwin, *The Diplomatic Protection of Citizens Abroad; State Insolvency and Foreign Bondholders*, 2 vols., especially the case histories in Vol. 2.

each State to change its laws and regulations at its will and expropriate private property whenever it considers that the public good so requires. The growth of the world economy is a larger consideration than these conflicts of ideology and interest; in reconciling them, the creative imagination can play a vital part; it can do so only by adopting as the fundamental basis of the law relating to international investment neither the rights of property of the investor nor the rights of sovereignty of the country of investment but the social function of the investment in the interest of the world community as a whole.

Among the measures necessary to sustain a high level of international investment are increased facilities for investment through official international lending agencies, new corporate structures and devices for international cooperation in private investment, the negotiation of international guarantees for the protection of private investment, and the development of international procedures for the settlement of disputes arising from such investment. In devising these measures a new approach to old problems is required.

Great progress has been made since the Second World War in the provision of facilities for investment through official international lending agencies. The International Bank for Reconstruction and Development (with its affiliates the International Finance Corporation and the International Development Association), the Inter-American, African and Asian Development Banks, and the European Investment Bank of the European Economic Community, all provide facilities of this type. Dams and hydro-electric stations; airfields, ports and highways; railroads and pipelines; irrigation and flood control, land clearance and improvement, and farm mechanisation schemes; mines; iron and steel plants and fertiliser industries; development banks which encourage small industries; these are some of the concrete manifestations in some eighty different countries of the practical outcome of these facilities. A novel body of autonomous law has been evolved to govern these multifarious operations;[1] it includes legal instruments of wholly new types such as the Articles of Agreement of these banks, their loan and bond regulations, and their loan, guarantee and credit agreements relating to particular transactions; these instruments establish procedures of compulsory arbitration which may in course of time make an important contribution to the law of international investment.

New legal forms are no less necessary for the maintenance and

---

[1] Broches, Aaron, 'International Legal Aspects of the Operations of the World Bank', 98 *Recueil des Cours de l'Académie de Droit international*, (1959 (III)), at pp. 297–409; Salmon, Jean, *Le Rôle des Organisations Internationales en Matière de Prêts et d'Emprunts*.

development of international cooperation in private investment. Two forces converge to make a new approach to the whole subject necessary: the increasing control of investment from external sources asserted by countries of investment, and the increasing complexity of international economic life which defies any possibility of rational control, international or national, on the basis of existing legal systems. The interplay of nationalist politics and economic entities with world-wide interests and responsibilities cannot be accommodated within the traditional pattern of public international law, the conflict of laws and national legal systems. There is one kernel of truth in the charges of neo-colonialism at present so rampant in the world, namely that the organisational structure of powerful economic interests frequently eludes any possibility of effective national control. The situation has a paradoxical aspect. On the one hand, governments increasingly insist on measures designed to accentuate the national character of the activities in their territories of foreign concerns. On the other hand, multiple incorporation devices and holding companies make it possible for the skilful lawyer to evade any effective control of many operations by any government.

In many cases important aspects of foreign investment, including in particular the constitution and much of the functioning of the investing company, were traditionally governed by the law of the investing State rather than that of the State of investment. Such a position is frequently no longer acceptable to the State of investment and there have been interesting experiments in joint international business ventures which represent new forms of cooperation between outside capital and a substantial measure of national control.[1] A wide range of new legal techniques have been developed to permit of such ventures.

The problems of devising any effective control in the public interest of far-flung international operations have proved more intractable. The legal system which we have inherited cannot cope with the international economic order which the thrust of ingenuity of commercial enterprise has now created. The essence of world-wide interdependence is, in the language of Max Radin, that 'any one grouping cuts through and across other groupings';[2] Radin described this as 'a fact which makes all social study so difficult';[3] it makes effective control in the public interest still more difficult. It is difficult to conceive of the problem being solved

---

[1] Friedmann, Wolfgang and Kalmanoff, George, *Joint International Business Ventures*.

[2] Radin, Max, *Law as Logic and Experience*, p. 126.

[3] Ibid., p. 126.

without the creation of some new international régime and status for economic concerns engaged in such operations. Such a régime and status might be a composite of three elements. The concern seeking international status under the régime would undertake to comply with agreed principles and to cooperate in prescribed arrangements for international supervision of its operations. Governments would give certain special facilities and privileges to concerns which had been granted such status. In areas of economic life in which international supervision was particularly desirable, governments would permit foreign concerns to operate in their territory only if they had applied for and been granted international status. Such an international régime for privately-conducted international operations would be a wholly new departure, but it may be the most satisfactory, and perhaps the only, solution for the dilemma which the conflict between nationalist politics and international economic operations increasingly presents. Both the clarification of the concept and the elaboration of the technical devices necessary for its implementation will call for creative imagination of a high order.

The political sensitivity of the problem of investment becomes increasingly acute when we proceed to consider the possibility of an international investment code, and such questions as multilateral investment insurance, investment guarantees and incentives, and international procedures for the settlement of investment disputes.

The concept of an international investment code is attractive and the common interest in economic stability and growth of the divergent interests involved may prove sufficiently substantial to make such a code a possibility. The prospect of success depends on the adoption of an approach much broader than the mere exercise of legal ingenuity in the interest of the investor. Such a code must represent a sufficiently fair compromise to be acceptable to capital exporting and importing countries alike as the basis of mutually profitable relations. It may perhaps take the form of a convention, acceptance of the provisions of which becomes a term of certain major international financial transactions.

Valuable work along these lines has been done by the Organization for Economic Co-operation and Development, which has prepared a Draft Convention on the Protection of Foreign Property designed to promote 'the flow of capital for economic activity and development' by 'a clear statement of recognised principles relating to the protection of foreign property, combined with rules to render more effective the application of these principles'. The Convention provides that 'each party shall at all times ensure fair and equitable treatment to the property of the nationals of the other parties'. It specifies three conditions to be complied with by any measures depriving, directly or indirectly, of his property, a national of another party; that they are taken in the public interest and under due process of law; that they are not discriminatory or contrary to any undertaking given; and that they are accompanied by provision for the payment of just compensation. 'Such compensation shall represent the genuine value of the property affected, shall be paid without undue delay, and shall be transferable to the extent necessary to make it effective for the national entitled thereto.' Each party should have regard to the principle that any measures taken by any State, whether or not a party, which are in conflict with these provisions should not be recognised within the territory of that party as valid. There is provision for an arbitral tribunal to which, under certain conditions, injured persons and companies would have access.[1] Along some such lines it may be possible to make progress.

A scheme for a multilateral investment guarantees corporation, designed to provide guarantees against risks of a non-commercial (political) nature for new private investment in developing countries, has been formulated but not adopted.[2]

Matters have proceeded somewhat further as regards arrangements for the settlement of investment disputes.

The International Bank for Reconstruction and Development has sponsored a Convention on the Settlement of Investment Disputes between States and Nationals of Other States. The Preamble to the Convention recites that the parties, 'recognising that, while such disputes would usually be subject to national legal processes, international methods of settlement may be appropriate in certain cases', attach particular importance 'to the availability of facilities for international conciliation or arbitration to which Contracting States and nationals of other Contracting States may submit such disputes if they so desire'. The Convention establishes an International Centre for Settlement of Investment Disputes which maintains a Panel of Conciliators and a Panel of Arbitrators designated in part by Contracting States and in part by the President of the Bank as Chairman of the Administrative Council of the Centre. A Conciliation Commission or Arbitration Tribunal is constituted from the panel for each case; failing agreement upon the constitution of the Commission or Tribunal the Chairman makes the necessary appointments. The jurisdiction of the Centre is limited to legal disputes arising directly out of an investment; it rests on consent; it extends to Contracting States and natural or juridical persons

---

[1] *International Legal Materials*, Vol. II, No. 2, pp. 241–267.

[2] *International Legal Materials*, Vol. V, No. 1, pp. 92–102.

who had or are deemed to have had the nationality of a Contracting State at the material date. The Convention is an attempt to strike a fair compromise between conflicting interests. To protect the investor it provides that 'when the parties have given their consent, no party may withdraw its consent unilaterally'. To protect the State of investment it provides that 'no Contracting State shall give diplomatic protection or bring an international claim, in respect of a dispute which one of its nationals and another Contracting State shall have consented to submit or shall have submitted to arbitration under this Convention, unless such other Contracting State shall have failed to abide by and comply with the award rendered in such dispute'. If conciliation proceedings fail, neither party 'shall be entitled in any other proceeding, whether before arbitration or in a court of law or otherwise, to invoke or rely on any views expressed or statements or admissions or offers of settlement made by the other party in the conciliation proceedings, or the report or any recommendations made by the Commission'. Arbitral tribunals are to decide disputes 'in accordance with such rules of law as may be agreed by the parties'. In the absence of such agreement 'the Tribunal shall apply the law of the Contracting State party to the dispute (including its rules on the conflict of laws) and such rules of international law as may be applicable'. The award is binding on the parties and 'each Contracting State' is to recognise an award rendered pursuant to the Convention as binding and to 'enforce the pecuniary obligations imposed by that award within its territories as if it were a final judgment of a court in that State'.[1]

6. Development aid

Fifty years ago there was no development aid as such; development was the function of speculative investment and intergovernmental finance was largely a matter of reparations, war debts and, at most, the monetary rehabilitation of shattered economies. Considerable legal inventiveness was applied to these problems[2] but there was no comparable body of law relating to development as a recognised object of policy to be pursued by concerted action.

Today development is the recognised keynote of world economic policy,[3] but is still a matter of policy rather than legal obligation. Will

---

[1] *International Legal Materials*, Vol. IV, No. 3, pp. 524–544; for the Provisional Regulations and Rules of the Centre see *International Legal Materials*, Vol. VI, No. 2, pp. 225–283.

[2] Cf. Jenks, C. Wilfred, 'Fischer Williams: The Practitioner as Reformer', 40 *British Year Book of International Law*, 1964, pp. 233–285.

[3] Black, Eugene, *The Diplomacy of Economic Development*.

the evolution of policy be arrested at this point or can we envisage a further stage at which the mutual relations of advanced and developing countries are governed by recognised legal obligations? Are we perhaps on the threshold of general principles of international law governing development and including an obligation of advanced countries to contribute to such aid on an agreed scale fixed for a reasonable period of years, obligations of developing countries to use such aid in an approved manner and to effect any social changes necessary to make it possible for such aid to fulfil its purpose, and safeguards to depoliticise the grant and receipt of such aid. Only if development aid is increasingly channelled through multilateral programmes can we hope to spell out from current policies principles which can be crystallised into legal obligations.

There is an increasing tendency to recognise the political advantages, to countries granting no less than to countries receiving aid, of multilateral programmes which transform aid 'from a national charity and an instrument of cold war competition' to 'a community responsibility characterised by continuity, predictability and dignity for all parties' which can be 'insulated from international political rivalries and internal political pressures';[1] only in such a manner can development aid be given a satisfactory rationale and provision be made for an equitable sharing of the burden.[2] The advanced aid-giving free economies have evolved in the Development Assistance Committee of the Organization for Economic Co-operation and Development a valuable instrument for comparing and concerting their aid programmes,[3] but multilateral aid remains a relatively small fraction of the whole.

The clearest institutional expression of development aid, as distinguished from development lending, on a multilateral basis is the International Development Association established as an affiliate of the World Bank for long-term low-interest development lending for programmes that cannot be financed by conventional loans.

The International Development Association is evolving a body of law and practice concerning development credits, based upon its Articles of Agreement, Development Credit Regulations and development credit and administration agreements, which is analogous to the body of autonomous law concerning investment transactions being evolved by the World Bank.

---

[1] See, for instance, Fulbright, Senator J. William, *The Arrogance of Power*, pp. 223–241.

[2] Mason, Edward S., *Foreign Aid and Foreign Policy*.

[3] Rubin, Seymour J., *The Conscience of the Rich Nations*.

Varied suggestions have been made for increasing the volume and diversifying the types of development aid available through multilateral schemes.

One of these, the Horowitz Plan of the Governor of the Bank of Israel, is designed to mobilise private capital for soft loans by a combination of an intergovernmental guarantee and an intergovernmental subsidy to provide market rates of interest organised through the World Bank or the International Development Association.[1] Alternative plans adumbrated in a World Bank study include a plan for increasing the resources of the International Development Association, which at present consists of outright grants from member Governments, by loans from Members made on the same terms as I.D.A. credits and repayable as and when borrowers from I.D.A. repay credits granted out of the proceeds of the loans,[2] and a plan whereby underwriting countries would meet part of the interest charges on a loan.[3]

One scheme of special interest prepared at the request of the United Nations Conference on Trade and Development of 1964 is designed to finance unexpected export shortfalls liable to disrupt long-term agreed development programmes which are dependent on the availability of anticipated foreign exchange resources'[4]; the purpose of the scheme would be to share with the country concerned the burden of adjustment to the shortfall in a manner compatible with the continuation of the development programme; it would apply to shortfalls for which provision cannot be made by the arrangements for temporary export shortfalls of a short-term character available through the International Monetary Fund facility for the compensatory financing of export fluctuations.[5]

The part which the law can play in shaping better schemes of development aid, and the effect of new schemes of development aid upon the law, may raise questions as significant for the future of the law of nations as those which the emergence of equity raised for the law of property in the English law of three centuries ago or those which modern labour and social security legislation have raised for the law of employment relationships in so many countries in recent times. New legal devices and techniques are being employed constantly and we appear to be feeling

---

[1] International Bank for Reconstruction and Development, *The Horowitz Proposal – A Staff Report.*

[2] Ibid., p. 31. [3] Ibid., pp. 31–32.

[4] International Bank for Reconstruction and Development, *Supplementary Financial Measures: A Study requested by the United Nations Conference on Trade and Development*, 1964.

[5] *International Legal Materials*, Vol. V, No. 6, pp. 1047–1079.

our way towards new fundamental principles. How large a part can the law of nations play in reducing the explosive inequalities between rich and poor nations which constitute so grave a threat to the peace and progress of mankind?

7. Know-how

In a world of constant scientific discovery and technological change, know-how is as vital an element in economic and social progress as investment and development aid. Fifty years ago the international law of know-how, then chiefly patent law,[1] consisted of rules to protect vested rights in know-how; today the organised transfer of know-how to developing countries has become a major objective of international policy which has found expression in a wide range of new legal devices; the shift of emphasis has reached the proportions of a reversal of general direction from the protection of vested legal rights to the diffusion of technical processes and skills. The United Nations Development Programme provides a legal framework for the transfer of know-how to developing countries on an ever-increasing scale. New legal concepts and techniques have been developed to facilitate the transfer of knowledge and skills.[2]

There is, for instance, an elaborate body of law governing the administration of the technical cooperation projects with member States in which the United Nations, the specialised agencies and a number of the regional organisations are involved. The agreements governing large pre-investment projects involving substantial expenditures are particularly important; they include the agreements with recipient States and executing agencies, and the detailed plans of operation, on the basis of which funds are made available from the United Nations Development Programme, and the substantial body of precedent which now governs the application of these agreements. A host of research and training institutes and centres for the transfer of know-how have been created in a large number of countries on the initiative or with the assistance of the United Nations or one of the specialised agencies; they include every possible variety and combination of international and national legal status and a wide range of new legal instruments, structures and devices have been evolved for their administration and gradual devolution from international to national responsibilitity. The OPEX scheme makes international personnel available to work as national government

---

[1] Ladas, Stephen P., *The International Protection of Industrial Property*.

[2] Schachter, Oscar, 'The Relations of Law, Politics and Action in the United Nations', *Recueil des Cours de l'Académie de Droit international*, Vol. 108, (1963 (I)), pp. 233–245; Feuer, G., *Les Aspects Juridiques de l'Assistance Technique*.

officials discharging operational and executive functions in developing countries; it is implemented through standard agreements between the United Nations and the employing governments, and standard contracts between the United Nations and the personnel concerned, which have important and novel features. All of these developments are experiments in new types of cooperative relationship between the world community and its members; their significance therefore far transcends the circumstances of individual cases.

8. Industrial development

Industrial development has become a primary objective of economic policy for much of the developing world, and the United Nations Industrial Development Organisation (UNIDO) has been established to foster such development. Has the international lawyer any significant contribution to make in the matter? Fifty years ago he clearly had not. His brief was often to protect the legal position and claims of established industrial interests. He is now as likely to be concerned in devising new legal instruments, rights and procedures to facilitate industrial development. In the formulation of general principles his part may well be more modest, for few of the aspirations of developing countries for assistance in their industrial development can at present be expressed as legal rights which the more advanced countries are prepared to recognise as such. Industrial development is, moreover, an objective rather than a department of policy, presupposing action in such fields as investment, know-how and trade; it may well be by developing new conceptions in these fields, and legal instruments and devices for their application, that the international lawyer will make his main contribution to industrial development.

9. Shipping

The law maritime has been from the earliest days of international law one of the leading traditional influences upon its development, and the legal régime of merchant ships in peace and war has passed through many phases of development from the Rhodian Sea Law, the Rolls of Oleron, the Black Book of the Admiralty and the Consolato del Mare, to the long succession of international conventions relating to merchant ships of modern times.[1] The law has been limited, however, to the legal

---

[1] For the whole process of development see Colombos, C. John, *International Law of the Sea*, 6th ed.

régime of shipping, with the emphasis upon jurisdiction over shipping and the regulation and safety of navigation,[1] and in more recent times the protection and conditions of employment of seamen;[2] the economics of shipping has lain beyond its scope and the Convention of 1948 creating the Inter-Governmental Maritime Consultative Organisation provides that matters concerning unfair restrictive practices by shipping concerns shall be dealt with in the first instance through the normal processes of international shipping business.

The question which now arises is how far the law should take cognisance of a wider range of political and economic considerations affecting shipping. The question has become acute in varied contexts.

How far should international law attempt to limit and regulate recourse to flags of convenience? The question was much debated by the United Nations Conference on the Law of the Sea of 1958,[3] which finally contented itself, after much debate, with providing in the Convention on the High Seas that 'there must exist a genuine link between the State and the ship' and that 'in particular the State must effectively exercise its jurisdiction and control in administrative, technical and social matters over ships flying its flag'.[4] The International Court of Justice has held that the flags of convenience States are among the largest shipowning nations within the meaning of the Convention establishing the Inter-Governmental Maritime Consultative Organisation.[5] How far is further regulation desirable in the matter?

How far should international law be developed to regulate international shipping cartels[6] and to become the equivalent of an international code of public utility regulation in respect of shipping services? How should it regard attempts by particular countries, notably the United States, to apply their national cartel regulations to international shipping?

What part can international law play in resolving the problems arising from the growing desire of developing countries to escape from their dependence on international shipping services?[7]

---

[1] Singh, Nagendra, *International Conventions of Merchant Shipping.*

[2] International Labour Office, *The International Labour Code, 1951*, pp. 755–925.

[3] Boczek, Boleslaw Adam, *Flags of Convenience;* Meijers, H., *The Nationality of Ships*, Roux, J. M., *Les Pavillons de Complaisance.*

[4] Article 5.

[5] *International Court of Justice Reports*, 1960, pp. 150–178.

[6] Marx, Daniel, Jr., *International Shipping Cartels.*

[7] United Nations, *Shipping in the World Economy;* United Nations Trade and Development Conference, *Establishment or Expansion of Merchant Marines in Developing Countries.*

It may well be that the international law relating to the economics of shipping will become as important as the law relating to the legal régime of shipping and the regulation of navigation.

10. Insurance

World-wide insurance, and in particular reinsurance, facilities have hitherto been provided by a small number of leading international insurance markets; this position is clearly changing and may be expected to change still further with the increasing interest of developing countries in establishing, by national or cooperative action, insurance facilities not involving the payment of premiums in foreign exchange or otherwise subject to foreign control or influence. Another factor tending in the opposite direction is the increased cover required for the risk incidental to advanced technology, including nuclear risks. These contradictory tendencies will both call for an important expansion of the international law relating to insurance.

Hitherto the international law relating to insurance, as distinguished from the principles of the conflict of laws relating to insurance transactions, has been concerned chiefly with such matters as the effect of war, changes of territorial sovereignty and measures of nationalisation on insurance transactions. Only recently have we begun to develop international rules concerning such matters as insurance against civil liability in respect of international transport, nuclear liability insurance, and the regulation of foreign insurance companies.[1]

Efforts to promote uniform international rules of marine insurance were made by the Institute of International Law as long ago as 1885 and by the International Law Association in 1901, but have had little success.

Must we not now envisage a larger role for the law in at least four respects?

As insurance markets become more numerous but less experienced, accepted international standards may become a factor in general confidence in their operations.

New insurance facilities for developing countries may require co-operative arrangements among a number of countries involving the creation of new legal entities and rules.

As the cover required for exceptionally large risks increases, international arrangements may be necessary to provide it.

Some measure of internationalisation of the traditional insurance

---

[1] Monaco, Riccardo, 'Les assurances en droit international', *Recueil des Cours de l'Académie de Droit international*, Vol. 101, (1960 (III)), pp. 389–471.

markets may prove desirable in order to enable them to continue to afford world-wide facilities on a basis acceptable to users in all countries.

There have not yet been any major developments in the international law relating to insurance comparable to those which have occurred in respect of other branches of economic policy and life; what contribution to such developments can we reasonably anticipate from the creative genius of the law?

11. Rural development, agriculture, and food production and distribution

In advanced and developing countries alike there is a tendency to regard industrial development as the essence and measure of overall economic growth, but historically an increase in the productivity of agriculture often precedes, and releases resources for, the process of economic growth;[1] as the process continues the magnet of industrialisation and urbanisation tends to draw vitality from the countryside and thereby to destroy the whole equilibrium of society. The complex repercussions of these tendencies are world-wide in their effects. The balance of town and country has become one of the gravest of social problems throughout the world. It has become so at a time when rapidly growing populations and rising standards and expectations have made increased food production one of the first priorities of enlightened statesmanship throughout the world.[2]

What bearing has international law on the question whether the coming generations are to be fed or to starve? Fifty years ago the answer would clearly have been none whatsoever. Famine and malnutrition were matters within the domestic jurisdiction of each State. The International Institute of Agriculture,[3] created in 1905, was primarily a body for the publication of statistical and other information; the convention establishing it placed no obligations in matters of policy upon adhering States; there was no significant development in this respect during the inter-war period, even when the League of Nations, during the 'thirties, made the problem of nutrition an international issue.[4] The Constitution of the Food and Agriculture Organization of

---

[1] Cf. Rostow, W. W., *The Stages of Economic Growth*, pp. 21–24.

[2] Castro, Josué de, *The Geography of Hunger*.

[3] Hobson, Arthur, *The International Institute of Agriculture*.

[4] *Final Report of the Mixed Committee of the League of Nations on the Relation of Nutrition to Health, Agriculture and Economic Policy*.

the United Nations, which came into force in 1945, represented a fundamental change of attitude. It expressed the determination of the nations accepting the Constitution 'to promote the common welfare by furthering separate and collective action on their part for the purposes of raising levels of nutrition and standards of living of the peoples under their respective jurisdiction, securing improvements in the efficiency of the production and distribution of all food and agricultural products, bettering the condition of rural populations, and thus contributing towards an expanding world economy'. This is, in the main, a practical task, calling primarily for a wider knowledge and use of already widely-known agricultural techniques, and the Food and Agriculture Organization has rightly so construed its mission;[1] but there is scope for a considered assessment of the extent to which the development of a network of more precise legal obligations would contribute to the accomplishment of this mission.

When the International Labour Organisation first adopted conventions and recommendations relating to agricultural labour in 1921 it was contended before the Permanent Court of International Justice that agriculture, by its nature, is not susceptible of uniform legal regulation even within the frontiers of a single State;[2] the Court rejected this contention.[3] During the almost fifty years which have elapsed since that time, legal regulation has become an increasingly important factor in the progress and prosperity of agriculture in many countries; has it a larger part to play than has yet been fully recognised in international action to promote rural development, the progress of agriculture, and the improvement of food production and distribution? In certain areas of policy, of which the conservation of game and fisheries, the prevention of the spread of animal and plant diseases, the control of locusts and other pests, the preservation from deterioration of food in transport and storage, and the grading of foodstuffs are illustrations, international agreements of unequal importance have received varying degrees of acceptance,[4] but in the main the progress of international law and international action relating to rural development, agriculture and food have followed different paths. Should this remain the position in a world in which the problem of the adequacy of future food supplies now looms so

---

[1] Hambidge, Gove, *The Story of F.A.O.*

[2] Permanent Court of International Justice, Series C, No. 1, pp. 545–567.

[3] Permanent Court of International Justice, *Collection of Advisory Opinions*, Series B, Nos. 2 and 3, pp. 29–33.

[4] On the whole matter see Velas, Pierre, *Introduction en Droit International Economique et Social*, Tome I, 'Droit International Agricole'.

large? Or has the law some significant part, not yet clearly visualised, to play in this as in other fields of economic growth?

12. Migration, refugees, and travel

Movements of people may be as important for the dynamic growth of the world economy as movements of goods and movements of capital. Fifty years ago freedom of migration could claim no warrant from international law and the law provided little protection for the immigrant as such.

During an earlier period freedom of migration had been exercised as almost a natural right; new countries were keen to attract migrants and the restrictive and selective immigration policies of later years were still to come; but the freedom was granted by national policies and when national policies changed there were diplomatic protests and sometimes, as in the case of the Gentlemen's Agreement of 1907–1908 between the United States and Japan,[1] diplomatic settlements, but the protests could not invoke and the settlements, far from establishing, denied any recognised rule of international law conferring or defining a right of freedom of migration. When the law in the matter did crystallise in the first quarter of the twentieth century, it crystallised on the basis of the right of every State to determine the composition of its own population. This remains, and in general international terms is likely to remain, the position; it is indeed significant that the United Nations Covenant on Civil and Political Rights provides that 'everyone shall be free to leave any country, including his own' but as regards the right of entry provides only that 'no one shall be arbitrarily deprived of the right to enter his own country'.[2]

The treaty establishing the European Economic Community provides for the free movement of workers within the community, the abolition of restrictions on the freedom of establishment of nationals of a member State in the territory of another member State, and the abolition of restrictions on the free supply of services within the community.[3] In this context immigration ceases to be a matter of domestic jurisdiction; freedom of migration becomes a characteristic feature of the economic life of the community. The Arab Common Market Plan of 6 June 1962 also provides for freedom of residence, work and economic activities. The establishment of a common market does not, however, necessarily imply, and that of a free trade area does not involve, such freedom of

---

[1] Griswold, A. Whitney, *The Far Eastern Policy of the United States*, pp. 333–379.

[2] Article 12. [3] Articles 48, 52 and 59.

movement of persons. The General Treaty for Central American Economic Integration[1] establishing the Central American Common Market, the Treaty for East African Co-operation of 6 June 1967 establishing the East African Community and Common Market,[2] the Agreement establishing the Central African Economic and Customs Union, and the Articles of Association for the Establishment of an Economic Community of West Africa of 4 May 1967[3] make no provision for the freedom of movement of persons; and the convention establishing the European Free Trade Association,[4] the Treaty instituting the Latin American Free Trade Association[5] and the Agreement establishing a Caribbean Free Trade Association are all silent on the subject. The Declaration of the Presidents of America of Intention to Establish a Latin American Common Market of 14 April 1967 envisages free movement of manpower within the Central American Common Market but contains no similar provision concerning the wider Latin American common market.[6] It seems probable that any further acceptance of the principle of freedom of movement of persons will be on a regional basis and related to other measures of economic integration. Meanwhile, not unnaturally in view of the complexity of the political and cultural as well as economic and social factors involved, migration is of all the potential elements of economic growth the one in respect of which the law is moving most slowly.

The treatment of migrants has a different history. Migrants have always enjoyed some protection from the general principles of international law relating to the protection of aliens,[7] but these have been a protection against arbitrary injustice rather than a guarantee of economic fairness and opportunity. From the early twentieth century onwards there has been a long succession of bilateral treaties for the protection of migrants,[8] and we now have, in the I.L.O. Migration for Employment Convention (Revised), 1949, a recognised international standard of treatment for such migrants which twenty-eight States have accepted as an international obligation; the outcome is that, while the right to control immigration normally remains, except within the

---

[1] Inter-American Institute of International Legal Studies, *The Inter-American System*, pp. 470–479.

[2] *International Legal Materials*, Vol. VI No. 5, September 1967, pp. 932–1057.

[3] *International Legal Materials*, Vol. VI, No. 4, July 1967, pp. 776–781.

[4] *European Yearbook*, Vol. VII, 1959, pp. 663–727.

[5] *The Inter-American System*, pp. 485–503.

[6] *International Legal Materials*, Vol. VI, No. 3, May–June 1967, pp. 535–544.

[7] Borchard, E. M., *The Diplomatic Protection of Citizens Abroad.*

[8] International Labour Office, *Migration Laws and Treaties*, 3 vols., 1928–1929.

European Economic Community and in any other case in which analogous arrangements may develop, a domestic matter, the duly admitted migrant is protected, in countries for which this convention is in force, by an international standard which covers recruitment, reception, medical care, placing, conditions of labour, social security, protection against arbitrary repatriation and similar matters. In this sense there is now a substantial qualification to the principle that immigration is a domestic matter.

The problem of refugees may be regarded as a special case of the problem of migration, in which the humanitarian prevails over the economic aspect. Prior to League of Nations days there was no organised international provision for the protection of refugees. During the last fifty years there have been constant changes in the organisational arrangements for the protection of refugees, reflecting changing estimates of the scale and prospective duration of the problem, changes in its incidence and political context, and changes in the policies and measures of resettlement and protection envisaged from time to time;[1] a number of these changes have been influenced by the repeated illusion, repeatedly destroyed by the facts, that the problem of refugees is essentially temporary. From this tortuous history two principles appear to have emerged. The first is that, while the refugee has no right to the refuge of his choice, the world community has a community responsibility, acknowledged although still inchoate and formless, for the resettlement and protection of refugees to the fulfilment of which the State from which they have sought refuge is not entitled to object, and which is discharged by cooperation with the United Nations High Commissioner for Refugees in the fulfilment of his mandate in a manner beneficial to the economic growth of the community. This responsibility, already implicit in established practice, is now formally recognised by the United Nations Declaration on Territorial Asylum, adopted by the General Assembly on 14 December 1967, which provides that asylum granted by a State in the exercise of its sovereignty shall be respected by all other States, that the situation of persons seeking such asylum is of concern to the international community, and that 'where a State finds difficulty in granting or continuing to grant asylum, States individually or jointly or through the United Nations shall consider, in a spirit of international solidarity, appropriate measures to lighten the burden on

---

[1] Simpson, Sir John Hope, *The Refugee Problem – Report of a Survey*; Vernant, Jacques, *The Refugee in the Post War Period*; Woodbridge, George, *The History of UNRRA*, 3 vols.; Holborn, Louise W., *The International Refugee Organization*; Schnyder, F., 'Les aspects juridiques actuels du problème des réfugiés', *Recueil des Cours de l'Académie de Droit international*, Vol. 14, (1965 (I)), pp. 335–450.

that State'. The second principle is that there is a recognised international standard of protection for refugees, now embodied in the United Nations Convention on the Status of Refugees of 25 July 1951.[1] The question is sometimes asked whether refugees are now to be regarded as subjects of international law; the answer to this question, whether positive or negative, is perhaps less important than the clear acceptance of a community responsibility in the matter and the formulation of a community standard of treatment. The fact that the responsibility and standard of treatment are still contested does not detract from the significance of the measure in which they are accepted as compared with the position a generation earlier.

Whereas the problem of refugees may be regarded as the pathology of the freedom of movement of persons, freedom of travel represents the everyday application of the principle. Before the First World War freedom of travel was the rule rather than the exception, no passport being required for travel in Europe west of Russia and Turkey. During the last fifty years freedom of travel has been limited by numerous, widely varying and constantly changing passport, visa, security and currency requirements and restrictions; the policies of 'closed' societies during this period have been a major complicating factor. In recent years there has been a substantial but precarious relaxation of these requirements and restrictions, chiefly by reciprocal agreement or unilateral action, but though the Universal Declaration of Human Rights declares that everyone has the right to leave any country, including his own, and to return to his own country, this liberalisation has fallen far short of freedom of travel becoming anything which can be described as a legal right. The law as yet plays little part in guaranteeing, or even facilitating, the freedom of travel without which there can be no true community. Must its role remain so limited?

13. Population

Mutual aid for economic stability and growth cannot cope with the problems of a population explosion. Nor can the world community accept a collective responsibility for the general welfare if its member nations do not so discipline their rate of population increase as to make the task a possible one. The facts are widely known. A World Leaders' Declaration on Population, signed by the heads of state or prime ministers of thirty countries and formally presented to the Secretary-General of the United Nations on 11 December 1967, records them in

---

[1] 189 *United Nations Treaty Series*, 137.

dramatic terms. 'It took mankind all of recorded time until the middle of the last century to achieve a population of one billion. Yet it took less than a hundred years to add the second billion, and only thirty years to add the third. At today's rate of increase, there will be four billion people by 1975 and nearly seven billion by the year 2000. This unprecedented increase presents us with a situation unique in human affairs and a problem that grows more urgent with each passing day.' Malthus now appears to have been less wrong than premature. Throughout the developing world the pressure of population upon resources is a stern reality. The quality of life succumbs to the quantity of life. The education of an élite cannot keep pace with the pressure of the masses. The political implications are startling and have been aptly and cogently stated by Secretary of State Dean Rusk. 'At the present time there is no nation that is putting forward the doctrine of *lebensraum* for territorial expansion or aggression against its neighbours. That is because there is considerable confidence that science and technology can somehow deal with this problem of people and resources. If that hope disappears, we could have new crises arising out of sheer pressure of population. It is a race between scientific and technological advance on one side, and limitation of the growth of the species on the other. In the 1980s and 1990s this problem could be at least as explosive as the nuclear weapons problem.'[1]

Fifty years ago it was taken as a matter of course that international law was unconcerned with population policy beyond recognition that immigration was a matter within the domestic jurisdiction of each State. It is widely assumed that the position in this respect remains unchanged. Is this assumption valid? Has the law nothing to say, and can we remain content that it should have nothing to say, upon this, the greatest of our economic and social problems? The ground is so new, and in some respects so controversial, that one cannot venture any clear prophecy. Eugenics by law, a favourite topic of the sponsors of ideal commonwealths from Lycurgus and Plato onwards, has not commended itself to any civilised jurisprudence. Population trends are determined by social habits expressed in myriads of decisions by individuals. Action by governments consists largely of using their immense influence to ensure that such decisions are taken in the light of knowledge rather than in the darkness of ignorance. The World Leaders' Declaration recognises this; it is not a legal instrument but a statement of beliefs concerning policy which places the accent on access to knowledge. Where do we proceed from this point on? It is clearly not for the law of nations to intrude

---

[1] *The Times*, Friday, 12 January 1968, page 4, column 7.

upon the privacy of intimate convictions and habits, but it is not alien to its function to promote access to knowledge which affects the fundamentals of world economic development. Can the law of nations encourage restraint by placing a premium upon the knowledge necessary for rational population policies, or facilitating its dissemination, and if so how?

Action by international organisations to disseminate such knowledge has already been initiated. The General Assembly of the United Nations, while 'recognising the sovereignty of nations in formulating and promoting their own population policies, with due regard to the principle that the size of the family should be the free choice of each individual family', has approved a work programme covering training, research, information and advisory services in the field of population; the World Health Organization, the International Labour Organisation, Unesco and the United Nations Children's Fund have all accepted appropriate responsibilities in the matter; and the United Nations has established a Population Trust Fund, financed by voluntary contributions from governments and private sources, to permit of the expansion of these activities.

Is an international agreement for freedom of access to such knowledge, pledging cooperation with these activities, conceivable in our time, and if so in what form? In the United States the constitutional right to such knowledge has been established by the Supreme Court.[1] Can we conceive of any international parallel?

Can the law do more than this? There is at least one principle which may serve as a point of departure. No State can derive any rights against its fellows from the lack of self-restraint of itself or its citizens. No State can expect to receive over a substantial period continuing international aid which its own rate of population increase makes wholly ineffective to revitalise its economy and trigger self-sustaining growth. Certain forms of aid might be granted only to States which had adopted rational population policies which made it possible for such aid to be practically effective in achieving its intended purpose of raising standards. If such an approach were to become accepted policy, it would remain to be seen whether such a policy must be its nature remain a policy or whether the creative imagination could give appropriate expression to the policy in the law. There is no inherent objection to aid being furnished only to those who eliminate the barriers to knowledge without which the aid cannot be effective for its purpose and if this is accepted policy there is no reason of principle for which the policy

---

[1] *Griswold* v. *State of Connecticut*, 85 S. Ct. 1678 (1965).

should not find expression in the law. Whether the policy can be wisely and effectually expressed in the form of legal conditions of eligibility for aid or any other legal form becomes essentially a practical matter to be gauged on the basis of specific proposals.

14. Wealth and welfare

The present stage of development of the law relating to economic stability and growth reflects the conflicts of economic ideology, structure and interest which divide the world. There have been far-reaching developments during the last fifty years, but there is nothing in the field of economic policy and action strictly comparable to the unanimity of acceptance of the Charter of the United Nations, the unanimous approval by the General Assembly of the Universal Declaration and United Nations Covenants on Human Rights, or the degree of consensus represented by the new treaties relating to scientific and technological developments such as the Antarctic Treaty, the Nuclear Test Ban Treaty and the Space Treaty. The implementation of the new basic instruments may be precarious in all these fields, but they represent a general consensus in matters of principle; in the economic field the uncertainties and difficulties are compounded by the more limited nature of the consensus achieved. The Fund, GATT, the World Bank Group and the regional development banks and O.E.C.D. have revolutionised the law in respect of their membership and operations and are constantly broadening both, but they still tend to be regarded as the symbols of a free economy. UNCTAD and UNIDO in their initial stages of development have tended to place in sharp relief, rather than to resolve as is their purpose, the gap between affluence and underdevelopment and conflicts of economic interest between the rich nations and the poor nations. The significance of these limitations must be fully recognised, but when every allowance has been made for them the transformation which has been effected in the law remains fundamental. The world now recognises a common responsibility for the common welfare and is in process of expressing this recognition in legal obligations, institutions and devices. The principle, stripped of its detailed applications, is clearly stated in two instruments which have been virtually universally accepted, the Charter of the United Nations itself and the Constitution of the International Labour Organisation.

By virtue of the Charter of the United Nations and the Constitution of the International Labour Organisation the common wealth and the common welfare are a common responsibility; our problem now is that we are only beginning to deduce the precise legal implications and consequences of this responsibility, to express them as obligations with a specific content, and to give them the necessary institutional and procedural form. In the Charter the responsibility is expressed in the pledge of all Members to take joint and separate action in cooperation with the United Nations to promote higher standards of living, full employment and conditions of economic and social progress and development.[1] In the Constitution of the International Labour Organisation we have an unequivocal acceptance of the principles that 'poverty anywhere constitutes a danger to prosperity everywhere', that 'all human beings, irrespective of race, creed or sex, have the right to pursue both their material well-being and their spiritual development in conditions of freedom and dignity, of economic security and equal opportunity', and that 'the attainment of the conditions in which this shall be possible must constitute the central aim of national and international policy'; we have an equally clear affirmation that these objectives can be secured only by 'the fuller and broader utilization of the world's productive resources', with the accent upon measures to expand production and consumption alike. When we reach back to fundamentals, the law relating to economic stability and growth has its foundation in the same human values as the law relating to the dignity of man. Major developments in the law presuppose a germinal principle with a vitality, breadth and depth of appeal, and range of potential applications adequate to the challenge to be met, and fertility of resource in applying the principle effectively and equitably with general consent. In the contemporary development of the international law relating to economic stability and growth we have the germinal principle; its effectiveness will depend on the fertility of resource shown in its equitable application. The common responsibility to create wealth and devote it to welfare is no less a challenge to the creative genius of the law than the call to 'save succeeding generations from the scourge of war' or the mission to uphold 'the dignity and worth of the human person'.

---

[1] Articles 55 and 56.

8

Science and technological progress

It has become a trite saying that the progress of science and technology has far outstripped the effectiveness of social control through the law.[1] True of municipal law, this is even more true of international law; international lawyers, as Philip Jessup has pointed out, 'have barely begun to address themselves to the challenge presented by the new frontiers of science'.[2] What contribution can the creative imagination make towards closing the gap between the achievements of science and technology and the inadequacies of our law and institutions?

We must expand the frontiers of the law to embrace the social discipline of science no less than that of economic forces. Civilisation cannot long entrust itself to the wisdom and moral responsibility of a technological élite to whom humanism, spiritual values and the common touch are equally alien. Why have we achieved so little where so much is at stake? The most plausible explanation is a disconcerting one. The imperative requiring the social discipline of economic forces is the claims of social justice and their political significance. The imperative requiring the social discipline of science is the preservation of civilisation against destruction by natural forces which man has shown greater skill in releasing than in controlling; the problem is even more fundamental but the political base for effective action less assured. We have nevertheless made some progress, though much less decisively than the needs require.

There are of course important areas within which the law has already become an established element in the recognised discipline of scientific and technological progress. Telecommunications and aviation are commonplace but none the less significant illustrations of world-wide facilities the daily operation of which presupposes world-wide regulation which has been in process of development for a century in the case of telecommunications[3] and half a century in that of aviation. The

---

[1] Patterson, Edwin W., *Law in a Scientific Age*.

[2] *The Use of International Law*, p. 11.

[3] International Telecommunication Union, *From Semaphore to Satellite*.

regulations which have made these facilities possible have been developed within an institutional framework embodying significant new legal devices such as the frequency registration arrangements of the International Telecommunication Union[1] and the standards and recommended practices of the International Civil Aviation Organization.[2] But these are routine matters as compared with the challenges which now confront us. Fifty years ago nuclear energy, space, the exploration and exploitation of the ocean depths and probing into the centre of the earth were the recognised domain of Jules Verne and H. G. Wells; Westlake and Oppenheim were not concerned with them. Polar exploration was the admired achievement of Nansen and Peary, Amundsen and Scott, but of marginal significance for the law. Sonic boom, cybernetics and molecular biology had not intruded upon the legal mind. Pollution was perhaps an old but a secondary problem. Deliberately induced large-scale changes of natural environment were inconceivable. The chief interest of international lawyers in scientific and technological development was in the effect of changes in the military art on the law of war and neutrality. Today the full spectrum of current scientific and technological development poses urgent questions for the law.[3]

1. Nuclear energy

Nuclear energy is the most immediately ominous of the challenges offered by the progress of science and technology to the effectiveness of the law as we inherited it.[4] The magnitude of the challenge was appreciated from the outset. Within twelve months of Hiroshima a comprehensive plan for the international control of nuclear energy was submitted to the United Nations. No agreement could be reached. Since that time a piecemeal approach has been adopted.

Some worthwhile progress has been achieved in this manner, both on the military front and in respect of the peaceful uses of nuclear energy.

By the Partial Nuclear Test Ban Treaty each of the parties, now over 100 in number, undertake 'to prohibit, to prevent, and not to carry out any nuclear weapon test explosion, or any other nuclear explosion, at any place under its jurisdiction or control, in the atmosphere, beyond its

---

[1] Codding, George A. Jr., *The International Telecommunication Union.*

[2] Schenkman, Jacob, *Internationl Civil Aviation Organization.*

[3] Jenks, C. Wilfred, 'The New Science and the Law of Nations', in 1968 *International and Comparative Law Quarterly*, Vol. 17, Part 2, April 1968, pp. 327–345.

[4] Bloustein, Edward J. (ed.), *Nuclear Energy, Public Policy and the Law.*

limits (including outer space) or under water'. Negotiations relating to underground explosions are still proceeding.

The Treaty on Principles Governing the Activities of States in the Exploration and Use of Outer Space, including the Moon and Other Celestial Bodies, which both the United States and the U.S.S.R. have now ratified, embodies an undertaking by the parties 'not to place in orbit around the earth any objects containing nuclear weapons or any other kinds of weapons of mass destruction, install such weapons on celestial bodies, or station such weapons in outer space in any other manner'.[1]

A Treaty on the Non-Proliferation of Nuclear Weapons has been approved by the General Assembly. By the Treaty each nuclear-weapon State Party undertakes not to transfer nuclear weapons or other nuclear explosive devices to any recipient whatsoever or to assist any non-nuclear-weapon State to acquire such weapons or devices; each non-nuclear-weapon State Party undertakes not to receive such transfer or to manufacture or acquire nuclear weapons or other nuclear explosive devices. Non-nuclear-weapon States Parties agree to accept safeguards for the prevention of diversion of nuclear energy from peaceful uses. Each Party agrees to ensure that potential benefits from any peaceful applications of nuclear explosions will be available to non-nuclear-weapon States Parties. The prospects of the Treaty securing the ratifications necessary to make it effective remain uncertain.

A Treaty for the Prohibition of Nuclear Weapons in Latin America has been signed on behalf of seventeen Latin American States.[2]

The Statute of the International Atomic Energy Agency, now in force for 93 States, provides a nucleus for enlarging 'the contribution of atomic energy to peace, health and prosperity throughout the world'.

The International Atomic Energy Agency has established and administers safeguards against the diversion of materials and facilities to military purposes; these are applicable to all Agency projects and to bilateral or multilateral projects placed under Agency safeguards by the States concerned; they provide for Agency inspection.

The International Atomic Energy Agency has adopted Basic Safety Standards for Radiation Protection.

The International Labour Organisation has adopted a Radiation Protection Convention, applicable to the industrial use of nuclear energy, and issued a Manual of Industrial Radiation Protection elaborating more detailed standards.

---

[1] Article IV.

[2] *International Legal Materials,* Vol. VI, No. 3, pp. 521–534.

The International Atomic Energy Agency has adopted regulations for the safe transport of radioactive material by air, land or water.

A convention concerning the disposal of radioactive waste into the sea is in preparation by the International Atomic Energy Agency.

A Convention on the Liability of the Operators of Nuclear Ships has been negotiated.

A Convention on Civil Liability for Nuclear Damage has been sponsored by the International Atomic Energy Agency.

This international action is paralleled by measures taken by the European Nuclear Energy Agency maintained by the Organization for Economic Co-operation and Development and by the European Atomic Energy Community.

These steps towards legal and social control of nuclear energy by the acceptance of international obligations are not to be despised. When the fundamentals of a problem are intractable by reason of political attitudes, the only way in which to create changed political attitudes may be to build habits of confidence and cooperation by concentrating in the first instance upon non-essentials. But such an approach will not in itself resolve the larger problems left temporarily in abeyance. The ultimate test of its value will be the extent to which it facilitates changes in the basic attitudes which made it a necessary expedient, the only alternative to a deadlock of utter sterility.

The problem of nuclear energy, like that of arms, ultimately resolves itself into that of the peaceful government of mankind and cannot be resolved in any lesser context.

2. Space

'Already', Cardozo said in 1921, 'there is a body of legal literature that deals with the legal problems of the air.'[1] There is now an extensive literature of the law of space.[2]

Space presented a second unique challenge to the creative imagination of international lawyers. Thus far, this second challenge has been nobly met. A new medium comparable in importance to the hydrosphere or the atmosphere became of immense political, strategic, scientific, and

---

[1] *The Nature of the Judicial Process*, p. 62.

[2] For a survey of the literature down to 1963 see Jenks, C. Wilfred, *Space Law*, pp. 95–179; and see in particular Jessup, Philip C. and Taubenfeld, Howard J., *Controls for Outer Space and the Antarctic Analogy*; McDougal, Myres S., Lasswell, Harold and Vlasic, Ivan A., *Law and Public Order in Space*; Haley, Andrew G., *Space Law and Government*; Chaumont, Charles, *Le droit de l'espace*; Christol, Carl Q., *The International Law of Outer Space*; Lachs, Manfred, 'Space Law', *Recueil de l'Académie de Droit international*, Vol. 113 (1964 (III)), pp. 7–103.

potentially commercial, importance within a matter of a few months.[1] Many influential voices counselled prudence in attempting to define the legal status of the new medium. But the general sense of legal opinion was, as I ventured to express it at the time, that 'while it is healthy that the evolution of the law should follow rather than anticipate that of life, there are circumstances in which the possibility of developing the law on sound principles depends primarily on an initiative being taken in the matter before *de facto* situations have crystallised too far'.[2]

Happily, this approach, fully endorsed by the responsible governments of the leading space powers at the highest level, prevailed. In the seventh year of the space age, the General Assembly of the United Nations adopted unanimously a Declaration of Legal Principles Governing the Activities of States in the Exploration and Use of Outer Space, representing a solid core of generally accepted principle around which the law of space could develop.[3] Three years later the General Assembly approved a Treaty on Principles Governing the Activities of States in the Exploration and Use of Outer Space, including the Moon and Other Celestial Bodies.[4] A series of more detailed agreements will be necessary to implement the Treaty on Principles: the first of these, an Agreement on the Rescue of Astronauts, the Return of Astronauts and the Return of Objects Launched into Outer Space, was approved by the General Assembly on 19 December 1967. These are the most imaginative achievements which the law of nations as yet has to its credit in the field of the social control of science and technology.

The Treaty on Principles provides that the exploration and use of outer space shall be carried on for the benefit and in the interests of all countries, irrespective of their degree of economic and social development, and shall be the province of all mankind; that outer space, including celestial bodies, is free for exploration and use by all States without discrimination of any kind, on a basis of equality and in accordance with international law, and there shall be free access to all areas of celestial bodies; that there shall be freedom of scientific investigation in outer space, including celestial bodies, and States shall facilitate and encourage international cooperation in such investigation; that outer space, including celestial bodies, is not subject to national appropriation by claim of sovereignty, by means of use or occupation, or by any other

---

[1] Braun, Werner von and Ordwaz, Frederick I., III, *History of Rocketry and Space Travel.*

[2] *The Common Law of Mankind*, p. 384.

[3] Jenks, C. Wilfred, *Space Law.*

[4] For the text see 61 *American Journal of International Law*, No. 2, April 1967, pp. 644–649.

means; that the activities of States in the exploration and use of outer space shall be carried on in accordance with international law, including the Charter of the United Nations, in the interest of maintaining international peace and security and promoting international peace and understanding; and that outer space, including celestial bodies, shall be denuclearised and demilitarised. These principles sum up the great debate concerning the legal status of space and the celestial bodies which dominated the early years of space law. They are an unequivocal statement of the law as governments now accept it, and represent a general framework within which more specific problems can be progressively resolved.

The Treaty also embodies working compromises in respect of two of the major controversies of the early years of the space age. It resolves the question of the extent to which private enterprise is permissible in space by allowing States to forbid or permit such enterprise in accordance with their own views of policy on condition that, if they permit it, they assume full responsibility for it. The question whether space experiments which may involve a risk of modifying natural environment should require some kind of international authorisation is dealt with in a similarly pragmatic manner, by requiring consultation but not consent prior to space activities which may cause harmful interference with activities of other States in the peaceful exploration and use of space.

The Treaty states the general principle of international liability for damage caused by an object launched into space; a more detailed agreement spelling out the application of this principle is in process of negotiation.

The Treaty envisages opportunities for the parties to observe the flight of space objects launched by other parties, and provides for the exchange and dissemination of information concerning space activities and for a reciprocal right of visit of stations, installations, equipment and space vehicles on the moon and other celestial bodies.

Within this general framework other important advances have been made, notably by the adoption of a code of space telecommunication regulations now legally binding on all Members of the International Telecommunication Union and, on a more limited basis, by the negotiation of Arrangements for a Global Commercial Communications Satellite System; new proposals for a communications satellite system have recently been formulated by the U.S.S.R. and seven other socialist republics. There is now a substantial exchange of information received from meteorological satellites through the World Meteorological Organisation and the United Nations has under consideration the possibility of a navigational satellite system.

There nevertheless remains a whole series of major unresolved questions which may within a few years become acute. These include: the role of international organisations in activities in space (including in particular the distribution of liability in respect of such activities between such organisations and their members); the organisation as world public services of certain types of operational activity in space; jurisdiction over persons in space; the legal régime of space resources; and the role of law in the regulation of space experiments and avoidance of space cluttering and contamination. Over this wide range we are now reaching the point at which it may be necessary to pass from speculation to action and to hammer out hard law by a combination of custom and precedent with negotiation and agreement. This task will call for a further creative effort of major proportions in which specialists in the law of international organisations, corporation lawyers and private international lawyers will all be called upon to cooperate with space scientists in resolving new problems.[1]

The success of such an effort will ultimately depend on the effectiveness of the demilitarisation of space and the measure in which we recognise that the problem of law and order in space is but a new phase of the perennial problems of peace on earth and goodwill among men and that ultimately there is no middle course between chaos and international control.[2]

3. The ocean depths

Current developments in oceanography and the exploration and exploitation of the ocean depths may during the coming years have consequences comparable in importance to those of nuclear energy and space exploration. They may add a new dimension, if not to the habitable world, at least to the world of readily accessible resources. If they should do so, the law relating to the public order of the ocean depths may become a major new chapter of the law of the sea.

Historically, the law of the sea has evolved through three main phases. The first phase was that of early claims to the sovereignty of the seas.[3]

---

[1] Jenks, C. Wilfred, 'Space Law Becomes A Reality', in British Institute of International and Comparative Law, *Current Problems in Space Law: A Symposium*, pp. 15–25.

[2] Jessup, Philip C. and Taubenfeld, Howard J., *Controls for Outer Space and the Antarctic Analogy.*

[3] Fulton, T. W., *The Sovereignty of the Seas*; Piggott, F. T., *The Freedom of the Seas, Historically Considered.*

During the second phase[1] the principle of the freedom of the seas established by Grotius furnished the basis of virtually the whole of the law; the controversies of this phase related primarily to the extent of the rights of neutral commerce in time of war; among the peacetime uses of the sea the law gave a clear primacy to freedom of navigation. In the third phase new means of using, and pressures upon, the resources of the sea and its bed, and the new threats to national security and other interests presented by the increased speed and mobility of ships and aircraft, have been reflected in the far-reaching changes in the law crystallised and sanctioned by the United Nations Conferences on the Law of the Sea; these have included recognition of the rights of the coastal State over the continental shelf and its resources, recognition of a contiguous zone within which the coastal State can exercise certain rights of control, changes in the method of demarcation and breadth of the territorial sea, and the formulation of general principles governing the conservation of the living resources of the high seas.[2]

We now appear to be entering upon a fourth phase.[3] The accessibility, through nuclear submarines and otherwise, of the ocean depths, and the possibility of exploiting their hitherto untapped resources, have added the equivalent of a new dimension to the hydrosphere. Sealabs are no less significant than spacelabs in extending man's dominion into a new medium. With the development of missile launching submarines, fish-farming and marine plant cultivation in the ocean depths, underwater mining, and the extraction of minerals and chemicals from the seas, aquanautics may prove to be of greater strategic importance and much more promising economic potential than astronautics. We must not permit an excessive preoccupation with the law of outer space to distract our attention from the need to develop an adequate law of inner space. The principles governing the activities of States in the ocean depths may be no less important than those governing their activities in the exploration and use of outer space. They will doubtless be drawn from, but may well require adaptation of, the traditional law of the sea. They call for the same intensive consideration as the principles of space law and it

---

[1] Gidel, G., *Le droit international de la mer*; Colombos, C. John, *The International Law of the Sea*; Smith, H. A., *The Law and Custom of the Sea*; Jessup, Philip C., *The Law of Territorial Waters and Maritime Jurisdiction.*

[2] McDougal, Myres S. and Burke, William T., *The Public Order of the Oceans*; Reiff, Henry, *The United States and the Treaty Law of the Sea*; Bowett, D. W., *The Law of the Sea.*

[3] Burke, William T., *Ocean Sciences, Technology and the Future International Law of the Sea*; President's Science Advisory Committee, *Effective Use of the Sea: Report of the Panel on Oceanography.*

may well be desirable that they should be formulated in a similar manner in a Declaration adopted by the General Assembly which at its 1967 Session envisaged clearly for the first time a comprehensive international approach to the whole question; such a Declaration might prepare the way for an Ocean Depths Treaty. In pursuing the matter we shall have to draw upon the social science, no less than the physical geography, of the oceans in finding imaginative solutions for this new challenge. As an initial step the General Assembly, by a resolution adopted on 18 December 1967, recognised the common interest of mankind in the seabed and the ocean floor, the importance of preserving them from actions and uses which might be detrimental to this common interest, and the desirability of practical measures to promote international co-operation in their exploration, conservation and use; it also established an *ad hoc* committee to pursue the matter. The questions relating to the seabed and the ocean floor now under active consideration include their legal status, the possibility of reserving them exclusively for peaceful purposes, the use of their resources in the interests of mankind, freedom of scientific research and exploration, reasonable regard to the interests of other States, and pollution and other hazards. On certain broad principles wide agreement may be reached without undue difficulty; these may well include the principle that the exploration and use of the seabed shall be conducted for the benefit and in the interest of all mankind, the principle that no State may claim or exercise sovereignty or sovereign rights over any part of the deep ocean floor, the principle that activities on the deep ocean floor shall be conducted in accordance with international law, including the Charter of the United Nations, and the principle of mutual assistance in the event of accident, distress or emergency arising out of activities on the deep ocean floor. The reservation of the deep ocean floor for peaceful purposes, being related to the questions of effective arms limitation measures and the verification of such measures, is likely to involve more difficult negotiations. Internationally agreed arrangements governing the exploitation of the resources of the deep ocean floor will have to be worked out in considerable detail; it would seem desirable that they should make provision for the orderly development of such resources in a manner reflecting the interest of the international community in such development, conditions conducive to the investment necessary for the exploration and exploitation of such resources, the dedication of a portion of the value of the resources recovered to international community purposes, and accommodation among the commercial and other uses of the deep ocean floor of marine environment. Detailed arrangements for international cooperation in the scientific investigation of the deep ocean floor, the avoidance of unjustifiable interference with other activities, the minimisation of pollution of the seas and disturbance of existing biological, chemical and physical processes and balances, and consultation concerning potentially harmful activities and experiments, will also be necessary. An internationally agreed precise boundary for the deep ocean floor may prove to be both more necessary and more feasible than the demarcation of outer space from airspace.

4. The polar regions

The polar regions, until recently among the most inaccessible on earth, have now become the hubs of complex strategic and scientific interests and communication systems.[1] The Arctic and Antarctic present markedly different problems, but in both cases there is need for increasing international cooperation and control. The Antarctic Treaty of 1 December 1959 has furnished a political stimulus and legal framework for further developments in the Antarctic. The Treaty provides for freedom of, and international cooperation in, scientific investigation in Antarctica; for the demilitarisation and denuclearisation of Antarctica; and for leaving in abeyance for the duration of the Treaty all territorial rights or claims in Antarctica. There is as yet no Arctic Treaty to deal with the even more urgent and difficult problem of the Arctic, which has been transformed by jet aircraft, guided missiles and anti-missile screens and the nuclear submarine from a barrier impassable to arms and commerce alike into the strategic hub of the rivalries of the greatest powers. The traditional law relating to the Arctic deals mainly with such matters as the application of the principles of discovery and occupation to barren lands, the susceptibility to occupation of frozen sea, and the sector theory as the basis of territorial claims.[3] The Antarctic Treaty was made possible by a wholly new approach to the problem based on leaving territorial rights and claims in abeyance for the duration of the treaty and developing a régime based on functional needs in the

---

[1] For the Arctic see Macdonald, R. A. J., *The Arctic Frontier* and for the Antarctic, Jessup, Philip C., and Taubenfeld, Howard J., *Controls for Outer Space and the Antarctic Analogy*.

[2] Smedal, Gustav, *De l'Acquisition de Souveraineté sur les Territoires Polaires*; Taracouzio, T. A., *Soviets in the Arctic*; Dollot, René, 'Le droit international des espaces polaires', in *Recueil de l'Académie de Droit international*, Vol. 75, (1949 (II)), pp. 115–200; Mouton, M. W., 'The International Régime of the Polar Regions', *Recueil de l'Académie de Droit international*, Vol. 107, (1962 (II)), pp. 175–284.

Antarctic.[1] An equally new approach to the problem of the Arctic, taking fully into account the major natural, geographical, political, strategic and economic differences between the two regions, will be necessary to eliminate the real danger that political and military rivalry in the Arctic may provide the occasion and theatre for a mutual exchange of nuclear missiles. Can we conceive of an Arctic régime including an element of scientific cooperation, an element of common services, and an element of demilitarisation and denuclearisation, and what contribution can the creative imagination make to giving such a régime an appropriate legal form and content, through the negotiation of an Arctic Treaty?

5. The centre of the earth

The journey to the centre of the earth was always the most fantastic dream of science fiction and still appears the least likely to be realised, but we may well have reached a point at which the law can no longer ignore the centre of the earth. Experiments designed to probe beyond the crust of the earth through the mantle towards the inner core are being undertaken by both the United States and the U.S.S.R.;[2] while they remain essentially sources of new geological and geophysical knowledge they may present no special legal problem, but if at any stage they release or set in motion volcanic or other unsuspected natural forces, the consequences of which may be far from local, some very large questions may arise. Our knowledge of the centre of the earth is still highly speculative.[3] We may hope that the scientists will be prudent but deep drilling for purposes of commercial exploration and exploitation is becoming increasingly common and is constantly extending its depth range; underground nuclear explosions are being envisaged for an increasing range of economic purposes. These varied developments, taken as a whole, are tending to raise acutely the question whether we do not need a legal régime for the centre of the earth defining what may and what may not be done without full international consultation; such a legal régime might take the form of a Centre of the Earth Treaty formulating a code to govern experiments and deep drilling operations liable to affect geological processes and forces in the centre of the earth. The idea of a Centre of the Earth Treaty may have the flavour of fantasy; but how

---

[1] Cf. Jenks, C. Wilfred, *The Common Law of Mankind*, 'An International Régime for Antarctica', at pp. 366–381.

[2] Bascom, Willard, *A Hole in the Bottom of the Sea;* Mahalkov, A., *The Mystery of the Earth's Mantle.*

[3] Gutenberg, B., *Internal Constitution of the Earth.*

long is it since an Antarctic Treaty, a Nuclear Test Ban Treaty and a Space Treaty would have seemed equally fanciful?

6. Environmental changes

Man has unlocked the energy of the atom and is exploring space and the ocean depths. He is mastering the polar regions and seeking to probe the secrets of the centre of the earth. The creative imagination is already playing a significant part in reshaping the law to cope with the problems of these new frontiers of human knowledge and action. But the changes in natural environment resulting from current scientific and technological developments may prove to be more varied in character and both more far-reaching and more immediate in impact than anything which we have yet experienced. They will not necessarily be limited to the effects of radiation, experiments in space, the opening up of the ocean depths, the bringing of the polar regions within the theatre of continuous and effective human action, and the penetration of the crust of the earth towards the inner core. Our immediate habitat may be more directly affected in matters profoundly transforming everyday life. As long ago as 1931 Carl Becker said that in our age 'novelty has ceased to excite wonder because it has ceased to be novelty';[1] how much truer that has now become. Let us for the moment postpone consideration of the problem of pollution which affects such fundamentals of life as air and water and the problems of noise and vibration which affect the resilience of the human nervous system, and consider only deliberately induced large-scale changes of environment. No one can yet foresee the outcome of current speculations and experiments concerning weather control, hurricane seeding, typhoon dispersion, the modification of climate, the rehabitation of arid zones, the desalination of sea water, the diversion of ocean currents, changes in the volume of polar ice which would affect the level of the oceans, new sources of energy, low and high temperature research, and suchlike matters. We know that ambitious plans are being canvassed in respect of all these matters. It is reasonable to suppose that they may be no more than a sample of things still to come, some of them veiled from informed discussion by military secrecy. In these circumstances, nuclear energy, space, and the ocean depths, while each constituting in itself a major challenge to the creative genius of the law, are only particular manifestations of a larger problem. We cannot but ask whether scientific and technological innovation and experiment have

---

[1] Becker, Carl L., *The Heavenly City of the Eighteenth Century Philosophers*, p. 23.

not reached the point at which a significantly larger measure of international consultation, and in some matters control, may not be necessary to ensure that unknown risks, which may adversely affect the natural environment of the whole human race, are not assumed without any proper evaluation of the issues at stake, on the exclusive responsibility of one State which may not have adequate knowledge of the relevant facts or any real concern for all the interests involved.[1] May this not be a further major challenge to the creative genius of statesmen and the creative imagination of international lawyers? Within the State we now accept it as self-evident that ultra-hazardous activities and experiments should be subject to public licence and control. How are we to apply the same principle in a world which has become one?

7. Pollution

Changes of natural environment are occurring constantly. Changes due to deliberate schemes to modify the environment are and will probably remain a small proportion of the changes due to the everyday activities of modern man. The cumulative effect of the increasing consumption of natural resources and use of chemical and, more recently, physical processes by an increasing population, and of the wastes and unanticipated ecological changes resulting therefrom, is a pollution of land, air and water which has become one of the gravest problems of contemporary societies. Within the State the problem is increasingly calling for legislative intervention and legal control. The problem is becoming increasingly international in scale and character. What part is international law called upon to play in the preservation of natural environment and the ecological balance of nature?

Pollution as a national problem[2] embraces many facets of the effect of human life in an industrial society in changing the face of the earth; it affects land, air and water; air pollution includes the effect of dust, smoke, exhaust gases and other noxious products from coal and oil burning, internal combustion engines (notably motor vehicles) and industrial processes; water pollution includes the effects of sewage,

---

[1] Jenks, C. Wilfred, *Law, Freedom and Welfare*, pp. 33–49 and 149–151.

[2] See, for instance, Thomas, W. J. (ed.), *Man's Role in Changing the Face of the Earth*; Goodman, G. T., Edwards, R. W., and Lambert, J. M., *Ecology and the Industrial Society*; Mellanby, Kenneth, *Pesticides and Pollution* (a book of broader scope than its title may suggest); Stamp, L. D., *Man and the Land*; Bergman, Jack and Lenormand, Sergei, *The Pollution Paradox*; Report of the President's Science Advisory Committee, *Restoring the Quality of Our Environment*; National Academy of Sciences – National Research Council, *Waste Management and Control*; Carson, Rachel, *Silent Spring*.

industrial effluents, detergents, and other wastes; pesticides may pollute land, air and water; radioactive pollution by military, industrial, research and medical activities may have equally general effects. How many of these aspects of pollution call for international action and in what form?

Fresh water and air pollution and the pollution of land are primarily regional problems. We may be able to formulate internationally general principles concerning them but the application of these principles becomes an international matter chiefly in frontier areas, drainage basins covering more than one State, and atmospheric zones with winds and air currents affecting more than one State. The pollution of the ocean and its shores and radioactive pollution whatever its incidence present problems calling for general international action of a more continuous and systematic character.

Fresh water pollution has been the subject of treaty provisions for upwards of a hundred years; the Institute of International Law formulated as long ago as 1911[1] the general principle that such pollution is illegal and the International Law Association approved tentatively a series of articles on the subject in 1964[2]; but there is no general international agreement on the matter. On air pollution we have a widely quoted arbitral authority, the *Trail Smelter Award*[3] of 1941 between the United States and Canada, but again no general international agreement.[4]

The absorptive capacity of the ocean is so much greater than that of fresh water or of the atmosphere in any one place that the pollution of the oceans and their shores has become a recognised problem only in respect of the extreme cases of the discharge of oil and radioactive wastes. The Geneva Convention on the High Seas of 29 April 1958[5] provides for measures to deal with both oil pollution[6] and radioactive pollution[7]; the International Convention for the Prevention of the Pollution of the Sea by Oil of 12 May 1956[8] and the International Atomic Energy Agency Draft Convention concerning the Disposal of Radioactive Waste into the Sea, represent important first steps in this

---

[1] *Résolutions de l'Institut de Droit International*, 1873–1956, at p. 81.

[2] International Law Association, *Report of the Fifty-First Conference*, Tokyo, 1964, pp. 132–147 and 175–186.

[3] 3 *United Nations Reports of International Arbitral Awards*, pp. 1905–1982.

[4] On fresh water and air pollution see further Jenks, C. Wilfred, 'Liability for Ultra-Hazardous Activities in International Law', in *Recueil des Cours de l'Académie de Droit international*, Vol. 117, (1966 (I)), pp. 121–124.

[5] 450 *United Nations Treaty Series*, pp. 82–103. [6] Article 24.

[7] Article 25. [8] 327 *United Nations Treaty Series*, pp. 4–33.

direction. Pollution in what have come to be regarded as its characteristic forms is normally a process of deterioration over a period of time resulting from successive increments of the pollutant, but experience has dramatically illustrated that the danger of radioactive pollution or fact of large-scale oil pollution may arise from a single catastrophic incident such as the crash of a plane carrying a nuclear device[1] or the wreck of a large tanker.[2] These incidents have raised acutely the question of how much larger a part the law should play in defining precautions to reduce both the danger of catastrophic incidents and the probability of progressive pollution, in recognising liability for both catastrophic and gradual pollution, and in requiring insurance or other adequate provision for the full discharge of such liability.[3]

Less dramatic but no less insistent is the question what measure of international regulation of potential sources of pollution entering into international commerce, including chemical products, has become necessary.

The law can draw upon a longer and wider experience of national and international action in relation to problems of pollution than in relation to some of the newer scientific developments, but the disproportion between the magnitude of the current problem and the limited effectiveness of the action already taken is no less great. Should we not be thinking in terms of a World Pollution Treaty embodying principles applicable to environmental pollution in all its forms and constituting a general framework for more detailed arrangements relating to the pollution of the oceans and their shores by oil, pollution by radioactivity, and other special cases which may call for special arrangements?

8. Noise and sonic boom

The threat of noise to the nervous vitality and recuperative power of the human organism has become comparable to the threat of pollution to the fresh air and fresh water which human life requires for health, vigour and, ultimately, survival. Should we regard noise as essentially a problem for engineers and doctors, or has the law some part to play in preserving the human values and amenities involved? Noise has long been a major problem of industry and urban life, and within the State noise control is becoming increasingly subject to legal regulation.[4]

---

[1] Szulc, Tad, *The Bombs of Palomares*.

[2] Gill, Crispin, Booker, Frank and Soper, Tony, *The Wreck of the Torrey Canyon*.

[3] International Maritime Committee, '*Torrey Canyon*', 1967.

[4] See, for instance, Council of Europe, *Noise Abatement: A Public Health Problem*.

Noise level is increasingly governed by legal regulations relating to such matters as traffic noise, railway noise and aircraft noise. Public health codes, building codes, and health and safety regulations for industrial establishments contain increasingly stringent provisions concerning tolerable levels of noise and constructional and operational requirements for the limitation of noise. With the growing importance of aircraft noise, the problem has become one of international proportions. What is the role of international law in noise control?

Jet aircraft have already made the problem of engine noise acute and it has been the subject of considerable international consultation.[1] The apparent imminence of the introduction of supersonic aircraft into commercial service[2] will add to the problem of engine noise that of sonic boom. This will be an international problem of new dimensions. The problem of engine noise is international in that aircraft generating noise exceeding a tolerable level fly into and out of the airports of other countries where restrictions, such as constructional requirements for noise abatement, provisions for noise reduction by the use of aircraft operating techniques, specifications concerning take-off and approach procedures, and limitations of night flight can be applied to their operations; an international scheme of noise certification of aircraft has been envisaged to facilitate the application of rules concerning these matters. The problem of sonic boom is international in a wider sense; the intensity and range of sonic boom are such that it affects not only the areas of departure and arrival of the aircraft but the whole of its flight path and a lateral band which, at a speed of Mach 3 and a height of 70,000 feet, may be some seventy miles broad for the full length of the flight path. In the problem of sonic boom the inconvenience and potential injury from noise are compounded by the danger of impact damage. This may have a wide and varied incidence ranging from damage to buildings, including historic monuments, or valuable equipment to the release of avalanches in mountainous areas. The elements in the problem which admit of international regulation are the constructional rules to be observed to reduce the boom effect, the operational rules (including rules requiring the craft to be flown subsonically in certain places or circumstances) to be observed to reduce the probability of damage from boom, and the questions of liability which may

---

[1] United Kingdom Board of Trade, *Aircraft Noise – Report of an International Conference on the Restriction of Noise and Disturbance Caused by Civil Aircraft.*

[2] International Civil Aviation Organization, *The Technical, Economic and Social Consequences of the Introduction into Commercial Service of Supersonic Aircraft: A Preliminary Study.*

arise. The questions of liability include the nature and extent of liability, the proof, directness or remoteness, and possibly in certain cases the presumption, of damage, and any provision for the discharge of liability required to be made by insurance or otherwise.[1] These issues are so much more far-reaching than those to which jet aircraft have already accustomed us that, whereas the question of engine noise can be left primarily to those responsible for international cooperation concerning the technicalities of aviation and town planning, that of sonic boom raises questions of policy needing a different type of consideration: 'It poses acutely the questions of how much disruption of established convenience is tolerable in the name of progress the benefits of which may be much less widely shared, at what point the law should intervene, and how it should resolve the questions of liability and indemnification for loss, damage and necessary readjustment which may arise. In a technological revolution the burden of change cannot be left to lie where it falls; it becomes increasingly a social cost which must be borne by society.'[2] What part is international law called upon to play in resolving these increasingly pressing questions?

9. Electronics and cybernetics

Electronics and cybernetics may at an early date present no less a challenge to the law than nuclear energy, space, changes in natural environment, pollution or sonic boom. Automata with 'sense organs, effectors and the equivalent of a nervous system to integrate the transfer of information from the one to the other' are no longer 'the dream of the sensationalist nor the hope of some future time', but have long been in widespread use 'as thermostats, automatic gyro-compass ship steering systems, self-propelled missiles – especially such as seek their target – anti-aircraft fire-control systems, automatically controlled oil-cracking stills, ultra-rapid computing machines, and the like'.[3] The basic ideas are not new,[4] but the range and impact of such developments is now affecting wide sectors of the life of society. Automation has transformed vital industries. Computers have replaced clerks for much large-scale routine office work. With the aid of magnetic ink and character readers they are revolutionising banking practice. They are used for world-wide

---

[1] Jenks, C. Wilfred, 'Liability for Ultra-Hazardous Activities in International Law', in *Recueil des Cours de l'Académie de Droit international*, Vol. 117 (1966 (I)), at pp. 119–120 and 176–196.

[2] Jenks, op. cit., p. 120.

[3] Wiener, Norbert, *Cybernetics*, 2nd ed., p. 43.

[4] *Charles Babbage and His Calculating Engines*, edited by Philip and Emily Morrison.

airline reservations. Transcontinental and transatlantic telephone calls can be automatically dialled. Automated local trains are operating or projected in London, Paris and San Francisco. Air traffic control and safety systems are increasingly automatic. The same techniques are being applied to the policing of cities; New York uses electronic devices and computers for the detection and recording of crime and to facilitate the arrest of criminals. The military applications of all these developments are far-reaching; new defensive weapons consist essentially of their radar and electronic components. Scholarship is no less affected than industry, commerce, the policing of cities and war; data retrieval systems are taking the place of research assistants. We are therefore reaching the point at which peace, personal freedom and the progress of knowledge are all at the mercy of, and increasingly dependent upon, electronics and cybernetics, and possibly robots. Nuclear and space technology are proving to be fast breeders of further developments with still unforeseen applications to everyday life. How much of a gap, of time or intrinsic feasibility, there still remains between these developments and the frightening possibilities of the robots of R.U.R. or current science fiction is, in this age of unpredictable achievements, an unanswerable question. But the question poses a dilemma for the law. What part can the creative imagination of the international lawyer play in ensuring that electronics and cybernetics do not evade and destroy the social discipline of the law? This is no longer a fantastic question. The implications for the future of this body of research and development 'are, if possible, more startling and decisive than the coming of astropolitics'.[1] To pose the question is no more premature than was speculation about the legal régime of space a dozen years ago. Man cannot entrust his children to a radar and computer operated nuclear trigger. Justice cannot entrust the future of freedom to concealed photographic and recording devices. Scholarship cannot entrust the future of wisdom to the storage and retrieval of factual information. No less an authority on cybernetics than Norbert Wiener has emphasised the dangers:

> There is nothing more dangerous to contemplate than World War III. It is worth considering whether part of the danger may not be intrinsic in the unguarded use of learning machines. Again and again I have heard the statement that learning machines cannot subject us to any new dangers because we can turn them off when we feel like it. But can we? To turn a machine off effectively

[1] Lasswell, Harold, *World Politics and Personal Insecurity*, pp. vii–viii.

> we must be in possession of information as to whether the danger point has come. The mere fact that we have made the machine does not guarantee that we shall have the proper information to do this. . . . The idea of non-human devices of great power and great ability to carry through a policy, and of their dangers, is nothing new. All that is new is that now we possess effective devices of this kind.[1]

The law must at least insist upon minimum standards of disclosure of what is done and plans in progress, upon certain precautions to be observed, and upon the retention of effective human control. No legal system can exact less from the inventors of 'machines that approximate advanced forms of life so closely that the differences are tenuous or indistinguishable'.[2] Civilisation must control its Frankensteins to escape destruction by their monsters. How are we to apply the principle on a world scale? We cannot apply it without resolving the problem of armament within the framework of an organised world community, but the problem is a wider one and calls for a new approach to the role of law in the discipline of scientific and technological innovation.

The immediate problem is to find an acceptable point of departure for international action in a field in which military and commercial secrecy compete in defying any attempt to assert the need for orderly control in the public interest. Efficiency and economy in the use of electronic equipment, the adequacy of servicing facilities on a world basis, the possibility of shared use of certain equipment involving heavy capital expenditure and the feasibility of international inspection of equipment for purposes calling for such inspection all presuppose some measure of uniformity and interchangeability based on common international standards. The need for a common international instructional language for computers is already preoccupying both makers and users. Lawyers and accountants are already wrestling with the new problems which the widespread use of computers presents for the law of evidence and audit practice. Liability for cybernetic error or damage calls for attention. Unless world standards governing the use of cybernetics are evolved by a combination of scientific and commercial practice based on the recognition of certain obligations of disclosure, it may be necessary to prescribe them by law on the basis of international conventions or regulations. Real time multiple access computer facilities for certain purposes may have to be organised as an international grid

---

[1] Wiener, Norbert, *Cybernetics*, 2nd ed., pp. 175–76.

[2] Lasswell, op. cit., p. viii.

comparable to the European Organization for Nuclear Research (CERN) or the Global Commercial Communications Satellite System. The international law of electronics and cybernetics will in due course take its place with the law governing nuclear energy, space, the ocean depths, natural environment and pollution.

10. Molecular biology and mind control?

The imminent possibility of mind control on a massive scale represents a further challenge. Electronic and cybernetic innovation, wisely controlled, can be to the drudgery of the mind what steam, electricity and internal combustion have been to the drudgery of the body – the release which begets freedom. Mind control can enslave what electronics and cybernetics set free. The concept of mind control is no longer a fantasy. Leading psychologists and neurologists assure us that molecular biology is now coming to grips, in a manner comparable to the achievements of nuclear physics, with the chemical basis of life, memory and learning. The mutation of plants and animals is an accepted routine. Medical science is experimenting with the transplanting of vital organs of the body, including the heart. We appear to be upon the threshold of the possible biological and psychological reshaping of man – for freedom or for slavery. The potential consequences, for ethics, politics and social control, are so far-reaching that no sophisticated jurisprudence can ignore them. As Sir Macfarlane Burnet has said, 'The human implications of what is going on in this sophisticated universe of tissue-cultured cells, bacteria, and the viruses which can be grown at the expense of one or other are at best dubious, at worst frankly terrifying' and 'it is becoming all too evident that there are dangers in knowing what should not be known.'[1] Conditioned reflexes and brain-washing can be as destructive of a free society as the H-bomb. Unless we grapple with the problem posed by the possibility of mind control, and find means of so controlling the possibility as to enlarge rather than subvert freedom and consolidate rather than destroy the moral unity of mankind, our efforts to humanise the progress in other respects of science and technology will inevitably and inexorably fail. What contribution can the creative genius of the law make to securing this end? How can we match the initial, if still tentative and halting, response of the law to resolving the problems posed for the welfare of society by the progress of nuclear physics and rocketry, and the prospect of a similar response to the problems now being posed by the progress of oceanography and

---

[1] 'Men or Molecules?', *The Lancet*, pp. 37–39.

cybernetics, with a comparable response to the more fundamental and subtle problems about to be posed by the progress of molecular biology? We have clearly reached a point at which 'what should not be known' will in fact be known and the role of the law must be to make it possible for man to live with such knowledge. The greatest danger is that the new knowledge may be used irresponsibly. The most effective safeguard against this danger may be to give some appropriate legal sanction to free trade in ideas throughout the life sciences. The fullest discussion, exchange and sharing of knowledge of the life sciences may be the surest possible guarantee against their becoming an instrument of thraldom.

11. Common standards and common services

The first stage in the progress of the law of nations to encompass the impact of science and technology upon society is normally the formulation of common standards; but further progress of international cooperation in scientific and technological matters increasingly requires the provision of a legal framework for common services.

There are anticipations of the need for such a framework in a number of important treaties. The International Civil Aviation Convention envisages joint air transport operating organisations or international operating agencies being subject to the provisions of the Convention.[1] The International Telecommunications Convention contains nothing of equally general scope but provides for its application to 'the telecommunication operating services of the United Nations'.[2] The Antarctic Treaty provides for cooperative working relations with 'international organisations having a scientific or technical interest in Antarctica'.[3] The Treaty on Principles Governing the Activities of States in the Exploration and Use of Outer Space applies to activities carried out by or within the framework of international organisations.[4] These provisions are almost certainly precedents which will be followed in treaties prompted by other scientific developments.

There is an increasing number of examples of experiments in the development of common services for the better exploitation of the possibilities of advanced science and technology. On the world scale we already have, in the field of satellite communications, the Global Commercial Communications Satellite System. In Europe we have a much more varied pattern. The embryos of common services now in operation in Europe or parts of Europe include Eurocontrol (which controls jointly the upper air space of the United Kingdom, France, the

[1] Article 77. [2] Article 26. [3] Article 3 (2). [4] Articles 6 and 13.

Federal Republic of Germany and the Benelux countries) in the field of aviation; the Eurovision and (for Eastern Europe) Intervision networks in the field of television; the European Organization for Nuclear Research at Geneva and Joint Institute for Nuclear Research at Moscow in the field of nuclear research; the European Company for the Chemical Processing of Irradiated Fuels as a servicing body for the atomic energy authorities of the participating countries; the European Space Research Organization and European Launcher Development Organization in the field of space research and development; and the projected European Molecular Biology Laboratory at Geneva. If we were to add to the list industrial partnerships under government sponsorship in such fields as aircraft construction, cybernetics and other branches of advanced science and technology the picture would become much more elaborate. It is not surprising that proposals for such common services should have evoked the keenest interest and most varied and effective immediate action in Europe, where the necessary technical sophistication is traditional and the scale of countries and resources makes international cooperation essential for the practical application of the new technology, but it may be anticipated that these European developments will be paralleled in other regions and on the world scale. What part will international law be called upon to play in controlling and guiding this development?

We are going to need the equivalent of an international law of public utilities dealing with the most sophisticated developments of advanced science and technology. A wide range of questions concerning the financing and ownership of joint ventures, the choice of systems and equipment, the placing of contracts in an equitable manner, tender arrangements, the availability of service on an equitable and non-discriminatory basis, rate-fixing, patent arrangements, and suchlike matters are going to need close consideration. The international law of advanced science and technology will inevitably, as scientific and technological development proceeds, be called upon to deal extensively and intensively with the economic aspects of the operation of common services for the practical application of successive new developments.

12. Science in the service of man

The question of the part which international law should play in the social discipline of science is much broader than any of the particular problems in respect of which it has already become acute. It will not be resolved by nuclear lawyers, space lawyers, cybernetic lawyers, and other new breeds of specialists claiming an authority which neither scientists nor lawyers generally have the detailed knowledge to contest, but which does not represent a real consensus of statesmenship, science and the law. A much broader approach involving fundamental principles which require the real assent of the world community as a whole expressed in the most responsible manner has become necessary to enable us to deal progressively in an appropriate general context with the innumerable special problems which will continue to arise and in many cases to take us by surprise.

A first but decisive step in the development of such an approach might be the adoption by the General Assembly of the United Nations, one would hope unanimously, of a Declaration of General Principles Dedicating Science and Technology to the Service of Man.[1]

Such a Declaration might formulate the principle that science is the common heritage of all mankind as a principle of the law of nations. Such a provision might be regarded from one standpoint as a generalisation of a principle already formulated in special contexts by the Antarctic and Space Treaties, but would be different in nature, vastly more significant, and correspondingly more difficult of acceptance, by reason of its generality. Its potential implications would be far-reaching. They would indeed be so far-reaching that it is only realistic to assume that their practical implementation would be a gradual process over a considerable period of time. Among them is the principle that scientific information should be freely exchanged and available to the whole world. This scientific counterpart of open covenants openly arrived at presents practical problems no less difficult than those of its analogue in diplomacy, but is no less vital for the establishment of an open world of freedom from fear.

The Declaration might formulate the fundamental principle that the common interest of mankind in ensuring that scientific and technological innovation and continuing ultra-hazardous activities do not destroy, disrupt, disintegrate or pollute the natural environment on which human life and welfare depend or release forces having such a tendency which are liable to escape from human control is a matter of public policy of general, profound and continuing international importance. From this principle the Declaration could deduce two major obligations. The first would be an obligation for every State to cooperate in preventive measures for the avoidance of known and foreseeable

---

[1] The proposals outlined in the following paragraphs were originally submitted by me to the Geneva World Peace Through Law Conference on 12 July 1967; they have since been published under the title 'The New Science and the Law of Nations', in 1968 *International and Comparative Law Quarterly*, Vol. 17, Part 2, April 1968, pp. 327–345.

hazards in accordance with appropriate international procedures and regulations; the fulfilment of this obligation would be secured primarily through the provisions of special treaties such as have already been envisaged. The second would be an obligation for every State to participate in procedures of consultation and enquiry for the avoidance of unforeseen hazards before authorising within its jurisdiction or under its authority scientific or technological innovations or continuing ultra-hazardous activities which may have a substantial influence on natural environment to the detriment of the world community or of other States or their nationals; this would be a new obligation similar in nature to but far more comprehensive in character than the corresponding provision of the Declaration of Legal Principles Governing the Activities of States in the Exploration and Use of Outer Space subsequently incorporated in the Treaty on Principles. It might well come to be regarded as the central principle of the international law concerning scientific and technological developments.[1]

The Declaration might embody the principle that the hazards of scientific and technological innovation and of continuing ultra-hazardous activities should be equitably borne and should not fall upon their chance victim. From this principle it might deduce that the obligation of every State to avoid injury to the world community or to other States and their nationals from ultra-hazardous activities occurring or originating within its jurisdiction or undertaken on its behalf or with its authority should exist without proof of fault and include responsibility for ensuring the provision of adequate financial security for the discharge of such liability.[2]

The Declaration might also formulate a broad policy of intensive mutual cooperation in working out in all the necessary practical detail arrangements for the proper regulation of specific scientific and technological developments as they reach the stage at which such regulation is possible and desirable and for proper consultation and enquiry before experiments or tests which may affect the future of scientific experiment or the natural environment of the earth or other celestial bodies, or, within a more modest range, the natural environment of other States, are undertaken.

At a later stage the proposed Declaration of General Principles

---

[1] I have discussed the matter more fully in Jenks, *Law, Freedom and Welfare*, pp. 33–49 which continues to be the fullest expression of the suggestion to this effect which I first made in the *Liber Amicorum J.P.A. François*, 1959.

[2] I have discussed more fully in Jenks, 'Liability for Ultra-hazardous Activities in International Law', in *Recueil des Cours de l'Académie de Droit international*, Vol. 117, (1966 (I)), at pp. 105–198.

Dedicating Science and Technology to the Service of Man could serve as the basis for the negotiation of a World Science Treaty defining comprehensively the fundamentals of the mutual obligations among States arising from the impact of science upon society in much the same manner in which the 1963 Declaration of Legal Principles Governing the Activities of States in the Exploration and Use of Outer Space prepared the way for the 1967 Space Treaty.

Taken together, the Declaration and the Treaty would furnish the framework for a concerted long-term effort to translate their provisions into established fact. Within such a framework we could proceed to make a reality of a comprehensive approach to the whole problem, continuing to develop the law as occasion may warrant and concluding such further treaties as occasion may require, but above all progressively developing the full partnership in action which must be our ultimate purpose.

In surveying the goals of creative effort we have said nothing of much of the traditional content of the law, of such matters as recognition, succession, territory, jurisdiction, responsibility and immunities. We must not underestimate the continuing importance of these matters. They remain, and will continue to remain, important, in any world of States. Sir Cecil Hurst described the world of States in 1944 in terms which remain fully appropriate today:

> There then is the picture of the world in which we live today; a world divided among a number of States; each of which is the equal of the others in the sense that it is entitled, except for self-imposed limitations, to regulate its own affairs as it wishes; each of which is bound by the conditions of existence in modern times to be in constant relations with other States; each of which is responsible for caring for the interests of its people. . . . A State cannot put forward a claim founded on a general rule of law if it is not bound by that same rule. . . . The result is that a State cannot escape from subjection to international law, or, to put it slightly differently, international law is the necessary concomitant of statehood.[1]

This remains a true picture, but it is only a part of the picture and it is because it is only a part of the picture that the law governing the existence, recognition and succession of States as elements in the structure of the international community, and the traditional core of

---

[1] *International Law – The Collected Papers of Sir Cecil J. B. Hurst*, pp. 6–9.

the law of peace, which comprises such matters as territory, jurisdiction, responsibility and immunities, must now be seen as elements in a common law of mankind of a more comprehensive nature.[1]

It may well be true that no change in the substantive content of the law will in itself change its technical status from 'the law not of a community, of men, but, as for centuries past, of a quasi community of States'.[2] But as the law acquires a substance which corresponds to community needs it becomes a social reality in the creation of a true community. The technical status of the law has no objective reality; it is a construction of the stage reached in social evolution. It is not primarily in the areas of the law which constitute its traditional subject-matter and define its traditional technical status that the gap between the legacy of the past and the needs of the future has become so dangerously wide. The normal labours of practitioners and scholars should be reasonably sufficient to reshape this part of the law in accordance with changing needs. There is an imposing mass of established authority concerning these matters which the devoted labours of the last half-century have made more readily available than ever before. We now have, thanks primarily to the pioneer work of Sir Hersch Lauterpacht and the early cooperation and sponsorship of Lord McNair and Sir John Fischer Williams, a solid set of international law reports covering almost half a century.[3] We have elaborate digests of United States,[4] British[5] and French[6] practice on matters of international law, with similar digests of German and Swiss practice promised; we have a valuable symposium of Australian practice[7] and excellent Canadian casebooks;[8] similar records of practice for a wider range of countries may confidently be expected to become available. We have valuable

---

[1] Jenks, C. Wilfred, *The Common Law of Mankind*, pp. 58–61.

[2] Manning, C. A. W., *The Nature of International Society*, pp. 178–179.

[3] *Annual Digest of Public International Law Cases*, 6 vols, 1919–1932; *Annual Digest and Reports of Public International Law Cases*, 10 vols., 1933–1949; *International Law Reports*, 16 vols, 1950 onwards, now edited by Eli Lauterpacht.

[4] Moore, John Bassett, *A Digest of International Law*, 8 vols; Hackworth, Green Haywood, *Digest of International Law*, 8 vols; Whiteman, Marjorie, *Digest of International Law*, 8 vols published.

[5] McNair, Lord, *International Law Opinions*, 3 vols; McNair, Lord, *The Law of Treaties*; Parry, Clive, *A British Digest of International Law*, 5 vols published; Lauterpacht, Eli, *British Practice in International Law*.

[6] Kiss, Alexandre-Charles, *Répertoire de la Pratique Française en Matière de Droit International Public*, 4 vols published.

[7] O'Connell, D. P. (ed.) *International Law in Australia*.

[8] Mackenzie, Norman A. M. and Laing, Lionel H., *Canada and the Law of Nations*; Castel, J. G., *International Law Chiefly as Interpreted and Applied in Canada*.

studies of recognition,[1] succession,[2] territory,[3] jurisdiction,[4] responsibility,[5] immunities[6] and similar questions which are proof of the vigour with which the law relating to these matters is being reshaped to meet modern needs. But these matters are not the crux of the problem of the adequacy of the law as we now know it to contemporary needs. Of these parts of the law we can perhaps reasonably say with John Bassett Moore in 1914 that 'international law is on the whole as well observed as municipal law'.[7] The problem lies elsewhere and involves more fundamental issues. The future of peace, the vitality of freedom, the outlook for welfare, the impact of science on society, the large issues which will determine the future of law in the world community, will be resolved upon another plane. We need today a much broader perspective. Whereas 'in the last century we studied law from within', today we 'are studying it from without'.[8] It is the responsiveness of the law to new challenges from without rather than its successful adaptation from within of traditional rules to changed needs which will determine the importance of its role in the future of world society. Our essential concern is the relationship of the law to the whole life of society, and the well-being of society depends on ends such as peace with justice, the dignity of man, economic stability and growth, the progress of science and technology rather than on means such as the formal structure of the mutual relations of States. It is in the light of our ends that we must consider whether we can be satisfied with the present intellectual and spiritual vitality of the law of nations, with the sufficiency of its legislative procedures, or with the adequacy of its institutional framework. It is the essence of the concept of a new world of law that the law should include within its scope and regulate effectively matters which have hitherto lain beyond its purview or effective influence. We cannot resolve our problems by the most devoted labours in the archives; they arise in everyday life and can be resolved only by bringing the creative

---

[1] E.g. Lauterpacht, H., *Recognition in International Law*.

[2] E.g. O'Connell, D. P., *State Succession in Municipal Law and International Relations*, 2 vols.

[3] E.g. Jennings, R. Y., *The Acquisition of Territory in International Law*.

[4] E.g. Mann, F. A., 'The Doctrine of Jurisdiction in International Law', *Recueil des Cours de l'Académie de Droit international*, Vol. 111, (1964 (I)), pp. 9–162.

[5] Amerisinghe, C. F., *State Responsibility for Injury to Aliens*.

[6] E.g. *International Law: The Collected Papers of Sir Cecil J. B. Hurst*, pp. 171–294; Hardy, M., *Modern Diplomatic Law*; Lee, Luke T., *Vienna Convention on Consular Relations*.

[7] Moore, John Bassett, *International Law and Some Current Illusions*, p. 300.

[8] Pound, Roscoe, *The Spirit of the Common Law*, p. 212.

imagination to their solution as they arise every day, using the richness of precedent as the point of departure and the source of much wise counsel, but no longer as authority circumscribing fertility of resource in response to unprecedented needs. The world can become an organised community only by inventing 'its own legal machinery as its course' proceeds 'instead of allowing its progress to be held up by legal obstacles, as has happened too often in international affairs'.[1] Statesmanship must rely on scholarship and professional skill and experience as its tools but it must remain its own master, in full command of the initiative, and this is no less true of statesmanship in the law than of statesmanship in other areas of policy; for the foundation of statesmanship is not the learning, skill and experience in which it is embodied but reason and morality, and ultimately it is reason and morality, remaining ingenuous in their sincerity as they become ingenious in their sophistication, which define, and inspire the will to seek, the goals of creative effort which we have postulated for the law.

---

[1] Lord McNair in 21 *British Year Book of International Law*, 1944, p. 241, describing the legal tradition of the International Labour Organisation.

part III

The law in motion

The goals of creative effort as they have emerged from our enquiry have not been subjectively determined; they have been defined by the current preoccupations of our society as measured by the major changes which have already occurred or are in process of occurring in the law and by the subjects of current international negotiation. They attest the need of a dynamic society for a dynamic legal system. How are we to achieve the dynamism in the law without which it cannot respond to the needs of the evolution of society? Clearly we need a law in motion. How are we to keep the law in motion without impairing its quality and effectiveness as law? To do so we need a living law in which all the traditional processes of legal development and growth retain their full vitality; we need effective international legislative procedures; and we need an effective institutional framework of the world community within which the law and the community contribute continuously to each other's further development. We must therefore consider in turn each of these three elements in the problem: the need for a living law; the need for more effective international legislative procedures; and the need for a more effective institutional framework for the law; only by complementary progress in the concept, ethos, climate, traditions and techniques of the law, in the development of the international legislative process, and in institutional development, can we hope to achieve a major breakthrough towards the rule of law in world affairs.

9

The living law

There continues to be an important school of legal thought which considers that the changes which have become necessary are so far-reaching that they can be achieved only by legislative and institutional development. The law, on this view, is what it is, not what it should be, and the duty of, for instance, the International Court is 'to apply the law as it finds it, not to make it'.[1] This view, it is submitted, underestimates both the gravity and urgency of the problem and the legitimate possibilities of a bolder approach. To attain the goals of creative effort which we have postulated, more effective international legislative procedures and a more effective institutional framework for the law of the world community are clearly necessary, but it is no less necessary, and is indeed a condition without which the necessary legislative and institutional developments are unlikely to take place, that the whole spirit of the law and all of its established and traditional processes of growth and change should be attuned to the expanded purposes of the community and the scale and rate of growth and change in the life of the community.

Nothing is gained by underestimating the dilemma which is inherent in the problem. The law cannot make its contribution to a dynamic society by endeavouring or purporting to transform itself into something other than itself. It is law and its value is that it is law, law with all its limitations but likewise law with all its potentialities as law. To measure the potentialities of the law we must combine a profound sense of history, a thorough understanding of the *ratio legis* as well as the technical modalities of past and present practice, and a keen sensibility to future need. How can the law grow rapidly without ceasing to be law?

Approaching our task in this perspective, let us now consider the bearing of such an approach on the general concept of international law and the traditional techniques and sources of the law. The conventional wisdom of the law clearly cannot provide an adequate answer to our problems. A new world requires a new outlook, a new vitality, a new

---

[1] *South West Africa Cases*, 1966 International Court of Justice Reports, 48.

courage. In the graphic language of Judge Wyzanski, 'when the world is in turmoil the study of first principles is not a luxury but an essential'.[1] It becomes vital to determine wherein the creative imagination can transform the impossible into the merely difficult. Having clarified our goals and measured the significant but halting progress already made towards achieving them, we must proceed to analyse the conditions of future progress, to estimate the potential contribution to such progress of each of the recognised elements of development and change in a growing legal system, to review the appropriateness and adequacy of our varied resources for the work in hand, to project the probable development of foreseeable trends, to evaluate the policy alternatives available to us, and then to move boldly forward by exploiting to the full successive opportunities of logical progression from the existing law and natural development of existing procedures and institutional arrangements. We cannot hope to discharge these tasks successfully without a Promethean gift of fire which brings to life the inert matter of fact, rule and precedent which the creative imagination must illuminate or succumb to in defeated frustration.

1. The concept of law

The contemporary development of international law reflects the evolution of municipal legal systems. Roscoe Pound has distinguished twelve conceptions of law and traced four stages in the development of conscious thinking about the end of law. The end sought may be to keep the peace; to maintain the social status quo; to secure the natural equality of the subjects of the law by permitting the maximum of free individual self-assertion; or to balance and reconcile claims, wants and desires so as to secure a continually wider recognition and satisfaction of such wants, claims and desires through social control.[2] International law has traditionally been chiefly concerned with keeping the peace, maintaining the status quo and securing the 'natural equality' of States; only now is it gradually becoming a positive instrument of social control in a dynamic society.

This concept of the function of law in the international community is the outcome of a long process of evolution in the course of which international law has been profoundly influenced at every stage of its development by the prevailing climate of legal philosophy.

Grotius and his successors reflected the belief in natural law which

---

[1] Wyzanski, Charles E., Jr., *Whereas – A Judge's Premises*, p. 251.

[2] *An Introduction to the Philosophy of Law*, pp. 59–99.

medieval scholasticism transmitted to the western world from Greek political and Roman legal thought.[1]

With Vattel the social contract replaced the law of the *civitas maxima* as the foundation of international law.[2]

The positivism of the late nineteenth century was a faithful reflection in the international field of the analytical jurisprudence of John Austin and his German counterparts and the theory of law as command;[3] like them it belongs to the same intellectual world as the basic principles of nineteenth-century science, determinism, measurement, continuity and impersonality; it is but natural that the contemporary recognition of discontinuity, uncertainty and chance as inherent in the laws of nature should have become one of the general intellectual influences shaping contemporary legal thought.[4]

It is still too soon to gauge with any accuracy the impact on the law of the new scientific thought of the twentieth century, but it is already apparent that the new jurisprudence which reflects the new science will have a far-reaching influence on the fundamentals of international legal thought.

All of the more recent schools of legal thought have been reflected in distinctive approaches to international law, the work of Léon Duguit in that of Nicolas Politis and Georges Scelle,[5] Kelsen's outstanding contribution to legal theory in the contributions to international law of himself and his disciples,[6] the philosophy of the common law as developed by such British writers on jurisprudence as Maitland, Pollock, Bryce and Dicey in the pragmatic idealism of Brierly[7] and Fischer

---

[1] Lauterpacht, H., 'The Grotian Tradition in International Law', in 1946 *British Year Book of International Law*, Vol. 23, pp. 1–53.

[2] Vattel, *The Law of Nations*, Vol. III, Introduction by Albert de Lapradelle, pp. I–LV.

[3] The early editions of Oppenheim's *International Law* may be regarded as the culmination of this phase.

[4] Cf. Jenks, C. Wilfred, 'The New Science and the Law of Nations', in *International and Comparative Law Quarterly*, Vol. 17, Part 2, April 1968, pp. 327–345.

[5] Politis, Nicolas, 'L'influence de la doctrine de Léon Duguit sur le développement du droit international' and Scelle, Georges, 'La doctrine de Léon Duguit et le fondement du droit des gens', in *Archives de philosophie de droit et de philosophie juridique*, t. II, 1932; Guggenheim, Paul, 'Duguit et le Droit International Publique', in *Revue Juridique et Economique du Sud Ouest*, Série Juridique, No. 34, 1959, pp. 1–8.

[6] See, for instance, in relation to each other Kelsen, Hans, *General Theory of Law and the State* and *The Pure Theory of Law* and Kelsen, Hans, *Principles of International Law*, 2nd ed. by Robert W. Tucker.

[7] Lauterpacht, Sir Hersch, 'Brierly's Contribution to International Law', in Brierly, J. L., *The Basis of Obligation in International Law*.

Williams,[1] the insights of Roscoe Pound in those of Myres McDougal.

There is one element common to many of these recent schools which is of outstanding importance at the present juncture in the development of international law. It is the concept that much of law is permissive rather than imperative; it does not consist of commands but of rules defining the legal consequences of certain types of conduct, specifying the conditions to be fulfilled or procedures to be followed in order to confer rights, create obligations or attain other legal results, and affording facilities whereby the parties to legal transactions can mould their legal relations with each other, together with adjective rules providing how the substantive law is to be determined and changed. This general approach has been brilliantly expounded by Professor Herbert Hart in *The Concept of Law*;[2] it has a wider validity than those of the details of Professor Hart's presentation which have attracted criticism; it also has a very much more far-reaching application to international law than Hart has recognised.

International law now has, if I may use Hart's terminology, rules of recognition, change and adjudication, however imperfect they may be. It has passed far beyond the stage of being, as Hart appears to consider it, a limited number of separate rules to be inductively verified and syllogistically applied. It is a body of living principle and developing precedent growing with the needs of international society.

It is characteristic of such a body of living principle that its mandatory rules, while remaining of fundamental importance and dealing with such crucial matters as the prohibition of recourse to force and the obligation to settle disputes by peaceful means, become a relatively smaller proportion of the whole as it develops. The concept of law as the rules to be followed to achieve the positive purposes of life in society becomes increasingly important. As Dennis Lloyd has put it, law has come to be envisaged 'not as a purely negative force, for the restraint of evil, but as a positive instrument for realising those goals towards which man's good or social impulses tend to direct him'.[3] This is as true and as fundamental of contemporary international law as of any municipal legal system. It affects profoundly the nature, the metabolism and the content of the law.

The outcome is to substitute for positivism, the natural counterpart of Austinian jurisprudence, and for the concept of law as command, a positive approach to the function of law in the progress of international

---

[1] Jenks, C. Wilfred, 'Fischer Williams – The Practitioner as Reformer', in *British Year Book of International Law*, Vol. 40, 1964, pp. 233–285.

[2] Oxford, Clarendon Press, 1961.

[3] *The Idea of Law*, p. 18.

society, a concept of law as a positive instrument rather than a negative restraint. Law becomes a means of doing things by cooperative action in a disciplined and equitable manner rather than a command to do or not to do them.

The positive approach implies, in the first place, that international law, like municipal legal systems, has an open texture, and much the same kind of open texture. Nothing could be more mischievously untrue than the suggestion that the whole of international law is uncertain and precarious. There is a solid core, universally accepted, which is unlikely to be greatly changed, but at any particular time there is a large number of uncertain questions, new questions, and questions in respect of which it is not clear how far established practice and precedent will be regarded as applicable to changed or changing circumstances. No approach to international law which overlooks or belittles this essential element in its nature permits of a fair appraisal of either its present effectiveness or its future potentialities. The uncertainty of the human predicament is nowhere more apparent than in the field of international relations. We must therefore not expect of the law a certainty in either its content or the effectiveness of its application which is equally foreign to the nature of law in a changing society and to the nature of international relations. But we can expect of it the acceptance of a common discipline in resolving successive problems peacefully within the recognised framework of the legal order.

The positive approach implies, in the second place, that international law, like municipal legal systems, has a recognised metabolism whereby it 'takes in, assimilates and uses matter from without and by so doing gathers the energy for its own growth'.[1] We find this process at work in all the various modes and agencies of legal development: in the growth of custom, in the evolution of the practice of international organisations, in the perpetual retesting and reformulation of the law in the course of international adjudication, in the recasting of old and framing of new law by the law-making treaty, and in the contribution of legal scholarship and speculation to the progress of the law. The history of international adjudication affords innumerable striking illustrations of the process in operation. If we examine the growth and proof of custom, the extent of recourse to the general principles of law recognised by civilised nations, the part played by equity in tempering the rigour of the law, and the influence of international public policy in the development of the law, we find in each case a constant interaction of factors of stability and factors of change, elements from within and elements from without

---

[1] Jenks, C. Wilfred, *The Common Law of Mankind*, p. 167.

the existing *corpus* of international law, transmuting each other in accordance with legal tradition by the established techniques of the law, within the limits recognised as permissible at a given stage in the development of the law. The established techniques include, but are not limited to, the logic of the law, inductive and deductive; logic no more excludes preference, policy and choice in international than in municipal law, but, internationally or municipally, preference, policy and choice operate interstitially. The limits recognised as permissible vary, but have widened conspicuously in our own time in recognition of the needs of a changing society.

The positive approach implies, in the third place, that the content of international law, like that of mature municipal legal systems, consists increasingly of rules designed to enable society to effect social change peacefully and accomplish its social purposes in a world and age of growing scientific and technological interdependence. The rules of international law are becoming increasingly rules designed to enable international society to adopt a more positive approach to its political, economic and social problems. In this context the law of international organisations, the law of international economic relationships, the law of human rights, the law of scientific and technological independence, the law of treaties and the law governing international adjudication cease to be an expression and bulwark of the sovereignty of the State; they become manifestations and instruments of a growing sense of world community; they are chapters of the common law of mankind.

How far the process has yet gone may be open to debate. It has been argued that 'international justice and morality are still in what may be called the *laissez-faire* or individual stage', that 'the conceptions underlying the "welfare state" have hardly begun to be seriously applied to the society of States', and that 'the rights of States are still regarded as inherent in each State independently of the rest, instead of defining the conditions in which States can live together and cooperate in the service of a good common to them all'.[1] Our review of the goals of creative effort and some of the steps taken to achieve them has demonstrated, it is submitted, that this appraisal underestimates the progress already made. Whatever scope there may be for divergences of view concerning the effectiveness of what has been achieved, the concept of law as a positive instrument of the progress of international society has now been clearly established.

Such a view of the responsibilities of the law to the future does not involve any denial of its origins or renunciation of its traditions.

---

[1] Ginsberg, Morris, *On Justice in Society*, pp. 12–13.

The concept of law, however we may refine it by analysis of the structure, content and method of operation of the law, cannot be divorced from that of justice which has been a constant theme of philosophical and legal debate from Plato and Aristotle[1] to Kelsen,[2] del Vecchio[3] and Alf Ross.[4] The concept of justice is a complex of varied elements, including pure virtue, social virtue, equilibrium and equality of consideration for all,[5] but when we proceed from these broad principles to their application in practice the upshot of the debate has been well expressed by Morris Ginsberg:

> The central core of the idea of justice is not the requital of desert but the exclusion of arbitrariness and more particularly the exclusion of arbitrary power. Hence the enormous importance of the growth of legality, the emergence of the notion that persons are under the rule of law and not of men.[6]

The full acceptance of this position as the foundation of international relations, throughout the field of action of the modern State, involves a revolutionary revaluation of the part which the law may be called upon to play in the practical conduct of world affairs.

It is this revaluation, this concept of law as the positive instrument of enlightened policy substituting the progress of international society for arbitrary power over the whole range of the preoccupations of the welfare state, which makes it both legitimate and realistic for us to call upon the law for a significant contribution to securing peace with justice, protecting human dignity and the rights of man, promoting the general welfare by fostering economic stability and growth, facilitating the inevitable processes of social change, and harnessing scientific and technological progress for the common good. It is in the light of this concept of law that we must proceed to examine the potential contributions to the attainment of these purposes of a creative and resourceful invocation of custom, general legal principle, equity, and international public policy, and a creative and resourceful development of international adjudication, international procedures and devices of a legislative nature, and the general institutional framework of international society.

The task is admittedly made vastly more difficult by the growing complexity of the problems which beset us every day. Geoffrey Sawyer has pinpointed the dilemma:

---

[1] Barker, Ernest, *The Political Thought of Plato and Aristotle.*

[2] *What is Justice?* [3] *La Giustizia,* 4th ed. [4] *On Law and Justice.*

[5] Allen, C. K., *Aspects of Justice.* [6] *On Justice in Society,* p. 63.

> The trend of the law is not towards the generalization and formal simplicity, and accompanying rigidity, against which Ihering and Gény protested; it is towards complexity and specificity with no organizing concepts.[1]

To attain the goals which we have postulated for creative effort we need organising concepts to orientate the redeployment of the traditional resources of the law. Vinogradoff credited Maitland with a unique gift of 'closing abstract reasoning into forms taken from the living world of shapes and sounds';[2] to mould the future is still more difficult than to understand the past and calls for a comparable mastery of the interplay of the general and the particular; our task is to subsume the complexities of the living world under broad concepts sufficiently dynamic but generally acceptable to shape its destiny constructively.

The broadest of such concepts already command wide acceptance. We have delineated them in identifying the goals of creative effort. They include the preservation of peace with justice, the protection of human dignity, the promotion of the general welfare by fostering economic stability and growth, and the social control of scientific and technological development. Each of these concepts can be broken down into more precise concepts, some of which we have already identified, such as, in the case of peace with justice, the renunciation of the threat and use of force, the subjection to review by the community of the right of self-defence, the control of armament, and obligations of collective security and peaceful settlement. The concept of law in general as a means for achieving these things and the comparable objectives which we have identified in the other broad areas of effort, and the validity of that concept in world affairs as the world seeks to organise itself as a community, emerge equally clearly from the contemporary reassessment of the concept of law and the experience which we have already gained from putting that concept to the test of practical application in seeking the goals which we have postulated for creative effort.

2. Sovereignty

Such a general approach to law implies the rejection of the concept of the sovereignty of the State in its international relations. In so doing it reflects the changed realities of international society. In this, as in so many other phases of current world affairs, we are confronted with a

---

[1] *Law in Society*, p. 209.

[2] Vinogradoff, Paul, *Collected Papers*, Vol. I, p. 255.

paradox. The almost inevitable result of the doubling in less than twenty years of the number of independent States in the world, and of the natural aspiration of these new States to full and obvious control of their own affairs, has been that, while the constant erosion of sovereignty continues, claims to sovereignty are more widely and sometimes more vigorously asserted than ever before. The concept has, moreover, tended to become a bulwark behind which groups in the world community which find themselves in a minority are apt to retrench themselves, and, within such groups, a protection for national freedom against super-power control or domination by extremist influences. But while the catchword of sovereignty continues to intoxicate national policies the facts of community life make the concept increasingly unreal.

The root of the difficulty is partly conceptual and partly real. The origin of the conceptual problem is that political thinkers evolved the doctrine of sovereignty by conceiving of the State in abstraction from its international relations. For the most part Bodin, Hobbes, Locke, Rousseau and Hegel, the leading formative influences upon the doctrine of sovereignty as enunciated by political thinkers, omit, underestimate or misinterpret 'just that aspect of the State in which the international lawyer is most interested'; as Brierly shrewdly observed, 'it is only within our own lifetime that writers on the State seem to have begun to recognise that we live in a world of plurality of States, or at any rate to regard that obvious fact as one that has an important bearing on the nature of the State as such'.[1] Even today there is still, but in the academic rather than the practical world, a school of thought which regards a continued belief in sovereignty as a proof of political realism and intellectual sophistication;[2] in the real world, where the future of mankind is at stake, it is no longer accepted as either.

The erosion of the general concept of sovereignty began at a much earlier date. Maine's analysis of sovereignty[3] pointed the way for later critics of Austin. Even in the realms of political theory where it originated the doctrine was, as Sir Frederick Pollock pointed out as long ago as 1890, 'found inadequate, like all dogmatic formulae, to account for complex facts'.[4] Dicey could find no recognisable sovereign in federal systems of government.[5] Henry Sidgwick, seeking for the sovereign in the modern constitutional State, found that political power 'is usually

---

[1] *The Basis of Obligation in International Law*, p. 30.

[2] Hinsley, F. H., *Sovereignty*.

[3] *Lectures on the Early History of Institutions*, Lectures XII and XIII, 'Sovereignty' and 'Sovereignty and Empire'.

[4] *An Introduction to the History of the Science of Politics*, p. 98.

[5] *Introduction to the Study of the Law of the Constitution*.

distributed in a rather complex way among different bodies and individuals'.[1] Bryce described international relations as 'the sphere in which no sovereignty *de jure* exists'.[2] Duguit, Krabbe, Kelsen, Politis and other thinkers progressively undermined the authority of the concept in legal thought until it is now widely agreed that sovereignty is not 'a real characteristic of a real thing' but 'a judgment of value';[3] many would add that it is a judgment based on discredited values.

The erosion of the concept in general legal thought made possible a revaluation of its significance for international law.

The concept can of course be given, and has often been given, a rational interpretation as the measure of discretion granted to States by the law. In *The Common Law of Mankind*[4] I attempted to express this now widespread view, which owes much to the work of Brierly and Fischer Williams[5] and received classical expression in the statement of Judge Anzilotti in the *Customs Union Case* that by sovereignty 'is meant that the State has over it no other authority than that of international law',[6] in the formula that 'the sovereignty of the State consists of its competence as defined and limited by international law and is not a discretionary power which overrides the law'.[7] This is the international corollary of the classical doctrine of English law as expounded by Bracton and reaffirmed by Fortescue and Coke:

> The king ought not to be under any man, but he ought to be under God and the law, since the law makes the king. Therefore let the king render to the law what the law has rendered to the king, namely dominion and power; for there is no king where will prevails and not the law.[8]

In a recent volume,[9] scholars versed in fifteen different legal systems or groups of legal systems have placed the concept in this rational perspective, and have shown that the necessary intellectual foundations for

---

[1] *The Elements of Politics*, Chapter XXXI, 'Sovereignty and Order', p. 641.

[2] 'The Nature of Sovereignty', in *Studies in History and Jurisprudence, 2*, p. 554.

[3] Kelsen, Hans, *What is Justice?*, p. 286.

[4] London, Stevens and Sons, 1958.

[5] Jenks, C. Wilfred, 'Fischer Williams – The Practitioner as Reformer', 40 *British Year Book of International Law*, 1964, pp. 238–243.

[6] P.C.I.J. 1931, Series A/B, No. 41, p. 57. [7] P. 3.

[8] Bracton, *De Legibus et Consuetudinibus Angliae*, 1–8–5; Fortescue, *De Laudibus Legum Angliae*; Conference between King James I and the Judges of England, 12 *Coke's Reports*, 63 (1612).

[9] Larson, Jenks and Others, *Sovereignty Within the Law*.

the acceptance of the concept that sovereignty consists not of freedom from any kind of external control but of full status in but subject to the law already exist in the major legal systems of the world. Some may regard so elaborate a demonstration as a work of supererogation leading to a foreseeable result; but the issue is one of such continuing and crucial practical importance that a marshalling of the full strength of the intellectual case against sovereignty is not to be despised.

Conceptually, therefore, sovereignty is no longer a problem; 'we are learning to come to terms with the paradox that to maintain freedom, even at a national level, it may be necessary to surrender sovereignty,'[1] at least to the extent of re-interpreting what we mean by sovereignty in these rational terms; the reality is still sadly otherwise. These rational concepts are not what governments normally mean when they invoke their sovereignty. Austin was entirely justified in his contention that 'supreme power limited by positive law is a flat contradiction in terms'[2]; when governments invoke sovereignty they are apt to be thinking in terms of supreme power rather than of rights recognised by law. They invoke it as a determined, unreasoning and at times highly emotional rejection of any external restraint or criticism. They have not substituted a rational for a traditional ideology of sovereignty. They mean red-blooded, and all too often red-clawed, sovereignty, sanctified lawlessness, a juristic monstrosity and a moral enormity. Sovereignty, in this political and emotional aspect, cannot be conjured away by the re-interpretation of a concept. It must be rejected by a deliberate act of policy as a snare and a delusion, which the new States will quickly recognise as such as they find that it cannot fulfil any of the essential purposes for which they value their freedom and independence, and which cannot serve effectively the long-term interest of any party to the ideological conflicts of our time. The essence of the matter is of the utmost simplicity. The world has outgrown sovereignty. As Max Huber has said, 'the concept of sovereignty, which existed long before the Renaissance, may have been necessary for transforming feudal medieval States into modern ones, but for any ethic of a supranational community it is mortal poison'.[3] It is a major intellectual obstacle to basing policy and action on a clear recognition that in the modern world the only choice open to us is one between 'alternative forms of

---

[1] Cowen, D. V., *The Foundations of Freedom with Special Reference to Southern Africa*, p. 196.

[2] *The Province of Jurisprudence Determined*, 2nd ed., p. 225.

[3] Carnegie Endowment for International Peace, *Perspectives on Peace, 1910–1960*, p. 157.

dependence'.[1] The concept that 'a State is not such, or at least is not perfectly such, if it lacks sovereignty'[2] has ceased to have any relationship to the facts of life in the modern world, the purposes of the modern State, or the place of the State in the wider community within which it now discharges all of its essential functions as a State. Sovereignty holds no promise of peace. It affords no prospect of defence. It provides no assurance of justice. It gives no guarantee of freedom. It offers no hope of prosperity. It furnishes no prescription for welfare. It hardens the opposition to orderly and peaceful social change. It disrupts the discipline without which scientific and technological innovation becomes the Frankenstein of our society (but a remorseless Frankenstein perpetually making new monsters). It is a mockery, not a fulfilment, of the deepest aspirations of humanity. The most eloquent refutation of the concept of sovereignty in the sphere of international relations is its futility, as tested by the professed purposes of contemporary politics.[3]

The concept is too obsessive an intellectual and emotional hangover for us to dismiss the part which sovereignty, as traditionally understood, has played in the traditional thinking of political philosophers and international lawyers as now belonging to history. We have, alas, not yet sufficiently purged ourselves of the past for this to be either wise or possible. The old Adam is still all too apt to plunge us back into the original sin of a self-sufficient approach to problems which call for a wider outlook. Mr. Justice Holmes once said that 'theory is the most important part of the dogma of the law, as the architect is the most important man who takes part in the building of a house'.[4] While the dogma of sovereignty retains its grip, the creative approach required to build a house of many mansions for human freedom and human dignity will continue to be inhibited. The conscious rejection of the dogma of sovereignty is therefore an essential step in so releasing our creative facilities that we can build together the prosperity and welfare of a free commonwealth, in which peace with justice, freedom and welfare rest solidly upon the common law of mankind. Only when we have rejected it can custom, general legal principles, equity, international public policy, adjudication and new legislative procedures and devices contribute their full potential to the contemporary development of the law.

Such a conscious rejection of the dogma is implied in the manner in

---

[1] Younger, Kenneth, *Changing Perspectives in British Foreign Policy*, p. 91.

[2] Vecchio, Giorgio del, *Philosophy of Law*, translated by Thomas Owen Martin, p. 364.

[3] I have elaborated these points more fully in *Law in the World Community*, pp. 31–41.

[4] 'The Path of the Law', *Collected Legal Papers*, p. 200.

which the General Assembly of the United Nations has assumed competence to discuss and in some cases act upon a wide range of questions which particular States have claimed to be essentially within their domestic jurisdiction within the meaning of the Charter.[1] The General Assembly has tended to be less respectful of sovereignty than the International Court, in whose pronouncements on the subject we have 'the elements, not always fully self-conscious and not always fully self-consistent, of an international public policy that sovereignty should be civilized by being treated as the creature rather than the master of the law'[2], but no outright rejection of the concept.

In this context Kelsen's most recent formulation of his attitude to sovereignty represents a challenge:

> In the sphere of international relations the view that the State is essentially sovereign is an individualistic philosophy, based on the individuality of the State. The dogma of sovereignty is not the result of scientific analysis of the phenomenon of the State, but the assumption of a philosophy of values. Consequently, it cannot be contradicted scientifically. One can only show that an interpretation which proceeds from another assumption – namely from that of the sovereignty of the international legal community – is just as possible, and that positive international law itself, so far as its validity is admitted, requires this interpretation.[3]

The sovereignty of the world community would, however, present problems no less formidable than those bequeathed to us by the sovereignty of the State. It may be that Dicey, Sidgwick and Bryce still have something relevant to tell us in the matter, that in the world community, as in the federal State, there is no recognisable sovereign, that it is by its nature a community in which power is distributed 'in a rather complex way', and that international relations are a sphere 'in which no sovereignty *de jure* exists'.

The world community is now in process of organising itself as a complex. The complex comprises the United Nations as the general world organisation (universal in its vocation though not yet in its membership); specialised and analogous agencies corresponding to the main departments of national governments but deliberately constituted as independent international organisations;[4] comprehensive regional organisations in all but one of the main regions of the world; an

---

[1] Rajan, M. S., *United Nations and Domestic Jurisdiction.*

[2] Jenks, C. Wilfred, *The Prospects of International Adjudication*, p. 500.

[3] *What is Justice?*, p. 286. [4] Pp. 233–239 below.

unprecedented number of national States; and a myriad of every possible kind of corporate and unincorporate bodies with an international membership or activities criss-crossing frontiers in such a manner that no effective control of them is conceivable unless they are ultimately brought within an international system. In this complex any concept of any sovereignty, wherever lodged, is as unreal as the concept that sovereignty in the United States rests with the legislatures of three-fourths of the several states, or conventions in three-fourths thereof, as Congress may decide, when acting upon amendments to the Constitution proposed by Congress by a two-thirds majority of both Houses or by a convention called on the application of two-thirds of the several states. The whole concept becomes meaningless; in its increasing meaninglessness it becomes increasingly mischievous; it is no less mischievous as an intellectual obstacle to clear thought than as a political barrier to resolute action; the plea that the concept still serves a useful function in clarifying and giving a healthy realism to political thought is wholly misconceived; it has lost all touch with reality and no longer carries weight with practical men.

There may at first glance appear to be some inconsistency between a plea for the reinterpretation of the concept of sovereignty as a competence conferred and circumscribed by law and a plea for the outright rejection of the concept in the sense in which the term continues to be invoked in political and diplomatic discussion. In reality, the reinterpretation and rejection of sovereignty are not mutually exclusive alternatives but complementary approaches. For purposes of juristic analysis the civilisation of sovereignty in the classical temper of the common law which has been characteristic of the pronouncements on the subject of the International Court of Justice[1] may continue to be the most natural and effective approach; in more political contexts only the clear rejection of the concept will unclutter the ground sufficiently to permit of effective constructive action; the difference of approach reflects the fact that the term continues to be used with widely different meanings.

The rejection of sovereignty has a direct relationship with all of the goals which we have postulated for creative effort. The renunciation of the threat and use of force, the subjection to review by the community of the right of self-defence, the control of armament, and obligations of collective security and peaceful settlement all presuppose the drastic curtailment of the right of the State to act unilaterally on the most vital issues of peace or war which was the essence of external sovereignty. A

[1] Jenks, C. Wilfred, *The Prospects of International Adjudication*, pp. 497–500.

community responsibility to restrain escalation and the maintenance of international peacekeeping forces are means of substituting collective for unilateral action. The international guarantee against the overriding authority of the State of the political freedom, civil liberties, economic and social rights, freedom of the mind and fullness of opportunity of its citizens leaves little place for the full authority of the State over its own citizens which was the essence of internal sovereignty. The emergence of obligations of mutual consultation and common action covering the whole field of monetary policy and trade and of a wide range of new obligations relating to investment, know-how and other matters, is in process of substituting economic solidarity for economic sovereignty. The law governing recent scientific and technological developments, the prototypes of which are nuclear energy and space, relates to matters so new that the concept of sovereignty has played little practical part in its development. In all of these fields the rejection or radical reinterpretation of the concept of sovereignty is essential for the attainment of our goals and the concept has in fact been rejected or ignored in the action taken with a view to their attainment.

Let us therefore consider the traditional techniques and sources of the law as avenues for its further development on the basis of the assumption that the world has substituted a positive for a positivist concept of law and no longer looks to the dogma of sovereignty as the basis of international relations.

3. Custom

Historically, custom holds pride of place among the sources of international law and it has not forfeited that place by the criticism of those who quibble with the term 'source' and prefer to describe custom as 'evidence'. 'Law everywhere begins with custom.'[1] Custom is "the original method of manifestation of the social will',[2] and 'the natural starting point of legal evolution'.[3] *Ius gentium*, to the Romans, meant 'the common law or usage of mankind'.[4] As the law of nations has developed custom has inevitably lost some of its original pre-eminence, but its continued vitality remains important for both the stability and the continued

---

[1] Bryce, *Studies in History and Jurisprudence*, p. 640.

[2] Vecchio, Giorgio del, *Philosophy of Law*, p. 306.

[3] Ross, Alf, *On Law and Justice*, p. 92.

[4] Pollock, Sir Frederick, *Jurisprudence and Legal Essays*, Selected and Introduced by A. L. Goodhart, p. 126.

growth of the law. In particular, we must proceed with caution in comparing the status of custom in contemporary international law with the shrunken role of custom in developed systems of municipal law.

In municipal law the part played by custom in the growth and development of the law tends to decline as a legal system matures. 'Custom', said Holland, 'exists as law in every country, though it everywhere tends to lose its importance relatively to other kinds of law';[1] or, as Sir Carleton Allen has expressed it, 'the scope of custom diminishes as the formulation of legal rules becomes more explicit and as a more elaborate machinery is set up for the making and administering of law'.[2] Judicial precedent tends to supersede, and, where the authority of precedent prevails, to crystallise, the custom which it recognises. 'Vague habits', Vinogradoff tells us, quoting Ulpian, are 'transformed in this way into technical formulae, either by judges determining their exact scope and effect, or by legal experts called upon to frame rules for the settlement of disputes'.[3] The upshot is that custom either operates as part of the general law or becomes a variation of the law which must be proved. It becomes increasingly difficult to fulfil the classical conditions of validity of an alleged custom. Blackstone, following in the main Coke on Littleton, formulated these as being that the custom must have existed from time immemorial, 'time whereof the memory of man runneth not to the contrary', that the custom must have been continuous, that it must have been enjoyed peaceably, that it must be reasonable, that it must be certain, that it must be compulsive, and that it must be consistent with other customs.[4] The requirement of antiquity, in particular, tends to freeze the vitality of custom. No scope is left for the emergence of new customs in changed situations. Legislation becomes the normal method of changing existing law. To this general proposition there are, of course, certain admitted exceptions, notably in respect of the custom of merchants which remains important in commercial law, largely as evidence of implied intention,[5] but the existence of such exceptions does not invalidate the general proposition. In the municipal law of modern societies custom has in practice become increasingly an exception to the law rather than a source or evidence of rules of law of general application; as Sir Carleton Allen has said, 'it does not apply to the generality of citizens, but only to a particular class of persons or to a particular place'.[6]

---

[1] *The Elements of Jurisprudence*, p. 39. [2] *Law in the Making*, p. 87.
[3] *Collected Papers*, p. 417. [4] *Ehrlich's Blackstone*, pp. 27–28.
[5] Pollock, Sir Frederick, *A First Book of Jurisprudence*, pp. 268–273.
[6] Allen, C. K., *Law in the Making*, p. 89.

International law has not reached the stage of development at which custom is, or can be allowed to be, devitalised in this manner. The part played by custom in the development of international law is limited by the relative frequency and importance of unique situations in international life,[1] but has not been rendered obsolete by adjudication, codification or legislation. The scope for adjudication remains limited by the fact that jurisdiction continues to be based on consent. Legislation and, under the current practice,[2] codification likewise require the consent of those to be bound thereby; they cannot be achieved by an authoritative decision independent of the will of those to whom the new rules are addressed. Nor can a breach of custom be regarded, in a society with inadequate means of law enforcement at its disposal, as necessarily destroying its authority. In many cases it may be difficult to determine 'whether an international custom will be accepted as law or merely considered as part of the *comitas gentium*' and 'the question of which customs shall be accepted as law can only be decided by future decisions or by codification'.[3]

Kelsen[4] has stressed the decentralised nature of the process of custom formation in contrast to the making of new law by authoritative decision; in this respect the process of custom formation and the technique of the law-making treaty are alike; they both reflect the decentralised nature of the structure and law-making processes of international society. In such a decentralised society the continuing fermentation of new custom has not been made unnecessary by more organised and sophisticated processes of legal development.

In these circumstances the continued vitality of custom is a condition of the continued vitality of the law itself.

Scholarship, legislative craftsmanship and the judicial process, far from superseding custom, all have distinctive and significant parts to play in preserving the vitality of custom.

Scholarship is both the philosopher and the scribe of custom. There has been much discussion, some of it highly recondite, on the nature of custom, the part played in its creation by the sense of legal obligation (or *opinio juris sive necessitatis*), and the extent to which acquiescence rather than the sense of legal obligation is the determining factor, particularly when the custom involves the recognition of a right rather than the performance of a duty. From Gentilis, Grotius and Pufendorf

---

[1] Dickinson, Edwin D., *Law and Peace*.

[2] Pp. 162–165 below.

[3] Ross, Alf, *On Law and Justice*, p. 95.

[4] 'Théorie du droit international coutumier', *Revue internationale de la théorie du droit*, 1939, pp. 253–274.

onwards, virtually every leading writer has discussed the nature and effect of custom.[1] Most of the general works on international law discuss the matter in greater or lesser detail and there is also an extensive special literature of the subject by contemporary writers amassing the elaborate learning to which it has given rise.[2] To recapitulate this elaborate learning is unnecessary for our purpose.

It will suffice to approach the matter in simpler terms. The old likening by common lawyers of the growth of usage and its development into custom to the formation of a path across a common has lost none of its picturesque cogency:

> At first each wayfarer pursues his own course; gradually, by reason either of its directness or on some other ground of apparent utility, some particular route is followed by the majority; this route next assumes the character of a track, discernible, but not as yet well defined, from which deviation, however, now becomes more rare; whilst in its final stage the route assumes the character of a well defined path, habitually followed by all who pass that way. And yet it would be difficult to point out at what precise moment this route acquired the character of an acknowledged path.[3]

Custom is constantly in *statu nascendi*. The line of demarcation between custom which has not become law and custom which has become law is at best ambiguous and often imperceptible. One cannot better Fischer Williams' characterisation of the difficulty: 'The Rubicon which divides custom from law is crossed silently, unconsciously and without proclamation.'[4] The difficulties remain, as they have always

---

[1] The literature is admirably summarised in Mateesco, Nicolas, *La coutume dans les cycles juridiques internationaux*.

[2] See, for instance, Visscher, Charles De, 'Coutume et traité en droit international public', *Revue générale de droit international public*, 3, pp. 353–69; Kelsen, Hans, 'Théorie du droit international coutumier', *Revue internationale de la théorie du droit*, 1939, pp. 253–292; Lauterpacht, Hersch, 'Decisions of Municipal Courts as a Source of International Law', 10 *British Year Book of International Law*, 1929, pp. 65–95; Guggenheim, Paul, 'Les deux éléments de la coutume en droit international public', *La Technique et les principes du droit public – Etudes en l'honneur de Georges Scelle*, 1; Kosters, Jan, 'Les fondements du droit des gens', *4 Bibliotheca Visseriana*, p. 115; Gianni, G., *La coutume en droit international*; Kopelmanas, Lazare, 'Custom as a Means of the Creation of International Law', *British Year Book of International Law*, 1937, pp. 127–151; Sørensen, Max, *Les Sources du Droit International*; Mateesco, Nicolas, *La coutume dans les cycles juridiques internationaux*; Kunz, Josef J., 'The Nature of Custom in International Law', 47 *American Journal of International Law*, 1953, pp. 662–69; Macgibbon, Ian O., 'Customary International Law and Acquiescence', *British Year Book of International Law*, 1957, pp. 115–145.

[3] Pitt Cobbett's *Leading Cases on International Law, 1, Peace*, p. 5.

[4] *Aspects of Modern International Law*, p. 44.

been, that of proof and that of determining at what stage a custom can be said to have become authoritative and binding.

We can accept as a fair summary of the position two recent statements, one by Myres McDougal, the other by Karol Wolfke, a recent Polish writer; while using widely different idioms, they do not diverge substantially in their conclusions. Myres McDougal describes the law of the sea as not 'a mere static body of rules' but 'a whole decision-making process, a public order which includes a structure of authorised decision-makers as well as a body of highly flexible, inherited prescriptions', a 'process of continuous interaction, of continuous demand and response' in which unilateral and competing claims are weighed and appraised by decision-makers external to the demanding State 'in terms of the interests of the world community and of the rival claimants', and 'ultimately accepted or rejected'.[1] Wolfke considers that 'in present international law there are no precise pre-established conditions for custom-creating practice, except for one general condition that it must give sufficient foundation for the presumption that the State concerned accepted it as binding'; that the decision as to whether this condition has been fulfilled in a particular case must be left to the 'organ ascertaining the existence of custom'; that whereas practice may be described as 'the raw material of custom, only the element of acceptance gives it the mark of the law'; and that the subjective element required does not consist of any element of conviction of legal obligation on the part of States but of their presumed acceptance of a practice as the expression of law.[2]

These statements throw into sharp relief the fluidity of the position and the measure of responsibility involved in the appraisal of custom.

Four points call for some special comment.

It is widely assumed that there is a major divergence between western and Soviet views of the validity and vitality of custom. The assumption reflects the discussion of custom in Soviet writings rather than any comprehensive objective evaluation of both Soviet and western practice. The Soviet literature of international law has tended to limit the law to what has been expressly accepted by States, preferably by treaty rather than by custom. It has emphasised the uncertainty of custom, the inapplicability of much of the custom of earlier times to socialist States in 'the international law of the transition period', and the need to prove the acceptance of the alleged custom by the State against which it is

---

[1] *American Journal of International Law, 49*, pp. 356 et seq.; the general approach is more fully developed in McDougal, Myres S. and Burke, William T., *The Public Order of the Oceans*, pp. 1–63.

[2] Wolfke, Karol, *Custom in Present International Law*, pp. 51–52 and 58.

invoked. In this respect it has shown a dogmatism equally characteristic of much of the western literature. There is high western authority for a pragmatic conservatism in the acknowledgement of custom, which in England found classical judicial expression in *West Rand Central Gold Mining Co.* v. *The King*.[1] Elihu Root, as a member of the Advisory Committee of Jurists of 1920 which drafted the Statute of the Permanent Court of International Justice, took an equally conservative view of custom and, with the full concurrence of Lord Phillimore, favoured the limitation of the law to be applied by the Court exclusively to rules accepted by States.[2] Manley O. Hudson, as special reporter of the International Law Commission of the United Nations in 1950, formulated requirements for the recognition of custom highly exacting in their insistence on the concordant practice of 'a number of States' over 'a considerable period of time' in conformity with the law and with the general acquiescence of other States; the general sense of the Commission was that the requirements were too exacting and it decided not to attempt to define them.[3] Neither Root's view nor Hudson's would now be regarded as acceptable statements of the contemporary outlook of western lawyers. The concept of the law as perpetually in motion and constantly renewing itself from forces outside itself has had too decisive an impact on our thought. In reviewing the Soviet literature on custom it is well to recall this historical perspective. The divergence of Soviet from western views may be at least in part a time lag rather than an irreconcilable antithesis of principle. Grigori Tunkin's analysis[4] is of special interest from this point of view. He acknowledges fully the importance of customary norms. States, he points out, refer constantly to them in their mutual relations. The problem of custom is one of the most important and complex in international law. Neither the antiquity nor the continuity of a custom is essential to its validity, and custom may be constituted by negative acts. It develops by a historic process whereby States accept customary norms as binding; these norms are then binding in the same manner as treaties. Up to this point there is no significant divergence of view. Only on the question of whether generally accepted custom binds States which have not accepted it does Tunkin take issue with such western writers as Basdevant, Charles De

---

[1] Law Reports (1905) 2 King's Bench Division, 391, 401.

[2] Permanent Court of International Justice, Advisory Committee of Jurists, Procès Verbaux, pp. 281, 286–287 and 293.

[3] United Nations, *Year Book of the International Law Commission 1*, pp. 4–6 and 275–276, *2*, p. 260.

[4] *Droit international public – Problèmes théoriques*, pp. 76–89.

Visscher, Guggenheim and Verdross. He insists that to regard a generally accepted custom as binding a dissenting minority would be inconsistent with the equality of States, that a norm cannot today be regarded as generally accepted unless it is recognised by the States of the two opposed social systems and that new States are not bound by the existing law, and he implies, particularly in his criticism of Guggenheim, that it is for States rather than international organs to determine whether or not a custom has been accepted. These are important issues but they are not primarily or inherently ideological. Except as regards the position of new States, these views are a current Soviet statement of what would have been regarded in the West a generation or two ago as established doctrine. The major question which they raise is whether they are compatible with the needs of a world community which is moving, and must move, towards a higher degree of integration than they are prepared to concede, whether they are sufficiently dynamic for the world of today, and whether Soviet doctrine can, consistently with its basic postulates, move further in the direction indicated by the needs of the times.

The acceleration of the rhythm of modern life has been reflected in an acceleration of the formation of custom. New questions calling for an urgent solution emerge with startling speed and frequency. Custom creating acts which would formerly have been few in number and spread over long or at least substantial periods of time now follow each other in such repeated instances and quick succession that regularity of conduct can be established in a brief period. The notoriety of practice necessary to presume general acquiescence in it no longer presupposes effluxion of time; modern communications have made it immediate. These fundamental changes in the process of formation of custom have given us the concept of 'spontaneous' or 'instantaneous' custom. The concept has secured widespread attention only in recent years, largely as the result of such developments as the recognition of the authority of States over the continental shelf and the emergence of generally accepted principles of space law, but it was anticipated by the spontaneous recognition of sovereignty over the airspace on the outbreak of the First World War. Expressing the matter on the narrowest basis the concept is a necessary adaptation to new and constantly changing technologies. As Max Sørensen has said, 'une pratique concernant les canaux internationaux ne peut évidemment remonter qu'à la construction du premier canal international et les coutumes du droit aérien dépendent de l'évolution technique des avions'.[1] If the inference drawn by Sir Frederick Pollock

---

[1] Op. cit., p. 102.

from the childhood of the individual to that of the race that 'one or two instances probably sufficed to make a good custom for our prehistoric ancestors'[1] is a valid one, the concept of spontaneous custom may be a reversion to the earliest origins of custom rather than an innovation. However this may be, it is now a crucial element in the continuing vitality of custom.

The practice of States embraces their collective as well as their individual acts. One of the significant consequences of the contemporary development of international organisation has been that the custom of international organisations has taken its place with the custom of States in the accepted corpus of international law.[2] Such custom forms a large part of the law governing the operation of such organisations and the relations between such organisations and States; it is of increasing importance for the law governing the relations of States and may ultimately supersede much of the earlier law relating to such matters as the recognition of States and governments, reservations to treaties, State succession, especially in respect of law-making treaties, title to disputed territory, responsibility for injury to aliens, and forcible means of redress short of war; it may add important chapters to the law relating to peace with justice, human rights, the general welfare, social change and scientific and technological progress. Custom evolved in this manner by the collective practice of States we shall call 'collective custom'.

The disappearance of any clear demarcation between international and domestic matters also has a significant bearing on the process of custom formation. As long ago as 1923, in the *Tunis-Morocco Nationality Decrees Case*, the Permanent Court of International Justice described the delimitation of domestic jurisdiction as 'an essentially relative question' dependent upon 'the development of international relations'.[3] In the light of contemporary developments the line of demarcation is not merely relative and changeable but frequently imperceptible. In these circumstances the old controversy concerning the extent to which the municipal conduct and decisions of States or their organs contribute to the formation of international custom has become singularly profitless; it had in any case been virtually resolved by a widespread consensus that such conduct and decisions are either an element or evidence of custom. The position has now been complicated by the fact that the

---

[1] *Jurisprudence and Legal Essays*, Selected and Introduced by A. L. Goodhart, p. 166.

[2] Cf. Jenks, C. Wilfred, *The Common Law of Mankind*, pp. 190–192.

[3] Permanent Court of International Justice, Collection of Advisory Opinions, Series B, No. 4, p. 24.

external relations of States are no longer conducted exclusively through the traditional machinery of foreign offices and diplomatic services. A substantial proportion of the departments of government intermesh with each other internationally and conduct external relations in their own fields of action. In the relations so conducted we have new occasions for custom formation of potentially far-reaching importance. Much of the customary law of the future may be evolved by patterns of conduct in which the traditional machinery for representing and binding the State plays little or no part; this may prove to be true in fields as varied as aviation, currency, finance, health, judicial cooperation, nuclear energy, shipping, space, trade, and perhaps many others. Custom evolved in this manner we shall call 'specialised custom'.

The appraisal of these developments calls for an imaginative grasp of the interplay of old and new which presupposes a solid knowledge of established practice no less than a lively appreciation of the significance of new facts, tendencies and potentialities. An adequate record of customary observance, authoritative in character, precise in detail, and covering the longest possible period of time and the widest geographical area is therefore an important element in the vitality of custom. The digests of international law and practice for which John Bassett Moore[1] set the pattern and which are now being compiled with the cooperation of an increasing number of governments and international organisations are invaluable as such a record and in some cases as a key to still richer unpublished resources.[2] The application of skilled scholarship to diplomatic and legal archives, exemplified by such works as McNair's *International Law Opinions*[3] and *Law of Treaties*,[4] has in our time made a notable contribution to placing the continuous growth of custom in historical perspective.

The International Law Commission of the United Nations and United Nations Conferences for the codification of the law on particular topics now play an important part in restating accepted custom. In the course of so doing they can exercise a salutary positive influence in revitalising the growth and acknowledgement of custom. Agreed restatements of the law by the International Law Commission already carry great authority and are particularly valuable as an indication of

---

[1] Moore, John Bassett, *Digest of International Law*.

[2] Hackworth, Green Haywood, *Digest of International Law*; Whiteman, Marjorie M., *Digest of International Law*; Parry, Clive, *A British Digest of International Law*; Kiss, Alexandre Charles, *Répertoire Français de Droit International Public*; United Nations, *Repertory of Practice of United Nations Organs*; see also Parry, Clive, *The Sources of Evidence in International Law*.

[3] Cambridge, University Press, 1956. [4] Oxford, Clarendon Press, 1961.

the extent to which changes in custom have met with general acceptance. The agreed conclusions of a United Nations codification conference carry still greater authority, even prior to the ratification of any conventions in which they may be embodied; in what degree such conclusions may come to be regarded as a binding repeal of obsolete usage or authoritative formulation of new customary rules which have come to be generally acknowledged remains to be determined.

No less significant is the role of the General Assembly. We have observed that the contemporary importance of unprecedented problems such as those arising from scientific and technological developments has given us the concept of 'spontaneous' or 'instantaneous' custom. In the recognition of such custom the General Assembly can, especially when it acts unanimously, play a uniquely important part. A striking illustration is afforded by the Declaration of Legal Principles Governing the Activities of States in the Exploration and Use of Outer Space which is now generally accepted as an authoritative statement of customary law recognised by States as binding upon them.[1] The significance of the Declaration in this respect has not been affected by the subsequent conclusion of the Treaty on Principles Governing the Activities of States in the Exploration and Use of Outer Space and it may serve as a precedent for similar action in respect of the ocean depths, the general problem of large-scale changes of natural environment and the broad principles governing scientific and technological development generally. How large a part the General Assembly may be called upon to play in crystallising custom in other fields we will have occasion to consider when examining its legislative potentialities. At this stage we are concerned with the matter only as a significant element in the importance and probable effectiveness of the continuing vitality of custom.

The judicial attitude towards proof of custom can have a decisive bearing on its continued vitality. Unduly exacting or rigid standards of proof can undermine the authority of widely accepted custom and inhibit further growth. A reasonable measure of judicial discretion may give much fairer and more satisfactory results. In this particular respect certain aspects of the jurisprudence of the International Court give cause for some concern and should be regarded as still open to further consideration.[2] It would, I submit, be entirely proper and appropriate for the International Court to regard the nature and extent of the proof

---

[1] Jenks, C. Wilfred, *Space Law*, especially pp. 183–186.

[2] I have reviewed the International Court cases in *The Prospects of International Adjudication*, pp. 225–265.

of custom required in international adjudication as a matter within its discretion. The Court is entitled to find that the custom invoked is sufficiently widely acknowledged not to require special proof. The Court is under no obligation to require affirmative evidence of the acceptance of the custom by the party against which it is invoked or such evidence that an accepted custom is based on an *opinio necessitatis juris*. These are matters for determination by the Court in its discretion and it has no obligation to require evidence which in the nature of the case it may frequently be impossible to furnish. In judging whether the available proof of custom is sufficient, it is legitimate for the Court to take into account the reasonableness and expediency of the alleged custom in the light of general principles of law, equity, public policy and practical convenience. The Court is entitled to recognise, and should increasingly recognise, the practice of international organisations as an element in the development of customary law, but it should not regard political controversy concerning the existence of a custom, in an international organisation or conference or elsewhere, as precluding it from finding that the custom is well established and is binding. It is for the Court to determine on the basis of the facts of the case whether any treaty provisions invoked are to be regarded as proof of or an exception to custom. Only by approaching the problem of proof of custom in this manner can the Court preserve the creative energy of custom from a process of judicial attrition.

In what areas of the law, and in respect of which of the goals which we have postulated for creative effort, continuing or new custom will play the largest part, cannot be foreseen with any accuracy. There are at least three major unknowns which affect in some measure all the main areas of the law. How far will old custom remain apposite, and how far will it be superseded by codification or legislative action? How far will new law be created by deliberate legislative action or the deliberate attribution of regulatory powers to international bodies and how far by the development of new custom? How far will alleged new customs command the consensus necessary to cross the Rubicon beyond which they become law and what will be the relative weight in the development of new law of custom, general principles of law, equity and public policy? Any answer to these questions must necessarily be speculative, but the principles involved are clear.

The potential range of new custom, including spontaneous, collective and specialised custom, covers every area of the law and all of the goals which we have postulated for creative effort. How dependent we will be in each field on the future vitality of custom will depend on the measure and rate of legislative and institutional progress in that field, but there is little prospect that legislative and institutional progress will be so comprehensive, continuous and rapid that we can afford to disdain the continuing vitality of custom as a significant factor in the further development of the law. The contribution of the General Assembly to the authoritative formulation of custom and the judicial attitude towards proof of custom may therefore have an important bearing on our capacity to attain, and success in attaining, the goals which we have postulated for creative effort. The General Assembly, in its successive pronouncements on space law, has shown an encouraging appreciation of the problem which may serve as a precedent for similar action in other fields; the part which the International Court will play in the matter awaits further clarification.

4. General principles of law

Custom, by its nature, presupposes recurrent situations, not necessarily identical with, but at least comparable to, each other. It provides no immediate answer for the new problem and no answer for the unique case. In an age of cataclysmic change the new problem is an everyday occurrence. In a legal system with a small number of subjects the unique case occurs with much greater relative frequency than in a legal system the subjects of which are counted in millions. In international law the creative energy of custom has not been neutralised at its source by other elements in the growth of the law, but the proportion of cases in which even spontaneous or instantaneous custom can provide a satisfactory answer for new or unique problems is relatively small. It is for this reason that the general principles of law recognised by civilised nations have been so important a factor in the development of international law at every successive stage of its development.

The early institutional writers on modern international law drew heavily, as Maine pointed out[1] with the unique authority of a Whewell Professor who was himself among the greatest of comparative lawyers, on Roman law; the law relating to territory, in particular, was based largely on the Roman rules. During the eighteenth and especially the nineteenth centuries the expansion of the common law in all five continents made it no less significant a source of international rules and practice.

During the nineteenth century and the early part of the twentieth century recourse to general principles of law became, as Hersch Lauterpacht's pioneer work[2] so brilliantly and convincingly demonstrated, a

---

[1] *International Law*, pp. 16–23.

[2] *Private Law Sources and Analogies of International Law.*

(perhaps, indeed, one should say *the*) characteristic feature of international arbitration. The range of questions in respect of which tribunals as varied as the leading British-American arbitral tribunals, the Permanent Court of Arbitration, the Central American Court of Justice and a large number of miscellaneous claims commissions had recourse to general principles of law was singularly wide. It included the legal nature, acquisition and loss of territorial sovereignty, state servitudes, acquisitive and extinctive prescription, property and possession in animals *ferae naturae*, treaties as contracts, state responsibility (with reference to absolute liability and fault), state succession, interest, measure of damages, estoppel, and *res judicata*, to give only particularly striking or common illustrations. Article 38 (1) (c) of the Statute of the International Court of Justice which, following the corresponding provision of the Statute of the Permanent Court of International Justice, provides that the Court shall apply, together with international conventions and custom, 'the general principles of law recognised by civilized nations', consolidates this long and well-established practice of recourse to such principles for the development of international law.

Concerning the nature of such recourse there has been much debate and Lauterpacht, Georges Ripert,[1] Jean Spiropoulos,[2], Alfred von Verdross,[3] Bin Cheng[4] and others have expressed divergent views of the extent to which the general principles of law are to be deduced from municipal law analogies or principles more general in character than any such analogy. These divergences are largely methodological rather than real. Whether the general principles applied by the Court are recruited directly from municipal law analogies or from principles so general that they are independent of any system of municipal law but find widespread expression in municipal legal systems may not be of any great importance as a practical matter.

The International Court has been cautious and sparing in exercising the authority conferred upon it by Article 38 (1) (c) of the Statute by referring specifically to general principles of law. As I have ventured to say elsewhere:

> The Court is frequently reluctant to rely on a general principle of law if the question at issue can be disposed of on some other basis.

---

[1] 'Les règles du droit civil applicables aux rapports internationaux', *Recueil des Cours de l'Académie de Droit international*, Vol. 44, 1933 (II), pp.569–663.

[2] *Die allgemeine Rechtsgüindsätze in Völkerrecht, Théorie générale du droit international.*

[3] 'Les principes généraux du droit dans la jurisprudence internationale', *Recueil des Cours de l'Académie de Droit international*, Vol. 52, (1935 (II)), pp. 195–249.

[4] *General Principles of Law as Applied by International Courts and Tribunals.*

> The general principles which it most readily invokes are, naturally enough, the most general and most self-evident. A principle which requires exposition or argument is much less likely to appear in a decision of the Court than one which can be expressed in a maxim, and is more apt to find a place in an individual or dissenting opinion. The Court, quite rightly in view of its unique status as the supreme judicature of mankind, is reluctant to invoke authority or precedent for any proposition which it formulates, with the result that it is inclined to refrain from stating general principles unless they are already so widely accepted that they can be expected to command a degree of assent which makes any argument in the matter or reference to precedent superfluous.[1]

This cautious attitude has not, however, precluded the Court from invoking as general principles such fundamental concepts as *nemo judex in re sua*, the right of a judicial body to determine its jurisdiction, the distinction between a corporate body and its members, the relevance of accepted practice to the determination of the extent of constitutional powers, the rule that error cannot be pleaded by a party which contributed to or could have avoided the error, and the principle of *res judicata.*

We may anticipate that international law will, as it develops further, continue to recruit its principles, rules and institutions from general principles of law. The scope for such development will be profoundly influenced by prevalent concepts of law, of the place of law in international relations, and of the relationship of law and sovereignty. The general concept of law which we have expounded, as a discipline of social control the emphasis of which has shifted from commands to do or not to do to rules defining the consequences of acts in the law and prescribing the conditions to be fulfilled and procedure to be followed to secure the desired result, narrows the range within which the invocation of general principles of law raises any question of how far they can be relied upon to limit the freedom of action of States. The attitude towards sovereignty which we have adopted, the concept so happily expressed by Sir Gerald Fitzmaurice that international law is the source of, rather than a restriction upon, the rights of States,[2] implies that any question which may arise concerning the extent to which the freedom of action of States is limited by a general principle of law is not governed by any general presumption in favour of freedom of action, but must be

---

[1] Jenks, C. Wilfred, *The Prospects of International Adjudication*, p. 305.

[2] 30 *British Year Book of International Law*, 1953, pp. 8–13.

determined in the light of all the relevant circumstances and considerations. The basic factor which determines the scope for and limits of recourse to general principles of law is not anything inherent either in the nature of international law and the international legal system or in the process of such recourse, but the extent to which judicial agreement can be secured on the principles applicable and the conditions of their application and the measure in which decisions resulting from the application of such principles command general confidence and support at a particular stage in our progress towards world community.

When the problem is approached in this manner it resolves itself into that of how far there exists a sufficient core of accepted principle common to all the main legal systems of the world to secure the measure of judicial agreement and general confidence necessary to permit of extensive recourse to such commonly accepted principles for the progressive development of the law. In *The Common Law of Mankind*[1] I have argued that there is a sufficient consensus on certain fundamental principles among the main legal systems to give us the necessary point of departure and that all the leading systems are subject to processes of development and change which afford significant opportunities for enlarging their common core. We may therefore, if I may borrow the jargon of the economists, reasonably envisage a take-off into self-sustaining growth. It has been argued that a far more detailed and critical analysis of the world's legal systems is necessary to warrant such a conclusion; that any such synthesis as I have suggested involves a task of such proportions as to be impracticable; that general principles cannot be determined by a lowest common denominator; and that the basic problems of international relations arise not from the differences of intellectual approach which such a synthesis represents an attempt to reconcile but from conflicts of interest. All of these are valid and significant points, but they imply a misconception of the original thesis. The thesis is not that we already have in the major legal systems of the world the essentials of a satisfactory world order, but that we have the elements out of which we can build such an order. May I perhaps quote the precise terms in which I originally stated the thesis in *The Common Law of Mankind*:

> The legal systems which we must lay under contribution for the purpose of building up from general principles a universal law of nations are not systems in their final stage of development, irrevocably committed to everything which has been characteristic

---

[1] London, Stevens and Sons; New York, Praeger, 1958.

> of their earlier stages of growth. The key to the situation is not whether in their present phase of development they are consistent with and will contribute to a universal legal order, but whether they are capable of developing in a manner which will be consistent with and will contribute to a universal legal order.[1]

The suggestion for a multi-cultural and multi-legal system approach[2] which accompanies this thesis is not that we should attempt to garner into an encyclopaedia from all the legal systems of the world everything which may at some time be internationally relevant, an academic undertaking of admittedly colossal and impracticable proportions, but that as questions assume practical importance they should be examined in the light of the legal systems of the world as a whole rather than with an outlook limited to the leading civil law and common law systems. The comparative method envisaged for this purpose is not one of deducing deceptive conclusions from superficial comparison and perfunctory analysis but one of penetrating through form and terminology to substance, which may prove on fuller examination to be more like or more unlike than a first glance suggests. We must learn 'not to be lured by homonyms and not to be afraid of synonyms'.[3] If the task is approached in this spirit with creative imagination, the recognition by the Statute of the International Court of the importance of the general principles of law recognised by civilised nations as an integral part of the law to be applied by the Court may prove to have been the decisive landmark in the development of a common law of mankind. Such general principles have a significant contribution to make in relation to all of the goals which we have postulated for creative effort. It is no more possible to anticipate the precise contexts in which there may be occasion to invoke general principles than to foresee with any precision the future development of custom, but there are certain areas in which recourse to such principles may prove to be particularly significant and illustrations of these, in no sense exhaustive, may serve to demonstrate the scope for creative effort. As such illustrations we may mention, without enlarging upon, the effect of the prohibition of the threat or use of force on the general body of international law, the discharge of treaty obligations, and liability for ultra-hazardous activities.

The prohibition of the threat or use of force affects the fundamentals of the law.[4] It has, as was demonstrated during the Second World War

---

[1] P. 116. [2] Pp. 87–89.

[3] Kahn-Freund, O., *Comparative Law as an Academic Subject*, p. 19.

[4] Cf. Jenks, C. Wilfred, *The Common Law of Mankind*, pp. 176–178.

by the practice of lend-lease, transformed the law of neutrality. It is the foundation of the concept of crimes against the peace embodied in the Nuremberg judgment and subsequently endorsed by the General Assembly. It is the basis of the principle, now accepted by the International Law Commission of the United Nations, that any treaty the conclusion of which was procured by the threat or use of force in violation of the principles of the Charter of the United Nations is void. It may, and doubtless will, prove to have many further applications.

The discharge of treaty obligations is perhaps the most crucial of the many areas of the law of treaties in which the capacity of the law to resolve problems arising in new contexts depends on the substitution for unilateral action by States of the application, preferably judicially, of the general principles of law governing the discharge of obligations by default, frustration and obsolescence.

Liability for ultra-hazardous activities illustrates the role of general principles of law in the development of the international law of tort. The principle of fault rendered a historical service to the development of international law by displacing the principle of collective responsibility for wrongs which found expression in the blood feud of early law. But it became clear as early as the *Alabama Case* that lack of due diligence constitutes fault. The diligence required increases, as the Alabama Tribunal indicated, with the risk involved, and some activities involve hazards so great that absolute liability as a risk of the enterprise is the only equitable principle. Contemporary scientific and technological developments, of which nuclear energy and space exploration are only the most immediately dramatic of many possible illustrations, have greatly increased the range of ultra-hazardous activities and given an altogether new importance to this branch of the law, in which the manner in which municipal law has responded to the same problem is the major source of development corresponding to needs which have now become urgent.[1]

5. Equity

General principles of law merge almost insensibly into equity, which differs from them chiefly in that, seeking initially to temper the rigour of consistent principle with fairness in particular cases by adapting principles to circumstances, or to provide remedies for grievances for which

---

[1] Jenks, C. Wilfred, 'Liability for Ultra-Hazardous Activities in International Law', *Recueil des Cours de l'Académie de Droit international*, Vol. 117 (1966 (I)), pp. 101–198.

no effective remedy exists at law, it tends to develop into a supplementary body of principle dealing in a spirit of fairness with matters for which the law in an earlier stage of development failed in substance or procedure to provide remedies satisfactory to the judicial conscience and law forming opinion generally. In some legal systems, including both Roman and English law, the development of equity has been associated with a special jurisdiction, but in others, such as Islamic and Jewish law, the equivalent of equity has been an element or attitude in the development and application of the law independent of the existence of any special jurisdiction. Equity as an element in international law is in the nature of the case a less technical concept than the equity of the English Court of Chancery.

Recourse to equitable principles and conceptions has been a commonplace of international arbitration throughout its history to a much greater extent than has been generally appreciated. The necessary distinction between a decision on the basis of respect for law and a decision *ex aequo et bono* which, as Lauterpacht pointed out, is 'a species of legislative activity',[1] and which the Statute of the International Court of Justice permits only 'if the parties agree thereto', has tended to obscure the significance of the wide range of cases in which equitable principles operate within the law, the frequency with which international tribunals have been specifically charged to decide cases submitted to them in accordance with law and equity, and the extent to which equitable considerations have been invoked before and by tribunals even in the absence of any such specific reference to equity in the terms of reference of the tribunal.[2] In international, as in municipal, adjudication, equity in this sense does not override the law; it operates within the general framework of the law, makes it more flexible, and mellows it. As equity is not, in international law, a technical concept, there is no clear distinction between the recognition of equities and a modified attitude to proof of custom, fuller recourse to general principles of law, and due regard to considerations of international public policy; all of these factors merge with each other as mellowing influences in the progress of the law towards greater maturity. The significance of the part which equity can play in the further development of international jurisprudence will depend in large measure on how far it evolves into a concept of established universality by drawing its inspiration from the equitable conceptions of a wide range of legal

---

[1] *The Development of International Law by the International Court*, p. 213.

[2] I have discussed this matter in detail in *The Prospects of International Adjudication*, pp. 316–427.

systems. The need to evolve such a synthesis is a major challenge to the creative imagination.

The recognition of equities, and procedures which for the common lawyer are essentially equitable, may be of significant importance in a wide range of contexts but perhaps chiefly in the law relating to economic stability and growth and the law concerning scientific and technological development. Equitable maxims, such as 'equality is equity', 'he who seeks equity must do equity' and 'come with clean hands', 'equity looks to the intent rather than the form', and 'equity regards the balance of convenience', equitable concepts such as estoppel, trust and unjust enrichment, and equitable remedies such as declaratory judgments, administration by a tribunal, injunction and specific performance, may all be fruitful elements of development.

6. International public policy

Public policy has been suspect among international lawyers. The only public policy for which there existed, until recently, any social or institutional foundation was national public policy which tended to be the negation of law. Only recently has it become possible to conceive of the vitality of the law as a major objective of the policy of a growing world community and the policy of the community as a significant influence upon the vitality of the law.[1] The policy of the community which may be expected to influence the development of the law is defined in general terms by the goals of creative effort which we have postulated.

The concept of international public policy as a positive influence upon the law rather than a ground for declining to enforce a foreign law or the terms of a contract has excited some surprise and provoked some criticism. That such a concept should not be congenial to private international lawyers is perhaps natural as it rests on a basis entirely different from that of the concept of public policy with which they are familiar. Constitutional lawyers in particular and, one may hope, equity lawyers and criminal and tort lawyers, will find themselves more at home with such a concept, which is not unlike preoccupations of public policy which have influenced their own specialities. The reception of the concept by public international lawyers will probably be determined partly by their general attitude to processes of growth and change in the law and partly by the extent to which the concept commends itself by its content as it becomes more specific.

---

[1] I have discussed the matter at length in *The Prospects of International Adjudication*, pp. 428–546.

Public policy, like equity, cannot be defined with precision in advance of the contingencies in which it is invoked, but the essence of the matter is that the law is an instrument of the policy of a growing world community. International public policy 'requires the effectiveness of international organisation, the civilisation of sovereignty, the full recognition throughout the law of the implications of the changed legal status of violence, the consolidation of the rule of law rather than its emasculation by insistence on unattainable standards of proof of custom, a law of contract and tort adequate to contemporary needs, and rules concerning prescription, acquiescence and estoppel which secure a necessary minimum of stability in a world of cataclysmic change.'[1] In all these matters the relevance of public policy will be so closely related to recourse to general legal principles and the requirements of equity that it may be difficult to distinguish the three elements as separate influences upon the development of the law; they will all tend towards a positive approach to the solution of new problems in a spirit of justice and convenience rather than by invoking a husk of principle or precedent the marrow of which has decayed. In developing and applying the concept of the public policy of a growing world community the creative imagination can make a major contribution to the contemporary development of the law.

The concept clearly has possible applications throughout the areas which we have postulated as the goals of creative effort. The general policy of eliminating recourse to force and substituting collective or third-party for unilateral judgment, of developing effective protection for human rights, of adjusting conflicts of economic interest on the basis of a common responsibility for promoting economic stability and growth in the common interest, and of establishing an effective social discipline of scientific and technological development, provides a broad intellectual framework for the multiplicity of decisions concerning specific and concrete issues which will determine the whole tone and temper of the legal system and the adequacy of its response to growing and changing need.

7. The judicial process

The creative energy of custom and general principles of law, and the scope for resourcefulness in coping with the unexpected to avoid unfairness and frustration provided by equity and public policy, cannot create new law effectively in an institutional vacuum. There must be

---

[1] Ibid., pp. 545–546.

recognised processes through which custom and legal principle come to be accepted as binding and appropriate recognition is given to equities and public policy. Among these, adjudication is of distinctive importance.

What are the prospects of international adjudication, and what contribution can the creative imagination make to improving them? I use the term in the broadest sense, to include the prospects of the submission to adjudication of a larger number and wider range of significant questions, the prospects of developing a more varied range of procedures and remedies which make international adjudication more flexible and effective in its operation, the prospects of the international judicial process being a major creative influence upon the development of the substance of the law, and the prospects of securing compliance with decisions strongly resented by the losing party. Some high authorities, and in particular Sir Gerald Fitzmaurice, have expressed the view that progress in these latter respects will help so little to increase the willingness of governments to submit a wider range of significant questions for impartial adjudication that these questions are best dealt with separately;[1] I prefer to regard them as distinct but related parts of a broader problem, that of so developing the international judicial process that impartial justice under law plays, within a wider framework embracing many other elements, its necessary part in the progress of an organised world community towards a lasting peace of freedom and welfare. In this process the acceptance of jurisdiction is perhaps the vital, but is only the first, stage.

As we have seen when discussing peace with justice as one of the goals of creative effort, the unwillingness of governments to depart from the voluntary basis of jurisdiction is not justified by anything inherent in the nature of justiciability but arises from a persistent reluctance to accept the consequences and risks of impartial judgment.[2] Of what avail, it will be asked, can the creative imagination be in such a situation? The paralysis is a paralysis of the will, not of the mind; the difficulty is one of policy, not of an imperfect technique which legal skill can and should improve. The objection is an important one, but calls for three comments. The first responsibility of the creative imagination when confronted with such a situation is to understand it; the most urgent need is the avoidance of misplaced ingenuity in creating a simulacrum of compulsory jurisdiction while preserving the freedom of action of the parties in cases to which they attach real importance by such devices as the Connally amendment (which excludes from compulsory jurisdiction

---

[1] *Kansas Law Review*, 13, 1965, pp. 442–50. [2] P. 42 above.

matters which the party concerned claims to be within its domestic jurisdiction) and the reservation of the right to terminate acceptance of jurisdiction at any time. Any real progress presupposes a major change of perspective as the result of which the relative importance of peace with justice and freedom of action are differently assessed; to such a change of perspective imaginative insight can make a significant contribution. Progress is likely to be gradual and to be made chiefly by grasping opportunities to provide for compulsory jurisdiction when negotiating arrangements of mutual advantage to the parties in the practical operation of which it can perform useful service; only a continuing alertness of imaginative insight can perceive and grasp such opportunities to the full as they occur.[1]

If, as we may anticipate, the progress of compulsory jurisdiction remains halting, it may be of great importance to consider whether it is practicable to take any more immediate step which would tend to re-establish the basic concept that objectivity is both possible and desirable, even in a dynamic and tragically divided world. Agreed arrangements for the impartial determination of disputed facts at the request of any party concerned would be a great step forward. To treat questions of fact as questions of fact or questions of evidence as questions of evidence might well be the decisive first step towards treating questions of law as questions of law.[2]

The impartial determination of disputed facts may be of primary importance in all four of the main areas which we have identified in discussing the goals of creative effort. Objectivity in ascertaining the facts is an essential element in evaluating the justification for measures alleged to have been taken in self-defence and restraining escalation; it is the heart of the problem of verification which has been the stumbling block in so much of the discussion of arms control. Objectivity in ascertaining the facts is the necessary foundation for any effective international action to protect civil liberties and promote social justice and the freedom of the mind. Objectivity in ascertaining the facts is a prerequisite of reconciling conflicting interests in the fields of economic stability and growth and in particular the emotionally charged conflicts of interest between the richer and the poorer nations. Objectivity in ascertaining the facts is the essence of the scientific evaluation of the questions requiring regulation without which the law cannot bite

---

[1] Jenks, C. Wilfred, *The Prospects of International Adjudication*, pp. 101–118.

[2] I have discussed the matter more fully in 'Universality, Coexistence and the Rule of Law', a lecture delivered before the Institute of Law of the Polish Academy of Sciences on 13 September 1965 and reproduced in *Law in the World Community*, pp. 15–30, especially at pp. 25–28.

effectively on the new problems posed by advanced science and technology.

International judicial procedure is relatively free of the technicalities which have been characteristic of the early phases of development of many municipal legal systems, but the range of parties, procedures and remedies normally available in international adjudication is narrow. Only in the Court of Justice of the European Communities do we find a range comparable to that of a developed system of municipal law. The provision of a wider range of parties, procedures and remedies may be no less important for the future of international adjudication than the broadening of compulsory jurisdiction and no less a challenge to the inventive ingenuity of the creative imagination.[1]

Two developments in matters of *locus standi* are particularly desirable for the attainment of the goals which we have postulated. One is to give international organisations a *locus standi* as parties to proceedings before international courts and tribunals; such a development would tend to facilitate proceedings in a wide range of cases in which an international organisation is a more natural and appropriate representative of the community interest than any of its members or any party to a particular controversy.[2] The other is to recognise more fully the existence of a legal interest in the general welfare entitling States to institute proceedings in circumstances such as those in which their right to do so was denied by a majority of the International Court in the *South West Africa Cases*.[3] Both of these suggested developments would have an important bearing on the potential contribution of the judicial process to all of the major goals which we have postulated.

In matters of procedure the need for expedition in certain types of case and for expertise in others may call for new developments.

It is, however, in the field of remedies that it is most necessary to test by our objectives the adequacy of our present means of attaining them. The remedies at present available from the International Court are in effect limited to a decision stating the law (in the form of a judgment or advisory opinion) or an award of damages. Are these the most appropriate remedies for attaining the goals which we have postulated or are there other possible remedies which should be considered? In questions of peace and security the political difficulties of experimenting with new types of remedy are at their maximum. In human rights areas,

---

[1] I have discussed the matter in some detail in *The Prospects of International Adjudication*, pp. 119–184.

[2] Jenks, op cit., pp. 185–244.

[3] Cf. Jenks, C. Wilfred, *Law in the World Community*, pp. 52–53.

something analogous to the issue of a prerogative writ may be possible. In matters relating to economic stability and growth and scientific and technological development, there may be cases calling for the equivalent of an injunction and cases best dealt with by the equivalent of a decree in equity settling the respective rights and obligations of the parties. The jurisdiction of the International Court comprises 'all cases which the parties refer to it and all matters specially provided for in the Charter of the United Nations or in treaties and conventions in force', including specifically legal disputes concerning 'the nature or extent of the reparation to be made for the breach of an international obligation'. There is nothing in the Statute to debar the development of a wider range of remedies;[1] this could certainly be done by instruments granting the Court jurisdiction in particular matters and envisaging new remedies being granted in the exercise of that jurisdiction; there may also be cases in which the Court could and should develop a new remedy by granting, in accordance with its Statute, 'reparation' of a 'nature' other than that which has hitherto been habitual in the form of a new remedy. How much can be done to provide more appropriate and effective remedies will depend on how far States, in conferring jurisdiction on the Court, and the Court in framing and applying its Rules and determining the nature of the reparation to be made for the breach of particular obligations, develop a fertility of procedural resource corresponding to the importance of the changes taking place in the substantive law. Some experimental experience before lesser bodies may be a natural and useful preliminary to any sustained attempt to provide a wider range of remedies in the International Court itself.

Jurisdiction and procedure are the framework of the international judicial process; the essence of the matter is the impact of adjudication on the law and, through the law, on international society. How does the attitude of international tribunals on such matters as proof of customary law, and resort to general principles, to equity and to considerations of public policy, affect the substance and development of the law? It may have a decisive influence on the continued vitality of custom; it will in large measure determine the extent to which general principles of law remain a fertile source of growth and to which equity and public policy make any significant contribution to the maturity of the law.

A wider acceptance of compulsory jurisdiction, the development of new procedures and remedies, and judicious valour in the judicial development of the law will be of little avail if international decisions

---

[1] On the whole matter see Jenks, C. Wilfred, *The Prospects of International Adjudication*, pp. 119–184.

and awards remain ineffective in practice and no adequate means exist of securing compliance with their terms. The record of compliance with international decisions has been good, so good that it has been widely assumed that the problem of securing compliance is not in practice one of the major problems of international adjudication, but there have been a sufficient number of cases in which international decisions and opinions have been ineffective in practice to raise a serious doubt whether the attitude continues to be warranted. The problem of compliance cannot usefully be considered in the abstract. The steps necessary to secure compliance, and the extent to which any organised procedure for securing compliance is possible or desirable, may vary widely with the nature and terms of the decision or award and the political context in which it is given. Certain types of decision or award present no enforcement problems because they are self-executory. Where measures of enforcement are necessary, they may take the form of enforcement by United Nations action, enforcement through specialised agencies and other international organisations in a position to use effective means of pressure or constraint in respect of the subject-matter of the decision, enforcement through regional organisations, enforcement through the cooperation of other States having assets of the judgment debtor within their jurisdiction, and enforcement through municipal legal procedures; special devices, such as the constitution of a special international fund to satisfy financial awards, are also conceivable. There is no immediate or comprehensive solution for the problem of developing effective methods of securing compliance with international decisions and awards, and a sustained attempt to develop with imaginative insight complementary approaches effective in particular types of case is therefore indispensable.[1] It follows that we should consider attentively the appropriateness of each of these possible types of enforcement action in respect of each of our postulated goals.

The value of the contribution which international adjudication can make to attaining the goals which we have postulated for creative effort will be determined in part by the progress of compulsory jurisdiction, in part by the range of procedures and remedies which become available, in large measure by the impact of the judicial process on the content of the law, and to a significant extent by the degree in which there is a reasonable certainty of compliance. In respect of all these matters the outcome will depend in substantial measure on how far, in seeking to widen jurisdiction, to evolve new procedures and remedies, to develop

---

[1] I have discussed the problem more fully in *The Prospects of International Adjudication*, pp. 663–726.

the content of the law, and to secure fuller compliance, we can relate experiments and innovations in method to the goals which we are seeking to pursue. However technical the problem of jurisdiction, procedure or execution for which we are seeking a solution may be, the criterion of the value of whatever may be proposed is how effectively it will operate in practice for the attainment of the goals which we have postulated, namely the preservation of peace with justice, the protection of human rights, the promotion of economic stability and growth, and the social control of science and technology.

8. Codification

Law evolved from custom, general principle and adjudication inevitably tends to be untidy in form, uncertain in content and uneven in application. Since the days of David Dudley Field,[1] Bluntschli[2] and Fiore[3] there has been a widespread desire among international lawyers for a more systematic approach designed to achieve by codification a more comprehensive and precise restatement of the law. The need for, feasibility and desirability of codification nevertheless remained until relatively recently a highly controversial issue. In League of Nations days many common lawyers were inclined to be wary of the codification of international law. Their hesitation in the matter was a composite of two elements, a fear that successful codification would crystallise the law prematurely at too early a stage of its development, and the converse fear that unsuccessful attempts to codify might unsettle much of what had previously been regarded as well-established law.[4] After the failure of the Hague Codification Conference of 1930 to reach agreement on the greater part of its agenda this second fear became almost an obsession. It was reflected in influential proposals to substitute the restatement of the law by authoritative bodies of international lawyers following the methods of work evolved by the Harvard Research in International Law for codification by treaty or other forms of intergovernmental action.[5] During the last twenty years there has been a

---

[1] *Outlines of an International Code*, 2nd ed.

[2] *Le Droit International Codifié*, 5th ed.

[3] *Il Diritto Internazionale Codificato*, 4th ed.

[4] E.g. Brierly, J. L., 'The Failure of Codification' (1931), reprinted in *The Basis of Obligation in International Law*, pp. 189–200.

[5] Hurst, Sir Cecil, 'A Plea for the Codification of International Law On New Lines' (1946), reprinted in *International Law – The Collected Papers of Sir Cecil J. B. Hurst*, pp. 129–151.

marked change of perspective.[1] The far-reaching changes which have occurred in the composition of, and weight of influence within, the international community have greatly increased the practical need for, and desirability of, codification. There has been a growing sense that the authority of certain parts of the law can and should be consolidated by a process of codification in which the newer members of the international community take a full part. Such a view does not impair the established principle that new members of the international community are bound by international law as they find it, but tends to promote among them a valuable sense of identification with and shared responsibility for the law. The International Law Commission of the United Nations has surmounted formidable initial difficulties and achieved a substantial measure of success in reformulating important segments of the law.[2] On the basis of its work a series of major conferences, the First United Nations Conference on the Law of the Sea of 1958 and the Vienna Conferences on Diplomatic and Consular Relations, have adopted, and the Vienna Conference of the Law of Treaties has adopted on first reading, conventions which have placed the prospects of codification in a wholly new perspective. The Geneva Convention on the High Seas proclaims its provisions to be 'generally declaratory of established principles of international law'. The Conventions on Fishing and Conservation of the Living Resources of the High Seas and on the Continental Shelf have been widely ratified and are in force. The Convention on the Territorial Sea and the Contiguous Zone is unlikely to come into force by reason of the subsequent failure to reach agreement on the breadth of the territorial sea but has had a marked impact on the law. The Vienna Convention on Diplomatic Relations of 1961, a modern codification of one of the oldest chapters of the law, is in force for over sixty States, and the Convention on Consular Relations of 1963 may be expected to come into force in due course. A similar measure of success in respect of the law of treaties and some of the matters now pending before the International Law Commission would give codification under the auspices of the United Nations a wholly new status among the recognised processes of growth in international law, comparable to that of the major codifications of the civil law systems or the most successful of the uniform laws of the common law jurisdictions.

There nevertheless remains one profoundly unsatisfactory element in the present procedure of codification in respect of which the position has

---

[1] Lauterpacht, H., 'Codification and Development of International Law', in *American Journal of International Law*, Vol. 49, No. 1, January 1955, pp. 16–43.

[2] Briggs, Herbert, *The International Law Commission.*

remained substantially unchanged since the First Hague Peace Conference of 1899. When the law has been restated at a codification conference, the convention restating it, much of which may be designed as a statement of existing law already binding upon States, is submitted for ratification by States in the same manner as a convention designed as a means of securing the acceptance of entirely new obligations which are clearly not binding on States which do not accept the convention. In these circumstances failure to ratify the convention may tend to throw doubt on the continued validity of obligations which already existed independently of the convention. There would be a great advantage in a codifying procedure which avoided this danger; when we come to consider the legislative potentialities of the General Assembly it may be possible to envisage an important new departure in the matter.[1]

It is particularly important to avoid anything which would tend to accentuate the precariousness of codification by treaty, such as the inclusion in a codification convention of provision for denunciation. The Hague Conventions of 1899 and 1907 and the Convention and Protocols on Nationality Questions adopted at the League of Nations Codification Conference of 1930 included denunciation clauses, but the United Nations Conventions on the Law of the Sea of 1958 and on Diplomatic and Consular Relations of 1961 and 1963 rightly make provision for their revision but omit any denunciation clause.

Codification, by its nature, can make little contribution to the earliest stages of the formulation of new law to govern new problems, but nevertheless has an important bearing on the attainment of the goals which we have postulated for creative effort. By clarifying and consolidating the existing law it defines the point of departure; the law can evolve more readily from well settled and generally accepted principles and rules than from complete uncertainty; if we can no longer rely on the foundations laid by the past we cannot build for the future without undertaking the immensely laborious task of completely relaying those foundations. When codification clarifies and consolidates the instruments and procedures which we must use to create new law, its relevance to new developments is even more direct; the codification of the law of treaties obviously facilitates the creation of new law by treaty; a further codification, at an appropriate time when circumstances are more favourable, of the law relating to peaceful settlement might render a similar service to the progress of adjudication in new fields of law. These considerations apart, the scope for codification in the newer fields of law may arise more quickly and directly than anything in the experience

[1] Pp. 200–211 below.

of more leisurely times would suggest. The rate of development of the contemporary world has already given us 'spontaneous custom'; 'spontaneous custom' may facilitate early codification by the measure of agreement which it expresses or place a premium upon prompt codification by the precariousness of such agreement which any uncertainty concerning such custom discloses. We cannot codify the law on any new subject before such law exists, but there is a clear possibility that we shall be called upon to codify the law on some of the new subjects at a very early stage of development. The newer the subject, the more imperceptible the line of demarcation between codification and legislation may sometimes become.

We thus come to the conclusion that, in an approach to the law which has substituted a positive for a positivist concept of law and rejected the dogma of sovereignty, all of the traditional sources and processes of legal development and growth, custom, general legal principle, equity, public policy, adjudication and codification, can make some significant contribution to the goals which we have postulated for creative effort and that as a practical matter the limits to that contribution will be set less by any inherent limitations of these sources or processes than by the extent to which their potentialities are fully exploited within these limitations. How much will be done along these lines will be determined not by how much can or could be done but by how much we in fact do within the limits of what we clearly can do. From this conclusion concerning the possibilities of the inherent vitality of a living law we must now proceed to review the parallel roles of legislative and institutional development in meeting needs for which the vitality of a living law is not a sufficient answer.

10

Towards the parliament of man

Legislation is the characteristic mode of legal innovation in a mature legal system. One of Maine's truest comments on the tendency of legal evolution was that 'the capital fact in the mechanism of modern States is the energy of legislatures'.[1] To place the matter in perspective we must recall his other observation that 'legislatures are of very recent appearance in modern Europe' and that 'the earliest attempt to distinguish clearly between legislative and executive power, between legislative and executive action, has been traced to an Italian writer of the fourteenth century'.[2] The vital role of the legislative function and its relatively late development in the normal evolution of legal institutions represent the gravest dilemma in the contemporary outlook for international law. Where do we stand in the matter in the institutional development of the world community?

1. Legislation as a creative force

In defining the ultimate problem of international jurisprudence as being 'to find international equivalents for the factors known to national law as legislation, jurisdiction and execution'[3] Lorimer placed first among these factors 'legislation', insisting that 'we live in a world of perpetual change, and provision for change must form an element in every scheme which we form for the guidance of our future life'.[4] Within the State, Westlake reminds us, 'the action of the legislature is required to supplement, to amend or to define those rules of law which the judicature has to apply';[5] the world community has no legislature, and 'till "the parliament of man" becomes a fact, States have to do for themselves what parliaments do for individuals'. There is no graver weakness in the contemporary structure of international society.

[1] *Lectures on the Early History of Institutions*, 1914 ed., p. 398.

[2] *International Law*, p. 19.

[3] *Institutes of the Law of Nations*, Vol. 2, p. 186.

[4] Ibid., p. 289 [5] *International Law, Part I, Peace*, pp. 301–302.

When we look back at the goals of creative effort, legislation has played a decisive part in bringing them nearer to fulfilment within the State. The authority of the State to maintain peace, order and good government may be inherent in the common law but has been defined and consolidated by statutory powers. Much of the organisation and procedure of the courts is governed by legislation. Civil liberties are protected by legislation. Economic and social rights are largely the creation of legislation. The law relating to economic stability and growth has been profoundly influenced by, and the law relating to advanced science and technology consists essentially of, contemporary legislation.

We must therefore assume that legislative action will be equally necessary to achieve these goals in the world community. The existing legal framework for achieving them – the Charter of the United Nations, the General Treaty for the Renunciation of War, the Statute of the International Court of Justice, the Universal Declaration of Human Rights and United Nations Covenants of Human Rights, the Constitution of the International Labour Organisation, the Articles of Agreement of the International Monetary Fund, the GATT Agreement, the Articles of Agreement of the World Bank and its affiliates, the Antarctic, Partial Nuclear Test Ban and Space Treaties, to mention only some leading examples – has indeed been created primarily by legislative processes. In exploring the goals of creative effort it has been natural to envisage a whole series of further treaties as means of achieving them. We must therefore think in terms of a vigorous programme of further international legislative action for the preservation of peace with justice, the protection of human dignity, the promotion of economic stability and growth, and the social control of science and technology. As the community develops the need for such action expands.[1] Such a programme must therefore be expected to embrace at any one time a wide range of the most varied, complex and controversial issues of public policy. It is likely to be comparable to the legislative programme of a major modern State in a dynamic phase of development.

Are the international legislative procedures at our disposal adequate for the legislative effort which the peaceful progress of the world community requires? If our existing procedures of international legislation fall short of the need, how can we so develop them as to meet the need?

---

[1] Cf. McDougal, Myres S., Lasswell, Harold D. and Miller, James C., *The Interpretation of Agreements and World Public Order*, at pp. 3–4.

At first glance the problem may appear to be of such scope and difficulty, and so essentially a matter for the political action of States, that the international lawyer can make no significant contribution to its solution. The energy of legislatures being a late development in legal systems, an international equivalent for the factor known to national law as legislation, even though it may come logically first in the analysis of the ultimate problem of international jurisprudence, must be regarded as the culmination of, not as a point of departure for, the institutional development of the world community. The principle that 'there is some quality in the people at large which enables them to impart the obligatory force of law to their desires when these are expressed in a certain way'[1] is nevertheless gradually coming to have a new application on the world scale. On closer examination the problem resolves itself into a number of elements, none of which permits of a dramatic solution but all of which call for continuing action undertaken to some extent concurrently and to some extent as successive stages. To each of these elements and stages the creative imagination of the international lawyer can make some significant contribution.

2. The law of treaties

The first gateway to world legislative action is to restate authoritatively the law of treaties in the light of modern needs. This has been done by the United Nations Conference on the Law of Treaties on the basis of the invaluable preparatory work of the International Law Commission.[2] While the restatement of the law of treaties will not in itself make procedures of international legislation more effective, the treaty is so important among the legislative devices at our disposal that the clarification of the law of treaties has a significant relationship to the more effective use of the treaty as a legislative device.

The potentialities of the treaty as an international legislative device are of course profoundly affected by national practice concerning the conclusion and operation of treaties, which varies widely[3] and in respect

---

[1] Corwin, Edward S., *The Twilight of the Supreme Court*, p. 105.

[2] United Nations, *Reports of the International Law Commission on the 2nd Part of its 17th and its 18th Session*, Supplement No. 9 (A/6309/Rev. 1).

[3] See, for instance: McNair, Lord, *The Law of Treaties*; Crandall, Samuel B., *Treaties: Their Making and Enforcement*; Triska, Jan F. and Slusser, Robert M., *The Theory, Law and Policy of Soviet Treaties*; Chailley, Pierre, *La Nature Juridique des Traités Internationaux*; Naurois, Louis de, *Les Traités devant les Juridictions Nationales*; Dehousse, Fernand, *La Ratification des Traités*; Visscher, Paul De, *De la Conclusion des Traités Internationaux*; and Blix, Hans, *Treaty Making Powers* and Holloway, Kaye, *Modern Trends in Treaty Law*, pp. 115–38 3 which contain particularly valuable comparative material.

of which any close uniformity seems unlikely to be attainable in view of differences of national tradition, constitutional law and practice, and interest, but greater certainty in the international law relating to treaties can nevertheless make a valuable contribution to the part played by the treaty in the legislative reshaping of the law.

The Vienna Convention on the Law of Treaties, adopted by the United Nations Conference on the Law of Treaties in 1968 is an imaginative restatement of the law in the light of changed practice and changing needs. They do not in any way resolve the problem of creating more effective international legislative procedures, but they establish a framework within which we can proceed to resolve it over a period of time. The primary significance from this standpoint of some of the most important provisions of the Convention is indeed not what they provide but what they permit or at least do not preclude.

Invalidity of treaties procured by the threat or use of force. The Convention states in simple and categorical terms that a treaty is void if its conclusion has been procured by the threat or use of force in violation of the principles of the Charter of the United Nations. This is a matter which has been subject to much debate for many years and is perhaps the boldest and most decisive innovation in the history of the law of treaties; its bearing on the first of the broad areas within which we have identified goals for creative effort, peace with justice, is readily apparent.

Jus cogens. The Convention affirms that a treaty is void if it conflicts with a preremptory norm of general international law from which no derogation is permitted and which can be modified only by a subsequent norm of general international law having the same character. In one aspect this provision that a treaty is void if it violates the *jus cogens* is the obverse of the provision that a treaty procured by the threat or use of force is void; illegal force invalidates a treaty and no treaty can validate illegal force. The concept of *jus cogens* is relatively recent in international law but now widely accepted though still of somewhat uncertain scope. The *jus cogens* clearly includes the rules and principles of international law which protect the foundations of law, peace and humanity in the international order, foremost among them the prohibition of the threat or use of force; it probably also includes the principles and rules which dedicate certain places or resources to the common use of all mankind, with the oceans and outer space and their potential resources as obvious illustrations; it may well include the fundamental principles of human dignity and the human rights derived therefrom. The scope of the principle of *jus cogens* in relation to treaties will tend to be a reflection of that of international public policy in the development of general principles of law. In matters of economic stability and growth it may have little immediate application, but in all three of the other broad areas within which we have identified goals for creative effort, the preservation of peace with justice, the protection of human dignity by securing respect for human rights, and the social control of scientific and technological development, the principle of *jus cogens* may become, in contexts of fundamental importance, a powerful reinforcement for the rule of law.

Treaties and other rules of international law. The Convention provides that the rule that a treaty does not create either obligations or rights for a third State without its consent, does not preclude a rule set forth in a treaty from becoming binding upon a third State as a customary rule of international law, and that the invalidity, termination or denunciation of a treaty, the withdrawal of a party from it, or the suspension of its operation as a result of the application of its provisions or of the terms of the treaty, shall not in any way impair the duty of any State to fulfil any obligation embodied in the treaty to which it is subject under any other rule of international law. These rules might be expanded to provide that the failure of a State to become a party to a treaty, or any reservation made by a State when becoming a party to a treaty, does not impair the duty of that State to fulfil any obligation embodied in the treaty to which it may be subject under any other rule of international law, but perhaps this is already implicit in them. The need for improved international legislative procedures to achieve the goals which we have postulated for creative effort does not make it any the less necessary to maintain the authority and vitality of other sources of legal obligation and development. A living law, as we have already seen, is an indispensable element of any law in motion. The concept that the embodiment of any principle or rule of law in a treaty does not impair whatever validity the principle or rule may have independently of the treaty is therefore a matter of fundamental importance at a time when the law is in process of rapid growth and it is essential that other processes and potential processes of growth should not be prejudiced by the hazards of the treaty-making process and the precariousness of many treaty obligations in a world of some hundred and forty separate States which still has no effective procedure of collective legislative action. It may be of special importance in areas such as the social control of scientific and technological development in which the parallel progress of 'spontaneous' and institutional or 'collective' custom and treaty action may tend to reinforce each other.

Agreements with subjects of international law other than states. The Convention relates only to treaties concluded between States, but provides that this limitation does not affect the legal force of agreements concluded between States and other subjects of international law or between such other subjects of international law or the application to such agreements of any of the rules set forth in the Convention to which they would be subject independently thereof. At one stage it had been envisaged that the Convention would apply to such agreements; at a later stage the International Law Commission thought it preferable to limit the scope of its proposals to treaties between States. The goals which we have postulated for creative effort will imply an increasing number of agreements between international organisations and States, and the implied recognition that such agreements are subject to many of the same principles as treaties between States may therefore be of substantial importance. At the same time one can understand the desire to deal separately and at a later stage with the special problems of agreements between international organisations and States, including that of the procedure to be followed by international organisations to conclude agreements creating obligations binding upon their member States.

Treaties adopted within international organisations. The Convention acknowledges that the application of its provisions to treaties which are the constituent instruments of an international organisation, or are adopted within an international organisation, is subject to any relevant rules of the organisation. This is a point of capital importance as a matter of both immediate practical convenience and long-term policy. The principle that treaties creating, or concluded by States within, an international organisation are governed by the general law of treaties except in respects in which they may be subject to a special rule or established practice of the organisation, and the full recognition of an exception to the principle for matters in respect of which there is a special rule, or established practice of the organisation, are equally important and essentially complementary to each other. The principle is important because we cannot, without creating utter confusion, have a different law of treaties for the instruments adopted within each of some forty different international and regional organisations, a number which will continue to increase; this is the more so as relatively few of these organisations are, or can be expected to be, equipped to evolve or maintain consistently a distinctive practice corresponding to some special problem, structure, procedure or opportunity. The exception is important because there are cases in which an organisation has special rules and a well-established body of practice governing an important and distinctive group of conventions and these rules and practice create a body of international obligations in respect of these conventions more coherent and stable and better adapted to the requirements of the subject-matter or situation than would be secured by applying the necessarily more elastic and less exacting provisions of the general law. The matter is of long-term as well as immediate practical importance because international legislative technique remains so defective, and both the need to improve it and the difficulty of doing so remain so great, that it is vital to leave the way open for the development of varied specialised international legislative procedures for special purposes as opportunities present themsevles.

Conclusion of treaties. The Convention treats a two-thirds majority as the normal practice for the adoption of the text of a treaty by a diplomatic conference, a clear acceptance of contemporary rather than traditional diplomatic practice; they recognise that the authentication of the text of a treaty no longer necessarily takes the form of signature or initialling by the representatives of negotiating States; and they assert an obligation of good faith to refrain from acts calculated to frustrate the object of a treaty prior to its entry into force.

These provisions should tend to facilitate the adoption of many of the large number of important general conventions which the achievement of the goals which we have postulated for collective effort will require, but they fail to come to terms with the problem of the treaty or convention which can be effective or significant in practice only if it secures certain indispensable acceptances by States in a predominant position in the particular field. For cases of this nature, procedures which combine special negotiation among States with a predominant interest, discussion between such States and a representative group of other States, and final adoption or approval by the General Assembly or a specially convened but widely representative conference, may continue to be of great importance; it was procedures of this nature which made possible the conclusion of the Partial Nuclear Test Ban Treaty and the Space Treaty and it would not be surprising if they were to become typical of further negotiation concerning the social discipline of advanced science and technology. It is, of course, particularly important that such procedures should combine arrangements which permit real negotiation among the States with a predominant interest and secure their full support, with arrangements which give other States a real voice in the formulation of the agreement which they are being asked to accept and the full effectiveness of which may depend on its acceptance by the great majority of other States no less than on that of the States with a predominant interest.

Reservations. The Convention formulates rules concerning the admissibility, acceptance and effect of reservations, the general effect of which may be summarised as being that, if it is desired to prohibit or limit reservations or to formulate any special conditions governing their acceptance, provisions on the subject must be included in the treaty. Otherwise a reservation will be admissible unless it 'is incompatible with the object and purpose of the treaty' (which may be controversial) and its effect will be that the treaty will operate between the State making the reservation and States accepting the reservation but not between the State making the reservation and a State objecting thereto except with the express consent of the latter.

Amendment and modification of treaties. The Convention lays down general principles concerning the amendment of multilateral treaties and their modification as between certain of the parties. In the nature of the case they do not establish any procedure of amendment of general application or define the conditions to be fulfilled for the adoption or entry into force of an amendment; so far from envisaging the circumstances in which the coming into force of an amendment may bind parties dissenting from the amendment, or alternatively discharge them or entitle them to discharge from the obligations of the treaty, they state as general principle that the amending agreement does not bind any State already a party to the treaty which does not become a party to the amending agreement. These principles are, however, all governed by the qualification 'unless the treaty otherwise provides'; their effect is therefore to define a point of departure in the light of which the draftsman of a treaty will know how to provide 'otherwise' if he wishes to secure a different result.

Invalidity, termination and suspension of the operation of treaties. The provisions of the Convention relating to the invalidity, termination and suspension of the operation of treaties, and particularly those relating to termination as a consequence of breach, supervising impossibility of performance, fundamental change of circumstances, and the emergence of a new peremptory norm of international law, are an imaginative attempt to reconcile the inevitable fluidity of human affairs with requirements of orderly procedure to avert the dangers of unilateral action and give a substantial measure of protection against arbitrary assertion of the nullity or termination of a treaty. The problems with which they are an attempt to deal have been for generations the Achilles heel of the binding force of treaties, and it has been widely recognised that a solution must be sought by combining an agreement upon principles with an agreed procedure for reviewing their application in particular cases.[1]

The procedure provided for in the Convention falls far short of compulsory jurisdiction. It consists essentially of an obligation to notify any claim that a treaty is invalid or that a ground exists for terminating, withdrawing from or suspending the operation of the treaty and, except in cases of special urgency, to await a period of three months during which any party may raise an objection; if an objection is raised the parties are, subject to their rights and obligations under any provisions in force between them concerning the settlement of disputes, to seek a solution through the means indicated in the Charter of the United Nations; any act declaring invalid, terminating, withdrawing from or suspending the operation of a treaty is to be carried out through an instrument communicated to the other parties. The principle of these provisions is perhaps more important than the limitations of their precise effect. They establish a clear relationship between the substantive law concerning the invalidity, termination and suspension of the operation of treaties and the procedure to be followed for the exercise of the rights and powers conferred by the substantive law and in so doing represent an important stage in the introduction of some measure of order and regularity into the treaty terminating process.

We have assumed that legislative action will be necessary for the achievement of all of the goals which we have postulated for creative effort. A reasonable stability and certainty in the treaty engagements in which such action is embodied is an essential condition of the achievement of those goals. The Convention is therefore of major importance in this connection both for what it does and for what it does not provide. It establishes general principles concerning the invalidity, termination and suspension of the operation of treaties and the principle of regularity of procedure in these matters, but where the nature of the case makes desirable a clearer understanding concerning a specific procedure or the unequivocal acceptance of compulsory jurisdiction or

---

[1] Fischer Williams, Sir John, *Chapters on Current International Law and the League of Nations*, pp. 86–110; Brierly, J. L., *The Basis of Obligation in International Law*, pp. 108–116; McNair, Lord, *The Law of Treaties*, pp. 493–535; Scelle, Georges, *Théorie Juridique de la Révision des Traités*.

some other form of third-party judgment an appropriate provision must be included in the treaty.

In brief, the Convention will, if widely ratified, constitute the framework within which a more ambitious and much longer-term effort to improve international legislative procedure must now be pursued.

3. Law-making treaties

The second gateway to world legislative action is to exploit more fully and consistently the potentialities of the law-making treaty.

Concept and development of the law-making treaty. The unprofitable controversy concerning the appropriateness of the term 'law-making treaty' need not detain us. It must be conceded that the Convention on the Law of Treaties does not use the term; only as regards reservations, amendments and suspension as between certain parties does it contain special provisions for multilateral treaties, and these apply to multilateral treaties as such irrespective of their function or legal character. The term is, moreover, admittedly a metaphor, but is no less useful as an element in clear thinking concerning the differences between different types of treaty with essentially different functions because misuse of it is dangerous. As Lord McNair so convincingly pointed out nearly forty years ago,[1] while all treaties are both law-making and contractual in the sense that they create legal obligations for the parties but normally only for the parties, there is a distinguishable class of treaties which are law-making in the sense that they fulfil in international society a function analogous to that of legislation within the State. They lay down rules of law relating to matters of interest to the international community which are designed to be of the widest possible application; while normally binding only upon the parties, they are open to accession by a wide range of States or by all States. McNair's concept of the law-making treaty is that of a common lawyer; it is empirical and practical and must be distinguished from the distinction between the *Verträg* (an exchange of promises to do different things) and the *Vereinbarung* (a mutual promise to do the same thing) imported by Oppenheim[2] from Triepel[3] into the English-speaking world. The valid criticism of Triepel's distinction which is so widespread in the literature of international

[1] 'The Functions and Differing Legal Character of Treaties', 11 *British Year Book of International Law*, 1930, pp. 100–118, reprinted in *The Law of Treaties*, 1961, at pp. 739–754.

[2] Oppenheim, L., *International Law*, Vol. II, *Peace*, pp. 23, 518 and 563–568.

[3] Triepel, H., *Völkerrecht und Landersrecht*, p. 53.

law[1] has little or no application to McNair's essentially practical approach.

The law-making treaty in its modern form began to be increasingly common from the mid-eighteen-sixties onwards and especially after the First World War. 'The establishment of the League of Nations, including the International Labour Organisation meant a great quickening of the legislative process. . . . The decade which began in 1919 saw the frequent assembling of international conferences at which numerous multipartite instruments were opened for signature. Much of the pre-war legislation was revised, and many subjects to which it had never been extended were brought within the range of legislative control.'[2] The process of legislative development by the law-making treaty was inevitably interrupted by the Second World War and was not immediately resumed with the same vigour thereafter but has now become even more important than during the inter-war period.

Defective technique of law-making treaties. We must, however, concede that the law-making treaty has remained a most imperfect legislative instrument and that all too little has been done to exploit fully its latent possibilities. Failure to grasp imaginatively the possibilities of the law-making treaty, to perfect its technique in respect of such matters as entry into force, reservations, effects in relation to third parties, interpretation, supervision of application, modification and termination, and to envisage clearly the mutual relationships of different law-making treaties in such a manner as to develop them into the elements of a coherent world statute book have remained all too common.[3] Delays in ratification, by no means confined to cases in which there is some real problem of policy or practical difficulty, result in many laboriously negotiated general conventions never coming into force, or only coming into force after such delay and between a group of parties so arbitrary in composition that their value is strictly limited.[4] The new technique of

---

[1] E.g. Lauterpacht, H., *Private Law Sources and Analogies of International Law*, pp. 156–160.

[2] Hudson, Manley O., *International Legislation*, Vol. I, p. xxxvi; the nine volumes of this collection by Hudson, covering the period from 1919 to 1945, give an invaluable picture of the international legislation of that period. A similar compact statute book of the international legislation of the subsequent period is most desirable.

[3] I have discussed the matter at length, in terms which still remain fully valid after the lapse of thirty years, in 'Les Instruments Internationaux à Caractère Collectif', *Recueil des Cours de l'Académie de Droit international*, Vol. 69, (1939 (III)), pp. 451–543.

[4] Wilcox, Francis O., *The Ratification of International Conventions*; Jenks, op. cit., pp. 456–470.

the adoption of conventions by majority decision of an international conference, while greatly facilitating their adoption, may result in a degree of disregard for strongly held and sometimes legitimate views which accentuates the difficulties of securing general ratification. It often happens that a convention is brought into force only by allowing the parties to make reservations of so far-reaching a character that the convention loses most of its value.[1] Unlike legislation which 'binds all persons subject to the jurisdiction of the body legislative whether they assent to it or not, whether their duly appointed representatives have assented to it or not', a law-making treaty, as such, 'only binds parties who have duly signed' it and 'where necessary, as it usually is, have ratified it';[2] the limitation of the direct binding force of law-making treaties to the parties[3] and the fact that it is exceptional for them to include special provisions designed to counteract this limitation upon their effectiveness by securing their indirect application in relation to third States, or protecting the parties against the consequences of their non-application by third States, both accentuates the difficulty of securing ratification by potential parties concerned with the effect of the prospective failure to ratify of third States and limits the effectiveness of the treaty when it enters into force for those who do become parties. The conception of general conventions as instruments concluded among States operates as a threefold limitation upon their effectiveness: it inhibits the participation in international arrangements on certain matters of States in the national life and political philosophy of which the voluntary principle plays an important part;[4] it limits the extent to which the provisions of certain conventions ensure directly for the benefit of individuals in the interest of whom they are frequently intended;[5] it makes no provision for conferring rights and imposing obligations on international organisations, which are now parties to a large number of international instruments and are increasingly affected by a wide range of general conventions;[6] in all three respects the concept

---

[1] Holloway, Kaye, *Modern Trends in Treaty Law*, pp. 467–548; Jenks, op. cit., pp. 471–477; Detter, Ingrid, *Essays on the Law of Treaties*, pp. 47–70.

[2] McNair, 'International Legislation', *Iowa Law Review*, Vol. 19 (No. 2), 1934, pp. 177–189; reprinted in *The Law of Treaties*, pp. 729–739.

[3] Roxburgh, Ronald F., *International Conventions and Third States*; Jenks, op. cit., pp. 478–487; Detter, op. cit., pp. 100–118.

[4] For one of the many types of case see Jenks, C. Wilfred, 'The Application of International Labour Conventions by Means of Collective Agreements', *Festgabe für A. N. Makarov*, pp. 197–224; and more generally Jenks, 'Les instruments internationaux à caractère collectif', pp. 488–497.

[5] Norgaad, Carl Aage, *The Position of the Individual in International Law*.

[6] Rosenne, Shabtai, 'United Nations Treaty Practice', *Recueil des Cours de l'Académie de Droit international*, Vol. 86, (1954 (III)), pp. 277–438.

represents an earlier phase in the evolution of international life and fails to reflect contemporary developments. General conventions frequently contain no provision, or no satisfactory provision, for any organised international supervision over the measures taken to give effect to the obligations assumed, with the result that, the responsibility for such measures being left entirely to the uncontrolled discretion of the parties or not subject to any continuing review of recognised impartiality, the degree of application secured is frequently very unsatisfactory.[1] The inclusion in general conventions of provision for the reference to an international judicial body of disputes concerning their interpretation or application has become the exception rather than the rule in the case of conventions of a general nature; even when a convention includes such a provision, the procedure for bringing matters arising thereunder before an international judicial body is almost invariably of such a character that few or no cases are brought by reason of the political implications of instituting such proceedings, although substantial questions may be at issue and the value of the convention much reduced by subsisting divergences of interpretation.[2] There is extensive precedent for the inclusion in treaties of all types of provisions defining the sanctions applicable in the event of non-observance,[3] but all too little progress has been made in devising sanctions so appropriate to particular cases that they operate effectively in practice with general approval. The position as regards the termination and modification of general conventions is in very many cases quite unsatisfactory.[4] Where there is any provision for termination, the provision generally takes the form of a unilateral right of denunciation which the parties are entitled to exercise at their uncontrolled discretion, sometimes only after the expiry of a certain period, or less frequently at certain intervals, but in some cases at any time from the outset.[5] As regards the modification of conventions, it is becoming increasingly common to include therein some provision on the subject,[6] but many of these provisions are

---

[1] Berthod, Paul, *Le Contrôle International de l'Exécution des Conventions Collectives* and Jenks, 'Les instruments internationaux à caractère collectif', pp. 498–506.

[2] Jenks, C. Wilfred, *The Prospects of International Adjudication*, pp. 31–54 and 'Les instruments internationaux à caractère collectif', pp. 507–520.

[3] Wild, Payson S., *Sanctions and Treaty Enforcement*.

[4] Tobin, Harold J., *The Termination of Multipartite Treaties*; Hoyt, Edwin C., *The Unanimity Rule in the Revision of Treaties: A Re-Examination*; Detter, op. cit., pp. 71–99.

[5] Jenks, 'Les instruments internationaux à caractère collectif', pp. 527–529.

[6] Engel, Salo, 'Les clauses de révision dans les traités internationaux multilatéraux de l'après-guerre', *Revue de droit international et de législation comparée*, 3rd series, Vol. XX, 1939, No. 3, pp. 529–558; Jenks, op. cit., pp. 530–542.

indications of a recognition that modification may some day be necessary rather than anything more precise or effective.

These weaknesses are not so inherent in the technique of the law-making treaty that they cannot be made significantly less crippling within the limits set by the nature of that technique. Many of them can be eliminated or made less serious by the inclusion of appropriate provisions in instruments when they are drafted. The authoritative restatement of the law of treaties in a United Nations convention will give the draftsmen of law-making treaties a body of clearer rules of law within which to operate, but will not eliminate the need for a sustained effort to improve the effectiveness of the law-making treaty as a legislative device by the inclusion of appropriate provisions in individual instruments as they are drafted. An imaginative appreciation of needs and opportunities will remain vital for this purpose.

Termination of law-making treaties. As illustrations we may take the problems of the termination and modification of the obligations resulting from law-making treaties. The United Nations Convention on the Law of Treaties provides (leaving aside details and exceptions not relevant to the point at issue) that a treaty may be terminated or a party withdraw therefrom in accordance with a provision of the treaty or at any time by consent of all the parties; specifies that a treaty which contains no provision regarding its termination and which does not provide for denunciation or withdrawal is not subject to denunciation or withdrawal unless it is established that the parties intended to admit the possibility of a denunciation or withdrawal; and lays down principles and procedures governing the termination or suspension of the operation of a treaty as a consequence of its breach. These general rules give the draftsman a point of departure but do not resolve any of the questions of policy which must be determined to frame an appropriate draft. The inclusion in a treaty of provisions prescribing suitable arrangements for its termination or modification when necessary will tend to reduce to a minimum the risk that the treaty will operate so rigidly as to invite repudiation. The draftsman will often be embarrassed in attempting to perform this task, more particularly if the instrument is of political importance and is the outcome of delicate negotiations, by the existence when it is drafted of general unwillingness on the part of all concerned to contemplate the future. Such unwillingness is, however, likely to diminish in proportion as the instrument is technical in character; where the subject matter is such that conditions are particularly liable to change an imaginative suggestion by the draftsman that the instrument should lay down some special procedure for the future termination or modification of the obligations to be created may materially assist those who are attempting to secure acceptance of a draft by difficult negotiations. The form in which provision for the termination of instruments not intended to create obligations binding in perpetuity is most commonly made is that of expressly reserving to each of the parties a right of denunciation. The practice is indeed so common that in the case of the majority of general conventions the undue rigidity of the obligations created which is often alleged to be a characteristic weakness of the technique of international legislation by means of the law-making treaty is entirely mythical. The avoidance of such rigidity by allowing the parties to release themselves from their obligations in the exercise of an unfettered individual discretion is, however, a mask for anarchy, a practice which weakens the whole structure of treaty-created international obligations and tends to justify the assertion of some writers[1] that the provisions of general conventions of a law-making character have not the status of rules of international law but are more transient in character. The right of denunciation is commonly limited so as to be exercisable only after the lapse of a prescribed period, calculated either from the first entry into force of the instrument or from its entry into force for the State desiring to denounce; this is, however, by no means always the position, even in the case of instruments which one instinctively thinks of as having been concluded for a considerable time, with the disconcerting result that a substantial proportion of the treaty obligations, by means of which an attempt is being made to build up a body of international law with the economic and social content necessary in the modern world, is precarious in the extreme. Where an instrument is open to denunciation at any time after the expiry of the period when the parties first become entitled to denounce it, the position is, unless the main interest in the instrument is concentrated within the period if its initial validity, only slightly better than where it is subject to denunciation at any time from the outset. A much greater degree of stability can be secured in the obligations resulting from an instrument by the inclusion therein of what is known as a tacit reconduction clause. This is a clause to the effect that, if the instrument is not denounced within a stated period from the date at which it becomes open to denunciation, the obligations resulting from the instrument will remain operative for another fixed period of years and will only be subject to denunciation during limited periods on the expiry of successive intervals of prescribed but sometimes varying length. The device is not at all a new one, but its use is still far

---

[1] Notably Dr. Torsten Gihl, *International Legislation.*

from general; a much wider use of it is desirable with a view to ensuring that the law created by general conventions has some measure of relative stability. The method adopted for calculating the times at which denunciation is permitted and the period of notice required are important factors in determining how much stability is secured, but even where denunciation is permitted only at periods which coincide for all parties and takes effect only on the expiry of a substantial period of notice, it nevertheless remains a device whereby undue rigidity in the provisions of law-making treaties is avoided at the price of being content to solve problems for limited periods on a highly precarious basis. This is a poor substitute for a legislature, a lawless expedient involving the substitution for an orderly process of change by collective decision of the restoration to the parties of the rights to take on their own behalf action the effect of which may be to terminate, for the denouncing party and in some cases for all the parties, the existence of any international rules on the subject. The resulting position is particularly serious if termination for one party involves termination for all, by operation of law or because it is no longer practicable or politic for them to remain parties. Some of the disadvantages of this position can to some extent be offset if the impending termination of the instrument brings into operation automatically a procedure intended to result in the substitution for the provisions about to be terminated, of some alternative arrangement. Another method by which some of the disadvantages of denunciation clauses can be avoided is the substitution for a discretionary right of denunciation of a provision (sometimes limited by a procedure) based on the conception of *rebus sic stantibus*. A more decisive step in the direction of collectivising the termination of law-making treaties is represented by provisions substituting for a unilateral right of denunciation vested in the parties a procedure for the termination of the treaty by the decision of an appropriate international body. The creative imagination of the draftsman of law-making treaties can play an important role in choosing among these alternative courses of action and developing the devices and procedures most appropriate to successive cases as they arise.

Modification of law-making treaties. The United Nations Convention on the Law of Treaties deals with the modification of treaties in terms no less general than those in which it deals with termination. It provides that a treaty may be amended by agreement between the parties and sets forth general rules concerning the amendment of multilateral treaties in relation to all the parties, agreements to modify multilateral treaties *inter se* between certain of the parties only, and the implied modification of a treaty by a subsequent treaty, subsequent practice or customary law. In the nature of the case it cannot specify the procedure to be followed in respect of modification of any particular instrument, the conditions to be fulfilled for the entry into force of a revised or amended text, or the effect of such revision or amendment; these are matters which can only be dealt with satisfactorily by imaginative foresight in the individual case.

The question is in some respects of even more crucial importance than the provision of orderly and where possible collective procedures for the termination of treaty obligations. When the obligations of a treaty are terminated without the entry into force of a new instrument, the subject matter will cease to be governed by international rules. What the world community most needs is not a legally irreproachable technique for the abrogation of the inadequate rules of law which it possesses, but an adequate procedure for the constant readaptation of these rules to the changing requirements of contemporary life. In the absence of any satisfactory procedure for this purpose of general application it is desirable to make provision for an appropriate *ad hoc* procedure in all international instruments in respect of which the question may prove to be important. This is now widely recognised to the extent of including in many instruments a reference to the possibility of modification, but many of these references are so lacking in solid procedural content that they are hardly more than a theoretical acceptance of the principle that modification may be desirable, with little practical effect.

One of the difficulties of discussing the matter is that the terminology relating to it is so inconsistent and confused. The terms modification, revision and amendment are sometimes used interchangeably and when any distinction is drawn between them different writers and draftsmen sometimes use them in different and even opposing senses. It would, it is suggested, conduce to clear thinking if writers, and in particular the draftsmen of treaty provisions, would develop a coherent and consistent usage in the matter. 'Modification', it is submitted, is the most general expression and can conveniently be used comprehensively to cover all possible types of modification of a treaty. 'Revision' appears to be the most convenient expression by which to describe procedures the effect of which is to substitute a new instrument for the original instrument, and 'amendment' the appropriate expression by which to describe procedures whereby some change is made in the provisions of an instrument which remains continuously in force. Modification for only some of the parties to a treaty can be conveniently described as '*inter se* modification' (or in the texts of instruments simply as modification) and the modification of a treaty by a subsequent but independent treaty or by subsequent practice or customary law as 'implied modification'. While there is not at present any established usage in the matter, such a clarification of the various terms in use would be helpful and it is in these senses that they are here used.

Whether a modification clause should provide for 'revision' or 'amendment' should be determined partly by the nature of the instrument and partly by the nature and scale of the changes which it is thought may be desirable. Where, as in the case of the constitution of an international organisation, it is imperative, or, as in the case of an instrument under which substantial funds are held, clearly preferable, that the instrument should remain continuously in force, it is essential or highly desirable to provide for amendment rather than revision. In other cases, much may depend on the probable nature and scale of such possible changes in its terms as can be anticipated.

A good modification clause of either type should provide for a method of initiating proceedings for the modification of the instrument which will work in practice without undue difficulty; unless the procedure to be followed consists of reference to an international conference which meets regularly at periodical intervals, the clause should embody an undertaking by the parties to participate in such proceedings; a clause which merely indicates that proposals for modification are to be communicated to some specified government, to which the responsibility for taking the necessary measures for convening and preparing the work of a revising conference is assigned in language of studied imprecision, is unlikely to be effective.

Wherever practicable the conditions for the taking effect of any proposal for modification should be made less strict than they would be in the absence of an agreed procedure for the purpose, either by providing that such proposals may be approved by some procedure which does not involve the formalism and delays characteristic of formal treaty procedure, or by qualifying the requirement of unanimity for the approval of the modification, or in both these ways; these desiderata tend to suggest that amendment may be preferable to revision wherever possible; the extent to which a binding majority decision is possible may depend in part on the nature and importance of the interests involved, and in part on the extent to which changes in municipal law may be required to implement the modification and the extent to which such changes relate to matters normally within the executive authority of governments or matters normally dealt with in legislation.

A good modification clause should define in exact terms the effects of the modification on the obligations resulting from the instrument in its original form or the original instrument as the case may be. It is important to distinguish between provisions which, by their nature, cannot be modified for certain parties while remaining in force for other parties and modifications which can be brought into force for a limited number of parties or progressively for different parties. The modification of an instrument may affect the obligations resulting from the instrument in its original form or the original instrument, both of which it will be convenient to include herewith in the term 'original instrument', in any one of three different ways. The original instrument may be abrogated for all the parties thereto by the entry into force of a revising instrument or modified for all of them by the taking effect of an amendment. The original instrument may remain in effect in its original form for the parties thereto which do not accept the revising or amending instrument, the parties which do accept the revising or amending instrument being released from their obligations under the original instrument in its original form and no longer having any continuing contractual nexus with the parties thereto. Alternatively, the original instrument may also remain in force in its original form as between parties which do not accept the revising or amending instrument and parties which do accept it, the relations between States which accept the revising or amending instrument being governed by the latter alone. Which solution is the most appropriate and convenient depends entirely on the circumstances of the case, and may depend on the nature and effect of the modifications adopted rather than any constant element in the subject matter of the obligations. The exact terms of the clauses governing the matter therefore need careful consideration both when drafting the original instrument and when drafting the modifying instrument; whenever feasible it may be desirable to adopt the practice followed by the International Labour Conference since 1934 of providing in the original instrument that the rules governing the extent to which the original and modifying instrument shall coexist shall be subject to the terms of the modifying instrument. Only imaginative insight into both the legal problems posed by the interrelationship of successive instruments and the factual problems of application which will arise can play a major part in making the procedure for modifying law-making treaties realistic and effective. This is a matter the technicalities of which are of more than technical interest and importance; they have a significant bearing upon the effectiveness of the whole corpus of law-making treaties which can make so important a contribution to the attainment of our major goals.

An international legislative drafting bureau? These are but illustrations; imaginative insight reflected in sustained initiative can play a similar role in making the other weaknesses of the technique of the law-making treaty significantly less crippling.[1] In exploiting the possibilities of the law-making treaty the legal advisers of international organisations and governments have unique and virtually continuous opportunities, all too rarely appreciated, still less grasped, to play a creative role. As Percy Corbett has said with reference to the legal advisers of governments:

> Theirs is the first chance to perceive those convergences of law and policies that can be made the stepping stones towards an effective law of nations. . . . Not a few of them bring to their work a conviction of mission to speed the coming of a universal legal community. If with this conviction they combine courage and a shrewd sense of the possible, they can exert steady pressure in that direction upon their governments.[2]

The full exploitation of these opportunities might be considerably facilitated by the maintenance by the United Nations of an International Legislative Drafting Bueau designed to service United Nations organs and conferences, miscellaneous international conferences, and specialised agencies and international and regional organisations which do not have a volume of such work justifying the maintenance of separate arrangements.[3]

One aspect of the problem which calls for special attention is the need to have more regard, when framing new law-making treaties, to their prospective effect on the international statute book as a whole and to avoid overlapping, inconsistencies and conflicts which may destroy the coherence, and greatly reduce the effectiveness and value, of the law-making treaties taken as a whole.[4]

Developments of this nature cannot, of course, fill the gap left by the absence of a legislative procedure capable of effecting major changes in international society, or in general international settlements such as the political, territorial and military provisions of peace treaties, but they can make a significant contribution to the effectiveness of the legislative

---

[1] For further illustrations see 'Les instruments internationaux à caractère collectif', *Recueil des Cours de l'Académie de Droit International*, Vol. 69 (1939 (III)), pp. 451–543.

[2] *Law in Diplomacy*, p. 34; and see Merillat, H. C. L., (ed.) *Legal Advisers and Foreign Affairs*, and *Legal Advisers and international Organisations*.

[3] I have elaborated this suggestion in 'The Need for an International Legislative Drafting Bureau', *American Journal of International Law*, Vol. 39, 1945, pp. 163–179.

[4] I have discussed more fully in 'The Conflict of Law-Making Treaties', *British Year Book of International Law*, Vol. 30, 1953, pp. 401–453.

machinery available for the conduct of its day by day business; they can be of substantial value in all of the main areas which we have identified in postulating goals for creative effort: in preserving peace with justice, protecting human rights, promoting economic stability and growth and establishing an effective social discipline of scientific and technological development. The number of law-making treaties at any time is now so considerable and the ground covered by them is so wide that a sustained determination to improve the technique of the law-making treaty could, if sufficiently widely shared, have within a decade far-reaching effects on the effectiveness of the international legislative process.

4. Quasi-legislation: functional

The third gateway to world legislative action is to develop new legislative procedures and regulatory powers for specialised purposes. Considerable ingenuity and practical acumen have been devoted to developing a wide range of such procedures and powers, of which the constitutions and practice of the specialised agencies of the United Nations afford varied illustrations.[1] Some of the innovations adopted have been substantial practical successes. Others remain suggestive but have been less significant in practice. There has been no consistency of progress in the matter. In some fields there have been, in the legislative technique employed as contrasted with the substantial results obtained, phases of apparent regression as well as phases of progress. In others we have the substance of an international legislative procedure but the technique remains at best untidy, the work of practical operators rather than of lawyers. In some cases legal skill of a high order has devised new types of legal instrument which are legislative in effect if not in form. In others the potentialities of specific constitutional powers have been unused or little used. Doubtless political and practical considerations have frequently been decisive, but the quality of the legal craftsmanship available has also been a relevant factor.

I.L.O. The International Labour Organisation was and remains a pioneer in the matter. The International Labour Conference has a unique composition, commonly described as its tripartite character,[2] the distinctive feature of which is that each government nominates two

---

[1] Detter, Ingrid, *Law-Making by International Organisations* is a most useful survey of these developments.

[2] Jenks, C. Wilfred, *The International Protection of Trade Union Freedom*, pp. 67–87 and 512–562.

government delegates and two delegates representing the employers and the workers respectively and chosen in consultation with the most representative industrial organisations. While the Conference (which the Constitution provides shall meet once a year) has no legislative powers, it plays the key role in an organised international procedure of a legislative character. Proposals adopted by the Conference take the form of either an international convention, or a recommendation to meet circumstances where the subject, or aspect of it, dealt with is not considered suitable or appropriate at the time for a convention. In either case a majority of two-thirds of the delegates present is required for the adoption of the proposal. Such adoption by the Conference replaces signature by plenipotentiaries as the first stage in bringing a convention into effect; an international labour convention is not signed on behalf of prospective contracting parties but authenticated by the President of the Conference and the Director-General of the I.L.O.; this device, now commonplace enough, was regarded in 1919 as a startling innovation. A convention or recommendation thus adopted is communicated to all Members for ratification or, in the case of a recommendation, for consideration with a view to effect being given to it by national legislation or otherwise. Each Member has a duty, whether its government delegates voted for or against the proposal,[1] to bring the convention or the recommendation within one year, or at most eighteen months, before the national authority or authorities within whose competence the matter lies, for the enactment of legislation or other action. It is now well settled that the competent authority is the body competent to implement the convention by making any necessary change in the municipal law and is normally the legislature.[2] When the consent of the competent authority is obtained, the Member communicates the formal ratification of the convention to the Director-General.[3] It binds the Members ratifying, but only them, and comes into force when the number of ratifications required by the convention (frequently any two ratifications) have been registered.[4] Reservations have always been regarded as inadmissible, but certain other types of limitations upon or explanations of the assent given to a convention are allowed in

---

[1] P.C.I.J., Series B, No. 13, p. 17.

[2] See International Labour Conference, 26th Session (1944), Report I, *Future Policy, Programme and Status of the International Labour Organisation*, Appendix, pp. 169–183 (Memorandum by the Legal Adviser of the I.L.O., Jenks), 29th Session (1946), Report II (1), *Reports of the Conference Delegation on Constitutional Questions*, pp. 42–43.

[3] Article 19 (5) (d) of the Constitution.

[4] See *The International Labour Code, 1951*, Vol. I, pp. xcviii–xcix.

virtue of the terms of particular conventions or established practice.[1]

Federal States are subject to the same obligations as unitary States in respect of conventions and recommendations which the federal government regards as appropriate under its constitutional system for federal action; the test is not one of strict legal power but of constituional propriety. In respect of conventions and recommendations which the federal government regards as appropriate, in whole or in part, for action by the constituent units rather than for federal action, the federal government is required (*a*) to make effective arrangements for the reference of such conventions and recommendations to the appropriate authorities and (*b*) to arrange coordinated action to give effect thereto.[2] These arrangements were designed as a procedure alternative to ratification; they were not conceived as a method of giving effect to such conventions when ratified, ratification involving the same obligations for federal as for unitary States. They were introduced in 1946 in substitution for a 1919 provision entitling federal States to treat conventions as recommendations in certain circumstances.

While ratification remains within the discretion of each member, the Constitution, as amended in 1946, provides that a State not ratifying shall report to the Director-General of the International Labour Office at appropriate intervals, as requested by the Governing Body, the position of its law and practice with regard to the matters dealt with in the convention. Such information is to show the extent to which effect has been given or is proposed to be given to the provisions of the convention. It is also to state the difficulties which prevent or delay the ratification of the convention. A similar obligation rests upon Members with regard to recommendations. This important innovation imposes upon Members a certain measure of obligation in respect of instruments to which they have not become a party. The result is that the difference between international labour conventions, which are designed as obligation-creating instruments, and recommendations, which are not designed for the creation of obligations but are exclusively standard-defining instruments, is less absolute in practice than in legal principle since conventions produce a substantial part of their practical effect as standard-defining rather than obligation-creating instruments.[3] The Constitution of the I.L.O. establishes mutually complementary procedures for the consideration of complaints, representations and periodical reports relating

---

[1] I.C.J. *Pleadings* (1951), 'Reservations to the Convention on the Prevention and Punishment of the Crime of Genocide', pp. 216–282.

[2] International Labour Conference, 29th Session (1946), Report II (1) *Reports of the Conference Delegation on Constitutional Questions*, pp. 173–186.

[3] See *The International Labour Code, 1951*, Vol. i, pp. lxviii–lxxvi.

to the application of ratified conventions.[1] The I.L.O. procedures of supervision are unique of their kind in their comprehensiveness and thoroughness;[2] while, directly or indirectly, they owe much of their effectiveness to the tripartite character of the International Labour Organisation, they represent a body of experience which should not be overlooked in the development of similar procedures for other groups or types of international conventions.

The value of the I.L.O. procedures relating to conventions, one of the most imaginative innovations in the historical development of new forms of treaty procedure, is attested by the measure of success achieved. On 1 January 1969, 128 conventions had been adopted by the Conference; 114 of these were in force for numbers of Members varying from two to 103 and 3,443 ratifications distributed over 126 conventions and 118 countries had been registered. The more important conventions relating to human rights had received from sixty-five to 103 ratifications each. The record of action taken by States to fulfil their obligations in response to criticism of failure to do so in full through the I.L.O. procedures is impressive.[3]

No less significant than the procedures of the I.L.O. is the extent to which the conventions adopted represent a comprehensive body of mutually complementary obligations, each convention being framed in the light of the provisions of the other conventions and the whole, which constitutes what is conveniently described as the international labour code, remaining continuously under review in the light of new problems and needs.[4]

F.A.O. Provision for a similar power to adopt conventions by a two-thirds majority was included in the Constitutions of F.A.O., Unesco

---

[1] See Jenks, C. Wilfred, *The International Protection of Trade Union Freedom*, pp. 75–81 and 492–498; but there have been major further developments since that time for which see Jenks, 'The International Protection of Trade Union Rights', in Luard, Evan (ed.), *The International Protection of Human Rights*, pp. 210–247; 'Human Rights, Social Justice and Peace', Nobel Symposium VII: *The International Protection of Human Rights, Proceedings of the Seventh Nobel Symposium*, Oslo, September 1967, edited by August Schou and Asbjörn Eide, pp. 227–260.

[2] Landy, E. A., *The Effectiveness of International Supervision: Thirty Years of I.L.O. Experience*; Valticos, N., 'Un Système de Contrôle Internationale: La Mise en Oeuvre des Conventions Internationales du Travail', *Recueil des Cours de l'Académie de Droit international*, Vol. 123, 1968, pp. 311–407.

[3] Landy, op. cit., pp. 67–78.

[4] *The International Labour Code, 1951*, 2 vols; Jenks, C. Wilfred, 'The *Corpus Juris* of Social Justice', in *Law, Freedom and Welfare*, pp. 101–136; Wolf, Francis, 'L'Interdépendence des Conventions Internationales du Travail', in *Recueil des Cours de l'Académie de Droit international*, Vol. 121, (1967 (II)), pp. 117–213.

and W.H.O., but without equally specific and precise obligations concerning submission to national legislative authorities and reporting; relatively little use has been made of these provisions in practice. The F.A.O. Conference may, by a two-thirds majority, approve and submit conventions to member nations for acceptance in accordance with their constitutional procedure; the F.A.O. Council may, under rules made by the Conference, approve and submit to member nations regulations or supplementary agreements designed to implement any general convention or agreement. The most important convention sponsored by F.A.O., the International Plant Protection Convention, was negotiated and signed as a diplomatic instrument without recourse to these constitutional powers.

UNESCO. The Unesco Conference has power to adopt conventions and recommendations for submission to national competent authorities; conventions require for adoption a two-thirds majority; for recommendations a simple majority suffices. The first important conventions sponsored by Unesco, the Universal Copyright Convention and the Convention for the Protection of Cultural Property in the Event of Armed Conflict, were adopted independently of these powers by diplomatic conferences convened by Unesco, but the practice now appears to have changed on the basis of regulations adopted by the Unesco Conference in 1950 and tends increasingly to be based on, though less developed than, that of the I.L.O.[1] The Convention against Discrimination in Education, for instance, was adopted by the Unesco Conference.

W.H.O. W.H.O. has a similar power to adopt conventions which has not been exercised in practice, but also has, within strictly defined limits, more significant regulative powers of a unique character. The Constitution of W.H.O. empowers the World Health Assembly to adopt regulations concerning sanitary and quarantine requirements and other procedures designed to prevent the international spread of disease; nomenclatures with respect to diseases, causes of death and public health practices; standards with respect to diagnostic procedures for international use; and standards with respect to the safety, purity and potency of biological, pharmaceutical and similar products moving in international commerce.[2] Such regulations come into force

---

[1] Saba, Hanna, 'L'Activité Quasi-Législative des Institutions Spécialisées des Nations Unies', in *Recueil des Cours de l'Académie de Droit international*, Vol. 111 (1964 (I)), pp. 605–686 at pp. 642–656.

[2] Article 21 of the W.H.O. Constitution.

for all Members after due notice has been given of their adoption by the Health Assembly except for such Members as may notify the Director-General of rejection or reservations within the period stated in the notice.[1] No positive act is required by a State desiring to become a party to the regulations, such an act being required only if it desires to reject them or notify reservations. W.H.O. has exercised these powers in two important fields by adopting the Nomenclature Regulations, 1948[2] (with Supplementary Regulations, 1949)[3] and the International Sanitary Regulations, 1951[4]. The Nomenclature Regulations provide that Members of W.H.O. shall compute and publish annually for each calendar year statistics of cause of death in accordance with the relevant articles of the Regulations and in accordance with the classification, nomenclature and numbering set out in the lists given in the *Manual of the International Statistical Classification of Disease, Injuries and Causes of Death*[5] annexed thereto. The International Sanitary Regulations supersede in whole or in part thirteen earlier conventions, agreements and protocols, including the basic International Sanitary Convention of 1926 and International Sanitary Convention for Aerial Navigation of 1933. Subject to minor temporary exceptions, they re-state in a single document the international sanitary law of general application which has been developed in a long series of instruments from 1851 onwards.[6] The Regulations lay down a special procedure for the consideration of reservations, the general effect of which is that reservations are not valid unless accepted by the World Health Assembly. The Health Assembly may, as a condition of its acceptance of a reservation, request the State making such reservation to undertake that it will continue to fulfil any obligation or obligation corresponding to the subject-matter of the reservation previously accepted by the State under existing conventions and agreements. If the Health Assembly objects to a reservation and the reservation is not then withdrawn, the Regulations do not enter into force with respect to the State which has made such a reservation and any existing conventions and agreements to which it is a party remain in force for the State. The International Sanitary Regulations came into force on 1 October 1952 and are now in force for 185 territories. This

[1] Article 22 of the W.H.O. Constitution.

[2] *Official Records of W.H.O.*, No. 13, pp. 349–52.

[3] *Official Records of W.H.O.*, No. 21, pp. 383–84.

[4] *Official Records of W.H.O.*, No. 37, pp. 335–53.

[5] Supplement 1 to the *Bulletin of the World Health Organization*, 2 vols, 1948 and 1949.

[6] *The First Ten Years of the World Health Organization*, pp. 259–277.

brilliant success of a new international legislative technique has not, however, been followed up by any further use of the regulative powers of W.H.O. in the other fields provided for in its Constitution. As a matter of policy W.H.O. has preferred to formulate the standards adopted in these other fields as scientific or professional standards not designed to be made effective primarily by means of legal instruments. This is particularly the case in respect of the international standards which have been adopted for drugs and other therapeutic substances. W.H.O. has also refrained from giving the character of a legal instrument to the international pharmacopoeia[1], which has been issued as an international standard and guide for national action on the understanding that it is not intended to be a legal pharmacopoeia in any country unless adopted by the pharmacopoeial authority of that country, largely because in some countries the pharmacopoeial authority is an official, whereas in others it is a professional or scientific, body; earlier international agreements have indeed been terminated in order to remove any legal barriers to general acceptance of the international pharmacopoeia. Unless there should be some future change of policy, the regulative powers of W.H.O. are therefore likely to be of little practical significance outside the limited field of sanitary and quarantine requirements. They nevertheless represent a precedent which may well be followed by other organisations, notably in cases in which detailed international regulations deal with matters within the regulatory powers of the executive departments of national governments. If at some stage of their further development the Universal Postal Union or the International Telecommunication Union should adopt a constitution which made it unnecessary to re-negotiate their basic conventions at each successive plenipotentiary conference, provision might well be made in such constitutions for specified regulative powers analogous to those of the World Health Assembly.

I.C.A.O. In the I.L.O. we have a case in which a new international legislative technique has become a characteristic feature of the work of the Organisation and achieved solid and permanent results. In W.H.O. we have a case in which a brilliant initial success in the use of a new international legislative technique has remained an isolated success, and subsequent policy has preferred other methods of action. In I.C.A.O., the International Civil Aviation Organisation, we have the curious paradox of an apparent regression of legislative technique accompanied by an increased effectiveness of legislative action. The Convention on

---

[1] World Health Organization, reissued from time to time.

the Regulation of Aerial Navigation of 1919 empowered the International Commission for Air Navigation, the predecessor of I.C.A.O., to amend with binding effect the annexes to the Convention which dealt with certificates of registration and airworthiness, log books, rules of the air, personnel licensing, aeronautical charts, meteorological information and customs arrangements. Such amendments required approval by three-fourths of the possible total number of votes, including (from 1926 onwards) the votes of three of five specified great powers, but then became binding upon all parties.[1] In the corresponding provisions of the Chicago International Civil Aviation Convention of 1944 which created I.C.A.O. there is an apparent regression of international legislative technique, clearly attributable in the first instance to the desire to facilitate wider ratification and in particular ratification by the United States. The annexes to the Chicago Convention, like those of the 1919 Convention, embody international standards and recommended practices and procedures for air navigation; these reflect fully the progress of the intervening years. They are not technically binding in law in the same manner, partly to permit of wider ratification of the Convention and partly because technical developments called for a degree and flexibility of regulation not permitting of binding legal obligations in all circumstances, but compliance with them is in practice a condition of free participation in international civil aviation. Annexes to the Chicago Convention may be adopted or amended by the I.C.A.O. Council by a two-thirds majority vote, but are not effective if disapproved within three months or any longer period prescribed by the Council by a majority of the contracting States. They are so drafted as to distinguish between standards, which in general consist of specifications, the uniform application of which is recognised as necessary for the safety or regularity of international air navigation, and recommended practices, the uniform application of which is recognised as desirable in the interest of safety, regularity or efficiency of international air navigation; contracting States are required to conform to the standards in accordance with the Convention, notification to the I.C.A.O. Council being compulsory in the event of impossibility of compliance, whereas in the case of the recommended practices the obligation of contracting States is to endeavour to conform. Divergences are to be notified to the Council and by it to other States, and are to be endorsed on certificates and licences; no aircraft or personnel having certificates or licences so endorsed may participate in international aviation

---

[1] Roper, Albert, *La Convention internationale du 13 octobre 1919 portant règlement de la navigation aérienne.*

without the permission of the State or States whose territory is entered. The annexes deal with personnel licensing, rules of the air, meteorological codes, aeronautical charts, air–ground communications, operation of aircraft in schedules, international services, aircraft nationality and registration marks, airworthiness of aircraft, aeronautical telecommunications, air traffic services, search and rescue, accident investigation, aerodromes, aeronautical information services, and measures to facilitate the handling of passengers and goods at airports. These regulations govern virtually the whole of international civil aviation except that of the U.S.S.R. and the People's Republic of China.[1]

The technique of annexes to the Convention embodying international standards and recommended practices and procedures applies only to the technical regulations governing air navigation. I.C.A.O. also has an important legislative role in the unification of air law but proceeds in this field by means of conventions, adopted in the first case which arose by the I.C.A.O. Assembly but more usually by a diplomatic conference.[2]

The freedoms of the air and air transport are dealt with partly by the transit and transport agreements appended to the International Civil Aviation Convention and partly by subsequent multilateral and bilateral agreements, based in part on the Form of Standard Agreement recommended in 1944 by the International Civil Aviation Conference (the Chicago Standard Form) and in part on the Standard Clauses recommended in 1959 by the European Civil Aviation Conference (the Strasbourg Standard Clauses).[3] In these standards we may, perhaps, have the germ of a further ingredient in the recognised legislative techniques of international civil aviation.

IMCO. In the field of shipping, the diplomatic conference and convention remain the normal method of international legislative action. The Inter-Governmental Maritime Consultative Organization has been granted powers in a somewhat limited field to provide for the drafting of conventions, agreements, or other suitable instruments and to recommend these to governments and to intergovernmental organisations. The powers of the IMCO Assembly are, however, limited in an unusual manner; it is required to refer proposals for the formulation of recom-

---

[1] Bin Cheng, *The Law of International Air Transport*, pp. 63–71; Schenkman, Jacob, *International Civil Aviation Organization*, pp. 257–290.

[2] Bin Cheng, op. cit., pp. 72–76; Schenkman, op. cit., pp. 364–381; and see McNair, Lord, *Law of the Air*, 3rd ed. by M. R. E. Kerr and A. H. M. Evans, pp. 9–14.

[3] Bin Cheng, op. cit., pp. 233–235, 241–246, and 504–507.

mendations or instruments to the IMCO Council thereon; any recommendations or instruments submitted by the Council which are not accepted by the Assembly are to be referred back to the Council; regulations concerning maritime safety are recommended to Members for adoption by the Assembly but must have been referred to it by the Maritime Safety Committee through the Council. The Council is so composed as to secure specially strong representation of the governments of the nations with the largest interest in providing international shipping services and those with the largest interest in international seaborne trade; the Maritime Safety Committee is so composed as to secure specially strong representation of nations with an important interest in maritime safety. These arrangements do not appear to preclude new regulative techniques comparable to that of I.C.A.O. but they give no express constitutional authority for innovations of such a nature.

There are of course old precedents in the maritime field for instruments which are virtually legislative in effect, such as the International Code of Signals[1] and the International Regulations for Preventing Collisions at Sea,[2] which have never been given the form of treaties, and IMCO has recently issued a revised International Code of Signals.

U.P.U., I.T.U. and W.M.O. The Universal Postal Union, the International Telecommunication Union and the World Meteorological Organization adopt international regulations which have *de facto* the effect of legislation in their respective spheres.[3] The Universal Postal Convention and International Telecommunication Convention are periodically revised by procedures which permit majority voting on most questions by the Universal Postal Congress and the Plenipotentiary Conference of the International Telecommunication Union; the revised conventions come into force on the dates provided for therein irrespective of the degree of ratification which they have then received. The Regulations annexed to the Conventions, and the Special Agreements governing particular services administered by the Universal Postal Union and International Telecommunication Union, are in most cases subject to amendment by special procedures providing for some form of

---

[1] For the history of which see Colombos, C. J., *International Law of the Sea*, 6th ed., pp. 335–338.

[2] *Final Act of the International Conference on Safety of Life at Sea*, Cmd 7491, Appendix B.

[3] For U.P.U. see Codding, George A., Jr., *The Universal Postal Union*; for I.T.U. Codding, George A., Jr., *The International Telecommunication Union;* for W.M.O. the most convenient account is in Detter, Ingrid, *Law Making by International Organisations*, pp. 228–234.

majority decision. The World Meteorological Organization Convention provides that all Members of W.M.O. shall do their utmost to implement the decisions of the W.M.O. Congress; if any Member finds it impracticable to give effect to some requirement in a technical resolution adopted by Congress, the Member is to inform the Secretary-General of the Organization whether its inability to give effect to it is provisional or final, and is to state its reasons therefor. There is neither provision for formal acceptance of the decisions of Congress nor a provision comparable to that of the W.H.O. Constitution that W.M.O. technical regulations will apply to Members in the absence of rejection or reservation within a given time-limit, but it appears to be assumed that decisions will in fact be implemented by action taken by the meteorological services. Without having any formal legal power to do so, the W.M.O., like its predecessor the non-governmental International Meteorological Organization, much of the practice of which it inherited, fixes dates on which changes in meteorological practice become widely effective. In postal, telecommunication and meteorological matters we have the substance of international legislation to a greater extent than the forms employed, which have not been the work of lawyers, recognise.

Fund. The International Monetary Fund, the International Bank and its affiliates, and the International Atomic Energy Agency, have regulatory powers governing the use of their own resources, or resources the management of which is committed to their care, which may be regarded as being in some measure legislative in nature by reason of the importance of those resources.

The International Monetary Fund is a complex of principles and devices which combines a body of obligations governing international monetary relationships with a fund the resources of which are designed to enable Members to fulfil those obligations.[1] The obligations are set forth in the Articles of Agreement of the Fund, as interpreted by the Executive Directors or, on appeal from them, by the Board of Governors who have final authority in the matter. Some of these obligations are expressed in terms of a general nature, and the power to interpret them may in certain cases be equivalent in substance to a delegated power to legislate in respect of matters covered by them. The Decisions of the Executive Directors of the Fund[2] do not fall clearly into any established category of legal instrument or document. They may be in

---

[1] Fawcett, J. E. S., 'The International Monetary Fund and International Law', *British Year Book of International Law*, Vol. 40, 1964, pp. 32–76.

[2] International Monetary Fund, *Selected Decisions of the Executive Directors as Selected Documents*, issued from time to time.

the nature of the exercise of a delegated legislative power to make more detailed regulations for the implementation of a general principle expressed in the Articles of Agreement; they may be comparable to a judicial decision; they may be a statement of the principles on which the Fund will exercise discretionary powers conferred upon it by the Articles of Agreement; they may be a continuing offer defining the circumstances in which a Member is entitled to have recourse to the resources of the Fund on which the Member is entitled to rely; they may, as in the case of the General Arrangements to Borrow of 5 January 1962, be in substance a supplementary international agreement effective in relation to Members adhering thereto by notification and compliance with its terms and conditions. In the field of international monetary policy the creative imagination has given us devices so new that we cannot conveniently label them in accordance with accepted legal terminology, but some at least of these devices contain a legislative element.[1]

World Bank Group. The lending and borrowing operations of the International Bank for Reconstruction and Development are governed, within the legal framework of the Articles of Agreement of the Bank, by a combination of national laws and regulations and distinctive legal instruments evolved by the ingenuity and skill of the legal advisers of the Bank. The national laws and regulations make effective the provisions of the Articles of Agreement; the Bank also relies on them to grant an appropriate status and facilities to its securities and transactions in respect of matters not covered by the Articles of Agreement, such as the classification of its bonds as eligible for institutional investment, the relaxation of capital market regulations and exchange control to permit or facilitate the introduction of its securities in capital markets, and enabling legislation to facilitate government guarantees of loans. The legal instruments evolved by the Bank itself are of three main types, namely: Loan and Bond Regulations issued by the Bank which are made applicable to particular loans or bonds by agreement or special resolution; Loan and Guarantee Agreements, with miscellaneous instruments subsidiary or incidental thereto, including project agreements and trust, guarantee and assignment indentures and mortgages; and bonds. The Articles of Agreement confer no specific authority on the Bank to issue Loan Regulations. The Regulations do not become effective directly in virtue of an international decision taken in exercise of powers conferred

[1] Broches, Aron, 'International Legal Aspects of the Operations of the World Bank', *Recueil des Cours de l'Académie de Droit international*, Vol. 98, (1959 (III)), pp. 297–409.

upon the Bank by its constituent instrument; they are, therefore, not comparable in legal nature or effect to the W.H.O. Regulations. The name may, indeed, be slightly misleading. The Loan Regulations can be construed as simply a device which the Bank has found convenient for the transaction of business; they are in the nature of standard clauses which are made applicable to loan and guarantee agreements by the terms thereof in the same manner in which the York–Antwerp Rules of General Average are incorporated in bills of lading and charter parties; they have, however, a practical importance as the legal basis of Bank loans comparable to that of the York–Antwerp Rules in maritime law; they are a substitute and equivalent for international legislation governing Bank loans. There are separate Regulations for loans to member governments and loans to other borrowers but many of the provisions are identical in the two sets of Regulations. Whereas the Loan Regulations bridge the concepts of contract and regulation by law, Loan and Guarantee Agreements, and the instruments subsidiary or incidental thereto, are clearly contracts and conveyances; they are acts in the body of law constituted by the Loan Regulations. The Bond Regulations are designed to cover, in a general authorisation, the voluminous procedural and administrative matters common to all bond issues and thus to avoid spelling them out in each resolution authorising a bond issue; they thus have the same legal character as the Loan Regulations. These various instruments constitute a body of law of an international character which is still in an early stage of development and may in course of time be expounded and elaborated by a series of arbitral awards given by the procedure provided for in the Loan Regulations. The autonomous character of this body of law is implicity affirmed by the provision contained in the Loan Regulations that the rights and obligations of the Bank, the borrower and (when applicable) the guarantor under the Loan Agreement, the Guarantee Agreement (where such exists) and the bonds, shall be valid and enforceable in accordance with their terms notwithstanding the law of any State, or political subdivision thereof, to the contrary.[1] The International Finance Corporation and International Development Association conduct their operations on the basis of similar instruments.

I.A.E.A. The Statute of the International Atomic Energy Agency empowers the Agency to establish and administer safeguards against the diversion of nuclear resources for military purposes and to establish

---

[1] Loan Regulations Nos. 3 and 4, Sections 7.01 in each case. I have discussed the matter further in *The Proper Law of International Organisations*, pp. 178–183.

or adopt safety standards. The Agency may establish and administer safeguards designed to ensure that special fissionable and other materials, services, equipment, facilities and information made available by the Agency, or at its request or under its supervision or control, are not used in such a way as to further any military purposes; it may also apply such safeguards, at the request of the parties, to any bilateral or multilateral arrangement, or, at the request of a State, to any of that State's activities in the field of atomic energy. The constitutional power thus granted would appear to entitle the Agency to apply such safeguards to Agency operations and certain other operations facilitated by the Agency by a decision of a legislative nature operative *per se*, but the safeguards as approved by the Board of Governors of the Agency specify that their provisions together with any other provisions which may be agreed upon in the course of negotiations 'will only become legally binding after the entry into force of a specific agreement including such provisions'. Their potential legislative quality has therefore not yet materialised in current practice. The agency is likewise authorised to establish or adopt standards of safety for the protection of health and minimisation of danger to life and property; it may provide for the application of these standards to its own operations as well as to operations making use of materials, services, equipment, facilities or information made available by the Agency or at its request or under its control or supervision, and may provide for the application of these standards, at the request of the parties, to operations under any bilateral or multilateral arrangement, or, at the request of any State, to any of the State's activities in the field of atomic energy. In this context also, the Agency appears to have constitutional powers to adopt standards of safety by a decision of a legislative nature operative *per se* in respect of Agency operations and certain other operations facilitated by the Agency. The Agency has adopted Basic Safety Standards for Radiation Protection and Regulations for the Safe Transport of Radioactive Material, but has refrained from giving them the formal legislative quality which it would appear to be authorised to give them by the terms of the Statute in respect of the operations specified therein. The development of Agency safeguards and standards is still at so early a stage that the initial practice of the Agency must not be regarded as precluding a fuller development in future of the legislative potentialities of its constitutional powers; the practical difficulty is, of course, to make a safeguard or standard legislatively effective *per se* administratively effective in practice. For this purpose a supplementary contractual undertaking may be valuable, and inclusion by a supplementary decision, effective *per se* in a more immediate manner, in the operational rules governing a particular facility or international service may be quite invaluable.

GATT. The basic obligations of the parties to the General Agreement on Tariffs and Trade are contained in the General Agreement but the concessions which represent much of the substance of the Agreement are contained in schedules of tariff concessions annexed to the Agreement which are varied from time to time to record the outcome of the continuing complex of multilateral and bilateral negotiations conducted within the framework of the Agreement. The procedure is one of negotiation rather than legislation but the result includes a legislative element. Special agreements such as the Long Term Cotton Textiles Arrangement, Grain and Chemical Products Agreements, and the Anti-Dumping Agreement which is expressed as an interpretation of the General Agreement in the form of rules for its application, have also been negotiated through GATT, but these also are perhaps more significant as an example of new techniques of negotiation than as an innovation in legislative procedure.[1]

In fine, the development of new legislative procedures and regulatory powers for specialised purposes is still in a highly experimental stage of development. The picture is a varied and in some respects uncertain one, but we may reasonably anticipate that a substantial further development of such procedures and powers will play a significant part in meeting the legislative needs of international society over a wide and increasing range of defined fields of international cooperation. The I.L.O. procedures afford a model which may be susceptible of wider application throughout the field of human rights, and the varied procedures which have been developed may be susceptible of manifold applications and adaptations in matters of economic stability and growth and of scientific and technological development.

5. Quasi-legislation; the General Assembly

The fourth gateway to world legislative action is to develop with cautious boldness the legislative potentialities of the General Assembly. True as it may be that 'the Assembly certainly has no right to legislate in the commonly understood sense of the term'[2] it exercises functions some of which have a legislative aspect. 'The General Assembly', it has

---

[1] Curzon, G., *Multilateral Commercial Diplomacy.*

[2] Higgins, Rosalyn, *The Development of International Law Through the Political Organs of the United Nations*, p. 5.

been well said, 'was not constituted as a world legislature, and its resolutions are not in themselves law in the same sense as are enactments of national parliaments', but this statement 'is by no means the equivalent of a negative answer to the question whether a resolution of the General Assembly possesses binding force'.[1] While the General Assembly is not the supreme legislature of the world community it is the most representative organ of the community and this gives the decisions of the Assembly an authority which is already unique, which will inevitably grow, and which, subject to measures to ensure that such decisions are responsibly taken after due deliberation, there is every advantage to the community as a whole in encouraging to develop rapidly. We have already emphasised, when discussing the continued vitality of custom, the increasing importance in the practice of States of their collective acts.[2] There is now a widespread recognition that the decisions of international organs are becoming an increasingly important source of international law.[3] While they do not fall neatly under any of the sources of law enumerated in Article 38 of the Statute of the International Court of Justice, they may qualify under any one of the three primary sources enumerated in that Article and sometimes simultaneously under more than one. 'As the subsequent practice of the parties to an international convention, they are evidence of the meaning of the convention. As the collective acts of States, they are evidence of custom, and in some circumstances they may appropriately be regarded as containing general principles of law recognised by civilized nations.'[4] Decisions of the General Assembly may have all these characteristics in a degree which gives them an almost legislative quality.

Matters within the authority of the General Assembly. Resolutions of the General Assembly are clearly binding when they are adopted under articles of the Charter by which the General Assembly is authorised to take specific action,[5] such as to adopt rules of procedure (Article 21),

---

[1] Sloan, F. Blaine, 'The Binding Force of a "Recommendation" of the General Assembly of the United Nations', 25 *British Year Book of International Law*, 1948, pp. 1–33; Qual, Lino di, *Les Effets des Résolutions des Nations Unies.*

[2] Pp. 144–146 above, and see also *The Common Law of Mankind*, pp. 190–192, reproduced from a paper originally published in 1951; the relative importance of collective acts has increased much further since that time.

[3] Tammes, A. I. R., 'Decisions of International Organs as a Source of International Law', *Recueil des Cours de l'Académie de Droit international*, Vol. 94 (1958 (II)), pp. 265–359.

[4] Asamoah, Obed Y., *The Legal Significance of the Declaration of the General Assembly of the United Nations*, p. 15.

[5] Vallat, F. A., 'The Competence of the United Nations General Assembly', *Recueil des Cours de l'Académie de Droit international*, Vol. 97 (1959 (II)), pp. 207–287.

to establish subsidiary organs (Article 22), to approve agreements with specialised agencies (Article 63) and agreements with governments concerning trust territories (Article 85), or, upon the recommendation of the Security Council, to determine the conditions upon which a non-member State may become a party to the Statute of the International Court of Justice (Article 93). Such resolutions may be in the nature of administrative or *ad hoc* decisions, but when of general or continuing validity they may be legislative in nature or include a legislative element. Resolutions are likewise clearly binding when they are addressed to organs subject to the authority of the General Assembly, an obvious illustration being the Staff Regulations of the United Nations. If budgetary powers (including the approval of proposed expenditures and apportionment of expenses) are regarded as legislative in nature, the General Assembly has, under Article 17 of the Charter, a further legislative power in respect of budgetary matters.

The matters within the direct control of the General Assembly which may be regarded as falling within this type of legislative authority are of growing importance.

Agencies established by the General Assembly. It is, for instance, becoming almost common usage to establish new international agencies or machinery by a decision of the General Assembly rather than by treaty. Such a decision can embody all the necessary organisational and procedural arrangements; it can place any necessary obligations on the agency created thereby, its organs and its officers; it can include the equivalent of obligations upon Members of the agency or States co-operating with it in the form of conditions for the enjoyment of the services of the agency; by constituting the agency within the framework of the United Nations, it can place financial obligations in respect of the agency upon the Members of the United Nations and give the agency the benefit of the privileges and immunities of the United Nations. Such a decision has the invaluable flexibility of being subject to amendment by the General Assembly without the re-negotiation of a treaty. The only thing which such a decision cannot do which a treaty could do is to place upon participating Members or States new obligations resulting directly from the decision itself which cannot be subsumed under the general obligations of the Charter.

It is therefore not surprising that the device should be used with increasing frequency for matters of growing importance. The United Nations Development Programme, the community chest of the United Nations constituted by the merger of the Expanded Programme of Technical Assistance and the United Nations Special Fund, was established, like its predecessors, by General Assembly decision. Whereas the Havana Charter for an International Trade Organization of 1948, which failed to come into force, was in the form of a treaty, the United Nations Trade and Development Conference and Board were established in 1965 by a decision of the General Assembly. The United Nations Industrial Development Organization has been established in the same manner.

The difficult questions begin to arise when we proceed beyond this point.

Recommendations with legislative effect. The circumstances in which a recommendation by the General Assembly to governments may be binding, and by being so binding may be legislative in its effect if not in its intrinsic legal nature, are exceptional. The parties to a treaty may have agreed to accept such a recommendation as binding;[1] the recommendation may become the basis of generally or widely accepted custom; a recommendation might conceivably recognize the applicability of the principle of *rebus sic stantibus* in such a manner as to release a State from any obligation of further performance of an obsolete treaty obligation. The Charter does not contain any precise equivalent for Article 19 of the Covenant, which provided that 'the Assembly may from time to time advise the reconsideration by Members of the League of treaties which have become inapplicable', but Article 14, which provides that 'the General Assembly may recommend measures for the peaceful settlement of any situation, regardless of origin, which it deems likely to impair the general welfare or friendly relations among nations' is sufficiently broad in its terms to cover much the same ground; it does not confer a power to revise treaties but it may include a power, to be exercised with the utmost caution, to recognise that they have become inapplicable.

Declarations of the General Assembly. It is becoming increasingly common for the General Assembly to formulate its conclusions on certain matters as Declarations. 'Sometimes these Declarations are interpretations of the Charter and other instruments; sometimes they are evidence of State practice and a developing customary international law; sometimes they formulate new principles which, in some cases, eventually lead to international treaties or new custom, or in other cases will be accepted as authoritative statements of international legal principles, in circumstances where a formal treaty cannot be attained. . . .

[1] See, for instance, Sloane, F. Blaine, op. cit., pp. 16–18.

A Declaratory Resolution of the General Assembly may, to some extent, bridge the gap between a legal vacuum and the full acceptance of a legal principle through treaty or custom.'[1]

These Declarations of the General Assembly have varied widely in their subject matter, their clear or presumed relationship to existing, growing or prospective future law, and the degree of consensus or approval with which they have been adopted. They include the Universal Declaration of Human Rights[2] (to which the Declaration on the Elimination of All Forms of Racial Discrimination,[3] the Declaration on the Elimination of all Forms of Religious Intolerance, the Declaration on the Elimination of Discrimination against Women, the Declaration on the Rights of the Child,[4] and the Declaration on the Right of Asylum may be regarded as complementary), the Declaration on Permanent Sovereignty over Natural Wealth and Resources[5] (which may be a precedent for further declarations in the economic field), the Declaration of Legal Principles Governing the Activities of States in the Exploration and Use of Outer Space[6] (which may be the prototype for further declarations relating to scientific and technological matters), and, in the political and military fields, the Declaration on the Granting of Independence to Colonial Countries and Peoples[7] and the Declaration on the Prohibition of the Use of Nuclear and Thermo-Nuclear Weapons.[8] It is perhaps significant that it is the declarations relating to political and military matters which have been the most controversial and criticised. It has been argued that the term 'declaration' has been so variously used over the last fifty years 'that it has now become dangerous to use this term at all'.[9] Practice is clearly taking a different course, and while the course which it is following may present some acute problems there may be great long-term advantages in the development of the practice of the General Assembly Declaration if it is responsibly guided. The position has been well stated in a memorandum by the Legal Department of the United Nations to the Commission on Human Rights which points out that a Declaration cannot be made binding, in

---

[1] Friedmann, Wolfgang, in Preface to Obed Y. Asamoah, *The Legal Significance of the Declarations of the General Assembly of the United Nations*, p. v.

[2] Schwelb, Egon, *Human Rights and the International Community*; Quadrangle Books, 1964, Asamoah, op. cit., pp. 186–191.

[3] Asamoah, op. cit., pp. 192–213.

[4] Asamoah, op. cit., pp. 214–224.

[5] Asamoah, op. cit., pp. 79–100.

[6] Jenks, C. Wilfred, *Space Law*; Asamoah, op. cit., pp. 129–160

[7] Asamoah, op. cit., pp. 163–185.

[8] Asamoah, op. cit., pp. 101–120.

[9] Johnson, D. H. N., 'The Conclusions of International Conferences', in *British Year Book of International Law*, Vol. 35, 1959, pp. 1–33 at p. 31.

the sense that a treaty or convention is binding, 'purely by the device of terming it a "declaration" rather than a "recommendation"', but that the solemn form of the Declaration 'may be considered to impart, on behalf of the organ adopting it, a strong expectation that members of the international community will abide by it', the upshot being that 'insofar as the expectation is gradually justified by State practice, a declaration may by custom become recognised as laying down rules binding upon States'.[1] The reasonableness of the expectation and the degree of probability of its being justified are largely a function of the measure of agreement secured in the General Assembly. 'While one concedes that the Assembly has no power to legislate, one must also admit that the Assembly has no power to prevent States from undertaking commitments in its halls';[2] the value of such commitments depends on their generality and genuineness. Little is gained except in political or propaganda terms if those whom it is chiefly sought to bind by the Declaration regard it as a political pronouncement without legal force, as those asserting the binding force of such Declarations would be the first to insist if it were to be asserted against their views or interests. A more general acquiescence than this is clearly necessary to create a new legislative competence. We may readily concede to critics of the whole trend of development that the value of declaratory pronouncements by the United Nations depends 'upon the degree of objectivity surrounding the circumstances in which they were adopted' and in particular 'upon the extent to which they can be regarded as expressions of the "juridical conscience" of humanity as a whole rather than of an incongruous or ephemeral political majority',[3] but subject to taking adequate procedural and other precautions for the fulfilment of these conditions and regarding their fulfilment as a test of the authority of the pronouncements made, the declaratory pronouncements of the General Assembly are a significant contribution to the development of a new legislative competence and procedure of great potential value for the achievement of the goals which we have postulated for creative effort.

Legislation by consensus. We are thus led to enquire whether we can find a broader and more generally acceptable basis for such a competence and procedure. Can such a basis be found in a right of the General

---

[1] United Nations, *Official Records of the Economic and Social Council*, 34th Session, Supplement No. 8, at p. 15 (1962).

[2] Asamoah, op. cit., p. 160.

[3] Johnson, D. H. N., 'The Effect of Resolutions of the General Assembly of the United Nations', *British Year Book of International Law*, Vol. 32, 1955–1956, at p. 122.

Assembly to legislate by consensus, which does not necessarily imply unanimity? Is there a further qualification to the principle that the General Assembly is not a legislature which may be expressed as being that the General Assembly may exercise by general consensus legislative functions which it has no authority under the Charter to exercise by the procedures of decision by a two-thirds or simple majority provided for in the Charter itself? The potentialities of such a consensus legislative jurisdiction of the General Assembly appear to be considerable. They may well include the formulation of agreed interpretations of the Charter itself defining more precisely the obligations of member States; the authoritative formulation or restatement of customary international law; and the exercise of legislative authority in respect of matters and over places beyond the legislative jurisdiction of any State. Future experience may add to these other cases of such jurisdiction.

The Charter makes no provision for any authoritative interpretation of its meaning or of the obligations which it embodies. The upshot is that while the International Court is, as the Court itself has made clear,[1] competent to interpret any provision of the Charter, failing reference to the Court each organ of the United Nations must act upon its own interpretation of the provisions governing its activities and the obligations which they place upon Members. The General Assembly, by reason of the range of its responsibilities and its representative character as the body which the Charter provides 'shall consist of all the Members of the United Nations' acting through their representatives,[2] plays an exceptionally important part in this process of interpreting the Charter by applying it. The extent to which a Member is bound by an interpretation from which it dissents depends, however, on the extent to which the action taken on the basis of the interpretation is binding by reason of its nature and the manner in which it was taken; the validity of the action as action taken by the General Assembly may not be open to question, but such action may be ineffective to place an obligation of performance or compliance, as distinguished from an obligation of acquiescence, upon the Member dissenting from it unless the Member is bound by some provision of the Charter or of some other legally binding instrument which is independent of the decision from which it dissents. An interpretation of the Charter approved by the General Assembly by general consensus is not subject to these limitations. It may reasonably be regarded as binding all Members of the United Nations, and if it

---

[1] *Article 4 of the Charter of the United Nations Case*, 1947–1948, I.C.J. Reports, p. 61; *Admission to the United Nations Case*, 9150, I.C.J. Reports, p. 6.

[2] Article 9.

gives a more precise content to a general provision of the Charter, it may be in substance a legislative act.

As an illustration we may take the provision that the United Nations shall promote 'universal respect for, and observance of, human rights and fundamental freedoms for all without distinction as to race, sex, language, or religion',[1] buttressed by the pledge of all Members 'to take joint and separate action in cooperation with the Organization' for the achievement of this purpose. Must we assume that the General Assembly has exhausted its potential authority and effectiveness in the matter by the adoption of the Universal Declaration of Human Rights and the approval of the United Nations Covenants on Human Rights. If at some future time (not yet foreseeable) the General Assembly, acting by consensus, were to take a third dramatic step forward by amending the Universal Declaration of Human Rights in such a manner as to transform it from a 'common standard of achievement for all peoples and all nations' into an agreed statement of the content of the obligation to respect and observe human rights and fundamental freedoms binding on all Members of the United Nations in virtue of the Charter, we should be in the presence of a legislative act of the most profound significance for the whole future of human society. No such consensus is at present foreseeable, and early progress in making more effective the international protection of human rights presupposes widespread ratification of the United Nations Covenants and the other more orthodox steps which we have already envisaged,[2] but a comprehensive approach to the problem of international legislation must envisage such long-range possibilities of General Assembly action.

Among other matters in respect of which we may envisage that the General Assembly might, as the world community grows in strength, give by a consensus procedure a more precise content to the general provisions of the Charter are the obligations of Members of the United Nations to 'settle their international disputes by peaceful means in such a manner that international peace and security, and justice, are not endangered', to 'refrain in their international relations from the threat or use of force', and to 'refrain from giving assistance to any State against which the United Nations is taking preventive or enforcement action'.

The Charter provides that the General Assembly shall initiate studies and make recommendations for the purpose of encouraging the progressive development of international law and its codification;[3] it does not confer any more far-reaching power to develop or codify international law and the General Assembly therefore has no authority under

---

[1] Article 55 (c). [2] Pp. 47–52 above. [3] Article 13 (1) (a).

the Charter to formulate or restate customary international law by majority decision. There does not, however, appear to be any valid reason why it should not do so by general consensus. The hesitation and opposition liable to be provoked by the novelty of such a procedure and difficulty of securing such a general consensus must not be underestimated, but there is something profoundly unsatisfactory in the present arrangements under which provisions which are designed to be, in the language of the Geneva Convention on the High Seas, 'generally declaratory of established principles of international law' become formally effective only by a process which involves their submission for ratification in accordance with the treaty-making procedures of some one hundred and twenty different States. Surely one can conceive of, and attempt progressively to develop, an alternative procedure. This might comprise three main stages, each possibly including a number of successive steps. The first would be the formulation or restatement of the international law on a given subject by the International Law Commission of the United Nations by the procedures which it has already evolved or some further development of those procedures. The second stage would be a United Nations Codification Conference for the purpose of reviewing the draft prepared by the International Law Commission and ascertaining the degree of consensus which can be secured on the subject. The third stage would be the reference of the matter to the General Assembly; the action taken by the General Assembly would depend on the degree of consensus secured; in the absence of general consensus the General Assembly would either decide that the draft should be embodied in a formal instrument for acceptance by States willing to accept it or refer it back for further consideration by the International Law Commission or the Codification Conference; in the event of general consensus, the General Assembly would embody the draft in a formal declaration promulgated by the Assembly as an authoritative statement of principles of international law. The practical advantages of such promulgation as an alternative to the ratification of an instrument of a treaty character by a large number of States might be a significant incentive to the mutual concessions necessary to permit of such an approach. The possibility of adopting such an approach in respect of any particular subject would doubtless be influenced by the extent to which the implementation of a Declaration promulgated by the General Assembly called for changes in municipal statutory law. This is a formidable difficulty which would tend to limit the occasions for such an approach; but the difficulty, though formidable, is not so unsuperable as to make it unprofitable to give the matter full and sympathetic consideration.

Legislative authority over places beyond the legislative jurisdiction of any State has become a matter of unforeseen and unforeseeable importance. I attempted in *The Common Law of Mankind* to state the challenge which the problem presents in respect of activities in space:

> Why cannot the United Nations, by action of the General Assembly, collectively assume jurisdiction in space in relation to all its Members? Hitherto no State has effectively exercised jurisdiction in space. There would, therefore, be no interference with any existing jurisdiction. Such action would be entirely without precedent, but the circumstances are equally unprecedented.[1]

While there may be no precedent for such action in past international experience, there is at least a partial analogy for such a concept in the manner in which federal authorities exercise legislative authority over territories outside the boundaries of any State in a number of federal systems. In the United States the earlier view that this authority was derived from the express power given to Congress 'to dispose of and make all needful rules and regulations respecting the territory or other property belonging to the United States' has been superseded, in particular since the Insular Cases of 1900,[2] by the view that it derives from the implied power to govern derived from the right to acquire territory and from the power implied from the fact that the States admittedly not having the power, and the power having to exist somewhere, it must rest in the federal government. By way of contrast, the legislative authority of the Parliament of Canada for those parts of Canada not within the boundaries of any province was specifically conferred by the legal instruments transferring Rupert's Land from the Hudson Bay Company to the Dominion of Canada.[3] The United Nations has no express title under the Charter or any other existing instrument to legislative authority over territories or media outside the boundaries or beyond the jurisdiction of any State; it does not, and should not, claim any territorial sovereignty or control over such territories or media, but it may reasonably assume and exercise legislative authority wherever, in the absence of such action, there would be a vacuum or conflict of such authority inconsistent with the purposes and principles of the Charter. The suggestion is no longer an idle fancy

---

[1] P. 407. [2] *De Lima* v. *Bidwell*, 182 U.S. p. 1.

[3] The relevant documents are conveniently available in Kennedy, W. P. M., *Statutes, Treaties and Documents of the Canadian Constitution, 1713–1929*, 2nd ed., pp. 639–658.

not matched by any attempt to put it to the test of practical experiment. The Declaration of Legal Principles Governing the Activities of States in the Exploration and Use of Outer Space is an earnest of what can be done in this manner; its precise legal status will inevitably remain subject to debate,[1] and has become less immediately important by reason of the successful conclusion of the Treaty on Principles Governing the Activities of States in the Exploration and Use of Outer Space, but in retrospect it may prove to have been a decisive step in the progressive assumption by the General Assembly of legislative authority over places beyond the legislative jurisdiction of any State. The cautious will, of course, continue to warn us not to read into the approval of the Declaration by the General Assembly more than is really there, but how much is there depends primarily on how much we wish to be there. When governments make it clear in the deliberations of the General Assembly that they regard a declaration about to be adopted as a statement of international law as it is accepted by the Members of the United Nations, it is altogether unseemly for responsible scholars to dismiss it as a statement of intention which has not created any new obligations incumbent on the Members of the United Nations. The precedent of the Declaration may well be followed at later stages in the development of space law or in respect of other matters. The General Assembly may, for instance, also assume a measure of legislative authority over the ocean depths in a similar manner.

The potentialities of a legislative authority based on consensus are necessarily limited by the reality of the prospect of securing consensus. For this reason alone it would be unrealistic to predicate any rapid development of such jurisdiction, but the existence of these possibilities is a necessary and important second qualification to the common assumption that the General Assembly has no legislative power. It has no plenary legislative power, but this limitation of its authority does not necessarily debar it from developing experimentally and exercising by consensus legislative functions which may be of increasing importance and significance for the evolution of an effective international legislative process.

In fine, the General Assembly has no statutory or plenary legislative power, and its composition and voting arrangements preclude giving it any such power, but it can nevertheless play a major role in the development of more effective international legislative procedures. It exercises by majority decision powers of a legislative nature in respect of matters directly subject to its control; these now include the establishment and

---

[1] Jenks, C. Wilfred, *Space Law*, pp. 183–188.

operation of important international agencies; it makes recommendations some of which may be legislative in effect; and when acting by consensus it can in practice formulate principles and adopt rules which are acknowledged by States as having the quality of law. Without having any statutory or plenary legislative authority it fulfils legislative functions out of which there may ultimately grow some measure of acknowledged legislative authority. How fast and how far this authority can or should be developed may depend primarily on the measure of success achieved in securing reasonableness and responsibility in the processes of community decision in which the General Assembly plays so large a part.[1]

6. The Security Council

The fifth gateway to world legislative action is to turn to good account the legislative potentialities of the powers of the Security Council. The Security Council is not well fitted to formulate law of general application but may exercise functions of a legislative nature in two ways: in the course of discharging its function of maintaining international peace and security it may give a new precision, in the form of decisions binding upon member States, to obligations implicit in the Charter and authorise Members to take action which would otherwise be illegal; secondly the legislative function includes that of making changes of a legislative nature in vested rights and in particular situations and we must therefore consider how far the Security Council is in a position to discharge this aspect of the legislative function.

Peace and security. The Security Council may, at the request of any Member of the United Nations, on its own initiative or on that of the Secretary-General, deal with any dispute or situation likely to endanger the maintenance of international peace and security or any threat to the peace, breach of the peace or act of aggression. In any such case it may investigate and recommend appropriate procedures or methods of adjustment; if it deems that the continuance of the dispute is in fact likely to endanger the maintenance of international peace and security it may recommend terms of settlement; in the event of a threat to the peace, breach of the peace, or act of aggression, it may call upon the parties concerned to comply with provisional measures, decide upon measures not involving the use of armed force to be employed by Members to give effect to its decisions, and take action involving the use of armed forces

---

[1] See pp. 247–249 below.

placed at its disposal by Members by agreements for the purpose. Members agree by the Charter to accept and carry out the decisions of the Security Council.

The powers of the Council become operative only in specific cases in which the conditions for their exercise have arisen, and for their exercise the Charter requires an affirmative vote of nine of the fifteen members including the concurring votes of the permanent members. It may well seem that powers so limited can hardly be regarded as legislative in character, but there are circumstances in which their exercise can be regarded as legislative in effect. In determining the measures to be taken by Members to give effect to its decisions the Security Council is in effect exercising emergency powers of a legislative nature, which place legal obligations upon member States and their citizens and may require changes of national legislation for their implementation; the measures to be taken may include complete or partial interruption of economic relations and may therefore directly affect private rights and financial interests. They may include an authorisation to a member State to exercise rights of visit, search, and diversion of ships upon the high seas which would otherwise be illegal; this is clearly an exercise of legislative power by the Security Council; it confers complete legality upon what would otherwise be wholly illegal. Peacekeeping operations by forces responsible through the Secretary-General to the Security Council require a 'legal foundation' for the 'regulation and guidance of the international personnel engaged in the operations' and must to a large extent 'take the form of general rules and prescribed procedures';[1] these, whether adopted as Security Council resolutions or given some other form, are in substance legislative in effect. One may indeed reasonably say that 'when an organ applies a Charter principle or any other rule of law to a particular set of facts, it is asserting, as a matter of logic, a new rule of a more specific character'.[2] At what point one describes this type of law-creating act as legislation depends partly on its form, partly on its substance, and partly on intellectual taste and fashion.

The future may disclose further possibilities in this direction. One can perhaps conceive that, if and when fuller confidence in international action for the maintenance of peace and security and understanding of

---

[1] Schachter, Oscar, 'The Relations of Law, Politics and Action in the United Nations', *Recueil des Cours de l'Académie de Droit international*, Vol. 108 (1963 (I)), at pp. 204–205.

[2] Schachter, Oscar, 'The Quasi-Juridical Role of the Security Council and the General Assembly', *American Journal of International Law*, Vol. 58, No. 4, October 1964, p. 962.

its importance has developed, the Security Council might, without in any way relinquishing the flexibility of its freedom of action in particular cases and power to adapt such action to the circumstances, approve standard measures including formulations of the obligations of Members to be applicable in given contingencies whenever the Council so decides. Such measures would be in effect legislation relating to peace and security becoming legally effective in respect of particular disputes or situations by the exercise of the powers of the Council to take action for the maintenance of peace and security in the particular case; they would be more than standard clauses as we generally use the term as they would become operative by the exercise of the powers of the Council irrespective of the concurrence of the parties concerned. A decision by the Council taken in accordance with the requirements of the Charter would of course be necessary for this purpose and would no doubt be regarded initially as no less substantive than the preliminary decision approving the standard measures, but we could perhaps conceive that at some future date a finding that the contingency in which the standard measures apply has arisen would be regarded as procedural. Such a development would clearly presuppose a degree of confidence in the Council and conviction of the importance of effective action by the Council which does not yet exist.

Vested rights. The express power of the Council to take decisions binding upon Members is limited to measures to maintain or restore international peace and security. It has no similar power to decide the merits of disputes. The power specifically conferred upon it in respect of disputes is a power to recommend appropriate procedures or methods of adjustment or, if it deems that the continuance of the dispute is in fact likely to endanger the maintenance of peace and security, to recommend such terms of settlement as it may consider appropriate. Hitherto the Security Council has had a better record in maintaining and restoring peace and security than in settling disputes, but you cannot permanently police explosive situations by cease-fires. Time is a great healer, but where it fails to heal the unsettled dispute is liable to erupt again with renewed and increased explosive energy. The power to maintain peace and security must therefore include some power to settle disputes by a decision when a recommendation is ineffective. The difficulty of fulfilling the voting requirements in the Security Council makes it improbable that any such power will be frequently exercised, but it does not exclude it from the range of types of possible international legislative action for the purpose of changing vested rights in particular situations. Seen in this light, the Security

Council is the contemporary equivalent of the role played by the Concert of Europe in reshaping international relations at the Congress of Vienna of 1815, the London Conferences on Belgium of 1830–1832 and 1838–1839, the Berlin Congress of 1878, the Berlin Conference on Africa of 1884–1885, the Algeçiras Conference on Morocco of 1905, the London Conference on the Balkans of 1912–1913, and similar meetings.[1] Provision of this nature for changing vested rights is an essential element in the development of an effective international legislative process.

Nor is the legislative potential of the Security Council wholly limited to action for the maintenance of peace and security and decisions changing vested rights in particular cases; throughout the exercise of its normal functions the line between applying law and making it is frequently imperceptible.

7. The Interparliamentary approach

The sixth gateway to world legislative action is to develop the interesting possibilities of interparliamentary assemblies, initially on a regional but perhaps subsequently on some wider basis. Only in Europe have experiments of this nature become of any significance and it is important to avoid any facile overestimate of their bearing in their present stage of development on the problem of international legislation. Only the European Parliamentary Assembly of the Communities of the Six has been given any real powers, even of a limited character;[2] these are limited to certain powers of supervision over the executive bodies of the Communities, the European Economic Commission, the Euratom Commission, and the High Authority of the Coal and Steel Community; they do not include any similar powers in relation to the Council of Ministers, which exercises the more important of the quasi-legislative regulative powers of the Communities. The Consultative Assembly of the Council of Europe,[3] as its name implies, is an advisory body; it is consulted concerning, and sometimes takes the initiative in proposing, European Conventions, but these are negotiated among governments by arrangements made by the Committee of Ministers; the Consultative Assembly has no quasi-legislative power to adopt such conventions and submit them for ratification to governments. The

---

[1] Webster, Sir Charles, 'The Council of Europe in the Nineteenth Century', in *The Art and Practice of Diplomacy*, pp. 55–69.

[2] PEP, 'The Parliament of the European Communities', *Planning*, Vol. XXX, No. 478, 9 March 1964; Ginestet, Pierre, *L'Assemblée Parlementaire Européenne*; Heidelberg, Franz C., *Das Europäische Parlament*.

[3] Lindsay, Kenneth, *Towards a European Parliament*, p. 958.

Western European Union Assembly[1] is similar in general nature to the Consultative Assembly; the Benelux[2] and Nordic[3] Council Assemblies work in more intimate cooperation with ministers and in the case of the Nordic Council, civil services. The Nato Parliamentarians Conference[4] is a periodical conference for discussion and debate rather than an institutionalised body. The Inter-Parliamentary Union, envisaged by some of its pioneers as the nucleus of a world legislature, serving as the Lower House with The Hague Peace Conference as the Upper House, is still marginal to world organisation; it operates as a pressure group to secure support within national legislatures for policies endorsed at its meetings and in particular for the policies of international cooperation which have always been its chief interest. The Commonwealth Parliamentary Association[5] is a body of the same nature. In practice the primary function of all these bodies is to establish and maintain, through varying degrees of institutional development, personal links among parliamentarians, rather than to exercise directly at any foreseeable future time the prospective responsibilities of an international legislature. Even within their limited range, the interparliamentary assemblies have not yet resolved the novel problems presented by their relationships with parliaments, governments and international executive bodies; their mandates and composition may well require review and their working methods are still experimental.[6] In all these circumstances is it not at least premature to regard them as a potentially significant element in an organised process of international legislation? Do they not, as a nucleus for further institutional growth, present problems as difficult as, though different from, those involved in the development of the legislative potentialities of the General Assembly and the Security Council? Would not the contrast between multi-party and single party political systems present problems of quite special difficulty if any attempt were to be made to introduce interparliamentary assemblies outside, or from an area wider than, their Western European cradle?

---

[1] Robertson, A. H., *European Institutions*, pp. 137–146.

[2] Kranenburg, J. L., 'The Consultative Inter-parliamentary Benelux Council', in Kenneth Lindsay, *European Assemblies – The Experimental Period*, pp. 261–267.

[3] Løchan, Einar, 'The Nordic Council', in Lindsay, op. cit., pp. 252–259.

[4] Hovey, J. Allen, Jr., *The Super-parliaments.*

[5] For a brief description see Walker, Patrick Gordon, *The Commonwealth*, pp. 218–219.

[6] Lindsay, Kenneth, *European Assemblies – The Experimental Period*, especially pp. 67–105.

To see the matter in perspective we must recall the origin and early history of parliamentary bodies and the manner in which different historical forces shaped so differently the development of the Houses of Parliament, the States General, the Cortes and the Diet. Parliaments were not, in their inception, legislatures. Their original function was to take the sense of the realm and secure wider support from the powerful and influential for the policy of the executive.[1] Only gradually was the function of taking the sense of the realm transformed into that of securing assent to legislation and the function of securing wider support for the policy of the executive into that of ensuring the accountability of the executive. Only in the United Kingdom did such a process of development lead without a major break of historical continuity to the constitutionalism of the modern democratic State. We may deduce from this that interparliamentary bodies which originate as a grand forum or grand assize are not thereby condemned to remain nothing more, but that their future role and potential significance as an element in an effective international legislative process presupposes favourable – one should perhaps say exceptionally favourable – conditions for gradual development. We can hardly conceive of interparliamentary bodies being given, in the foreseeable future, any autonomous or overriding legislative powers, but we can perhaps conceive of them being gradually associated with intergovernmental assemblies, conferences or councils in an international legislative process including both intergovernmental and interparliamentary, and perhaps both international and national, elements. It may be possible, in regional groupings of like-minded States if not on any wider basis, to vest defined and limited legislative, quasi-legislative or pre-legislative powers in an appropriate intergovernmental or supranational body. There may be less objection to so doing if that body is required to secure the assent to proposed action of an interparliamentary body. Where fully executory legislative powers cannot be granted, the consultation of an interparliamentary body may make possible arrangements whereby an international decision becomes executory unless it is disallowed by a government or parliament within a prescribed period. In still other cases such consultation may facilitate securing parliamentary approval which remains necessary. We have not reached a stage of development at which the picture can be foreseen at all clearly, but these varied possibilities are worthy of further consideration in appropriate contexts and circumstances.

---

[1] Maitland, F. W., *Memoranda de Parliamento*, reprinted in *Selected Essays*, edited by H. D. Hazeltine, G. Lapsley, P. H. Winfield; Pasquet, D., *The Origins of the House of Commons*, translated by R. G. D. Laffan.

8. The ultimate problem

Only as a seventh stage in the development of international legislative procedure need we approach the final gateway to world legislative action and tackle what James Lorimer described as the 'ultimate problem of international jurisprudence',[1] the creation of a true international legislature, analogous in function and authority, though not necessarily in composition and procedure, to national legislatures. Many plans for an international legislature have been formulated by writers from Sully, Leibnitz and Penn onwards. Of the most recent proposals some, like those of Clarence Streit,[2] envisage a federal legislature for like-minded States, while others, like those of Grenville Clark and Louis Sohn,[3] provide for a world legislature. All of these plans pose four major problems; the manner in which the representation of States with varied populations, cultural development, resources and power is to be weighted; the manner in which representatives are to be chosen; the nature and extent of the legislative powers to be entrusted to the international legislature and their relationship to national legal systems; and the relationship between the international legislature and executive action on the international and national planes. Ingenious, and in some cases sensible, solutions have been suggested for all these problems. There remains, however, a wide gap between the thinking of the prospective Hamiltons and Madisons of the world community (or perhaps we should say of the forerunners of Hamiltons and Madisons still unidentified or unborn) and the current estimate by statesmen of the possibilities of practical action. Throughout the field of political and legal thought there is no greater challenge to the creative imagination than the bridging of that gap. We are unlikely to bridge the gap by projecting into the international arena existing stereotypes of political thought and institutional organisation. The United Nations is not, and can never be, the United States or the U.S.S.R. writ large. The world is so much more complex than the most complex of existing political communities that the ultimate political structure of the world community will inevitably be more complex than our inherited patterns of political thought. The outcome remains in the womb of the future. It may even be that if we develop the other elements of international legislative action sufficiently the seventh stage may prove to be both less vital and less difficult than we at present suppose.

In what combinations these various possibilities will contribute to the

---

[1] *The Institutes of the Law of Nations*, Vol. II, pp. 183–299.

[2] *Union Now.* [3] *World Peace Through World Law*, pp. 19–60.

ultimate result remains unpredictable. 'In certain matters of politics', Westlake remarked, 'it is easier to look forward a thousand years than fifty. By observing the point towards which the great streams of tendency in history converge, a glimpse may sometimes be obtained of a distant goal, but the route by which that goal will be reached will depend on those unpredictable combinations which we call chance.'[1] Westlake's time scale has no relationship to the rhythm of our own time, but fundamentally his approach remains valid. The ultimate problem of international jurisprudence will be resolved not by a blueprint for a world legislature, complete with a formula determining the basis of representation and elaborate rules of procedure, but by the concurrent operation of irresistible social forces which make it essential to devise means of discharging the legislative functions without which international society cannot grapple with either its everyday problems or its emergencies. The world legislative pattern is unlikely to follow any existing national model or to consist of any single known institutional or procedural device. It may well be something as new among political institutions as were representative government and federalism in their time. It will almost certainly be a complex comprising a number of specialised authorities and procedures for dealing with recurrent problems in defined areas of policy falling within the responsibility of particular departments of national governments, some residuary general authority, possibly including both intergovernmental and interparliamentary elements, normally acting by consensus, and some effective means of legislative action in respect of matters of a general nature concerning which no general consensus can be secured. The Parliament of Man will not be a reincarnation in the United Nations of the House of Commons, the Chamber of Deputies, the Congress of the United States or the Supreme Soviet; it will be some wholly new expression of institutional imagination in a wholly new political context.

---

[1] *International Law*, Part I, *Peace*, 2nd ed., p. 353.

11

The architecture of the world community

To achieve the goals which we have postulated for creative effort, to maintain peace with justice, protect the dignity of man by securing respect for human rights and facilitating orderly social change, promote the general welfare by fostering economic stability and growth, and ensure that scientific and technological progress remains our servant and does not become our master, we must exploit to the full all of the resources potentially available to us for the creative development of the law: the continuing vitality of custom, the fertilising influence of general principles of law, the mellowing effect of equity, the guidance of international public policy, the possibilities of the international judicial process, the growing opportunity for codification, the conscious and deliberate reshaping of the law to meet changed needs by law-making treaties and other international procedures of a legislative nature which are gradually developing. But in order to exploit these potential resources successfully we must establish a firmer institutional framework for the law than we have yet brought into being. It will not suffice to revitalise the processes of natural development and growth in the law or lay the foundation stones for the parliament of man; we must concern ourselves with the whole architecture of society. Nature, we are assured by Marlowe's Tamburlaine, 'doth lead us all to have aspiring minds', with souls 'whose faculties can comprehend, the wondrous architecture of the world'. To comprehend and perfect, in matters political, the 'wondrous architecture of the world' is the most challenging of the responsibilities of contemporary statemenship. What can the creative genius of the law contribute to enabling statesmanship to meet this challenge?

The one world in which the law now operates is a world which, despite constant setbacks, is in process of organising itself as a world community.

To give this world community an effective minimum of organisation and government we must fulfil certain minimum conditions.

Fulfilling these conditions is primarily a task for statesmanship, but is a task which statesmanship cannot fulfil without the imaginative cooperation of legal skill of a high order.

Of these conditions, eleven call for special mention.

We must secure the universality and stability of the institutional framework of the world community.

We must develop a fertility of resource in the practice of world organisations capable of devising an appropriate solution for each new problem and some new line of advance in every successive impasse; we must recognise that in creating such organisations as organs and instrumentalities of the community we have brought into being lives the development of which cannot be foreseen by the most gifted of their begetters.

We must, in order to make possible such a fertility of resource, recognise that the organs and instrumentalities of the world community have certain inherent or implied powers to develop new methods of action, and new legal instruments, devices and procedures, to accomplish the purposes of the world community and the functions entrusted to them on its behalf.

We must harmonise the need for overall coordination in the work of the organs and instrumentalities of the world community as a whole with the need for vigorous autonomy in the main fields of action and the effective intermeshing of world with national action in particular fields.

We must so relate universal and regional action that they reinforce each other in a world community in which regional organisations have an acknowledged status, function and authority within the more comprehensive framework of the world community as a whole.

We must develop in the world community traditions of due process and respect for orderly procedure, sufficiently resistant to the political strains of a divided world of cataclysmic change.

We must develop processes of community decision which reconcile the need for a wide consensus among those whose cooperation is necessary to effective action with the need for decision by a majority, or in certain cases a suitably composed majority, as the only safeguard against the paralysis of community action.

We must, in order to enable the world community to secure the effective implementation of its decisions:

ensure that the world community can rely on the independence and loyalty of a world public service of the highest integrity and competence responsible only to the world community which it serves;

ensure that the world community can rely on the continuing availability of financial resources adequate for the discharge of its responsibilities;

ensure, by developing an appropriate legal régime of world services, that the community, and its organs, instrumentalities and agents, can rely on freedom from interference by any one government or group of governments with the discharge of the functions of the community; and

ensure that the community has at its disposal adequate means of, and procedures for, securing respect for its policies and decisions.

This is of course far from being an exhaustive list of the problems of institutional development which confront us, but it indicates certain immediate priorities the significance of which has been heightened by the recurrent crises of recent years.

None of these minimum conditions presupposes any particular structure of the world community or pattern of world organisation. They do not prejudge the question how far or in what manner we can or should create international equivalents for the executive, judicial and legislative function of the State. They do not call for a process of formal constitution-making such as has hitherto been practicable only in the aftermath of world wars. None of them presupposes any impracticable rewriting of the Charter in the immediate future. They all call for bold and vigorous action, but, while affording a basis for any revision of the Charter which may ultimately be desirable and feasible, they can all be achieved in substantial measure by natural development and growth if the creative imagination is alert to its opportunities.

1. The universal community

The oneness of the world implies the universality of the world community and the permanence of membership thereof. In this respect the Charter, and even more so the practice based on the Charter, are defective in three respects. The procedure governing the admission of Members, which requires a recommendation of the Security Council subject to the veto, is an obstacle to, not an incentive to, and still less a guarantee of, universality; the Charter permits expulsion; and a right of withdrawal is generally assumed, though the Charter is silent on the subject.[1] The concept of a universal world community implies the inclusion in its membership of every political and legal order created by man on earth. 'It is by its nature an inclusive, not an exclusive, community; and being inclusive it cannot be select or selective. It cannot, without being untrue to its own nature, and thereby partially destroying

---

[1] On the whole matter see Singh, Nagendra, *Termination of Membership of International Organisations.*

itself, reject any political or legal order as unworthy of membership.'[1]

The concept of a universal world community implies that no State should be excluded as an act of policy from membership of the United Nations. The procedure provided for in the Charter is, as we have seen, unhelpful in this respect, but the substantive provisions of the Charter present no special difficulty, especially if we accept the view of the majority of the International Court of Justice in the *Conditions of Admission of a State to Membership to the United Nations Case*[2] that a Member is not juridically entitled to make its consent to the admission of another State dependent on conditions not expressly provided for in the Charter. While this opinion of the Court was ineffective in practice at the time, and there were significant dissents, it remains a valid statement of an important principle. The Charter provides that membership 'is open to all other peace-loving States which accept the obligations contained in the present Charter and, in the judgment of the Organisation, are able and willing to carry out these obligations'.[3] There is nothing in this language which is restrictive in tendency or which justifies the existing membership or any particular Member in evaluating subjectively the peace-lovingness of the applicant; the question submitted to the judgment of the Organisation is indeed specifically limited to the ability and willingness of the applicant to carry out its obligations under the Charter. Procedurally the Charter does not facilitate universality, but there is no problem which a policy of deliberately seeking universality cannot overcome.

The concept of a universal world community likewise implies that the effective government of a member State should never be excluded as an act of policy from membership of the United Nations. Once a State is a Member of the United Nations, it is entitled to be represented by its effective government and representation cannot be denied on the ground that another rival government is more likely to act in the interests of the Organisation.[4] This position involves no change in the Charter but it does involve a major change in the practice of the United Nations concerning the representation of Members and changes therein. The change involved is primarily one of policy, but two questions of law may arise, one in the Security Council, the other in the General Assembly. It appears to be widely assumed that if the question whether a State is represented by its effective government arises in the

---

[1] Jenks, *Law in the World Community*, p. 18.

[2] *I.C.J. Reports*, 1948, p. 57.

[3] *I.C.J. Reports*, 1948, p. 57.

[4] Higgins, Rosalyn, *The Development of International Law Through the Political Organs of the United Nations*, p. 158.

Security Council the sitting representative of that State is entitled to veto any proposal to seat the representative of a new government. This view, it is submitted, is erroneous, both on the ground that the question is essentially procedural, as was admitted by both the United States and France in the Security Council when the question first arose in 1950,[1] and because the sitting representative of the State concerned is a party to a dispute within the meaning of Article 33 of the Charter and is therefore required to abstain from voting by paragraph 3 of Article 27; any vote cast by such a representative should be disregarded in the calculation of the vote in accordance with the principle applied to the Council of the League of Nations by the Permanent Court of International Justice in the *Interpretation of the Treaty of Lausanne Case* that 'the votes of the representatives of the parties are not therefore to be taken into account in ascertaining whether' the voting requirements are fulfilled on the ground that 'the well-known rule that no one can be judge in his own cause holds good'.[2] The General Assembly has repeatedly taken the view that a decision to recognise that a new government is entitled to represent a Member in substitution for the government previously regarded as entitled to represent it is a decision on an important question which must be made by a two-thirds majority of the Members present and voting. The logic and even the legality of this position are highly questionable. The rationale of the two-thirds rule for important questions is that no decision should be taken until a two-thirds majority is secured. Where the question at issue is what government shall represent the Member a decision is unavoidable; a decision to make no change in the representation of a Member when the facts have changed is as much a decision, and as grave a decision, as a decision to recognise the changed facts, and the effect of the two-thirds rule is to prefer the view of the minority to that of the majority. When no major case remains outstanding it will be desirable to consider the questions of long-range policy involved, formulate principles for future guidance in the matter, and devise a procedure which ensures that in any future case which may arise the matter is dealt with objectively on the basis of principle by an appropriate impartial authority.

It is equally implicit in the concept of a universal world community that the expulsion of any Member from the United Nations as an act of policy is unjustifiable. The power of expulsion conferred by the Charter on the General Assembly acting on the recommendation of the Security Council should be regarded as an obsolete survival from an earlier age.

---

[1] *Security Council Official Records*, 5th year, 460th meeting.

[2] P.C.I.J. 1926, Series B, No. 12, p. 32.

Expulsion is at best a clumsy gesture of moral indignation, an ineffective substitute for coercive action by the community, a confession of defeat by which the community, powerless to fulfil the common purpose, destroys itself.[1] There may be, and no doubt will be from time to time, extreme situations in which the maintenance of normal relations with a particular government within the world community becomes impossible. In such situations the suspension of a government rather than the expulsion of a people is the appropriate remedy. The Charter permits the suspension from the exercise of the rights and privileges of membership of the United Nations of a Member against which preventive or enforcement action has been taken by the Security Council.[2] The implications of such suspension might come to be regarded as far-reaching. It might be held to debar the suspended government from exercising any of the prerogatives or functions of a government not only within the United Nations but in any aspect of international relations; its decisions would cease to have extra-territorial validity and it would no longer be entitled to control assets abroad. We might even reach a stage at which such suspension would be regarded as branding the suspended government as an illegal régime for municipal as well as international purposes, thus releasing the citizen from his allegiance. Such a trend of development would no doubt present many difficulties, and the full potentialities of such an evolution would be unlikely to be realised in the first, or even the first few, of any cases which might arise, but whereas expulsion by its nature can lead nowhere a power of suspension so construed could be a step towards the forging of a higher loyalty binding all peoples together in the acceptance of a common rule of law.

It is no less implicit in the concept of a universal world community that the United Nations should not recognise the right of a Member to withdraw. The Charter leaves the matter open. The understanding at the time expressed in a statement adopted by the San Francisco Conference in 1945 was that 'the highest duty of the nations which will become Members is to continue their co-operation within the Organisation for the preservation of international peace and security' but that 'if a Member because of exceptional circumstances feels constrained to withdraw, and leaves the burden of maintaining international peace and security on the other Members, it is not the purpose of the Organisation to compel that Member to continue its co-operation in the Organisation'.

---

[1] I have developed the point more fully in *Law in the World Community*, pp. 106–109 and earlier writings there cited, from 1935 onwards.

[2] Article 5.

It was recognised that 'withdrawals or some other form of dissolution of the Organisation would become inevitable if, deceiving the hopes of humanity, the Organisation was revealed to be unable to maintain peace or could do so only at the expense of law and justice'. This statement by fifty nations in the prenuclear age, deliberately not included in the Charter although the Covenant had made specific provision for withdrawal, cannot be regarded as binding the United Nations in perpetuity. It is now clear that the right of unilateral withdrawal at the discretion of the withdrawing member is as inconsistent with the historical mission of the United Nations as the right of secession was inconsistent with the historical mission of the United States. Precedents for withdrawal and threats of further withdrawal may undermine the whole structure of contemporary world organisation. The right cannot be renounced by amending the relevant provision of the Charter; there is no relevant provision to amend. Nor is it realistic to envisage its renunciation by the inclusion in the Charter of a new provision renouncing any right of withdrawal. The future of the matter will be determined by the attitude adopted by the United Nations as cases arise. Whether the United Nations has deceived 'the hopes of humanity' in such a manner as to make withdrawals or some other form of dissolution of the Organisation inevitable is not a matter to be determined by a disgruntled or recalcitrant State or group of States; it is a question to be settled by the general consensus of mankind expressed in the first instance in the General Assembly itself; unless and until such a situation exists, and is generally recognised to exist, the extreme contingency envisaged in the San Francisco statement has not arisen and the 'inevitability' of withdrawals in such a situation cannot be invoked. There remains the possibility mentioned in the statement of 'exceptional circumstances' in which a Member feels 'constrained to withdraw'. It is for the United Nations, not the particular Member, to determine whether the circumstances are in fact so exceptional that it should 'not compel that Member to continue its co-operation in the Organisation'. The purported withdrawal cannot in any event release the State concerned from all of its obligations under the Charter and any other relevant instruments or United Nations decisions. The Charter itself provides that 'the Organisation shall ensure that States which are not Members of the United Nations act in accordance with' the principles of the Charter 'so far as may be necessary for the maintenance of international peace and security'.[1] Nor would a valid withdrawal terminate all of the other obligations incurred by the withdrawing

[1] Article 2, paragraph 6.

Member by reason of or during its membership; such release from such obligations as the withdrawing Member might claim would have no retroactive effect. Certain obligations would remain operative in respect of the period of membership and happenings during that period but cease to be binding for the future; further obligations would, of course, cease to vest or accumulate; but the withdrawal would not extinguish obligations which had already materialised, including obligations of a continuing character which had already vested. This represents a minimum estimate of the continuing obligations of the Member seeking to withdraw; it may well be, however, that the right of withdrawal should be regarded as open to question. The United Nations and the other Members on whom 'the burden of maintaining international peace and security' remains, are entitled to take the view that they will not regard the Member purporting to withdraw as being released from any of its obligations under the Charter or otherwise; they may not be in a position to compel its positive cooperation, but we may be reaching a stage in the evolution of world society at which they are entitled to proclaim, in the historic language of Lincoln's First Inaugural, that 'perpetuity is implied, if not expressed, in the fundamental law' of the world, and to regard the 1945 statement concerning withdrawal as a failure, not unnatural at that time, to appreciate the inevitable logic of the contemporary evolution of world society, not as a limitation upon our freedom today to deduce from the logic of the contemporary evolution of world society consequences unforeseen by, and unacceptable to, the founding fathers, who brought to the problems of a generation ago the conceptual approach of still earlier generations.

2. The Community as an organism

The process of institutional development will inevitably follow a chequered course. Events will unfold in so unanticipated a manner that no foresight can make adequate provision for the contingencies which prove to be practically important. Without a resourcefulness fertile in devising an appropriate solution for each new problem and some new line of advance in every successive impasse, no institutional framework of society can withstand the stresses and strains of these turbulent times. McIlwain said of constitutional history that it 'is usually the record of a series of oscillations'.[1] The constitutional arrangements of the world community will inevitably evolve through a comparable series of

---

[1] McIlwain, Charles Howard, *Constitutionalism: Ancient and Modern*, Revised Edition, p. 136.

oscillations. Fertility of resource in coping with the unforeseen is therefore a vital element in institutional effectiveness and constitutional order. When construing the Charter of the United Nations and the constituent instruments of other international organisations we must at all times recall with Marshall that 'it is a constitution we are expounding' and that a constitution is 'intended to endure for ages to come, and consequently, to be adapted to the various crises of human affairs';[1] we must realise with Holmes that 'we are dealing with words that are also a constituent act' which 'have called into life a being the development of which could not have been foreseen completely by the most gifted of its begetters';[2] we must be content to know that we have created an organism and leave it to coming generations to prove that we have created a world community; we must approach each successive problem 'in the light of our whole experience' and anticipations; we must unequivocally adopt a dynamic rather than a strict constructionist approach to the constitutional problems of international society.

The League of Nations, understandably though not inevitably in the circumstances of the time, was conservative in its constitutional tradition, but the constitutional history of the International Labour Organisation abounds with illustrations of such an approach[3] which played a significant part in its surviving the League. From the outset the Permanent Court of International Justice placed a broad construction on the competence of the Organisation. A system of membership based in principle on identity of membership with the League of Nations was transformed, when it became clear that the League could never achieve universality of membership, into a system whereby membership of the League continued to involve membership of the I.L.O. but the I.L.O. could also admit to, or retain in, membership States which had not become, or had ceased to be, Members of the League. Employer and worker representation was construed as early as 1935 as the representation of functions rather than classes; this interpretation was formulated authoritatively and generally accepted when the Constitution was under revision in 1945 and, though subsequently challenged, has remained the continuing basis of policy. A wide range of functions and agencies not specifically provided for in the Constitution has been developed. The competence of the Organisation to deal with matters not explicitly specified in the Constitution has been recognised. The authority of the

[1] 4 Wheaton 316 (1819). [2] 252 U.S. 416 (1920).

[3] 'The Future Development of the Constitution and Constitutional Practice of the International Labour Organisation: Memorandum by the Legal Adviser of the International Labour Office (Jenks)', *Official Bulletin of the International Labour Office*, Vol. XXVII, No. 2, 10 December 1945, pp. 114–145.

Organisation to include in its decisions and recommendations any economic or financial provisions which it might consider appropriate, at one time contested, was subsequently fully acknowledged. Important adjustments have been effected from time to time in the technique of conventions and recommendations. Within the International Labour Organisation there is an established tradition that the Constitution of the Organisation 'is not a strait waistcoat but the skeleton of a living body'.[1] When the Constitution was revised in 1945–1946 some of the results of this process of dynamic interpretation were embodied in the revised text; other matters, including the important question of socialised management, were dealt with by authoritative commentary on an unchanged text; still others were left to be determined by the course of future evolution; and as soon as the revision of the Constitution came into force the process of dynamic interpretation was resumed in relation to new issues which were not foreseen, or could not be dealt with satisfactorily, at the time of the revision. In 1945 it was still considered premature to include in the Constitution, as then revised, a series of provisions envisaged by the International Labour Office in 1944 relating to possible new types of I.L.O. action of a diplomatic, advisory, quasi-judicial and operational nature; provision was made in the Constitution for granting to governments at their request appropriate assistance in connection with the framing of laws and regulations on the basis of the decisions of the Conference and the improvement of administrative practices and systems of inspection, but it was thought inadvisable or premature to give any further specific powers. By the late 'forties the emphasis on new operational tasks had become so pronounced that the question whether there was any constitutional or legal obstacle to the assumption of such tasks was thought to require special consideration; the view taken, predictably in the light of the tradition of the Organisation, was that there was no constitutional or legal obstacle to such a development.[2] This dynamic tradition of the I.L.O. has not been limited to matters of constitutional interpretation; it has also found expression in procedural inventiveness. In 1950 the Governing Body of the I.L.O., acting in agreement with the Economic and Social Council, established a Fact-Finding and Conciliation Commission on Freedom of Association to provide facilities for the impartial investiga-

---

[1] Ibid., p. 143.

[2] 'The Constitutional Capacity of the International Labour Organisation to Undertake Operational Tasks and Sponsor Executive Agreements between Governments: Memorandum by the Legal Adviser of the International Labour Office (Jenks)', *Official Bulletin of the International Labour Office*, Vol. XXXI, No. 3, 31 December 1948, pp. 287–292.

tion of trade union situations which had become the subject of international controversy. The arrangements provided that no complaint could be referred to the Commission without the consent of the government concerned. When it became apparent that such consent would rarely be forthcoming, a Governing Body Committee on Freedom of Association, originally established to make a preliminary review of the desirability of asking the government concerned to give its consent to allegations being referred to the Fact-Finding and Conciliation Commission for formal investigation, was gradually developed, by general consent, with the cooperation of governments in all parts of the world, into a less formal alternative to the Fact-Finding Commission examining the merits of cases and making recommendations. For these proceedings, by reason of their less formal character and the fact that they continued to be in form a preliminary review by a committee advising the Governing Body, the formal consent of governments was not required. The practical upshot was that by the time the Fact-Finding Commission was seised of its first case (fourteen years after the establishment of the procedure) the Governing Body Committee had dealt with some four hundred cases,[1] in many, though by no means all, cases not less effectively than the Fact-Finding Commission could have done, and frequently in circumstances in which consent to the reference of the case to the Fact-Finding Commission could never have been secured.

The overall result has been to facilitate the membership in the Organisation, at critical stages of its history, of the United States and the U.S.S.R., both of which had originally remained aloof from it; to enable it to survive the transition from the League of Nations to the United Nations system; to widen its horizon from protective labour legislation to social justice in all its aspects including its foundations in economic policy and fundamental human rights; to transform a primarily informational and standard-setting organisation into an organisation discharging the full range of the varied functions of contemporary international bodies, including quasi-judicial and operational responsibilities; and to transform a highly centralised body into one with varied regional and industrial activities. The dynamic I.L.O. of today, constantly readapting itself to new needs, has been made possible by the dynamic tradition of constitutional interpretation.

A dynamic approach has been equally characteristic of the constitutional tradition of the United Nations, which in this respect owes

---

[1] For the story down to 1956 see Jenks, C. Wilfred, *The International Protection of Trade Union Freedom*, and for later development Jenks, 'The International Protection of Trade Union Rights', in Evan Luard (ed.), *The International Protection of Human Rights*, pp. 210–247.

more to the example of the I.L.O than to that of the League. The concept of 'the living Charter' was adopted from the outset by the legal advisers of the Secretary-General as the basis of their work and the record of the United Nations shows 'an accelerating current towards broad construction of its basic instrument' inspired by the fundamental concept that it is the constituent instrument of 'an embryonic community which the Charter hopes to guide in the direction of a world order'.[1] In the Security Council, the first important constitutional development was the acceptance of the principle that abstention does not constitute a veto. In the General Assembly, the decisive landmark of the early years was the Uniting for Peace Resolution of 1950 whereby the General Assembly assumed, or perhaps one should say formalised, the power to recommend when the Security Council fails to decide. The development of the powers of the Secretary-General to include executive responsibilities not originally envisaged is a further manifestation of the same general approach. The erosion of the concept of domestic jurisdiction by the broadening of international responsibilities, a process in which virtually all Members of the United Nations have at some stage played some part[2], has radically changed the balance between the collective responsibility of the community and the quondam sovereign rights of its members. In the United Nations we have indeed now reached in some respects, and we may be approaching in others, a stage of development at which the problem changes, to the extent of almost inverting, its nature. The problem ceases to be one of avoiding a paralysis of decision and becomes one of ensuring the responsibility of the decision making process; it ceases to be one of a vacuum of executive authority and becomes one of a vacuum of constitutional control of executive responsibility; the danger ceases to be that the Charter will be interpreted so rigidly that the United Nations cannot discharge its collective responsibilities in situations which were not foreseen and becomes that it will be interpreted so loosely that Members will cease to honour their several responsibilities in situations which were foreseen quite clearly. The principle that the Charter must be dynamically interpreted affords no justification for any ideological qualification of its obligations. In particular, the obligation of Members to refrain in their international relations from the threat or use of force is absolute and without such an obligation the prospect of maintaining world

---

[1] Feller, A. H., *United Nations and World Community*, p. 42.

[2] Rajan, M. S., *The United Nations and Domestic Jurisdiction*, 2nd ed.; Higgins, Rosalyn, *The Development of International Law through the Political Organs of the United Nations*, pp. 58–130.

peace by more effective international organisation becomes altogether illusory. The obligation becomes meaningless and inoperative if we allow it to be qualified by anything other than the necessary right of individual and collective self-defence, reasonably construed and subject to impartial review. The Charter of the United Nations will inevitably lose its political, its legal and its moral authority unless we are prepared to discharge in full the obligations which it implies for ourselves.[1] In fine, the province of dynamic interpretation is to consolidate, not to emasculate, the authority of the Charter.

In this changed situation the challenge to the creative imagination changes but remains no less insistent. It has become a challenge to evolve procedures of consensus and techniques of responsibility within a context of dynamic action, a challenge still more exacting than that of freeing dynamic action from institutional paralysis. In responding to the challenge we must be guided by the wise counsel of Paul Henri Spaak: 'When a principle is pressed to its logical conclusion and maintained against all reason, reality is not slow to take revenge.'[2] The fruitfulness of the creative imagination in its influence upon institutional development is determined primarily by the firmness of its imaginative grasp of reality.

3. The implied powers of the community

The Charter of the United Nations does not, like the Constitution of the United States, contain an express grant of the powers 'necessary or proper for carrying into execution' the specified powers, but in the *Reparation for Injuries Suffered in the Service of the United Nations Case*[3] we have a decision of the International Court of Justice equivalent to that of the Supreme Court of the United States in *McCulloch* v. *Maryland*,[4] in which Chief Justice Marshall held that if 'the end be legitimate' and 'within the scope of the Constitution' then 'all means which are appropriate which are plainly adapted to that end, which are not prohibited, but consist with the letter and spirit of the Constitution, are constitutional'.[5] In the *Reparation for Injuries Case*[6] the International Court held that 'under international law the Organization must be deemed to have those powers which, though not expressly

---

[1] Jenks, C. Wilfred, *Law in the World Community*, p. 58.

[2] Carnegie Endowment for International Peace, *Perspectives on Peace, 1910–1960*, p. 87.

[3] *I.C.J. Reports*, 1949.

[4] 4 Wheaton, 316.

[5] Ibid., p. 421.

[6] *I.C.J. Reports*, 1949, at p. 182.

provided for in the Charter, are conferred upon it by necessary implication as being essential to the performance of its duties'. It pointed out that 'this principle of law was applied by the Permanent Court of International Justice to the International Labour Organisation' in the *Case Concerning the Competence of the I.L.O. to Regulate, Incidentally, the Personal Work of the Employer*[1] and held that it must also be applied to the United Nations.

The Court applied the principle of implied powers again in the *Effect of Awards of Compensation Made by the United Nations Administrative Tribunal Case*[2] in which the main question at issue was whether the General Assembly had legal powers to establish a tribunal competent to render judgments binding on the United Nations. There was, the Court pointed out, 'no express provision for the establishment of judicial bodies or organs and no indication to the contrary'.[3] Invoking the statement in the *Reparation for Injuries Case* that the Organisation 'must be deemed to have those powers which, though not expressly provided for in the Charter, are conferred upon it by necessary implication as being essential to the performance of its duties', the Court proceeded to enquire whether the provisions of the Charter 'implied for the Organization the power to establish a judicial tribunal to adjudicate upon disputes arising out of the contracts of service' of its staff. It found that 'the power to establish a tribunal, to do justice between the Organization and the staff members, was essential to ensure the efficient working of the Secretariat, and to give effect to the paramount consideration' enunciated by the Charter 'of securing the highest standards of efficiency, competence and integrity'; capacity to establish such a tribunal therefore 'arises by necessary intendment out of the Charter'.[4] The Court dismissed a contention that 'an implied power can be exercised only to the extent that the particular measure under consideration can be regarded as absolutely essential' on the ground that the precise nature and scope of the measures by which the power should be exercised 'was a matter for the General Assembly alone';[5] it also rejected as irrelevant to the question before it contentions that 'an implied power to impose legal limitations upon the General Assembly's express Charter powers is not legally admissible'[6] and that 'the implied power of the General Assembly to establish a tribunal cannot be carried so far as to enable the tribunal to intervene in matters falling within the province of the Secretary-General'.[7]

---

[1] P.C.I.J. 1926, Series B, No. 13, p. 18.
[2] *I.C.J. Reports*, 1954, pp. 47–97. [3] P. 56.
[4] P. 57. [5] P. 58. [6] P. 59. [7] P. 60.

In the *Certain Expenses of the United Nations Case*[1] the Court was called upon to consider the principle of implied powers in reverse in the form of a contention that the budgetary powers of the General Assembly are subject to an implied limitation arising from the powers of the Security Council in matters of international peace and security; it rejected the contention.

How much wider an application the principle of implied powers may and should have, and what bearing it may have on the goals which we have postulated, remain uncertain and debatable. Differences of view concerning the legal foundation and extent of implied powers will tend to reflect profound divergences of policy concerning the measure of authority which should be granted to the world community, the rate at which such authority should be granted, and the extent to which it should be granted in broad and generous or more specific terms. The scope and potentialities of the doctrine of implied powers for the United Nations and for international organisations generally[2] is therefore one of the largest issues of the institutional development of the world community. The general purposes of the United Nations embrace the whole political future of man and every aspect of his freedom and welfare in organised society. On a generous and liberal view the potential scope of the implied powers of the United Nations and the specialised agencies to develop new methods of action, and new legal instruments, devices and procedures, to accomplish the purposes of the world community and the functions entrusted to them on its behalf, is therefore almost unlimited. Whether these powers grow with expanding public confidence, are disavowed by widespread public distrust, or atrophy through general public indifference, will largely depend on the vision and sense of responsibility with which they are invoked and exercised.

4. The whole and the parts

In developing the institutional structure of the world community we must harmonise the need for overall coordination with the need for vigorous autonomy in the main fields of action and the effective intermeshing of world with national action in particular fields. The parts cannot thrive if dissected from the whole; the whole cannot thrive without the vitality of the parts. Only a composite of autonomy and coordination can give tone and vigour to the whole system.

---

[1] *I.C.J. Reports*, 1962, pp. 151–308.

[2] Rouyer-Hameray, Bernard, *Les Compétences Implicites des Organisations Internationales.*

The United Nations system[1] is a complex of bodies falling into five main groups. The United Nations Organisation itself operates through six principal organs, each having certain independent powers, and a wide range of subsidiary organs of varying importance and autonomy. Thirteen specialised agencies operate under autonomous constitutions but have the relationship to the United Nations defined by the Charter and the agreements made thereunder; they fall conveniently into three sub-groups, the first sub-group consisting of the four promotion of the general welfare agencies, the International Labour Organisation, the Food and Agriculture Organisation, Unesco (for education, science and culture), and the World Health Organization, the second sub-group of the four financial agencies, the International Monetary Fund, the International Bank for Reconstruction and Development, the International Finance Corporation and the International Development Association, and the third sub-group of five highly specialised agencies, the Universal Postal Union, the International Telecommunication Union, the International Civil Aviation Organization, the Intergovernmental Maritime Consultative Organization, and the World Meteorological Organization. The International Atomic Energy Agency is not a specialised agency but is in a similar position and the General Agreement on Tariffs and Trade lies somewhat outside the pattern but may be regarded as analogous to a specialised agency. A third group of bodies, typified by the United Nations Trade and Development Conference, the United Nations Industrial Development Organization, UNICEF and the High Commissioner for Refugees, have an operational autonomy comparable to that of the specialised agencies but were created by decisions of United Nations organs, notably the General Assembly, which can modify their constitutional arrangements and retain financial control and a voice in the nomination of their executive heads. The fourth group consists of regional agencies of the United Nations system, such as the Regional Economic Commissions, legally the creation of their parent bodies but tending to become political realities in their own right. The fifth group comprises inter-agency arrangements evolved as a collective enterprise of the whole system or a substantial number of its parts, in particular the United Nations Development Programme.

This general pattern calls for a number of comments.

It is not the chaotic product of sporadic growth but the creation of deliberate policy at the highest level. While the details of the picture

---

[1] Goodrich, Leland M., *The United Nations*; Asher, Robert E., Kotschnig, Walter and Others, *The United Nations and Promotion of the General Welfare*.

reflect successive phases of development and historical accidents, the basic assumption 'that there cannot be, in the modern world, any single focus of authority where decisions on matters of international concern can be centralized'[1] is a deliberate and valid proposition of high policy.

It reflects the desire to secure the largest possible measure of international cooperation in as many fields of international action as possible and give such cooperation a maximum chance of success by removing as much of it as possible as far as possible from political influences and control.

It reflects the need to intermesh international action in the many fields of policy in which such action becomes effective by complementary national action with the complementary national action necessary to make it effective.

It reflects the unmanageability of bigness beyond a certain scale which has become a major problem of modern government as of modern industry.

As the modern State has become the welfare State, government has ceased to be the prerogative of a small number of central departments of State, notably treasuries and foreign offices. It has become a complex of public services embracing every aspect of the life of the community. Within this complex there are recognised arrangements for evolving general policy, but as the life of the community becomes more complex, and the machinery and procedures of government are increasingly adapted to its changing needs, these arrangements seek essentially a coordinated diffusion of responsibility. World organisation is evolving in the same direction and manner. Twentieth-century world affairs cannot be conducted by foreign offices and treasuries; they embrace too broad a spectrum of human affairs and interests. To be practically effective contemporary world organisation must interlock at innumerable different points with national arrangements with a continuing responsibility for policy and action; it must actively involve in continuous international cooperation all the major departments of government with substantive responsibility for the increasing range of questions with important international aspects and leave them the freedom of action necessary to enable them to conduct their collective business successfully and implement their decisions by action within the scope of their recognised departmental responsibilities.

These are fundamentals of policy and political structure which outweigh the admitted inconveniences of the decentralised system. A

---

[1] Jenks, C. Wilfred, 'Co-ordination in International Organisation: An Introductory Survey', *British Year Book of International Law*, Vol. 28, 1951, p. 88.

compelling case can, moreover, be made for the system by the most important of all tests – that of results.

The decentralisation of the United Nations system has made possible a vitality and growth in world organisation which a more orderly and disciplined approach could not have attained. The rate of growth is still too slow, and the solidity of the results achieved much too uncertain, by the test of the world's needs, but under this system the human race has, as Secretary of State Dean Rusk has said, 'been moving steadily, and in recent years more rapidly, to build up expected standards of conduct and instruments of co-operation' which are 'bringing a great deal of order in international affairs, even in the face of some of these most violent ideological problems, and security problems, that we are all aware of'.[1]

The decentralised structure of the United Nations system, while both inevitable and wise, nevertheless presents both difficulties and dangers.

The degree and type of decentralisation of functional responsibility which is desirable at any particular time within a system of this nature is so much a question of judgment rather than principle that questions will constantly arise concerning the appropriate balance of responsibility, measure of autonomy and method of coordination in some new context. There is a real danger that every new problem, and even every new phase of a problem, may precipitate some new institutional experiment rather than a sober appraisal of the adequacy of the existing institutional arrangements and the most appropriate manner of using or adapting them to cope with the new situation. Institutions grow in strength by proving their adaptability, and ease of institutional innovation may, by dispersing the thrust of change rather than harnessing it, weaken rather than strengthen the institutional structure as a whole. There is what Dag Hammarskjöld called 'a risk of disintegration of the international framework through a proliferation of organs' and a need to seek 'the optimum balance between a system with a large number of autonomous bodies and a system with strong concentration of tasks within a lesser number of organisations'. In seeking such a balance new forms may be necessary for both 'an integration of activities among autonomous organisations' and 'the delegation of powers within this or that organisation without breaking of its unity'.[2]

The rationale of the functional decentralisation of the United Nations

---

[1] 'United Nations Charter Amendments, Hearing before the Committee on Foreign Relations United States Senate, 89th Congress, 1st Session, April 28 and 29, 1965', p. 34.

[2] 'The Development of a Constitutional Framework for International Co-operation', reprinted in *Servant of Peace*, p. 258.

system is the importance of the close and continuous interlocking of international and national action in particular fields. The system provides a world counterpart for each of the main departments of national government and puts the counterpart in close relationship with the national departments to which it corresponds. There are, however, three difficulties. In the first place, public policy is a seamless web. However imperative it may be to divide it into segments for purposes of practical action, the interactions between different segments are so numerous that effective coordination must be secured if chaos and frustration are to be avoided. If such coordination cannot be secured internationally it is forced back to the national level. 'If this occurs, national action of a potentially disruptive character is liable to be substituted for co-operative international action, and the policies evolved within their respective spheres by the different international bodies will frequently fail to secure practical application.'[1] In the process, the whole concept of effective international action tends to be discredited. Secondly, the departmental structure of national governments varies widely and no conceivable allocation of responsibilities among world bodies with a substantial autonomy can therefore be wholly convenient to any particular government. Thirdly, in the contemporary world virtually half the membership of the United Nations consists of States which have recently attained their independence and are still in process of developing their own national systems of government and departmental structures. Many of these States have great difficulty in participating effectively in so complex a world structure.

One of the primary purposes of functional decentralisation was to take the politics out of the widest possible area of international co-operation. The concept was that each specialised agency would, within a broader framework of concerted action, be responsible for its own field, leaving political matters to be dealt with by the central political organs of the United Nations system as a whole. The general principle has been challenged at various times, and in particular since the great increase in the membership of the United Nations in recent years, as the direct result of which the issue has become specially acute in respect of South Africa and Portugal and may arise in other political contexts of the greatest delicacy. The principle remains of fundamental importance.

If once we depart from the general principle that the responsibility for political matters rests primarily with the United Nations, the

---

[1] Jenks, C. Wilfred, 'Co-ordination in International Organisation: An Introductory Survey', *British Year Book of International Law*, Vol. 28, 1951, p. 30.

> whole scheme of functional decentralisation on the basis of which so much progress in world organisation has been made during the last generation becomes unworkable. The political organs of the United Nations lose control of political issues; the technical work of technical agencies is disrupted; within individual governments as well as in international organisations technical departments become involved in political matters for which they have no continuing responsibility and which they are ill-equipped to handle; . . . a decentralisation which operates in practice to multiply the occasions for political conflict defeats its own purpose and frustrates both the political and the technical effectiveness of the system as a whole.[1]

The bearing of effective coordination on the law is not limited to its impact on the pattern of institutional development; it also affects the substantive content of international law. We have seen that the practice of international organisations has now become a significant element in the growth of international law itself.

> In so far as such practice is uniform and is based on clear and consistent principles, it can be a major factor in the development of an effective system of international law. In so far as it is so varied and inconsistent that it tends to destroy the authority of existing principles and usage, or to make it difficult for new principles or usage to secure general acceptance, it can be a major retarding factor. It is therefore of primary importance for the whole future of international law that the practice of the different international organisations in regard to matters of international law should be sufficiently uniform to operate as a constructive influence in the development of the customary law of nations.[2]

It is in the context of these far-reaching considerations of policy that the creative imagination must play its part in evolving an institutional framework which permits and achieves the reconciliation of vitality and discipline. Great progress has been made in the matter during the first twenty years of the United Nations system. The Charter embodies a considered scheme for the coordination of the activities of the United Nations and the specialised agencies, and the constitutions governing the specialised agencies, while having an independent validity, envisage

---

[1] Jenks, C. Wilfred, *Law in the World Community*, p. 111.

[2] Jenks, C. Wilfred, 'Co-ordination in International Organisation: An Introductory Survey', *British Year Book of International Law*, Vol. 28, 1951, p. 33.

their functioning to a greater or lesser degree as parts of a wider structure. An elaborate network of agreements governs the mutual relations of all the various bodies concerned, and a wide range of rules of procedure and administrative instruments has been developed to make these agreements effective. Complex institutional arrangements have been developed for handling the innumerable practical problems involved. Among these the Economic and Social Council and the Administrative Committee on Co-ordination (which consists of the Secretary-General of the United Nations and the executive heads of the specialised agencies) play the central roles, and the Advisory Committee on Administrative and Budgetary Questions of the General Assembly, the International Civil Service Advisory Board, the Joint Panel of External Auditors, and the Joint Inspection Unit have functions of special importance. The Resident Representatives of the United Nations Development Programme provide focal points for facilitating the cooperation of new States in this complex international system.[1] Continuing dissatisfaction and controversy concerning the working of the system has perhaps been inevitable. There has been much exaggeration of its weaknesses, and it has shown at its best on the successive occasions on which it has been called upon to mobilise the energies of the whole United Nations family to meet an emergency. Certainly there remain many problems to be solved, but a reasonable framework for further creative effort has been established.

5. Universal and regional action

The one world of our time remains a divided world. It has become one as an 'inclusive activity area'; it is far from one as a 'sentimental area', an 'interest area', or an 'organisation area'.[2] It is, moreover, so vast and varied a world that regional decentralisation must be expected to be no less important than functional decentralisation in the future structure of the world community and conduct of its affairs.[3]

The problem was only partly foreseen when the Charter of the United Nations was drafted. Article 52 of the Charter provides that nothing in the Charter 'precludes the existence of regional arrangements or agencies for dealing with such matters relating to the maintenance of international

---

[1] For a fuller account of the legal framework of the arrangements for coordination see Jenks, C. Wilfred, 'Co-ordination: A New Problem of International Organisation', *Recueil des Cours de l' Adadémic de Droit international*, Vol. 77 (1950 (II)), pp. 3–149.

[2] P. 6 above.

[3] Cf. Jenks, C. Wilfred, *The World Beyond the Charter*, pp. 140–142.

peace and security as are appropriate for regional action, provided that such arrangements or agencies and their activities are consistent with the Purposes and Principles of the United Nations'. It requires Members of the United Nations entering into such arrangements or constituting such agencies to 'make every effort to achieve pacific settlement of local disputes through such regional arrangements or by regional agencies before referring them to the Security Council' and requires the Security Council to 'encourage the development of pacific settlement of local disputes through such regional arrangements or by such regional agencies either on the initiative of the States concerned or by reference from the Security Council'. The article specifies that these provisions in no way impair the powers of the Security Council to investigate disputes and situations or the right of any Member to bring any dispute or situation before the Security Council or the General Assembly. Article 53 provides that the Security Council shall, where appropriate, use regional arrangements or agencies for enforcement action under its authority, but that no enforcement action shall be taken under regional arrangements or by regional agencies without the authorisation of the Security Council. Article 54 adds that the Security Council shall at all times be kept fully informed of activities undertaken or in contemplation under regional arrangements or by regional agencies for the maintenance of international peace and security. There is no other provision in the Charter concerning regional arrangements. The question is treated as though it arose only in respect of matters directly relating to the maintenance of international peace and security; as a matter of history it was envisaged at San Francisco as a question which was of foreseeable importance in relation to only one region, namely the Americas.

The perspective has now wholly changed. The relationship of universal and regional action has become one of the central issues of broad international policy, affecting all parts of the world and every sector of public policy and involving all of the functions of government, legislative, executive and judicial, in the nascent world community. 'Simultaneously with the unparalleled development of world organisation . . . there has been an equally unparalleled development of regional organisations of varying importance, stability and functions in virtually all parts of the world.'[1] No more difficult task confronts the architects of the world society than that of so articulating the world system and the regional systems that they reinforce instead of destroy each other. We cannot articulate them by legal norms or institutional devices unless we first succeed in clarifying certain fundamentals of policy.

---

[1] Jenks, C. Wilfred, *The Common Law of Mankind*, p. 211.

The necessary starting point is that all concerned, the universal organisations, the regional organisations, and the governments which, of set though frequently instinctive rather than deliberate purpose rather than by a mere failure of internal coordination, divide their allegiance between them, should clarify the basic assumptions underlying their respective policies. There can be no worth-while clarification of the policies of either universal or regional organisations without a corresponding clarification of the policies of large numbers of governments, and in general the policies of governments in the matter tend to be highly complex variables. There is sometimes a significant difference between the attitude of a government to regional organisations of which it is a member (and which it regards as beneficient or defensive) and regional organisations of which it is not a member (which it regards as aggressive or superfluous) but such attitudes tend to be predispositions rather than constants. The views of governments concerning the relations between universal organisations and regional organisations of which they are members are apt to fluctuate with changing evaluations of the relative support for policies to which they currently attach importance in the universal and world organisation respectively. Their attitude towards regional organisations of which they are not members are apt to reflect in a similar manner shifts in the current relations between alliances and alignments and changing rivalries within alliances and alignments. How can these shifting views be transmuted into a coherent and consistent continuing policy?

We must consistently see the picture as a whole. We must start from the firm proposition that universal and regional action can no longer be regarded as rival and contradictory approaches to the problem of world organisation. In a one world which remains, and in some respects will always remain, divided, and which is too vast and varied for any single pattern of world government, they are necessary counterparts to each other. Triple rather than dual federalism, with the world community, more integrated regions, and member States progressively evolving more organic relationships with each other, represents the type of world order most likely to command general acceptance and to be effective in practice.

Somewhat different problems arise in respect of the maintenance of peace and security, the judicial settlement of disputes, the codification of international law, the unification of private law, economic development programmes, measures of economic integration, the promotion and control of science and technology, the protection of human rights, social policy and cultural cooperation.

As we review these various fields of action we will find that in respect of many and perhaps most of them we must be content to propound a dilemma rather than any immediate solution.

In respect of the maintenance of peace and security the Charter itself states the broad principles applicable. They resolve themselves into the overriding responsibility of the whole world community for the maintenance of peace and security as a major interest of the community as a whole, qualified by the recognition that regional action may be preferable and more effective in particular cases. Acute political and practical problems, of which we are likely to hear much more, have arisen in regard to the application of these principles. Where universal action proves impracticable regional action may be imperative, but there is always the danger that appeal from a universal to a regional forum may substitute less responsible and more controversial courses of action for policies and measures evolved by compromise on a wider basis.

The debate concerning the desirability or otherwise of establishing regional courts for the settlement of international disputes has continued for half a century, without any great progress being made in the matter. Certain regional courts of special jurisdiction have been established, notably the Court of Justice of the European Communities[1] and the European Court of Human Rights,[2] but the movement for regional courts analogous to the International Court of Justice has remained a somewhat academic one. This represents, it is believed, a wise appraisal of the realities of the situation. The volume of major litigation between States does not at present justify the creation of regional courts parallel to the International Court of Justice. The International Court affords a guarantee of greater impartiality than could be afforded by a system of regional courts. The unity of international law is not something to be lightly lost by the conflicting jurisprudence of a plethora of regional tribunals in all parts of the world. There may be special cases in which such tribunals are desirable, but any such tribunals should be created to meet a specific need and not to give effect to any general assumption that regional tribunals are in principle desirable. If and when they are created every effort should be made to evolve principles and procedures which maintain a general world framework for regional development.[3]

The universality of international law is an essential element in the welfare and progress of the world community as a whole. The codification of international law on a regional basis is therefore a questionable

---

[1] Bebr, Gerhard, *Judicial Control of the European Communities.*

[2] Robertson, A. H., *Human Rights in Europe.*

[3] Jenks, C. Wilfred, *The Prospects of International Adjudication*, pp. 175–181.

enterprise to be undertaken with great caution. There may be subjects, in respect of which, and circumstances in which, regional codification presents a balance of advantage or there is no strong reason for resisting a desire for such codification which commands wide support, but such cases should be regarded as exceptional. Variations of regional customs or practice, justified by difference of geography, culture, economic and social structure, or political systems, or explained by differences of history, there will of course always be, but in principle the common law of mankind must be a law for all mankind. Concepts of a distinctive regional system of international law may prove to be no more than a phase in the development of the relationship between the region concerned and the world community as a whole. It is not without significance that Alejandro Alvarez, the leading protagonist of a distinctive American international law in the early years of the present century, will be remembered in future as the prophet of a 'new international law' of universal scope.[1]

A quite different situation exists in respect of the unification of private law (including the civil law, and in particular questions of personal status and capacity, commercial law, and certain aspects of private international law) and judicial cooperation in civil and criminal matters. The natural areas for such cooperation sometimes differ widely from the regional groupings evolved for other purposes. They define themselves by the origin and development of their legal systems, by the extent of their acceptance in the particular field of some recognised variant of the common law, the civil law, Islamic law or some other major legal tradition. Whereas regional experiments in the codification of international law may, unless they are limited to problems peculiar to a particular region or arising there in some peculiar form, tend to have the effect of disintegrating international law, such experiments in the unification of private law, if successful, have the effect of integrating municipal law. In the one case the effect is to narrow, in the other to widen, the law area of a common law.

In matters of economic development and economic integration and the promotion and control of science and technology we are confronted with a wholly different balance of considerations and interplay of forces. Economic development presupposes initiative, resources and skills; these elements may come from beyond or within the regional area concerned and the appropriate balance and modalities of universal and regional action depend on the origin and nature of the resources available, the extent to which an extra-regional contribution is desirable and

---

[1] *Le droit international nouveau.*

possible, and the arrangements most likely to promote initiative and self-sustaining growth within the region. Economic integration is in its nature a regional concept but its desirability and impact depend in substantial measure on its effect on the trading relations between the integrated area and the rest of the world. The promotion of scientific and technological development may be facilitated by joint action on a regional basis to undertake projects beyond the resources of all but the largest States; regional measures may also be desirable where some specifically regional problem calls for some new or special application of science and technology; but the fundamental problem of ensuring that scientific and technological development does not so outrun social control as to plunge the world into disaster can hardly be dealt with effectively on anything less than a world basis.

It is perhaps in respect of human rights that the dilemma is most acute. Is regional action the most effective means of making human rights a reality based on and supported by the *mores* of the community in which we are seeking to establish them? Or would a regional approach sometimes be tantamount to abdicating the concept of fundamental human rights which man everywhere can claim as man?

Social policy and cultural cooperation pose similar dilemmas.

In all these varied fields there lies before us an immense task of defining the frontiers of universal and regional action and organising relationships which make them effectively complementary to each other. We have not yet reached the point at which the part which the international lawyer will ultimately be called upon to play in this process is at all clear, but it is already evident that the long-term institutional relationships between the world community and regional organisations are among the major problems to which he will increasingly be called upon to devote his skill.

6. Due process and orderly procedure

Within this universal framework with its complex pattern of functional and regional diversity there must be a recognised rule of law based on traditions of due process and respect for orderly procedure. The problem arises in different forms for the deliberative, judicial or quasi-judicial, executive or administrative organs of the world community, but is important in respect of all of them.

Among the requirements of due process in deliberative bodies such as the General Assembly and other international conferences, the inherent right of freedom of speech of all duly accredited representatives participating in a meeting of an international organisation, the principle that no State or government should be condemned unheard, and respect for regularity of procedure are of outstanding importance. These were almost taken for granted until they became an issue in a wide range of international organisations as the result of the passion aroused by growing resentment against the continued practice of *apartheid* in South Africa. It is now apparent that due process and orderly procedure in deliberative bodies, and indeed the rule of law generally, will not long commend themselves to human impatience unless the record shows that they provide an effective means of redressing burning grievances within reasonable periods of time. Freedom of speech, fair hearing and due process are none the less vital for the whole future of freedom under law in the world community; they must be harmonised with a dynamic approach to the claims of justice and morality in effective forms of action.[1]

Due process and orderly procedure in deliberative bodies presuppose rules for the conduct of international business which have been worked out in some detail, are generally accepted and understood, and are reinforced with general support of firm and impartial chairmanship. The parliamentary practice of international organisations is of crucial importance for the responsible discharge of their responsibilities and may be a substantial factor in determining whether international discussion of emotionally charged issues contributes light or heat in critical situations. Philip Jessup[2] is perhaps the only leading scholar who has sufficiently appreciated the full importance of the matter and the part which must be played in the international law of the future by United Nations equivalents of Jefferson's Manual[3] and Erskine May[4].

Due process is so much the essence of judicial procedure that we may tend to assume that no special measures are now necessary to ensure it. In the case of the International Court of Justice, the procedure of which is governed by its Statute and Rules of Court[5] or other reputable international tribunals which operate in accordance with The Hague Convention for the Peaceful Settlement of International Disputes or the United Nations Model Rules of Arbitral Procedure framed by the International Law Commission, there is of course no problem,[6] but the

---

[1] Jenks, C. Wilfred, *Law in the World Community*, pp. 117–118.

[2] 'Parliamentary Diplomacy: An Examination of the Legal Quality of the Rules of Procedure of Organs of the United Nations', *Recueil des Cours de l'Académie de Droit international*, Vol. 89, (1956 (I)), pp. 185–318.

[3] *Manual of Parliamentary Practice*.

[4] *A Treatise on the Law, Privileges, Proceedings and Usage of Parliament*.

[5] Rosenne, Shabtai, *The Law and Practice of the International Court*, 2 vols.

[6] Simpson, J. L. and Fox, Hazel, *International Arbitration: Law and Practice*.

position in respect of international commissions of enquiry discharging quasi-judicial responsibilities on behalf of political bodies such as the General Assembly of the United Nations and certain of its committees is at best precarious. The value of such bodies depends on their impartiality and thoroughness being established beyond question by either party and no safeguards for these purposes embodying the duty of impartiality, opportunity for full and fair hearing, and reasonable criteria of relevance and proof, have as yet been institutionalised. The full rigour of international judicial procedure may well be inapplicable to such bodies, but the fundamental principles of due process and orderly procedure are not. Some of the precautions taken in the matter by the International Labour Organisation, which combine safeguards for the personal independence of those to whom the enquiry is entrusted consisting primarily of the method by which they are chosen, thorough staff-work on their behalf, and a full opportunity for all interested parties to express their views and comment fully on any allegations, evidence, or information relating to them before conclusions are reached, may well be of wider application.[1] Perhaps we need model rules for international enquiries analogous to the Model Rules of Arbitral Procedure. There may be cases in which such rules are not acceptable, or are departed from, for political reasons, but there is every advantage in there being a clear distinction between cases in which they are, and cases in which they are not, followed.

As the range of international executive and administrative action expands, due process and orderly procedure become no less necessary for sound and equitable administration than for wise deliberation and fair decision and enquiry. In respect of matters arising within the international public service, substantial provision for due process and orderly procedure has already been made by the adoption of staff regulations and similar instruments and the establishment of international administrative tribunals, one of the primary functions of which is to ensure due process and orderly procedure in all staff matters.[2] No comparable arrangements yet exist to ensure due process in in the exercise of international executive or administrative powers which may affect third-party interests; as such powers become increasingly significant, the development as a counterpart to international immunities of international procedures of redress against decisions of international organs which materialise in executive or administrative action

[1] Jenks, C. Wilfred, 'The International Protection of Trade Union Rights', in Evan Luard (ed.) *The International Protection of Human Rights*, pp. 239–246.

[2] Jenks, C. Wilfred, *The Proper Law of International Organisations*, especially pp. 70–84.

affecting third-party interests may become a matter of great importance.[1]

Due process and orderly procedure are the essence of civilised government and the world community will be unable to attain the goals which we have postulated for creative effort unless it makes a reality of them in every phase of its activities, in the discharge by representative bodies of such functions as formulating policy and taking decisions of a legislative character, in the fulfilment of judicial and quasi-judicial responsibilities and the conduct of enquiries into controversial matters, and in the performance of the executive and administrative tasks which are increasingly being entrusted to the community and its organs, agencies, and agents.

7. The processes of community decision

The processes of community decision are the crux of the problem of more effective world organisation. The transition from the interplay of forces which is the substitute for, rather than the equivalent of, a process of decision in a decentralised society of States to a formal procedure whereby particular questions are decided in a particular way by an organ of the community, represents a decisive stage in institutional development. 'There is no more difficult problem confronting international organisations today than that of evolving modes of taking important decisions which command general respect and give such decisions the weight necessary to make them effective in practice.'[2] Unanimity, even unanimity tempered by constitutional convention, is now discredited as a mode of taking international decisions; though not completely obsolete, it is no longer usual and cannot afford a workable basis for any new developments of importance in world organisation. The veto, though less unreasonable in concept and as a stage in historical development than its bad name suggests, likewise affords no solution for our present and prospective dilemmas. Weighted voting, familiar today chiefly in the financial agencies, in certain commodity councils and in certain European bodies, may have further applications in special contexts, but is unlikely to afford a solution in any unforeseeable future for the problem of existing or projected world organisations with general responsibilities. 'Where an organisation has a wide range of

---

[1] Jenks, C. Wilfred, *International Immunities*, pp. 161–165.

[2] Jenks, C. Wilfred, 'Unanimity, The Veto, Weighted Voting, Special and Simple Majorities and Consensus as Modes of Decision in International Organisations', in *Cambridge Essays in International Law: Essays in Honour of Lord McNair*, pp. 48–63, where I have discussed the matter more fully.

responsibilities, the factors to be taken into account in assessing the relative interest of its Members either in its work as a whole or in particular decisions are likely to be too varied and imponderable and the relative weight to be attached to the different factors is likely to be the subject of acute controversy.'[1] Contemporary international organisation is therefore based increasingly on the majority principle, a two-thirds or other specially calculated majority being required for certain matters, and other matters being determined by a simple majority. On balance this represents a great, but not an unqualified, gain; it liberates creative initiative from the paralysis which the requirements of unanimity and the veto are so liable to involve; but the possibility of a majority decision can be heady wine to the uninitated. When 'voting tends to become a substitute for negotiation rather than a measure of the amount of agreement reached or a final resort when negotiation fails',[2] parliamentary manipulation within international bodies over-reaches itself; it does not afford an effective substitute for diplomacy because only diplomacy can evolve the consensus without which the decision taken is unlikely to be effectively implemented by those whose cooperation is necessary for its implementation. A growing appreciation of this element in the problem has attracted widespread attention to the desirability, particularly in matters relating to trade and development, of institutional arrangements to facilitate a wider consensus, based on a fuller understanding of conflicting views and genuine negotiation, before matters are submitted for a simulacrum of decision by a majority vote. How clear the trend in this direction will be, and what measure of success it will attain, remain uncertain. The creative imagination may have an important part to play in devising procedures which place a premium upon securing general agreement without involving the potential paralysis of the unanimity rule or the veto. 'Whatever can be done to institutionalize the provision of opportunities for expanding the scope for reasonableness may represent the most important contribution that can be made in the immediate future to resolving the problem of how international decisions should be taken.'[3]

Effectiveness in action is the primary test of processes of community decision. Until the world community can secure the effective implementation of its decisions, its processes of community decision will be at best embryonic in character. Complex as is the problem of securing

---

[1] Jenks, C. Wilfred, 'Some Constitutional Problems of International Organisations', *British Year Book of International Law*, Vol. 22, 1945, pp. 41–42.

[2] Jenks, C. Wilfred, *The Common Law of Mankind*, p. 56.

[3] Jenks, C. Wilfred, in *Cambridge Essays in International Law*, p. 63.

compliance with international judicial decisions and arbitral awards,[1] the development of techniques of international executive action presents a range of difficulties perhaps even wider. The question arises in every sphere of public policy, from military action in defence of peace and security, through the broad expanses of economic policy, and the protection of human rights, to the implementation of uniform international regulations in the most technical fields. The development of executive responsibility and action on an international scale may take different forms in different areas of policy and administrative responsibility, but some of the indispensable elements of progress common to every sphere of policy are already clear. The effective implementation of community decisions involves the exclusive responsibility to the community of its agents, finance, and the freedom and independence of the organs and instrumentalities of the community from legislative or executive control or interference by individual governments acting in their own national interest.

8. The public service of mankind

The future of the world community as an effective instrument of government presupposes the exclusive responsibility to the community of its agents.[2] I may perhaps quote from a memorandum of mine written in 1945 and communicated to a number of the delegations at the San Francisco Conference which formulated the Charter of the United Nations:

> Experience has shown that the effectiveness of international secretariats depends largely on the extent to which they are genuinely international in character and consist of persons whose sole allegiance is to the international organisation which they serve. There is a clear-cut functional incompatibility between the international duties of the officials of such secretariats and the responsibility for upholding the national interests and policies of the countries of which they are nationals, and it is desirable that this incompatibility of function should be explicitly recognised by definite rules which are binding on officials and governments alike. A recognition of the importance of the matter born of a

---

[1] Pp. 160–161 above.

[2] There is now an extensive literature on the subject; see the comprehensive but by no means complete bibliography in Bedjaoui, Mohammed, *Fonction Publique Internationale et Influences Nationales*; Basdevant, Suzanne (now Mme Bastid), *Les fonctionnaires internationaux*, remains an important pioneer work.

> decade of experience led the Assembly of the League of Nations to require all League officials to make a solemn declaration that they would discharge their functions and regulate their conduct with the interests of the League alone in view, and would not seek or receive instructions from any government or other authority external to the League. League experience showed these arrangements to be seriously defective in that under them the obligation of officials to exercise the functions entrusted to them with the interests of the League alone in view was not paralleled by any corresponding explicit obligation of the governments concerned not to seek to influence their nationals in the discharge of international duties.[1]

The concept was embodied in the Charter, as it had already been embodied on the initiative of the I.L.O. in the constitutions of F.A.O., the Fund and the Bank, and thereafter it became a common form provision of the constitutions of new international agencies. It is now rightly regarded as a vital element in the constitutional structure of the world community, made still more vital by the unprecedented development of the diplomatic and executive responsibilities of the Secretary-General of the United Nations.

These responsibilities are, as was pointed out by Dag Hammarskjöld, 'a reflection, in some measure of the American political system, which places authority in a chief executive officer who is not simply subordinated to the legislative organs but who is constitutionally responsible alone for the execution of legislation and in some respects for carrying out the authority derived from the constitutional instrument directly'.[2] The viability of this concept, which is but one of the possible types of relationship between the chief executive officer of an international organisation and its representative organs,[3] still remains debatable, but the 'original idea of a dedicated international civil service responsible only to the organisation in the performance of its duties and protected insofar as possible from the inevitable pressures of national governments'[4] is independent of any particular concept of the most appropriate relationship between the chief executive officer and the

---

[1] Jenks, C. Wilfred, 'Some Comments on the Dumbarton Oaks Proposals', 1945, quoted in *The Proper Law of International Organisations*, pp. 28–29.

[2] 'The International Civil Servant in Law and Fact', reprinted in *Servant of Peace*, p. 336.

[3] Cf. Jenks, C. Wilfred, 'Some Constitutional Problems of International Organisations', in *British Year Book of International Law*, Vol. 22, 1945, at pp. 42–44.

[4] Hammarskjöld, op. cit., p. 342.

representative organs. Whatever form that relationship may take 'the chief executive of a world institution must . . . assume the duty of systematically presenting the challenge of a world outlook to policy-making bodies consisting of members whose responsibilities are likely to be primarily national and it will fall to him to defend the decisions of these bodies if they are questioned and to implement them insofar as their execution is a matter for international rather than national action'.[1] This concept of his responsibility is not a recent accretion to the international tradition; it is essentially the legacy of Albert Thomas, the first Director of the International Labour Office.[2]

The principle of an independent service has, of course, been challenged, and not from one quarter alone; it presupposes that 'anyone of integrity, not subjected to undue pressures, can, regardless of his own views, readily act in an exclusively international spirit and can be guided in his actions on behalf of the Organisation solely by its interests and principles, and by the instructions of its organs';[3] but the principle has survived, strengthened, the successive challenges offered to it. To switch from an international to an intergovernmental secretariat would, and not merely 'might well' as Dag Hammarskjöld said, 'prove to be the Munich of international co-operation'.[4] We should be reverting from the concept of a world public service to that of recording the precarious dealings of governments with one another. The danger constantly recurs in new and subtle forms but the provisions of the Charter have been an effective rallying point against any overt regression in the matter. The writing into the Charter of the twin principles of the exclusive loyalty of the international service to the community and the obligation of governments to respect that exclusive loyalty is therefore a striking illustration of the contribution which the creative imagination can make to strengthening the constitutional structure of the world community.

9. The sinews of peace

Ample and assured financial resources are the sinews of peace no less than of war. The creation of a reliable fiscal system is the central problem of good government. The power of the purse is one of the continuing

---

[1] Jenks, C. Wilfred, 'Some Problems of an International Civil Service', *Public Administration Review*, Vol. III, No. 2, Spring 1943, pp. 93–105.

[2] Phelan, Edward J., *Yes and Albert Thomas.*

[3] Hammarskjöld, op. cit., p. 369.

[4] 'The International Civil Servant in Law and Fact', reprinted in *Servant of Peace*, at p. 349.

themes of constitutional history in every country with a significant constitutional history. No competent student of federalism would fail to include the financial basis and structure of the federal system under investigation among the main factors determining its strength or weakness.[1] Only recently has there been any similar recognition by scholars of the homely truth so long familiar to international civil servants that finance is as much the crux of world organisation as of good government everywhere.[2] Until the *Certain Expenses of the United Nations Case*[3] in 1962 the financing of international institutions remained beyond the periphery of the recognised preoccupations of international lawyers.

Throughout the League of Nations period financial stringency was a continuing limiting factor of policy. There was a comprehensive budget (averaging 27 million gold francs or 5·4 million dollars and never exceeding 33·75 million gold francs or approximately 6·75 million dollars) for all League activities, including the Permanent Court of International Justice and the International Labour Organisation; this budget required the unanimous approval of the Assembly of the League; there was no prescribed date by which contributions became due and no sanction for financial default; the funds of the League remained, with the exception of certain reserves partly converted into real estate, the property of its Members, who were entitled to surpluses and responsible for deficits; League funds were generally recognised to be tax exempt but there was no effective guarantee of their convertibility or mobility. In retrospect there will be little or no dissent from the view that the League was financially starved throughout its history. These institutional weaknesses were, however, so offset by brilliant financial management that, once the initial difficulties had been overcome, the League was, on the scale of its authorised operations, financially strong and continued to meet its obligations during the Second World War. It was nevertheless apparent that when the international system came to be reconstructed on a more ambitious basis its financial arrangements would have to be radically recast.[4]

The new arrangements as conceived in the nineteen-forties had four

---

[1] See, for instance, Adarkar, B. P., *The Principles and Problems of Federal Finance*; Shirras, G. F., *Federal Finance in Peace and War*, and see Wheare, K. C., *Federal Government*, pp. 97–125; the literature on the subject for particular federations constitutes a library.

[2] Nicholas, Calvin J., *Financing the United Nations: Problems and Prospects*; Singer, J. David, *Financing International Organisations*; Stoessinger, John G. and Associates, *Financing the United Nations System*; *Institut Royal des Relations Internationales, Brussels, Les Difficultés Financières des Nations Unies et Les Obligations des Etats Membres.*

[3] *I.C.J. Reports*, 1962, pp. 151–308.

[4] Jenks, C. Wilfred, 'Some Legal Problems of the Financing of International Institutions', *Transactions of the Grotius Society*, Vol. 28, pp. 87–132.

distinctive features. The League system of a consolidated budget was replaced by the autonomous financing of the United Nations and the various specialised agencies within a general framework for comprehensive review by the General Assembly established by the Charter. A two-thirds majority replaced unanimity as the normal method of voting international budgets. As a sanction for financial default provision for the suspension of the voting privileges of States more than two years in arrear was included in the Charter and, with variations, the constitutions of a number of the specialised agencies. The financial agencies, but only the financial agencies, of the United Nations system were financed by the provision of capital resources. To these arrangements the 'fifties added a major new source of finance and a major problem: voluntary funds constituted by national pledges in lieu of international assessment as the source of the greatly expanded resources necessary to finance large-scale operational programmes of aid to developing countries; and the problem of financing peace and security operations involving the maintenance of substantial international forces.

These new arrangements have permitted the financing of international action on an incomparably larger scale than the old, but have thrown new problems into sharp relief. Decentralised financing was the only practicable arrangement in a scheme of world organisation as complex and experimental as the United Nations system, but it involves a continuing danger that widely divergent standards of financial responsibility and evaluation of the availability of resources in relation to needs may prevail in different agencies and sectors of policy. Majority voting, with provision for two-thirds or some other specially calculated majority, was likewise the only practicable alternative to the paralysis which a requirement of unanimous approval would represent under present and prospective conditions, but it involves a continuing danger that there may be no relationship between voting on financial matters and prospective financial liability and responsibility; the danger is the greater because the apportionment of expenses as well as the approval of estimates are decided by majority voting; it is therefore open to the majority to increase the estimates while reducing its own share of the burden. The financing of aid programmes by pledges rather than assessment made possible the rapid expansion of these programmes but left their future precarious and their long-term effect on the administrative and financial stability of the organisations administering them conjectural. The scale, unpredictability and urgency of the financial consequences of peace-keeping operations hardened the resistance to payment for such operations of those who questioned the authority with which they were undertaken or were opposed to them on political grounds. It was apparent by the early 'sixties that there would be major long-term problems, and by 1964 their interaction provoked a major crisis which the opinion of the International Court, in the *Certain Expenses of the United Nations Case*,[1] that the expenditures of the United Nations operations in the Congo and the operations of the United Nations Emergency Force in the Middle East were 'expenses of the Organisation' within the meaning of the Charter, failed to avert or resolve. No provision had been made (except in the I.L.O.) for the automatic operation of the sanction of the suspension of voting privileges provided for in the Charter, and in these circumstances the applicability and application of the sanction itself became a political issue which paralysed the General Assembly. The solution found for the crisis after twelve months of negotiation, in September 1965, left grave uncertainty whether the sanction provided for in the Charter can be effectively invoked in the future and was accompanied by statements which could be interpreted as impairing or qualifying the fundamental concept of the legal obligation of each Member to bear its share of the expenses of the United Nations as apportioned by the General Assembly. In the course of the crisis the precarious nature of pledges to the voluntary aid funds became transparent, and the possibility of maintaining or undertaking operations required for the discharge of the primary responsibility of the United Nations for the maintenance of peace and security ceased to be a function of the need for such operations as determined by the Security Council or the General Assembly and became a function of the willingness of the States most immediately concerned to pay for them.

The reconstruction of the finances of the United Nations system has therefore become of vital long-term importance for the whole future of world organisation. What contribution can the creative imagination, using legal skill to give institutional expression to the financial policies of a statesmanship seeking to endow the world community with more assured resources adequate to its responsibilities, make to this end? Clearly it can achieve little or nothing unless statesmanship wills the end and is prepared to make available the resources necessary to accomplish it. It is all too true that 'the financial problem of the United Nations is, in reality, a political problem' and that 'the financial crisis is first a political crisis over the political role the United Nations is to play in the national policies of its member States' and only secondarily 'a crisis over the financial burdens of membership in the United Nations'.[2]

---

[1] *I.C.J. Reports*, 1962, pp. 151–308.

[2] Stoessinger, John G. and Associates, *Financing the United Nations System*, p. 3.

It involves the whole question of the extent of the executive role of the United Nations in both the political-security and the economic-social areas and the related questions of the direction and control of United Nations executive operations.

No plan for a financially independent United Nations system could eliminate the political problem and dilemma in the foreseeable future. The vision of the world community levying its own taxes, and financing its executive operations from its own revenue producing resources, may be both less fanciful and less distant than practical men are apt to suppose, but it remains, unless some unexpected opportunity passes within our grasp, a vision of the longer rather than the more immediate future. The many suggestions of this nature which have been made should not, however, be dismissed as unrelated to practical realities. They should be regarded as possibilities of experiment to be tested whenever opportunities allow. The expansion of income from United Nations services, United Nations levies on international activities and transactions, the allocation to the United Nations of new revenue producing resources, and the mobilisation of private charity for United Nations humanitarian programmes[1] are all possibilities which should be put to the test of attempting to make institutional provision for them in appropriate contexts as circumstances permit. Only practical experience can determine how much they can ultimately contribute to the integration and long-term financing of the world community. How far, for what purposes and on what scale such devices are acceptable will depend primarily on the measure and certainty of consensus which exists on the matters of policy at stake and the extent to which there are other claims upon the potential revenue in issue. How far they are profitable will depend on their administrative feasibility, the prospective revenue involved, the cost-revenue ratio and, in the case of revenue from the exploitation of resources, the capital expenditure required.

There have been some interesting experiments along these lines over an extended period in the pre-1914 public international unions, in League of Nations days, and within the United Nations system, but mostly on a small, indeed an almost insignificant, scale. The mobilisation of private charity has yielded substantial resources for refugees, relief from natural disaster and, in particular, children, but even in these cases the resources so raised have been only a fraction of the contributions made by governments in fulfilment of voluntary pledges. Income from services and levies have yielded little more than miscellaneous

[1] For some of the various possibilities see Jenks, op. cit., 1942, pp. 92–94 and 125 and Stoessinger and Associates, op. cit., 1964, pp. 249–292.

receipts, the chief exception being the Suez Canal Clearance Surcharge Scheme whereby the cost of clearing the canal after the military operations of 1956 was charged to users of the canal.[1] A system of revenue producing charges provided for in the Statute of the International Atomic Energy Agency has not been practically effective in the early years of the Agency.[2] In the European Communities one bold experiment has been conspicuously successful. The European Coal and Steel Community finances its operations by an annual levy on coal and steel enterprises subject to its jurisdiction supplemented by borrowing on the security of a pledge in the hands of the Bank for International Settlements for the benefit of the lenders. Neither Euratom nor the European Economic Community has a comparable financial autonomy, though the Euratom Treaty envisages the possibility of introducing a similar levy by unanimous consent and the Common Market Treaty provides for a study of the conditions under which contributions from member States might be replaced by other revenues such as receipts from a common customs tariff. The experimental approach to these longer-range possibilities must not be abandoned, but presupposes a long view.

Somewhat more conventional devices may yield more immediately tangible, but still limited, results. The constitution by government quotas or subscription of an initial capital fund has been the basis of the successful operations of the International Monetary Fund and of the International Bank for Reconstruction and Development and its affiliates. For certain contingent expenditure, such as that of a compensatory finance scheme to offset export shortfalls, commitments largely in the form of immediately negotiable promisory notes may be appropriate and adequate. For certain activities such as education and training institutes, endowment funds may be possible, though experience in the matter has not been entirely reassuring. The right of international organisations to appropriate to reserve miscellaneous income and interest upon current balances may in time permit the building up of significant reserves.

The problem of sanctions for financial default covers a wide spectrum of possibilities ranging from the immediate through the hypothetical to the conceivable but clearly remote. The practice of the Universal Postal Union and International Telecommunication Union of charging interest upon late payment has much to commend it. The withholding of specified services from States in default may be reasonable and effective. The sanction of the disqualification from voting of States in arrear

[1] Stoessinger and Associates, op. cit., pp. 275–278.

[2] Ibid., pp. 231–234.

remains in the Charter and the constitutions of the specialised agencies and cannot be assumed to have been abrogated or obsolete, though the conditions under which it can be applied in the future will clearly need much careful consideration. Nor should we rule out the long-range possibility that financial obligations to the world community should be subject to recovery by the adaptation to international relations of one of the oldest of legal procedures, the procedure of attaching assets, wherever they may be found and despite any plea of sovereign immunity, to secure the payment of debts.[1] Long-range thinking on all these matters remains vital, but cannot be relied upon to resolve the immediate problems. Their solution presupposes five conditions.

We must at all costs maintain the principle that expenses of the United Nations apportioned by the General Assembly are a binding legal obligation of member States; if this principle is eroded there is no foundation on which the world community can develop its financial system.

We must resist the temptation to attempt to correct the anomalies in the budgetary patterns and practices of the different specialised agencies by seeking a consolidated budget; there is no unequivocal obligation in the Charter to bear apportioned shares of such a budget and until the world community has the working financial system which it so conspicuously lacks it is premature and unwise to entrust the future of international cooperation in all fields to a budgetary system which affords no assurance of making adequate provision for the maintenance of essential world services.

We must devise new financial procedures which promote and so far as possible achieve a consensus between those who control the votes and those who control the funds. The International Labour Organisation was confronted with an analogous problem when it assumed direct responsibility for its finances on the dissolution of the League of Nations. In both the Governing Body and the Conference governments control only half the votes but the ultimate responsibility for finance necessarily rests with the governments which bear the expenses of the Organisation. To reconcile these factors in the position the amendment to the Constitution establishing an autonomous budgetary procedure for the Organisation provides that the arrangements for the approval, allocation and collection of the budget of the Organisation shall be determined by the Conference by a two-thirds majority and shall provide for the approval of the budget and of the arrangements for the allocation of expenses among the Members of the Organisation by a committee of government representatives; the approved arrangements provide that

---

[1] Jenks, op. cit., p. 113.

the budget shall be adopted in the first instance by the Governing Body in which the States of chief industrial importance, which are the largest contributors, are strongly and permanently represented. The outcome has been that the International Labour Organisation has in practice something approximating to a consensus budget. An analogous device, including at some appropriate stage a committee in which there is some relationship between voting power and financial liability, not as a substitute for but as a counterweight to a two-thirds majority vote in the General Assembly, might afford a means of achieving the fuller consensus between those who control the votes and those who control the funds without which the legal obligation to pay may become unenforceable in practice.

We must devise some means of placing the operational programme of the United Nations system in the economic-social area on a less precarious basis than that of voluntary annual pledges with 40 per cent of the income dependent on the pledge of one State; as a minimum precaution against utter disaster, all sizeable projects should be funded for their full duration before they are undertaken, in accordance with the practice established by the United Nations Special Fund at the instance of Mr. Paul Hoffman.

We must devise some wisely acceptable method of constituting a Peace and Security Fund which makes it possible to finance emergency political-security expenditures on a substantial scale without delay and without disruption of the financial equilibrium of the United Nations system; in this context the close relationship of finance and policy will be a continuing source of special difficulty.

To these manifold tasks the creative imagination can make a twofold contribution, an imaginative understanding of the issues of long-range policy involved and institutional dexterity in evolving devices and procedures to make accepted policy effective.

10. The legal régime of world services

The legal régime of world services is an important further element in their freedom and independence from national control or interference. The elements of this régime which have been most clearly and fully defined thus far are the status and immunities of international organisations and their agents.

In League of Nations days the position was profoundly unsatisfactory.[1] The Covenant provided that the representatives of the League and

[1] Hill, Martin, *Immunities and Privileges of International Officials, The Experience of the League of Nations.*

officials of the League when engaged on the business of the League should enjoy diplomatic privileges and immunities and that the buildings and other property occupied by the League or its officials or by representatives attending its meetings should be inviolable. Apart from the conclusion of a *modus vivendi* with Switzerland and occasional *ad hoc* arrangements elsewhere, no attempt was made to spell out from these pointers (for they were pointers rather than principles) a systematic body of rules, applicable everywhere, reflecting the fundamental requirements of effective international cooperation. Sir Cecil Hurst,[1] Åke Hammarskjöld,[2] Charles De Visscher[3] and others displayed imaginative insight in important contributions to the clarification of the basic principles involved, but no significant progress was made in expressing these principles in widely accepted legal instruments. Save as regards the inviolability of 'buildings and other property' the League as such had, apart from the special arrangements made in Switzerland, no recognised legal personality, either for international purposes or in municipal law, and no clear-cut immunity; even its immunity from suit derived from the diplomatic privileges and immunities of its officials. In August 1940 the I.L.O., having decided as a matter of policy to maintain its activities to the fullest possible extent and therefore concerned to maintain the freedom of its lines of communication, transferred to Canada a working centre which was in effect its temporary operational headquarters. At a time when the United States, all of the American republics and a number of European and other countries which were Members of the I.L.O. still remained neutral, it was a matter of immediate political importance to ensure and emphasise that this transfer of the effective centre of operations to belligerent territory did not impair the independent international status of the I.L.O. This was the origin of the arrangements defining and guaranteeing the international status of the I.L.O. in wartime Canada which owed much to the political imagination and understanding of the long-range implications of the matter shown by Prime Minister Mackenzie King and his advisers, notably Dr. O. D. Skelton, Mr. Norman A. Robertson and Mr. John Read. The post-war régime of international immunities grew directly out of this wartime experience of the I.L.O. which was consciously taken by the architects of the postwar arrangements as a point of departure. The law on the matter no longer consists primarily of a general principle resting

[1] *International Law – The Collected Papers of Sir Cecil Hurst*, pp. 115–126.

[2] 'Les immunités des personnes investées de fonctions internationales', *Recueil des Cours de l'Académie de Droit international*, Vol. 56 (1936 (II)), pp. 110–209.

[3] *Annuaire de l'Institut de Droit International*, Vol. 31, 1924, pp. 1–17 and 179–180.

on the questionable analogy of diplomatic immunities; it has become a complex body of rules set forth in detail in constitutional instruments, conventions, agreements, statutes and regulations.[1]

The corporate personality of international organisations has now been unequivocally established. The question remained obscure and debatable until provisions on the subject were included, from 1944 onwards, in the Charter of the United Nations and the Constitutions of the specialised agencies; a number of these provisions were equivocal or logically defective[2] but further controversy was set at rest by the inclusion in the Conventions on the Privileges and Immunities of the United Nations and the Specialised Agencies respectively of specific provisions that each of the organisations to which they apply enjoys 'juridical personality', including 'the capacity to contract, to acquire and dispose of immoveable and moveable property, and to institute legal proceedings'; similar action has since been taken in respect of most of the regional organisations. The clear recognition of the corporate personality of international organisations is one of the great imaginative steps forward in the transformation of the law of nations from a law 'between States only and exclusively'[3] into a common law of mankind giving expression to the life of 'the great community, the universal commonwealth of the world'.[4]

Some of the implications of the corporate personality of international organisations are already generally acknowledged.[5] Their right to conclude with States, and with each other, agreements in the nature of treaties, and their enjoyment of the passive and (more recently) the active right of legation, are now a commonplace. The right of the United Nations to espouse an international claim was upheld by the imaginative and, on the basic issue, unanimous decision of the International Court of Justice in the *Reparation for Injuries Suffered in the Service of the United Nations Case*.[6] There remain other matters in respect of which an equally imaginative approach has still been lacking. International organisations still have no general *locus standi in judicio* before international courts and tribunals, though special arrangements have

---

[1] I have described and discussed the process of development in *International Immunities*.

[2] Jenks, C. Wilfred, 'The Legal Personality of International Organisations', in *British Year Book of International Law*, Vol. 22, 1945, pp. 267–275.

[3] Oppenheim, *International Law*, Vol. I, 1st ed., p. 340.

[4] Phillimore, *Commentaries upon International Law*, Vol. II, 3rd ed., p. 1.

[5] Weizberg, Guenther, *The International Status of the United Nations*, with a useful but not exhaustive bibliography at pp. 212–219.

[6] *I.C.J. Reports*, 1949, pp. 174–219.

been made in certain cases and inventive ingenuity has devised a variety of ways in which an international organisation can be made a party to such proceedings, including technically advisory proceedings in the International Court of Justice, in substance though not in form.[1] Only gradually is provision being made in general international conventions for the application to international organisations of the benefit and burden of their provisions, and satisfactory procedural arrangements for the purpose of enabling international organisations to accept the obligations of such conventions and acquire clearly vested rights thereunder remain to be elaborated. The Universal Copyright Convention of 1952, and the International Convention for the Protection of Industrial Property of 1958, for instance, contain provisions illustrative of the tendency to take account in general conventions of the possible incidence of the régime created thereby on international organisations,[2] but no provision whereby international organisations concerned can become in effect a party to the Convention. The provisions of the Convention on the Privileges and Immunities of the Specialised Agencies, which is subject to accession by States and acceptance by specialised agencies, may contain some of the elements of a possible technique for this purpose.

The developments which have occurred in regard to international immunities were at the outset greatly facilitated by the formulation of certain guiding principles which are now generally accepted as the rationale of such immunities. These were formulated in an I.L.O. Memorandum of 1945 in three basic propositions, namely:

1. that international institutions should have a status which protects them against control or interference of any one government in the performance of functions for the effective discharge of which they are responsible to democratically constituted international bodies in which all the nations concerned are represented;
2. that no country should derive any national financial advantage by levying fiscal charges on common international funds;
3. that the International Labour Organisation (for which we may substitute any other international organisation the position of which we may be considering) should, as a collectivity of member States, be afforded the facilities for the conduct of its official business customarily extended to each other by its individual member States.

This thinking was institutional in character. It was not preoccupied

---

[1] Jenks, C. Wilfred, *The Prospects of International Adjudication*, pp. 139–148 and 185–224.

[2] Jenks, C. Wilfred, *The Proper Law of International Organisations*, pp. 190–191 and 197–198.

with the status, dignity or privileges of individuals, but with the elements of functional independence necessary to free international institutions from national control and to enable them to discharge their responsibilities impartially on behalf of all their members. 'Historically it derives from two main sources, the contribution made by diplomatic immunities to the conduct of diplomatic intercourse as an element in the peaceful relations of States and the writings and decisions of the great federalists, and notably of Hamilton and Marshall, on the arrangements necessary to give reasonable independence and authority to newly created federal instrumentalities'.[1] To these main sources the analogies of parliament and judicial immunities have made a further contribution. In the light of these imaginative propositions, completed by the recognition that immunities must operate within the law and that differences between governments and international organisations concerning the interpretation or application of immunities agreements should be justiciable by some organised procedure, wide agreement has been reached on the immunities to be conferred on international organisations and various classes of persons connected therewith. The immunities granted to organisations include jurisdictional immunity, inviolability of premises, the protection of property and assets, the inviolability of archives, currency immunities and facilities, fiscal immunities, and immunities in respect of communications. The general principle that the international immunities of international judges and international officials are applicable in relation to the State of which the judge or official is a national is no longer contested in respect of their official acts, though the extent to which it has a wider application remains a matter of controversy (notably in respect of jurisdictional immunity for private acts, taxation and military services). A balanced evaluation of international immunities requires an imaginative grasp of their basic institutional function and the importance of that function at the present stage of world organisation:

> The basic function of international immunities is to bridle the sovereignty of States in their treatment of international organisations. This bridling of sovereignty is as much in the interest of States as in that of international organisations. While it debars each State from illicit interference, it also protects it from illicit interference by other States. It represents indeed an indispensable guarantee to each member State that the organisation will not become, by means of pressure and constraint

[1] Jenks, C. Wilfred, *International Immunities*, pp. 17–18.

which are not fully apparent and over which there is therefore no possibility of control, an instrument of the policy of other States directed against its own policy and interests, but will serve legally the common interest as determined by the recognised constitutional processes of the organisation.[1]

The desire to coordinate the action taken to define the immunities of a whole series of independent organisations in such a manner as to reconcile the desirability of reasonable uniformity with the possibility that the functional needs of different organisations might vary presented a further challenge to the creative imagination. The solution adopted, which owes much to the inventive ingenuity of Sir Eric Beckett, then Legal Adviser of the British Foreign Office, was the negotiation of a Convention on the Privileges and Immunities of the Specialised Agencies consisting of standard clauses approved by the General Assembly with an annex for each of the agencies to which the Convention becomes applicable; the annexes, which may modify the standard clauses, are recommended in draft by the General Assembly (or in the case of new agencies, by the Economic and Social Council) but subject to variation by the agency concerned in accordance with its constitutional procedure. This ingenious innovation succeeded in reconciling the conflicting claims of uniformity and diversity, of coordination and autonomy, by means of a new type of instrument to which, by different procedures, governments and international organisations both become parties.

In the recognition of corporate personality, the clarification of its implications for the rights and obligations of international organisations as international persons, and the definition of international immunities, great progress has been made. The substantive law governing many of the transactions of international organisations remains less determinate. 'Private international lawyers are apt to assume that the legal transactions of international organisations can be satisfactorily subsumed under existing concepts and rules of the conflict of laws. Administrative lawyers, particularly those trained in highly developed systems of municipal law, are apt to make the same assumption as regards the applicability to the administrative problems of international organisations of the established concepts and rules of developed municipal systems of administrative law'.[2] Both assumptions reveal a failure of imaginative insight, for the first seriously underestimates, while the second equally seriously overestimates, the progress achieved in the

---

[1] Jenks, C. Wilfred, *International Immunities*, p. 166.

[2] Jenks, C. Wilfred, *The Proper Law of International Organisations*, p. xxi.

development of a coherent body of law governing the legal transactions of international organisations. When broaching these matters 'we are not dealing with the clearly settled principles of an established legal system, but with experimental developments which have not yet passed beyond their infancy'.[1] In respect of a wide range of matters of property, contract, tort and procedure it has become necessary to rethink the whole question of the law applicable to the legal transactions of international organisations. The task calls for sustained imaginative insight of a high order.

11. The effectiveness of community decisions

A world public service of the highest integrity and competence, responsible to the world community alone, ample and assured financial resources, and a legal régime of world services which ensure their freedom of action and independence from national control or interference, are essential elements of the institutional structure of an effective world community; but these will be inadequate to secure effectiveness in action unless the community has at its disposal effective means of, and procedures for, securing respect for its policies and decisions. How are we to secure full faith and credit for, and full cooperation in the implementation of, international decisions?

Broadly speaking, international policies and decisions can be made effective in four different ways: by so involving national authorities in the process of international discussion and decision that they become the natural executing agencies of policies and decisions in framing which they have themselves participated; by the direct exercise of executive authority over matters within international control, or over which such control can be developed; by invoking a legal obligation of compliance by States with a decision relating to a matter within their executive authority; or by invoking a legal obligation of compliance by States with a decision involving changes in their internal legal order. These different types of decision involve widely different legal and practical problems, though the differences may be clearer conceptually than in the constantly shifting confusion of practical affairs. The organisation of a United Nations military force, for instance, as undertaken hitherto, normally involves national decisions for contributing forces, transport and supplies by the States participating in the establishment of the force, United Nations decisions determining the command structure and service regulations of the force, and obligations upon the contingents

---

[1] Jenks, C. Wilfred, *The Proper Law of International Organisations*, p. 255.

constituting the force to give effect to decisions concerning them. Financial sanctions against a State having resorted to force in violation of the Charter or against an illegal régime may involve measures taken in the spontaneous exercise of their national authority by States applying such sanctions, measures by an international body debarring access to resources under international control, and obligations by virtue of an international decision to take national measures some of which may be within the authority of the executive while others may involve legislative authorisation. The practical entanglement of such measures with each other does not affect the proposition that we must analyse clearly the differences of political and legal technique involved if we wish to be in a position to develop, deliberately and imaginatively, the potential elements of more effective executive action to implement the decisions of the world community.

The problem raises four large issues: how can States be equipped to fulfil more adequately and promptly their responsibilities as natural executing agencies of decisions in which they have participated; how can the range of rights, privileges, facilities and services which the community can withhold from its members as a sanction for its decisions be broadened, and how can they be effectively withheld without disruption of the community; how can the aid of municipal law and municipal courts be more fully enlisted to give effect to community decisions which create a legal obligation for a member in a matter within its executive authority; how, by some institutionalisation of the principle of the primacy of international law, or of the doctrine of incorporation, or otherwise, can community decisions be given the force of law when they involve a change in the municipal legal order? In respect of each of these issues there is much to be done to develop concepts, devices and procedures which make community decisions effective in action.

12. Law and institutional development

Our excursion into the architecture of society confirms the outcome of our review of the processes of growth and change in the law. Legal and institutional development presuppose and are complementary to each other; only by institutional development can the law be made effective as it is, or be developed into what it needs to become in order to play its part in attaining the goals which we have postulated for the community; only by developing the legal order can institutions be given the powers necessary for the effective discharge of the responsibilities entrusted to them, and subjected to the obligations necessary to discipline the exercise of those powers in the interest of the community. On the plane of thought the progress of the conceptual framework of world community presupposes the international lawyer becoming institutionally minded and the political thinker recognising to the full the place of law in the orderly government and peaceful progress of the community. On the plane of action the lawyer must become a statesman and the statesman a believer in the human values embodied in the rule of law; as statesman, the lawyer must be guided by the goals which we have postulated for creative effort; as believer in the human values embodied in the rule of law, the statesman must be guided by the concept of law as a positive instrument rather than a negative restraint, a means of doing things by cooperative action in a disciplined and equitable manner. The general trend is and must increasingly be from a decentralised to an institutionalised society, from a world of States to a world community. A marked degree of decentralisation will of course remain inevitable. The world is too big and too various to be governed as a single unit. Despite the increasing concentration of military power, and of some elements of economic power, political authority is very much more widely diffused than a generation ago. No one State or group of States with a common ideology or common interests will ever again be in a position, as Britain was for a century, to act as the world's policeman or the world's banker, still less to pass muster as the nucleus of the orderly government of mankind; Britain was able to fulfil these functions for so long because her position was at the time unique; the political evolution of mankind has now passed beyond the point at which any of the present or prospective super powers is or can ever hope to be in a similarly unique position; the age of empire has gone. World institutions will continue to grow in authority, but any attempt to oversimplify or overcentralise the structure of international society will inevitably sap their vitality; the world community will be both regionally and functionally decentralised. We are not in process of replacing a world of States by a world of men governed on the world scale as men are now governed within the State. What is in process of evolving is something infinitely more complex, a world community in which world organisations and services, States, and innumerable corporate bodies of an international character operating in accordance with international rules all play their parts in the service of man within a cooperative framework established and defined by the common law of mankind. We must therefore reconcile ourselves to the emerging picture of a complex institutional structure reflecting the complexity of the problems with which it must deal. The complexity of the institutional structure affects the prospects for the development of the law in many ways; in some ways it facilitates, while in others it complicates and may retard, such development; by affording ample scope for experiment it rightly places a premium on the bold initiative in specific fields so necessary for the attainment of the goals which we have postulated; by distributing authority, rightly and inevitably in view of the scale and complexity of the problems, it recognises the difficulty of giving a uniform and mandatory character to many of the new rules which will be required without a high degree of co-operation embracing a wide diversity of interests and institutional arrangements.

The general conclusion which emerges is much clearer than the modalities of its application; the progress of the law cannot be divorced from institutional developments, and neither can be achieved without a new creative spirit fully attuned to the needs and urgencies of a world which has become one. On the institutional side this involves a searching reappraisal of the whole structure of the community: the unequivocal establishment of its universality and permanence; a dynamic approach to the problem of its powers; a sophisticated view of the vital importance in so complex a picture of functional and regional action; respect for due process and the development of viable processes of community decision; a public service, financial resources and a legal régime which gives it the necessary independence of action; and effective means of, and procedures for, securing respect for its policies and decisions. Unless we can achieve these things on the institutional side, there will be no new world of law.

part IV

Creative scholarship and the law

Having defined the goals which we must seek by creative effort, examined the scope for creative purpose and experiment in respect of each of the major contributory influences to the growth of the law, reviewed the possible approaches to the problem of endowing international society with more effective legislative processes, and discussed some of the fundamentals of the more adequate institutional framework within which alone the law can play the part without which there can be no organised world community, we must now enter upon the final stage of our enquiry and explore the potential contribution of creative scholarship to the growth of world community. The ultimate responsibility for attaining our goals must necessarily rest with the world of action, but the world of thought can greatly facilitate or gravely embarrass the task of the world of action. The whole climate of the venture can be profoundly affected by the spirit in which creative scholarship envisages and discharges its responsibility. In a world which has become one there can be no ivory tower; scholarship must play an active part in building a new world of law or share in the responsibility for failure to achieve it.

12

Orthodoxy and vision

We must at this stage return briefly to our point of departure. Have we not departed too far from the conventional wisdom and sought too much of the law? Have we not forgotten that most respectable and respected of legal sayings, sanctioned by no less an authority than that of Maitland, that we saluted briefly at the outset of our enquiry: 'the lawyer must be orthodox otherwise he is no lawyer'.[1]

Orthodoxy and vision are clearly not twins, and are rarely regarded as first cousins; but it is for this reason that the offspring of their union have such noble vigour. The contrast appears less sharp if we visualise clearly the role which the vision of creative imagination is called upon to play. The creative imagination is not a refuge from reality, but a command of reality which rehabilitates the freedom of the human will; its office is to understand changing realities, to detect unsuspected relationships, to illuminate practice and precedent by principle, to perceive opportunities for decisive action while they can still be grasped, and to devise arrangements and procedures for giving practical expression to the values recognised by the law. In law, as in poetry, imagination never operates in a vacuum. 'Its stuff is always fact of some order somehow experienced; its product is that fact transmuted.'[2] Insistence on the role of the creative imagination in the law is not an alibi for 'rule scepticism' or 'fact scepticism'. We may say of the creative imagination as Cardozo said of the law of nature: 'it does not override human or positive law. It is the stuff out of which human or positive law is to be woven, when other sources fail.'[3] So understood, the creative imagination has played a vital role in every decisive crisis in the growth of the law. The contribution of Coke to the rule of law, of Nottingham to equity jurisprudence, of Mansfield to commercial law and Stowell to the law maritime, of Hamilton and Marshall to federalism, of Holmes, Brandeis and Cardozo to the judicial process in an age of social change, of Bentham to the

[1] *Collected Papers*, Vol. I, p. 491.

[2] Lowes, John Livingston, *The Road to Xanadu*, Chapter XXII, p. 427.

[3] *The Nature of the Judicial Process*, p. 132.

science of legislation and Thring, Ilbert and Ernst Freund to its craft, of Maine and Maitland himself to legal history, of Story and Westlake to the conflict of laws, of Francisco de Vittoria, Gentili and Grotius to the classical corpus of international law, were all outstanding achievements of the creative imagination fermenting the yeast of progress in a changing world.

In this perspective orthodoxy and vision are not competitors for the allegiance of the mind. Unless their mutually complementary nature is fully recognised, we are left with the bleak choice between an orthodoxy which is sterile and a vision which is a mirage. In partnership they can achieve what neither can achieve alone. A plea for faith and creative vision in the development of the law, in the renovation of its structure and techniques, and in giving imaginative and effective expression to the aspirations and priorities of our society therefore does not preclude the assurance which the orthodox will clearly require that the faith is not illusion, the vision not myopia, the imagination not hallucination. It is wholly reasonable for them to call for title-deeds of the faith and vision in the name of which I have presumed to plead that creative scholarship should give imaginative leadership in the future development of the law. We cannot find them in the law itself. We must look beyond the law to the fundamental values which shape the whole life of human society. Peace with justice, the dignity of man secured by respect for human rights and orderly social change, the promotion of the general welfare by achieving economic stability and growth, and the social discipline of science and technology are not postulates or axioms of law or even objectives of the legal system as a legal system. They are broad purposes, the fulfilment of which by the world community has become indispensable to the happiness of individual human lives in a world which has become one. We must seek in other studies the stimulus, and much of the know-how, for new development, and find its ultimate justification in reason and morality.

13

Law and other studies

Law, morals and politics are not autonomous provinces of the mind. They may be separable, and both clarity of thought and effectiveness in action may require that they should be separated, for purposes of analysis, but they are intertwined in operation and in the contemporary world are all profoundly affected by the impact of science and technology. 'When I emphasise the difference between law and morals', Holmes explained, 'I do so with reference to a single end, that of learning and understanding the law.'[1] Kelsen himself has told us in somewhat similar terms that the pure theory of law 'seeks to discover the nature of law itself, to determine its structure and its typical forms, independent of the changing context which it exhibits at different times and among different peoples'. He explains that 'as a theory, its sole purpose is to know its subject' and that 'it answers the question of what law is, not what it ought to be'.[2] It is, therefore, essentially an exercise in intellectual analysis, not a dynamic of legal development in a world of cataclysmic change, but an analytical abstraction as remote from as it is unconcerned with the constantly shifting welter of conflicting forces which constitutes social reality. In his later years Kelsen has been careful to add that the pure theory of law 'by no means denies the validity' of sociological jurisprudence. They operate on different planes. 'Sociological jurisprudence stands side by side with normative jurisprudence; neither is able to replace the other because each deals with different problems.'[3] But the clear distinction on which Kelsen insists between 'the science of law', 'the philosophy of justice' and 'the cognition of social reality'[4] belongs to the mind rather than to the world of affairs and men. As a practical matter, sound law, true morals and wise policy merge imperceptibly into each other and are shaped by a wide range of cultural, economic, psychological, and sociological considerations and

[1] 'The Path of the Law', in *Collected Legal Papers*, p. 120.

[2] 'The Pure Theory of Law and Analytical Jurisprudence', in *What is Justice?*, p. 266.

[3] Ibid., p. 269. [4] Ibid., p. 266.

influences. They owe much to history and even more to philosophy.

There is therefore abundant justification for the contemporary insistence that law must be studied in the context of society. There can be no rational dissent from the proposition in which Ehrlich summarised the whole thesis of the sociological school: 'the centre of gravity of legal development lies not in legislation, nor in juristic science, nor in judicial decision, but in society itself'.[1]

International law, in particular, must be studied in the context of the strains and stresses of contemporary international society.[2] The law of nations is not a self-contained and self-sustaining system of thought. As a framework for all human endeavour it must needs be a recapitulation of all human experience and a reflection of every human dilemma. Only by clearly separating the law from other disciplines for purposes of legal analysis can we determine, establish and maintain the binding force of legal principles and rules but the law must be studied in the context of the whole life of man in society. Only so can its development and the relationship of form to substance be understood and only so can a developing legal system be so fashioned and re-fashioned that it can be applied to changing circumstances and problems.

Such an approach is a necessary corollary of a dynamic concept of the part which the law should play in resolving our current problems. The vitality of the law draws sustenance from beyond the frontiers of the law itself. Roscoe Pound has once more given memorable expression to the essence of the matter:

> Growth in law takes place chiefly by assimilation and adaptation of materials drawn from other legal systems or from outside of the law.[3]

Vigorous growth presupposes ready access to all the resources of the human mind. Creative scholarship in the law is governed by the general laws of the art of thought. The legal imagination quickens in the same manner as the processes of scientific discovery and artistic creation. Newton and Darwin, Freud and Einstein did not create from nothingness; their creative originality did not consist in 'creating or originating a system of ideas out of nothing but rather out of the combination of well-established patterns of thought – by a process of cross fertilization, as it were'.[4] This they fully acknowledged. 'If', said Newton, 'I have been

---

[1] *Fundamental Principles of the Sociology of Law.*

[2] Visscher, Charles De, *Théories et réalités en Droit International Public.*

[3] *Law and Morals*, p. 32.

[4] Koestler, Arthur, *The Act of Creation*, pp. 121–177.

able to see farther than others it was because I stood on the shoulders of giants.' If there are now new opportunities for expanding the ambit of the law, they exist by reason of the changes which have occurred in its sociological foundations; we can take advantage of these opportunities because there were giants, from Grotius and his predecessors onwards to our immediate masters, on whose shoulders we can stand; to understand and exploit the changes which have created these opportunities our view must embrace a host of related disciplines.

For growth and change we must look both to 'other legal systems' and 'outside the law'.

The importance of this contribution of jurisprudence and comparative law to the process of growth we have already seen when discussing the concepts of law and sovereignty and the part played by general principles of law, and it has been implicit in our discussion of institutional development that the jurisprudential concepts and comparative analogies of public law may be particularly illuminating.

When we look beyond 'other legal systems' and begin to assimilate and adapt 'from outside the law' fundamental questions of legal method and the relationship of law to other studies and disciplines arise.

How can we draw most effectively on the full range of the social sciences for the purposes of the law?

The distinctive function of those of us whom Myres McDougal describes as decision makers 'is that of making choices, committing the community, between alternatives in action and of relating (those) choices to fundamental community policies'. As he acknowledges, the theory we require for this purpose 'is that which most fully assists in the economic prescription and application of community policy'. Reversing his conclusion I deduce from this that 'the theory which is appropriate for the conduct of international relations and law' may be quite different from the 'theory which is appropriate for the study of international relations'.[1] The sophistication of a theory of action is measured not by its subtlety but by its simplicity. The scholarship of the man of action will always have a different emphasis from, and a less refined presentation than, that of the pure scholar. It will glow with the impatience of his zest for action.

The interdisciplinary approach has become indispensable, but it involves a major dilemma. Interdisciplinary studies have not, by becoming a vogue, become a discipline, with an intellectual rigour or vigour comparable to that of the law. They lack, and are bound to lack, the

---

[1] 'Some Basic Theoretical Concept About International Law: A Policy Orientated Framework of Enquiry', *Conflict Resolution*, Vol. IV, No. 3, (September 1960), p. 338.

established standards of thoroughness and objectivity evolved by each of their contributory disciplines in the light of its own needs. The lack of such standards imports a pronounced element of chance and at times of whimsy into the venture upon new ground. The dangers are apparent. There is no new freedom, no broader opportunity, no promise of more effective impact on society, in becoming the captive audience of the Marxist superstition, the cult of power, the cant of moralising, or the hypnosis of sociological jargon.

The law is not to be dismissed as the product of economic forces, the expression of the economic structure of society and of the interests of its governing class. Economic forces play their part, and it is a major part, in shaping the law,[1] but they are also shaped by it, within a more complex interplay of historical, political, cultural, economic and social forces which mould and remould legal tradition and the economic organisation of society in the context of changing moral values and growing scientific and technological capabilities. As Eugene Rostow has so aptly said, 'our lives are dominated, for better or for worse, by ideas as well as by economic interests, technologies, and the impersonal tides of social change'[2] and 'the power of men's loyalty to their ideas is nowhere so visible as in the law'.[3] Our estimate of the law must not depreciate the extent to which it can and should play a positive role in this complex interplay of forces.

The leading economists, of both the liberal and the socialist schools, have indeed been the first to recognise the limitations of economic analysis and to call for a broad humanism in politics. It was Keynes who asserted that 'the economic problem is not – if we look into the future – the permanent problem of the human race'[4] and urged us not to 'overestimate the importance of the economic problem, or sacrifice to its supposed necessities other matters of greater and more permanent significance'.[5] It was Tawney who wrote that 'obsession by economic issues is as local and transitory as it is repulsive and disturbing' and that 'to future generations it will appear as pitiable as the obsession of the seventeenth century by religious quarrels appears today'.[6] Ours is

---

[1] See, for instance, Beard, Charles A., *An Economic Interpretation of the Constitution of the United States*, and Renner, Karl, *The Institutes of Private Law and Their Social Functions.*

[2] Rostow, Eugene, *The Sovereign Prerogatives: The Supreme Court and the Quest for Law*, p. 6.

[3] Ibid., p. 7.

[4] 'Economic Possibilities for our Grandchildren', in *Essays in Persuasion*, p. 366.

[5] Ibid., p. 373.

[6] Tawney, R. H., *The Acquisitive Society*, Chapter XI, last paragraph.

admittedly an age of economic tension and preoccupation, but we must not deduce the nature of the law from the nature of our present discontents. 'History', it has been said, 'is always, individually or collectively, a confrontation of the spirit of man with a choice', its real inevitability being 'the need to choose, not what is chosen'.[1]

Economic analysis has nevertheless a vital part to play in defining the problems with which the contemporary law must wrestle and developing the solutions for such problems which the law should seek to express in the form of legal rights, obligations and procedures. For the substance of the developing law of economic stability and growth we must look primarily to the economists, but at the stage at which economic policy requires for its effectiveness legal rights, obligations and procedures the economist must turn to the lawyer. Their partnership has already recast the law of international monetary policy and appears to be about to recast it further; it is in process of recasting the law relating to trade and investment; and it may be expected to operate increasingly over the whole field of international economic policy.

As law is more than economic forces, so it is also more than the margin of respectability conceded by power to the promptings of morality and humanity and the danger of retaliation. Morality and humanity apart, the *real politik* of scholarship is the least real of all policies; it tends to be proof of frustration rather than worldly wisdom. The relationship of law and power has always been the central problem of government. Pascal stated the principle in terms which have not been bettered: 'La justice sans la force est impuissante; la force sans la justice est tyrannique.'[2] Civilisation is a process of tempering power by law and enlisting it as the strong right arm of justice. This is no less true in the world community than in the city State. 'Power cannot be dissolved in law';[3] law cannot ignore or destroy power; it can and should seek to transmute power into 'a rational instrument to be used for desired and desirable ends';[4] in fine, the function of law in relation to power is to make power responsible. The facts of power are among the problems with which the law must wrestle; they are not a roadblock from which the law must ignominiously retreat. 'Power tends to corrupt, and absolute power corrupts absolutely';[5] it corrupts all things, beginning with the foundations of its own strength. History abounds with examples of the law proving more durable than the power which defied it.

---

[1] Post, Laurens van der, *Journey into Russia*, p. 323.

[2] *Pensées de Pascal*, Article VI, paragraph 8.

[3] Neumann, Franz, *The Democratic and the Authoritarian State*, p. 7.

[4] Ibid., p. 7. [5] Lord Acton in a letter to Mandell Creighton.

This general approach to the relationship of law and power is relevant to all of the major areas in which we have postulated goals for creative effort. In all of them the essence of the problem is to temper the exercise of power by the acceptance of responsibility and to ensure that responsible power is available to make responsible decisions effective. Peace with justice is a problem of making power responsible for ensuring that force is used only for purposes sanctioned by law in the common interest but is available to restrain unlawful recourse to force and to implement international decisions. Human rights is a problem of making the power of governments responsible to the governed in the interest of their freedom and giving the wider community of mankind power to protect those who are powerless to protect themselves. Economic stability and growth is a problem of qualifying unrestrained economic power by the recognition of a common responsibility for the common welfare and the resulting obligation of wealth and power to match their status and influence in the positive nature of their contribution to welfare. The social control of scientific and technological development is a problem of ensuring that the power which their knowledge and skill inevitably gives the scientific technocracy is held in check by a proper regard for broader and at times more human considerations.

When we pass from goals to methods of attaining them the relationship of law to power remains no less significant. A living law presupposes that power acknowledges its responsibility to respect the authority and dynamic vitality of a growing legal system and that sufficient power is available in the last resort to enforce that authority; without the acknowledgment of such a responsibility and the availability in the last resort of sufficient power to enforce it, the acceptance by the community necessary to the effectiveness of any legal system is lacking. The development of more effective international legislative processes presupposes some measure of delegation of power to the organs of the community. The institutional development of the world community poses at every stage problems of power and of making power responsible; of vesting power effectively in the community and its organs and of providing guarantees to ensure that the power so vested is used responsibly.

No realistic approach to a new world of law can ignore power any more than it can ignore economic forces, but an approach mesmerised by pride of, or fear for, power cannot come to grips with the crucial problem of the role of law in making power responsible. There is no more place for the cult of power in a sophisticated philosophy of international politics than there is in any rational theory of the State. The State exists to replace arbitrary power by social discipline and becomes a civilised State as it fulfils this function; the world community is being created to replace arbitrary power by social discipline on the world scale, and will become real as it achieves this purpose.

The ethical foundations of the law are a fundamental matter to which we must soon pay special attention,[1] but there is a gulf between morality and moralising. Morality is a sense of obligation addressed primarily to one's own conscience, moralising a practice of finding self-satisfaction in a sense of one's own virtue. The wellsprings of the creative imagination are reason and morality. Moralising inhibits the creative imagination by erecting barriers to an understanding transcending cultural differences. There is no greater impediment to virtue than a consciousness of virtue. This is not a proposition of higher morality remote from the world of politics. It is the first principle of successful diplomacy. As such it has a direct bearing on the prospect of bringing conflicting cultures and ideologies within the framework of a commonly accepted rule of law.

Sociology is the newest, the most tentative, and the least well-defined of the social sciences. Despite the advances of the last thirty years it is still difficult to proceed far in sociological discussion 'without becoming involved in the abundant quarrels of its students over its definition and the limits of its subject-matter'.[2] While sociology remains at this stage of development, it is inevitable that its contribution to the law, while vital, should still be a matter of debate and experiment. There are, as Cardozo has it, 'vogues and fashions in jurisprudence as in literature and art and dress'.[3] They appear to be no less arbitrarily determined; they are certainly no less precarious in duration. The architecture of the law is shaped by structural needs which outlive the fleeting fashions of the schools; these affect at most the decorative detail. A particular sociological approach cannot, by clothing itself in a language for the initiated, invest itself with a valid title to unique insight and effectiveness in evaluating, delimiting and consolidating the role of law in the life of the world community. The great pioneers of a sociological approach to international law, Max Huber,[4] Georges Scelle[5] and Charles De Visscher,[6] were sure-footed because they were great lawyers with a profound dedication to reason and morality as the bedrock of the law. The future contribution of sociology to the law depends on the extent to

---

[1] Pp. 291–299 below.

[2] Cairns, Huntington, *Law and the Social Sciences*, Chapter IV, opening paragraph.

[3] *The Nature of the Judicial Process*, p. 58.

[4] *Die soziologischen Grundlagen des Völkerrechts.*

[5] *Précis de Droit des Gens*, 2 vols.

[6] *Théories et Réalités en Droit International Public.*

which it remains experimental rather than dogmatic in temper, the degree to which its spokesmen show the humility of the enquiring mind, the clarity of their thought and expression, and the measure in which they recognise the obligations of moral responsibility and are conscious of and responsive to the creative opportunities of the great society. The true task of sociology in relation to the law 'is not at all to define law or to work out a system of jural categories or jural values',[1] but to give the lawyer a fuller understanding of society and the potentialities and limitations of social forces. It is the illumination of particular problems by descriptive sociology rather than the 'grand theories'[2] of sociology which can at this stage make the most important contribution to the progress of the law, if only because the grand theories remain debatable even when not actively controversial and what the law needs for its growth is the facts established by other disciplines rather than the speculative theories concerning those facts which have been evolved by students with a different training for other purposes. We must look to Ihering,[3] Duguit,[4] Gény,[5] Holmes,[6] Pound[7] and Cardozo,[8] rather than to the professional sociologists, for the foundations of sociological jurisprudence. Law *is* a means to an end; it *is* an expression of social solidarity; the geometrical jurisprudence of logical inference from abstract concepts *does* result in arbitrary rather than reasonable answers to the problems of choice with which the law is constantly confronted; 'weighing considerations of social advantage' *is* the essence of the judicial duty; the law can fulfil its function in society only as an element of social discipline responsive to the social purposes of the society; the 'reconciliation of the irreconcilable' and the 'merge of antitheses' are 'the great problems of the law'. We may and must be guided by these fundamental considerations in evolving the law in a manner consistent with its own nature, traditions and techniques. The basic concern of the international lawyer, as of any lawyer, with sociology is 'the futility of law which does not have a reasonable degree of social support or at least tolerance';[9] the

---

[1] Gurvitch, Georges, *Sociology of Law*, p. 52.

[2] Mills, C. Wright, *The Sociological Imagination.*

[3] *Law as a Means to an End* (trans. Hussik), Modern Legal Philosophy Series No. 5.

[4] *L'Etat* (1901–3); *Le Droit Social, le Droit Individuel et les Transformations de l'Etat*, 1911, translated into English as *Law and the Modern State*, 1919; *Les Transformations du Droit Public*, 1921; *Souverainté et Liberté*, 1922; and other works.

[5] *Méthodes d'Interprétation et Sources en Droit Privé Positif*, 2nd ed.; *Science et Technique en Droit Privé Positif.*

[6] *Collected Legal Papers.*

[7] *Social Control Through Law*, and *Jurisprudence.*

[8] *Paradoxes of Legal Science.*

[9] Sawyer, Geoffrey, *Law in Society*, p. 183.

primary contribution of sociology to the present phase of development of the law is to clarify the new community needs to which the law must respond and the social forces on which it can draw to satisfy those needs. To establish a fruitful partnership of law and sociology in our progress towards world community, the creative imagination of the international lawyer must be equal to the task of using the findings of sociology for his own purposes in a manner which commands the respect of his colleagues trained in the law and commends itself to the good sense of statesmen and citizens. Only so can the enlistment of sociology among the sources and resources of the law play its part in preserving peace with justice, protecting human dignity, promoting the general welfare by economic stability and growth, and providing the necessary social discipline for scientific and technological development.

The other studies on which the law must draw increasingly include the natural as well as the social sciences. The changed intellectual temper of the natural sciences has, as we have seen when discussing the concept of law,[1] affected the general climate of thought in a manner which affects the fundamentals of legal thinking, particularly by destroying the illusion of certainty in the law.[2] The law is also called upon to come to closer grips with specific scientific and technological developments. If the contemporary international lawyer is to make any effective contribution to the social discipline of science and technology he must have an understanding of scientific and technological processes comparable to that of the best patent lawyers. A sustained educational effort to bridge the gap between the 'two cultures' in respect of the relations of law, science and technology in an international perspective has become an essential key to the creation of an 'outward-looking' rather than an 'inward-looking' law.[3]

---

[1] Pp. 124–130 above. [2] Pp. 287–290 below.

[3] Jenks, C. Wilfred, 'The New Science and the Law of Nations', *International and Comparative Law Quarterly*, Vol. 17, Part 2, April 1968, pp. 327–345.

14

Logic, experience and intuition

Studies of other disciplines and interdisciplinary studies give us a wider range of data concerning the facts out of which legal problems arise and the forces which may make suggested solutions of legal problems effective or ineffective in practice; they do not in themselves resolve legal problems. Anthropology, economics, sociology, psychology, and political theory all have a bearing on jurisprudence, but their function is to define the problem, not to resolve it. As Hohfeld so rightly insisted, we must at all times recall 'the importance of differentiating purely legal relations from the physical and mental facts that call such relations into being'.[1] The facts never suffice to resolve any disputed question of law; they may create a strong prejudice in favour of a particular solution; they may show that past practice supports it or practical advantage recommends it; but, whatever the problem may be, the attitude of the law towards any given set of facts involves, and will be determined by, values and outlook. The facts contributed by other disciplines and interdisciplinary studies are no different in this respect from the other facts at the lawyer's disposal. They define the magnitude of the problem but do not determine whether it is soluble; that is the privilege of patient circumspection, diplomatic skill, moral pugnacity and the creative imagination.

1. Logic and experience

In the evaluation of facts, logic, experience and intuitions of public policy play mutually complementary parts. Without logic the law would be wholly at large, at the mercy of every gust of chance and favour; without experience, without clear intuitions of public policy, the consistency of concepts would exact too high a price of inconsistency with history, practical convenience and the welfare of society. The logic of the law is the discipline which gives it such form and consistency as it may attain at successive stages of its development. Experience

[1] Hohfeld, Wesley Newcomb, *Fundamental Legal Conceptions*, p. 27.

is the rich inheritance of its past development. Neither logic nor experience affords a sufficient, nor sometimes a relevant, answer to essentially new problems. To resolve such problems we must have recourse to the deeper recesses of the mind. The facts define the problem. Neither they nor logic can solve it. Imagination furnishes an answer. The answer must be reconcilable with the facts and defensible in logic, but the test of its relevance and adequacy is neither the facts nor logic but purposes and values. A biological analogy may illuminate the process:

> Imagination, not reason, creates the novel. It is to social inheritance what mutation is to biological inheritance; it accounts for the survival of the fittest. Reason or logic, applied when judgment indicates that the new is promising, acts like natural selection to pan the gold grains from the sand and insure the survival of the fittest.[1]

In the natural selection of the law, reason, which embraces the ideal of justice and the promptings of morality guided by the fruits of experience, plays a larger role than logic alone can fill.

While the language of legal reasoning is mainly the language of logic, 'you can', as Holmes so pungently declared, 'give any conclusion a logical form'.[2] It is for this reason that inductive positivism is the most sterile of legal dogmas. It promotes logical processes and scientific methods which are no more than tools of the art of thought into a self-styled legal philosophy which is incompatible with the normative character which is the essence of law.

Induction as one of the mutually complementary processes of the logic of the law plays, of course, a necessary and important part in legal reasoning. The inductive approach, as a distinctive school of thought, becomes objectionable only if and when it emasculates and devitalises the law. My contention is that it inevitably has this tendency. It can tell us how far we have advanced along a particular road, but not where we are going and still less where we should be going. The protagonists of the inductive approach show a marked inclination to question new developments in the law, dismissing them as subjective or extravagant even when they rest upon the authority of the International Court of Justice, on the ground that there is no sufficient warrant for them in an inductive review of precedent. Lord Chancellor Sankey, who is sometimes quoted

---

[1] Gerard, R. W., 'The Biological Basis of Imagination', in *The Creative Process*, edited by Brewster Ghiselin, p. 237.

[2] 'The Path of the Law', in *Collected Legal Papers*, p. 181.

as having given the authority of the Privy Council to the proposition that international law is 'a process of inductive reasoning', was quick to add in the same paragraph that 'in embarking upon international law their Lordships are to a great extent in the realm of opinion, and in estimating the value of opinion it is permissible not only to seek a consensus of views, but to select what appear to be the better views upon the question'.[1] Later in the same opinion he gave an important clue to what should be regarded as the better views. 'International law was not crystallized in the seventeenth century, but is a living and expanding code. . . . The area within which it reigns beyond dispute . . . has been greatly enlarged within the memory of living man.[2] Unquestionably, the existence of a substantial and growing body of established precedent is immensely serviceable; it reduces the extent to which we are 'in the realm of opinion'; it circumscribes the margin of uncertainty in the law and by so doing both promotes and facilitates a higher standard of respect for law; but it fails to resolve any of the problems of choice and judgment which are the essence of every new step forward in the development of any legal system. As I have ventured to say elsewhere:

> Law develops and progresses by the constant interaction of practice and principle; practice alone remains static and becomes archaic; principle alone remains abstract and becomes illusory; practice and principle together correct each other's limitations and enable law to give practical expression to the ideal of justice.[3]

2. Intuition and public policy

Such an approach inevitably implies a constant reliance on intuitions of public policy. Such intuitions cannot be reduced to mathematical precision or calculated like the motions of the planets. As Cardozo phrased it 'We may try to see things as objectively as we please. None the less we can never see them with any eyes except our own.'[4] A margin of human error is inseparable from the freedom of choice which constitutes the grandeur of human destiny. In the life of the law, as in that of man, such a margin of error is less noxious than the lethargic fertility of the unenquiring mind.

It is easy to sneer at intuition as an element in the growth of the law and to dismiss intuitions as subjective fantasies which can afford no objective basis for legal obligation or impartial judgment; but no great

---

[1] *In Re Piracy Jure Gentium* (1934) A.C. 586; 588–589. [2] Ibid., p. 592.

[3] Jenks, C. Wilfred, *The Prospects of International Adjudication*, p. 627.

[4] *The Nature of the Judicial Process*, p. 13.

judge or statesman, conscious of how he reaches big decisions on vital matters, ever does so. Misguided intuitions, undisciplined and perhaps prejudiced, untested by logic and experience, and perhaps defying both morality and humanity, can of course be the most disruptive of all destructive forces in law no less than in politics. Too many of the most sinister figures of history have believed in their stars. It does not follow that intuition is misplaced or that we can afford to dispense with or belittle it. The remedy is to improve the quality of intuition, not to deny the vital part which it plays in every great leap forward in thought and action. Moral integrity, intellectual discipline and political sophistication are the leading ingredients of healthy and sound intuition; in the nature of the case there can be no magic formula for these, but they are all recognisable qualities and without them there can be no progress in the law and the law cannot respond to the needs of a changing society. The renunciation of force, the recognition of the dignity and worth of the human person, the acceptance of a common responsibility for economic stability and growth, the concept of new scientific and technological developments being at the service of all mankind, all have their origin in intuitions of public policy which have progressively found expression in successive specific contexts, been formulated in treaty provisions, and been weighed in the balance in reaching judicial and arbitral decisions. Intuitions of public policy correspond in the analysis of the intellectual processes of legal developments to public policy itself in the analysis of the potential sources of new concepts and applications in a living law. Intuitions of public policy are the running streams which bring into the law the life-giving qualities of fresh water; without them it becomes a stagnant pool.

3. Precedent and inventiveness

Logic, experience and intuitions of public policy are the alchemist's potion of the judicial process. They have some bearing on all the varied processes of legal growth, and in particular on the evolution of custom, but only as international adjudication develops can they play fully the part which Holmes and Cardozo ascribed to them in the development of the common law. There is, however, a similar potion available to the craftsmen of the other processes of legal growth. The mortar and pestle of legislative and institutional development are precedent and inventiveness. It is inventiveness hammering upon precedent which grinds out the new from the old. Without the constant accumulation of precedent, inventiveness has only a transient effect. Without the constant resourcefulness of inventiveness, precedent confirms established ways, and frustrates emerging ways of thought and modes of action. I do not use the term 'precedent' in this context in the narrower Anglo-American sense in which it refers primarily if not exclusively to judicial decisions, but in the broader sense in which it has been used by the International Court as meaning any accepted practice.[1] The precedents of legislation and institutional development are treaty provisions and decisions of international organs. The scope for inventiveness is not limited to the interstitial freedom of action of the judge; it embraces the wider opportunities open to the legislator. It is for this reason that the fertile mind has such a vital part to play in the development of international legislative technique, the elaboration of new forms of legal obligation, the introduction of new procedural devices, and, more generally, the evolution of the constitutional practice of international organisations. We have, in surveying the contribution which the creative imagination has made and can make to the law-making treaty and institutional development, had some opportunity of glimpsing how great the opportunities are. In so hovering over the broad perspective we have adumbrated, not defined, them.

---

[1] E.g. *Wimbledon Case*, 1923 P.C.I.J., Series A, No. 1, p. 28; *Asylum Case*, 1950 I.C.J. Reports, p. 286; *Effect of Awards of Compensation Made by the United Nations Administrative Tribunal Case*, 1954 I.C.J. Reports, p. 62.

15

Doubt, chance and mutability

The approach which we have explored recognises the inevitability of a wide margin of uncertainty in the law. It acknowledges that there can be no certainty of attaining the political objectives which it postulates. It accepts these uncertainties as inseparable from a mature outlook on law and politics. It concedes with Jerome Frank that 'when human relationships are transforming daily, legal relationships cannot be expressed in enduring form' and that 'much of the uncertainty of law is not', in these circumstances, 'an unfortunate accident' but is 'of immense social value'.[1] It holds that, so far from being a paralysis of action, such a philosophy widens the range for creative action in rising above 'doubt, chance and mutability'.[2]

1. Uncertainty in the new jurisprudence

In this general philosophy there will be nothing new to the student of jurisprudence. It has much in common with the general outlook which Holmes and his successors have made an imperishable part of the tradition of American legal thought, and the validity and limits of which have been the subject of so much debate by the sociological and realistic schools and their critics. Into this debate we do not need to enter; certainly we are not called upon to concede with Felix Cohen that 'the law of the present is a tenuous abstraction hovering between legal history and legal prophecy';[3] rather may we insist with Jolowicz that 'it is just not true that there is no fixity in law',[4] and hold with Karl Llewellyn that the law is 'ambiguous within margins which in the main are reasonably defined'.[5] It is unnecessary for our purpose to distil from contemporary jurisprudential thought a consensus, the elements of

[1] *Law and the Modern Mind*, pp. 6–7.
[2] Shelley, Percy Bysshe, 'Hymn to Intellectual Beauty'.
[3] *The Legal Conscience*, p. 79.
[4] Jolowicz, H. F., *Lectures on Jurisprudence*, p. 137.
[5] Llewellyn, Karl N., *Jurisprudence – Realism in Theory and Practice*, p. 110.

which are not yet readily discernible, concerning the frontiers of certainty and uncertainty in the law; it suffices to note that a significant margin of uncertainty, so far from being inconsistent with the nature of law as a recognised body of binding obligations, is inherent in its nature as a body of obligations derived from principles which are constantly being applied to unforeseen facts in unpredictable situations. In this perspective the capacity to live with the inevitability of uncertainty is a test of the maturity of any legal system.

2. Uncertainty in the law of nations

There will properly be a major question in many minds concerning the applicability of such a philosophy to the field of international law. Does not the possibility of living with a philosophy which acknowledges the inevitability of so much uncertainty in the law presuppose a greater certainty in the underlying moral basis of law and society, a more solid core of accepted law, a stabler framework of accepted institutions, and more reliable habits of law observance and respect for the general interest, than the world community has achieved? Is not such a philosophy a luxury which only a more integrated community and developed system of law can afford? Can we reasonably, in the United Nations, be as open-minded concerning the margins of the law as contemporary legal thought in the United States without impairing the fundamental sense of legal obligation without which there can be no law and no progress in the law?

The question would be highly pertinent if it were a real one, but the answer surely is that it is not a real question in this form. The open texture of the law of nations is a fact of everyday experience. The answer of experience is that we can neither afford this degree of uncertainty in the law, nor afford certainty, nor develop an adequate institutional structure for the world community, unless we recognise that only on the basis of a less equivocal world political morality and within a more adequate institutional structure of the world community can the inevitability of uncertainty and the need for certainty in the law be reconciled.

We cannot afford the uncertainty concerning fundamentals which is inevitable in respect of their applications. It is the immutable certainty of the abiding moral values of which the law is essentially the expression which makes tolerable the persistent uncertainty inseparable from the determination of successive problems and cases in a growing legal system. It is the confident certainties of the great moral leaders of mankind which enable man to 'envisage circumstance all calm'.

We cannot afford uncertainty without an institutional structure which makes it possible to resolve uncertain questions as they become acute within a framework in which the overriding values and interests of the whole community are beyond question. To this extent it is clearly true that uncertainty is a luxury of freedom made possible by the relative stability of the maturity of a legal system which expresses such values and interests and is equipped with an institutional structure effective enough to circumscribe the danger that uncertainty in the law may have a disintegrating effect on society so far-reaching as to undermine the foundations of peace, order and good government. It is no accident that in a weak community with a primitive legal system and static ways of life the law tends to be as certain as it is fragmentary. The certainty of a few rules of limited scope is typical of a society which has not learned to live with change. As change becomes the normal rhythm of the life of society the compass of the law expands, discretion tempers rigidity, growth presses upon stability, and the exercise of discretion and processes of change are institutionalised by the community.

As the compass of the law expands the relative certainty of its earliest and simplest rules ceases to be typical of the law as a whole. In growing measure we cannot have certainty without an institutional structure which makes it possible to give widening areas of the law the certainty which so much of it still lacks. We are increasingly confronted with the difficulty expressed by Hersch Lauterpacht that 'once we approach at close quarters practically any branch of international law, we are driven, amidst some feeling of incredulity, to the conclusion that although there is as a rule a consensus of opinion on broad principle – even though this may be an overestimate in some cases – there is no semblance of agreement in relation to specific rules and problems'.[1] Only a vigorous institutional life, combining the potentialities of adjudication, codification, legislative action and the international administration of a widening range of common interests and services, can contribute the central core of certainty without which the inevitable margin of uncertainty becomes intolerably wide. Conversely, we cannot afford a certainty which would inevitably crystallise the inadequacies of our inheritance and paralyse growth without an institutional structure which makes possible the conscious and deliberate adaptation of the law to changing needs. The more certain the law, the more does it tend to give effect to established rights arising out of past transactions rather than to reflect the needs and aspirations of the present and the future.

---

[1] 'Codification and Development of International Law', *American Journal of International Law*, 49 (January 1955), pp. 16–43.

All historical experience attests that 'an absolutely rigid framework is bound in the end to collapse and to collapse violently'.[1] A sophisticated legal system must allow for this. Fischer Williams, pointing out that 'no civilised system of private law permits the dead hand to govern indefinitely the property of the living', said of territorial settlements 'nor can the world be ruled by a system of a perpetual and unbreakable international entail'.[2] The evolution of the general body of the law can no more be controlled by the dead hand than the devolution of territorial authority.

The dialectic interplay of certainty and uncertainty which characterises the life of the law corresponds to the interplay of stability and growth which characterises the life of society and is reflected in the nature of the institutions required to make the law effective. We cannot have an institutional structure which reflects and responds to the needs of society without combining therein institutional protection for stability and institutional provision for change. So to institutionalise the relationship between stability and change that they are complementary rather than antithetical to each other is the ultimate problem of world organisation.

Seen in this perspective, the general philosophy of legal evolution which we have adumbrated is no less appropriate to contemporary international society than to the mature legal systems of civilised nations which have already developed a more solid core of accepted law and a stabler framework of accepted institutions. The process is at a much earlier stage of development, but only by following the same process can we hope to resolve the dilemmas which confront us. We can hope to resolve them successfully only by a vigorous creative imagination guided by reason and morality.

---

[1] Fischer Williams, Sir John, *International Change and International Peace*, p. 1.

[2] Ibid., p. 2

16

Reason and morality

The creative imagination must draw both the vigour of its inspiration and the sureness of its touch from reason and morality. The relation of law and morality is one of the perennial themes of legal philosophy, an ever recurrent topic of new phases of a continuing debate. 'Law and morality', as Professor Ralph Newman has reminded us, 'have not only a common source but a common goal; social justice'.[1] But their sphere and methods of operation do not coincide.

There has indeed been much discussion of late, chiefly in England, of the extent to which sin and crime are coextensive with each other and the degree in which there is a sphere of private morality beyond the purview of the law.[2] In the law of nations the question takes a different form. There is no scope internationally, except as a limitation upon cooperation among States in criminal matters, for a private morality too personal for appraisal by the law. The corresponding but converse doctrine that matters of State lie beyond the pale of moral judgment has indeed played a conspicuous and nefarious role in the history of international relations; transposed from the politics of Macchiavelli and the philosophy of Hegel to the submissive acceptance of power by a succession of schools of legal thought, it has been the negation of international law. The popularity of this pernicious doctrine is not yet wholly spent, despite its unequivocal and authoritative condemnation by the Nuremburg Tribunal. No more challenging responsibility awaits the creative imagination than that of developing a constructive alternative to it.

The interplay of law and morals is no less complex in world affairs than in personal life. The law cannot embrace the whole of public morality. Law may be of varying degrees of precision and susceptible of different types and degrees of enforcement. But some measure of tangibility and some legal consequences of failure to conform are of its essence.

---

[1] *Equity and Law: A Comparative Study*, pp. 17–18.

[2] Devlin, Patrick, *The Enforcement of Morals*; Hart, H. L. A., *Law, Liberty and Morality*; *The Morality of the Criminal Law.*

There is clearly an important area of international morality which cannot meet these standards.

1. Magnanimity and generosity

In general, magnanimity and generosity cannot be a matter of legal obligation. They are nevertheless the only salve for the resentment and mistrust which lie at the core of all our most crucial problems. There is, however, one element in magnanimity for which we can already claim a firmer status in the law. Professor Lon Fuller, who distinguishes the morality of aspiration which 'starts at the top of human achievement' and the morality of duty 'which starts at the bottom'[1] has suggested that there is one matter in which 'the morality of aspiration offers more than good counsel and the challenge of excellence' and 'speaks with the imperious voice which we are accustomed to hear from the morality of duty'. This voice, unlike that of the morality of duty, can, he urges, 'be heard across the boundaries and through the barriers that now separate men from each other'; it evokes 'one central indisputable principle of what may be called substantive natural law', namely the injunction to 'open up, maintain and preserve the integrity of the channels of communication by which men convey to one another what they perceive, feel and desire'.[2] Toleration and open-mindedness are now an obligation of international law. The obligation flows directly from the determination expressed in the Preamble to the Charter to practise tolerance and live in peace with each other as good neighbours. It is being given a more precise content by the wide range of agreements between States with divergent ideologies concluded every year. With this major qualification the higher morality of international relations will only gradually find expression in legal standards and procedures. Our present concern is with the basic elements of world political morality which can find a more immediate expression in the law. Without this much the world community cannot develop the minimum public order indispensable for its life as a community.

2. The basic elements of world political morality

To some even this degree of reliance on reason and morality may seem both a debatable and a dangerous conclusion. The Inquisition claimed to enforce morality. The goddess of reason presided over the guillotine. Are not both reason and morality concepts which are either so clearly an

---

[1] *The Morality of Law*, p. 5. [2] P. 186.

expression of a particular accepted order or so essentially subjective in character as to forfeit any claim to wide and lasting allegiance? Is not world society 'morally a plural structure comprising a number of different mutually tolerant moralities?'[1] Certainly it is true, as Max Huber has said, that 'the ethos of international relationships is the most difficult to grasp and perhaps the most uncertain, since it is valid for men of different religions and of different, in part conflicting, political and social ideologies, as well as for the many groups whose attitude towards transcendental values is indifferent or nihilistic'.[2] But the distinctive nature of the common ethos of the ideal of human unity does not deprive that ethos of its validity or power.

The answer must be found in certain simplicities which are as lasting as they are simple. The sophistication of the schools may reject them as trite but the experience of practical idealists is that they have outlived and will continue to outlive successive sophistries. In these simplicities we have the elements of a political morality valid for the whole world.

The essentials of such a common political morality valid for the whole world can be formulated in eight basic propositions.

The unity of mankind. The first principle of world political morality is the unity of mankind. The whole concept of world community presupposes this principle; the other principles of world political morality are all derived from it; it is the foundation of the concepts of the brotherhood and equality of man; the religions with an oecumenical outlook endorse it, even when they draw a sharp distinction between those who accept and those who reject the faith; it is implicit in the greater philosophies, however diverse they may be in other aspects. In the nature of the case the principle, like those derived from it, rests on faith in, rather than proof of, its validity. If we believe in the unity of mankind, we can reasonably seek to establish an organised world community and a new world of law; if we do not believe in the unity of mankind, the necessary moral, emotional and intellectual basis for an organised world community and a new world of law is lacking. Here we are dealing with fundamentals, and the question is not one of weight of reasoned argument but of convictions and attitudes formed in the deepest recesses of man's moral nature. The law can ask no better justification than the deepest instincts of man.

---

[1] Hart, H. L. A., *The Morality of the Criminal Law*, p. 40.

[2] Carnegie Endowment for International Peace, *Perspectives on Peace, 1910–1960*, p. 161.

The immorality of arbitrary force. The second principle of world political morality is the immorality of arbitrary force. The principle finds expression in the provision of the Charter of the United Nations that armed force shall not be used save in the common interest.

The principle is not based on any idle belief that force settles nothing. Napoleon, who is sometimes quoted as an authority for this comfortable tenet, espoused it only in St. Helena. Force has throughout history shaped the future of mankind, for good as well as for ill. It was force which preserved the future of Greek culture at Marathon. It was by force that the Roman legions laid the foundations of western civilisation. It was force, not principle, which drove Hitler to his bunker beneath Berlin. It was force which contained Stalinism. And so throughout the intervening years. Force could have made, but was never invoked to make, a reality of the Covenant of the League of Nations. Without collective reliance on force to repel force the United Nations cannot become a reality; this is indeed the heart of the Charter.

The justification of the principle is that without it society can no longer survive. In an age of nuclear weapons, long-range delivery systems and instant retaliation, the use of armed force on behalf of anything less than the world community as a whole disrupts the community, involves an incalculable danger of escalation and threatens all mankind with irrevocable disaster.

> The world is one. It must be thought of as one, governed as one, kept in peace as one. And if it goes to war, it goes to war as one – i.e., against itself.[1]

There has been much pleading – perhaps one should say special pleading – that the principle is not absolute and the legitimacy of recourse to force should be judged by context rather than precept. The difficulty with this approach is that every case becomes a special case to be judged by criteria the application of which inevitably involves a subjective element. Unless the principle is unqualified, it will disappear by erosion. The solution for the practical difficulties which will inevitably arise is not to qualify the principle, but to make effective the action in the common interest of the community as a whole.

The principle, expressed in these terms, is no new chapter in the wishful thinking which has so often destroyed the effectiveness of international action. It is the basis on which power politics have been precariously transmuted in our time into the politics of mutual restraint. The position will remain precarious until the undefined margins of the

---

[1] Madariaga, Salvador de, *Disarmament*, p. 52.

principle become less treacherous with the development of more effective and assured community action to maintain the peace.

Sovereignty limited by law. The third principle of world political morality is that sovereignty is limited by law. The State is the creature of the law, not the law the creature of the State. Whereas the renunciation of the right to use or threaten force is a contemporary development, the principle that the State is the creature and not the master of the law has its roots in Greek political thought, Roman law, and medieval scholastic theology; it is to be found in some form in all of the leading non-European legal systems, religious and secular. The most persistent challenge to this view has come from the protagonists of metaphysical theories for whom the morality of the State has consisted of the fulfilment of its own nature unfettered by standards of morality or concepts of moral or legal obligation external to itself. Of these theories the chief survivor is the Marxist theory of law and the State. Even Marxism is not impervious to change; some of its current exponents go so far as to deny its character as a dogma and to present it as an essentially dynamic philosophy constantly adapting itself to new needs. These needs are essentially those of what has now become an established order concerned with its own future stability under the stress of changing and growing pressures. In this there is nothing surprising. Every enduring revolution becomes in course of time an establishment which evolves its own legality. In this perspective the vital long-range question ceases to be whether the law binds the State but how the law which binds the State grows and develops. Paradoxically, but not surprisingly, it is the revolutionary forces in the world which tend to take a conservative and static view of the growth of the law and to seek to perpetuate what progressive opinion has long regarded as its weaknesses; the evolutionary forces, by instinct and experience, take the more dynamic view that orderly readjustment to changing situations being one of the essential purposes of the law, the metabolism of the law itself must reflect and meet the needs of the changing nature of society and the growing pressure of world community. The manner in which this issue is resolved will determine the future of the law, but the current joinder of issue concerning it, however far-reaching its consequences, does not in itself place in jeopardy the basic principle of world political morality that the law, once acknowledged to be such, is not subject to the will of the State.

Third-party judgment. The fourth principle of world political morality is third-party judgment. No one may be judge in his own cause. In this matter, as in so many others, there has been during the present century a revolution in accepted ways of thought. Half a century ago the right to be judge in its own cause was still the characteristic prerogative of the State in its international relations with its ultimate sanction in the right to threaten and use force. Today the right to use or threaten force has gone. The obligation to show 'a decent respect to the opinions of mankind' is less clearly acknowledged in respect of matters not involving the use of force beyond the frontiers of the State. There is perhaps no other principle in respect of which a double standard is more prevalent in this allegedly neo-colonial age. But even those who continue to reject impartial judgment by due process of law can no longer escape multipartisan review by United Nations procedures. The sovereign prerogative o freedom of choice is ceasing to be the privilege of the individual State and becoming a social function vested in the community. There could be no profounder change in international morality. The completion of the process will take time, but the outcome is no longer seriously in doubt.

Good faith. The fifth principle of world political morality is good faith. Good faith is no recent accretion to international morality. It has been since Regulus returned to Carthage the foundation of international morality. It has been recognised since Callières to be the first principle of successful diplomacy. It is the most fundamental and comprehensive of all legal principles. It is the basis of contract, a major element in tort, the essence of equity, the most paramount of all considerations of public policy. Without good faith neither treaty, nor custom, nor general principles of law, nor equity nor public policy can conjure law from lawlessness or fairness from injustice. Concerning this much there can be no debate. The problems begin when we attempt to define the standard of good faith required in the varied transactions of public life. When does the honesty which the law requires become a disinterestedness on which it hesitates to insist? When does quick-wittedness in our own interests which the law condones, and reasonable men may applaud, become the dishonesty which the law condemns? These problems may well prove to be innumerable, but they are marginal. They are the staple of scholastic dialectics. They recur in new guises constantly in every legal system. They are a continuing challenge to the conscience of diplomacy. They do not in any way affect the validity of the basic principle which transcends and may even mellow deep divergences of ideology and interest.

Fair play. The sixth principle of world political morality is fair play. This principle transposes that of good faith to conduct not governed by agreement. Expressed in the more technical language than thou shalt not wrongfully harm thy neighbour the principle is the foundation of the law of tort in every mature legal system. We find it in Ulpian: '*Juris praecepta sunt haec: honeste vivere, alterum non laedere, suum cuique tribuere.*'[1] We find it reaffirmed by Sir Frederick Pollock: 'All members of a civilised commonwealth are under a general duty towards their neighbours to do them no hurt without lawful cause or excuse.'[2] When the principle is so expressed the scope of the duty, the determination of who is one's neighbour, the definition of 'lawful cause or excuse', may give rise to many problems, in international as in municipal law, but the general direction in which the law should and must evolve is clear. Reason and morality require us to be guided in resolving these problems by a comprehensive theory of liability, a generous recognition of the obligation of neighbourliness, and a ready willingness to accept absolute liability for special and in particular novel risks created by one's action. The principle of fair play can, however, and it is submitted should, be more broadly conceived. It is the link between good faith and mutual aid. Fair play includes respect for the rules of the game in the conduct of international relations; it includes the discharge of obligations towards the community which are measured by a growing sense of community, a new awareness of need and responsibility, and the scale of the resources which one enjoys under the protection of the community.

Mutual aid. The seventh principle of world political morality is mutual aid. The principle is part of the imperishable tradition of every great civilisation, and much of the explanation of how it became a great civilisation. It is the basis of the collective responsibility for the general welfare which has so profoundly transformed the modern law of every civilised State. All that is new is the need to extend the range and scope of the concept to correspond to a scale and content of human relationships which now encompass the world and embrace an ever more complex pattern of activities. We must, of course, recognise its reasonable limitations. Rich States cannot be expected to tax their thrifty poor in order that the rich of poor States may become richer and their poor breed more thriftlessly. With this important qualification wealth, in the world community as in a well-ordered State, is not a privilege to do as one will with one's own but a responsibility to be discharged as a trust with public spirit. By its nature the principle does not, while it remains a general principle, admit of precision or enforceability. It can have no other sanction than a general recognition that it is more blessed to give

[1] Justinian, *Institutes*, paragraph 3. [2] *The Law of Torts*, p. 1.

than to receive, but with this as its only sanction it has in the last twenty years begun to transform the world.

Human dignity. The eighth principle of world political morality is human dignity. It is the essence of Christianity, Islam, Judaism and Buddism; it has influenced in varying degrees the other higher religions; it constitutes both the rational and the emotional appeal of successive philosophies of enlightenment. 'Man is born free' is the most explosive of social dogmas. It is the touchstone by which the adequacy of every political theory, system of government, economic order, social structure and legal doctrine is now tested. Without having the precision or enforceability of a legal principle, the concept of the dignity of man is one of the abiding moral values constantly seeking expression in the law.

These general concepts of world political morality do not in themselves resolve any of our problems but they provide a basic intellectual framework within which our problems can be peacefully resolved. They will no doubt be reformulated from time to time. When I had completed my own formulation I compared it with that of Nicolas Politis in *La Morale Internationale*,[1] written at the close of his life against the tragic background of 1941. Politis distinguishes six leading rules of international morality: loyalty, moderation, mutual aid, mutual respect, the spirit of justice, and solidarity. The language differs, but the essence of the matter is much the same.

What is the relationship of this basic intellectual framework to such concepts as power, values and strategies; goals, trends, conditioning factors, and alternatives; inclusive and exclusive sharing of resources; and so forth? The relationship is that of a dynamic force to a subtle analysis. The subtle analysis can prove an invaluable tool for more sustained progress. The dynamic force gives the indispensable momentum without which there can be no progress.

These principles have a staying power which will survive our present discontents. They satisfy Hart's test, intended to be an exacting one, for taking legal cognisance of morality; they 'are not merely the moral convictions or mores of a particular society but are matters of justice which may be said to enter very deeply into the heart of morality at all times and places, and even where men do not conform to them they pay lip service to them'.[2] They will remain the moral basis of the world community when many contemporary analyses of power, the sociology of

---

[1] Neuchatel, Editions de la Baconnière, 1943.

[2] Hart, H. L. A., *The Morality of the Criminal Law*, p. 53.

international politics and systems and games theories, have passed away. They have the ever renewed vitality of natural law.

3. The ultimate values of international jurisprudence

Recognising the dilemma presented by doubt, chance and mutability, but taking our stance upon reason and morality, our final conclusion must be that the creative imagination, through which alone we can achieve the new world of law so central to the fulfilment of the vocation of our age, draws its vitality from the ultimate source of all right conduct: faith, hope and charity. Nor has it ceased to be true since the days of St. Paul that 'the greatest of these is charity'.[1] These concepts are not the special heritage of any particular culture, philosophy or religion; they are as universal as they are eternal. They are not a theological prepossession; they are the ultimate values of sophisticated wisdom no less than of simple faith and they are the ultimate values of international jurisprudence. They are the foundation of the positive law of the world community; they constitute the essentials of the Preamble to the Charter of the United Nations, which expresses the determination of the peoples of the world to reaffirm faith, justify hope, and practise charity. To 'preserve succeeding generations from the scourge of war' we must, in the philosophy of the Charter, undertake three related tasks. We must 'reaffirm faith in the dignity and worth of the human person', a task which involves making the writ of freedom run everywhere. We must 'promote better standards of life in larger freedom', a task which involves enlisting the law to make hope triumphant over poverty, ignorance, hunger, disease and despair. We must 'practise tolerance and live together in peace with one another as good neighbours', a task which involves so transcending our present conflicts of ideology by charity that they take their place in history with the ideological conflicts of the past: the Crusades, the Wars of Religion and the wars following the French Revolution, to mention only the classical examples of western cultures.

The task is primarily one for statesmanship.

As the lieutenant of such statesmanship, the creative imagination of the international lawyer also has its part to play. We must, in the language of Holmes, 'live greatly in the law'.[2] Dangerous the times may be, but danger does not legitimise despair. The nuclear age remains the confident morning of humanity.

---

[1] *First Epistle to the Corinthians*, Chapter 13, verse 13.

[2] *Collected Legal Papers*, p. 30.

If we are to 'live greatly in the law', if our thought is to have any impact on a world with problems of such unparalleled complexity and so unprecedented a momentum of change, we must think freshly, think in breadth, think in depth, and above all think clearly. There is but one objective test of clearness of thought: clearness of expression, with a lucidity accessible to all, needing no cypher for its comprehension.

If we respect these standards we can and must be bold. In measuring our task we must hearken to the voice of statesmanship. 'If we are guided by prudence alone to the neglect of imagination, we shall deny to the United Nations any possibility of growth.' Only by constant and vigorous exercise of our intellectual muscles can we, as the servants of the law, play our proper part in making it possible for the United Nations so to grow in stature 'that it becomes an effective guardian of the rule of law and an instrument through which the law itself can be constantly refashioned so that it can produce political freedom and social justice and meet the needs of mankind'.[1] To live and work by such a vision is no idle fancy but plain common sense responding to the call of duty and guided by sober statesmanship.

The world is one, and as one mankind will fulfil his destiny. That destiny is not mutual immolation, but the endless adventure of the freedom of the human spirit in a brotherhood 'not only of some but of all peoples'[2] living in peace under the common law of mankind.

---

[1] Rt. Hon. Michael Stewart, M.P., addressing the General Assembly of the United Nations as Foreign Secretary on 7 October, 1965.

[2] His Holiness Pope Paul VI addressing the General Assembly of the United Nations on 4 October 1965

Works cited in the text

The list of publications below is to facilitate reference to the works used in the text in illustration of the argument. It is not intended to be a comprehensive bibliography.

Official and semi-official sources

AMERICAN SOCIETY OF INTERNATIONAL LAW, THE. *International Legal Materials*, Washington D.C., January 1965.

International Legal Materials, March 1967.

COUNCIL OF EUROPE. *Noise Abatement: A Public Health Problem*, Strasbourg 1964.

'Les Difficultés Financières des Nations Unies et Les Obligations des Etats Membres', *Chronique de Politique Etrangère*, Institut Royal des Relations Internationales, Brussels, XVI, No. 1–2, Janvier-Avril 1963.

European Yearbook, VII, 1959, Martinus Nijhoff, The Hague 1960.

Final Act of the International Conference on Safety of Life at Sea, Cmd 7491, Appendix B.

GENERAL AGREEMENT ON TARIFFS AND TRADE. *Basic Agreement and Selected Documents*, Geneva 1952, with subsequent annual supplements.

GROUP OF TEN. *Report of the Study Group on the Creation of Reserve Assets, Report to the Deputies of the Group of Ten*, 31 May 1965, U.S. Government Printing Office, Washington 1965.

INTER-GOVERNMENTAL MARITIME CONSULTATIVE ORGANIZATION INTERNATIONAL MARITIME COMMITTEE. *Torrey Canyon*, 1967.

INTERNATIONAL BANK FOR RECONSTRUCTION AND DEVELOPMENT. *The Horowitz Proposal – A Staff Report*, Washington D.C. 1965.

Supplementary Financial Measures: A Study requested by the United Nations Conference on Trade and Development, 1964, Washington D.C. 1965.

INTERNATIONAL CIVIL AVIATION ORGANIZATION. *The Technical, Economic and Social Consequences of the Introduction into Commercial Service of Supersonic Aircraft: A Preliminary Study*, Montreal, August 1960.

INTERNATIONAL LABOUR CONFERENCE. 26th Session (1944), Report I:

Future Policy, Programme and Status of the International Labour Organisation, Appendix.

INTERNATIONAL LABOUR CONFERENCE. 29th Session (1946) Report II (1): *Reports of the Conference Delegation on Constitutional Questions.*

INTERNATIONAL LABOUR OFFICE. *The International Labour Code, 1951*, 1952.

INTERNATIONAL LAW ASSOCIATION. *Briand Kellogg Pact of Paris: Articles of Interpretation as adopted by the Budapest Conference 1934*, Sweet and Maxwell, London 1934.

Report of the Fifty-First Conference, Tokyo 1964.

International Military Trials, Nürnberg, Nazi Conspiracy and Aggression, Opinion and Judgment, United States Government Printing Office, Washington 1947.

INTERNATIONAL MONETARY FUND. 'The Adequacy of Monetary Reserves' in *Staff Papers*, III, No. 2, October 1953.

International Financial News Survey, XIX, No. 36, 15 September 1967; also reprinted in THE AMERICAN SOCIETY OF INTERNATIONAL LAW, *International Legal Materials*, VI, No. 5, September 1967, Washington, D.C.

International Financial News Survey, XIX, No. 45, 17 November 1967.

Selected Decisions of the Executive Directors as Selected Documents.

International Reserves and Liquidity, 1958.

INTERNATIONAL TELECOMMUNICATION UNION. *From Semaphore to Satellite*, Geneva 1965.

NATIONAL ACADEMY OF SCIENCES – NATIONAL RESEARCH COUNCIL. *Waste Management and Control*, Washington D.C. 1966.

Proposals for an International Clearing Union, His Majesty's Stationery Office, London, Cmd 6437 of 7 April 1943.

REPORT OF THE PRESIDENT'S SCIENCE ADVISORY COMMITTEE. *Effective Use of the Sea: Report of the Panel on Oceanography*, Government Printing Office, Washington D.C. 1966.

Restoring the Quality of Our Environment, Government Printing Office, Washington D.C. 1965.

Résolutions de l'Institut de Droit International, 1873–1956.

Security Council Official Records, 5th year, 460th meeting.

Trail Smelter Award – 3 *United Nations Reports of International Arbitral Awards.*

UNITED KINGDOM BOARD OF TRADE. *Aircraft Noise – Report of an International Conference on the Restriction of Noise and Disturbance Caused by Civil Aircraft*, Her Majesty's Stationery Office, London 1967.

United Nations Charter Amendments, Hearing before the Committee on Foreign Relations, United States Senate, 89th Congress, 1st Session, 28 and 29 April 1965, U.S. Government Printing Office, Washington 1965.

UNITED NATIONS OFFICE OF PUBLIC INFORMATION. *The United Nations and Disarmament, 1945–1965.*

UNITED NATIONS. *Official Records of the Economic and Social Council*, Supplements No. 8, 1962, and No. 11, 1965.

Repertory of Practice of United Nations Organs.

Reports of the International Law Commission on the 2nd Part of its 17th and its 18th Sessions, Supplement No. 9 (A/6309/Rev. 1).

Shipping in the World Economy.

Year Book of the International Law Commission 1, and 2, New York 1950.

UNITED NATIONS TRADE AND DEVELOPMENT CONFERENCE. *Establishment or Expansion of Merchant Marines in Developing Countries.*

United Nations Treaty Series.

WORLD HEALTH ORGANIZATION. *The First Ten Years of the World Health Organization*, Geneva 1958.

Official Records of W.H.O., Nos. 13, 21, 37.

Cases, opinions, pleadings and reports

Annual Digest of Public International Law Cases, 6 vols., 1919–1932.

Annual Digest and Reports of Public International Law Cases, 10 vols., 1933–1949.

Asylum Case, 1950, I.C.J. Reports.

Conditions of Admission of a State to the United Nations Case, 1948, I.C.J. Reports.

Customs Union Case, P.C.I.J., 1931, Series A/B, No. 41.

De Lima v. *Bidwell*, 182, U.S.

Effect of Awards of Compensation Made by the United Nations Administrative Tribunal Case, 1954, I.C.J. Reports.

I.C.J. *Pleadings*, 1951, 'Reservations to the Convention on the Prevention and Punishment of the Crime of Genocide'.

International Court of Justice Reports, 1948, 1949, 1954, 1960, 1962.

International Law Reports, 16 vols., 1950 onwards, now edited by Mr. Eli Lauterpacht.

Permanent Court of International Justice, *Collection of Advisory Opinions*, Series B, Nos. 2, 3, and 4.

Serbian Loans Case, 1929.

P.C.I.J., 1926, Series B, No. 12, No. 13.

Secondary sources

ADARKAR, B. P. *The Principles and Problems of Federal Finance.* P. S. King & Son, London 1933.

ALLEN, Sir Carleton. (C.K.) *Law in the Making*. 2nd edn., Oxford, Clarendon Press 1930.

Aspects of Justice. Stevens and Sons, London 1958.

ALVAREZ, Alejandro. *The droit international nouveau*, Paris, 1959.

AMERISINGHE, C. F. *State Responsibility for Injury to Aliens.* Oxford, Clarendon Press 1967.

ASAMOAH, Obed Y. *The Legal Significance of the Declaration of the General Assembly of the United Nations.* Martinus Nijhoff, The Hague 1966.

ASHER, Robert E., KOTSCHNIG, Walter, and OTHERS. *The United Nations and Promotion of the General Welfare.* The Brookings Institution, Washington D.C. 1957.

AUBOIN, Roger. *The Bank for International Settlements, 1930–1955.* Princeton Essays in International Finance, No. 22, May 1955.

AUBREY, Henry G. *The Dollar in World Affairs.* Harper and Row for the Council on Foreign Relations, New York 1964.

AUFRICHT, Hans. *The International Monetary Fund: Legal Bases, Structure, Functions.* Stevens and Sons, London 1964.

BARKER, Ernest. *The Political Thought of Plato and Aristotle.* Dover Publications, New York 1959, reproducing the 1906 edition.

BASCOM, Willard. *A Hole in the Bottom of the Sea.* Weidenfeld and Nicolson, London 1962.

BASDEVANT, Suzanne (now Mme Bastid). *Les fonctionnaires internationaux.* Paris 1931.

BEARD, Charles A. *An Economic Interpretation of the Constitution of the United States.* The Macmillan Company, New York 1935.

BEBR, Gerhard. *Judicial Control of the European Communities.* Stevens and Sons, London 1962.

BECHHOEFER, B. G. *Post-War Negotiations for Arms Control.* Brookings Institution, Washington D.C. 1961.

BECKER, Carl L. *The Heavenly City of the Eighteenth Century Philosophers.* Yale University Press, New Haven 1932.

BEDJAOUI, Mohammed. *Fonction Publique Internationale et Influences Nationales.* Stevens and Sons, London 1958.

BERGMAN, Jack, and LENORMAND, Sergei. *The Pollution Paradox.* Spartan Books, Washington D.C. 1966.

BERTHOD, Paul. *Le Contrôle International de l'Execution des Conventions Collectives*. Geneva 1946.

The Bible, First Epistle to the Corinthians, 1 Cor. 13 (Authorised version).

BLACK, Eugene R. *The Diplomacy of Economic Development*. Harvard University Press, Cambridge, Mass. 1960.

BLIX, Hans. *Treaty Making Powers*. Stevens, and Sons, London 1960.

BLUNTSCHLI, J. C. *Le Droit International Codifié*. 5th edn., Guillaumin, Paris 1895.

BLOUSTEIN, Edward J. (ed.). *Nuclear Energy, Public Policy and the Law*, Oceana Publications Inc., New York 1964.

BOCZEK, Boleslaw Adam. *Flags of Convenience*. Harvard University Press, Cambridge, Mass. 1962.

BORCHARD, Edwin. *The Diplomatic Protection of Citizens Abroad.* The Bankes Law Publishing Co., New York 1928.

State Insolvency and Foreign Bondholders. Yale University Press, New Haven 1951.

BOWEN, Catherine Drinker. *The Lion and the Throne: The Life and Times of Sir Edward Coke*. Little, Brown and Co., Boston 1956.

BOWETT, D. W. *Self-Defence in International Law*. Manchester University Press 1958.

United Nations Forces. Stevens and Sons, London 1964.

The Law of the Sea. Manchester University Press 1967.

BRACTON, Henry de. *De Legibus et Consuetudinibus Angliae*, 1–8–5.

BRANDEIS, Louis D. 'An Essential of Lasting Peace', reproduced in *The Curse of Bigness*. The Viking Press, New York 1934.

'The Living Law', reproduced in *The Curse of Bigness*. The Viking Press, New York 1934.

BRAUN, Werner von, and ORDWAZ, Frederick I. *History of Rocketry and Space Travel*. Nelson, London 1966.

BRIERLY, J. L. *The Basis of Obligation in International Law*. Oxford, Clarendon Press 1958.

'The Failure of Codification' (1931), reprinted in *The Basis of Obligation in International Law*. Oxford, Clarendon Press 1958.

BRIGGS, Herbert. *The International Law Commission*. Cornell University Press, Ithaca, New York 1965.

BROWNLIE, Ian. *International Law and the Use of Force by States*. Oxford, Clarendon Press 1963.

BRYCE, J. 'The Nature of Sovereignty' in *Studies in History and Jurisprudence, 2*. Oxford University Press, New York 1901.

Studies in History and Jurisprudence. Oxford University Press, New York 1901.

BURKE, William T. *Ocean Sciences, Technology and the Future International Law of the Sea*. Ohio State University Press 1966.

BURY, J. B. *The Idea of Progress*. Dover Publications, New York 1955 edn.

CAIRNS, Huntington. *Law and the Social Sciences*. Harcourt, Brace and Co., New York 1935.

CAMPBELL, Alan, and THOMPSON, Dennis. *Common Market Law*. Stevens and Sons, London 1962.

CARDOZO, Benjamin N. *The Nature of the Judicial Process*. Yale University Press, New Haven 1921.

Paradoxes of Legal Science. Columbia University Press, New York 1928.

CARSON, Rachel. *Silent Spring*. Houghton Mifflen Co., New York 1962.

CASTEL, J. G. *International Law Chiefly as Interpreted and Applied in Canada*. Oxford University Press, London 1966.

CASTRÉN, Erik. *Civil War*. Suomalainen Tiedeakatemia, Helsinki 1966.

CASTRO, Josué de. *The Geography of Hunger*. Little, Brown and Co., Boston 1952.

CHAILLEY, Pierre. *La Nature Juridique des Traités Internationaux*. Recueil Sirey, Paris 1932.

CHAMBERLAIN, Neil W. *The West in a World Without War*. McGraw-Hill Book Company, New York 1963.

CHAPUT, Roland Aimée. *Disarmament in British Foreign Policy*. George Allen and Unwin, London 1935.

CHAUMONT, Charles. *Le droit de l'espace*. Les Presses Universitaires de France, Paris 1960.

CHENG, Bin. *General Principles of Law as Applied by International Courts and Tribunals*. Stevens and Sons, London 1953.

The Law of International Air Transport. Stevens and Sons, London 1962.

CHRISTOL, Carl Q. *The International Law of Outer Space*. United States Naval War College, International War Studies, 1963, Government Printing Office, Washington D.C. 1966.

CLARK, Grenville, and SOHN, Louis. *World Peace Through World Law*. Harvard University Press, Cambridge, Mass. 1958.

COBBETT, Pitt. *Leading Cases on International Law*, 4th edn., Sweet and Maxwell Ltd., London 1922.

CODDING, George A., Jr. *The Universal Postal Union*. New York University Press, New York 1964.

The International Telecommunication Union, E. J. Brill, Leiden 1952.

COHEN, Felix. *The Legal Conscience*. Yale University Press, New Haven 1960.

COHEN, Morris Raphael. *Reason and Law*. Free Press, Glencoe 1950.

COLOMBOS, C. John. *International Law of the Sea*. 6th edn., Longmans, London 1967.

CONAN, A. R. *The Problem of Sterling*. Macmillan, London 1966.

Conference between King James I and the Judges of England, 12 *Coke's Reports* 63, 1612.

CORBETT, Percy E. *Law in Diplomacy*. Princeton University Press 1959.

CORWIN, Edward S. *The Twilight of the Supreme Court*. Yale University Press, New Haven 1934.

COWEN, D. V. *The Foundations of Freedom with Special Reference to Southern Africa*. Oxford University Press, Cape Town 1961.

CRANDALL, Samuel B. *Treaties: Their Making and Enforcement*. John Byrne and Co., Washington D.C. 1916.

CURZON, G. *Multilateral Commercial Diplomacy*. Michael Joseph, London 1965.

DE VISSCHER, Charles. *Annuaire de l'Institut de Droit International*. Vol. 31, 1924.

Théories et réalitiés en Droit International Public. Editions A. Pedone, Paris 1953.

De la Conclusion des Traités Internationaux. Brussels 1943.

DEHOUSSE, Fernand. *La Ratification des Traités*. Paris 1935.

DETTER, Ingrid. *Law-Making by International Organisations*. P. A. Norstedt and Söners Förlag, Stockholm, 1965.

Essays on the Law of Treaties. Norstedt and Söners, Stockholm 1967.

DEVLIN, Lord Patrick. *The Enforcement of Morals*. Oxford University Press, London 1964.

DICEY, A. V. *Introduction to the Study of the Law of the Constitution*. Macmillan and Co., London 1885.

DICKINSON, Edwin D. *Law and Peace*. University of Pennsylvania Press, Philadelphia 1951.

DOMKE, Martin (ed.). *International Trade Arbitration*. American Arbitration Association, New York 1958.

DUGUIT, Léon. *L'Etat*, 1901–1903.

Le Droit Social, le Droit Individuel et les Transformations de l'Etat, 1911, translated into English as *Law and the Modern State*, 1919, Allen & Unwin, London.

Les Transformations du Droit Public, 1921.

Souveraint é et Liberté, Paris 1922.

ERLICH, Eugen. *Fundamental Principles of the Sociology of Law*, Harvard University Press 1936.

FALK, Richard A. *Law, Morality and War in the Contemporary World*. Frederick A. Praeger, Inc., New York 1963.

FALK, Richard A. 'The International Law of Internal War' in Rosenau. *International Aspects of Civil Strife*. Princeton University Press 1964.

The Vietnam War and International Law. Princeton University Press for American Society of International Law, 1968.

FALK, Richard A., and BARNET, Richard J. (eds.). *Security in Disarmament*. Princeton University Press 1965.

FELLER, A. H. *United Nations and World Community*. Little, Brown and Co., Boston 1952.

FEUER, G. *Les Aspects Juridiques de l'Assistance Technique*. Librairie Générale de Droit et de Jurisprudence, Paris, 1957.

FIELD, David Dudley. *Outlines of an International Code*, 2nd edn., Baker, Voorkis and Co., New York 1876.

FIFOOT, C. H. S. *Lord Mansfield*, Oxford 1936.

FIORE, Pasquale. *Il Diritto Internazionale Codificato*. 4th edn. Unione Tipograficco, Editrice Torinese, Torino 1909.

FISCHER WILLIAMS, Sir John. *Aspects of Modern International Law*. Oxford University Press, London 1939.

Chapters on Current International Law and the League of Nations. Longmans, London 1929.

International Change and International Peace. Oxford University Press, London 1932.

Some Aspects of the Covenant of the League of Nations. Oxford University Press, London 1934.

FORTESCUE, Sir John. *De Laudibus Legum Angliae*. Translated, London 1775.

FRANK, Jerome. *Law and the Modern Mind*. Brentano's, New York 1930.

FRIEDMANN, Wolfgang. *Anti-Trust Laws*. Stevens and Sons, London 1956.

The Changing Structure of International Law. Stevens and Sons, London 1964.

FRIEDMANN, Wolfgang, and KALMANOFF, George. *Joint International Business Ventures*. Columbia University Press, New York 1961.

FRYE, William R. *A United Nations Peace Force*. Stevens and Sons, London 1957.

FULBRIGHT, Senator J. William. *The Arrogance of Power*. Jonathan Cape, London 1967.

FULLER, Lon. *The Morality of Law*. Yale University Press, New Haven 1964.

FULTON, T. W. *The Sovereignty of the Seas*. Edinburgh 1911.

GARNER, J. W. *Recent Developments in International Law*, University of Calcutta 1925.

GENY, François. *Méthodes d'Interprétation et Sources en Droit Privé Positif*, 2nd edn., Librairie Générale de Droit et de Jurisprudence, Paris 1919.

Science et Technique en Droit Privé Positif. Sirey, Paris 1913–1924.

GERARD, R. W. 'The Biological Basis of Imagination', in *The Creative Process*, edited by Brewster Ghiselin. University of California Press, Berkeley and Los Angeles 1954.

GIANNI, G. *La coutume en droit international.* Paris 1931.

GIDEL, G. *Le droit international de la mer.* Paris 1932–1934, 3 vols.

GIHL, Torsten. *International Legislation.* Oxford University Press, London 1937.

GILL, Crispin, BOOKER, Frank, and SOPER, Tony. *The Wreck of the Torrey Canyon.* David and Charles, Newton Abbott, Devon 1967.

GINESTET, Pierre. *L'Assemblée Parlementaire Européenne.* Presses Universitaires de France, Paris 1959.

GINSBERG, Morris. *On Justice in Society.* Penguin Books, Harmondsworth, Middlesex 1965.

GOLD, Joseph. *The Fund Agreement in the Courts.* International Monetary Fund, Washington 1962.

The International Monetary Fund and Private Business Transactions. International Monetary Fund, Washington 1965.

GOODMAN, G. T., EDWARDS, R. W., and LAMBERT, J. M. *Ecology and the Industrial Society*, Blackwell, Oxford 1965.

GOODRICH, Leland M. *The United Nations.* Stevens and Sons, London 1960.

GOODRICH, Leland M., and HAMBRO, Edvard. *Charter of the United Nations: Commentary and Documents.* 2nd edn., World Peace Foundation, Boston 1949.

GOTLIEB, Allan. *Disarmament and International Law*, The Canadian Institute of International Affairs, Toronto 1956.

GREENSPAN, Morris. *The Modern Law of Land Warfare.* University of California Press 1959.

GRISWOLD, A. Whitney. *The Far Eastern Policy of the United States*, Harcourt, Brace and Co., New York 1938.

GUGGENHEIM, Paul. 'Les deux éléments de la coutume en droit international public', *La Technique et les principes du droit public – Etudes en l'honneur de Georges Scelle.* 1, Paris 1950.

GURVITCH, Georges. *Sociology of Law.* Routledge and Kegan Paul, London 1947.

GUTENBERG, B. *Internal Constitution of the Earth.* Dover Publications, New York 1951.

HACKWORTH, Green Haywood. *Digest of International Law*. Government Printing Office, Washington D.C. 1940–1944, 8 vols.

HALEY, Andrew G. *Space Law and Government*, Appleton-Century-Crofts, New York 1963.

HALL, William Edward. *International Law*, 3rd edn., Oxford University Press 1889.

HALLAM, Henry. *The Constitutional History of England*. John Murray, London 1899.

HAMBIDGE, Gove. *The Story of F.A.O.*, D. Van Nostrand Co., New York 1955.

HAMMARSKJÖLD, Dag. 'The Development of a Constitutional Co-operation', reprinted in *Servant of Peace*. Harper and Row, New York 1962.

HAMMARSKJÖLD, Dag. 'The International Civil Servant in Law and Fact' reprinted in *Servant of Peace*. Harper and Row, New York 1962.

HARROD, Roy F. *The Life of John Maynard Keynes*, Macmillan, London 1951.

The Dollar. Norton, New York 1963.

HART, Herbert L. A. *Concept of Law*. Oxford, Clarendon Press 1961.

Law, Liberty and Morality. Oxford University Press, London 1963.

The Morality of the Criminal Law. Magnes Press, Jerusalem 1965.

HAWKINS, C. H. *Commercial Treaties and Agreements: Principles and Practice*. New York 1951.

HEIDELBERG, Franz C. *Das Europäische Parlament*. Lutzeyer, Badan-Badan 1959

HENKIN, Louis. *Arms Control and Inspection in American Law*. Columbia University Press, New York 1958.

HEXNER, Ervin. *International Cartels*. University of North Carolina Press, Chapel Hill 1945.

HIGGINS, A. Pearce. *The Hague Peace Conferences*. Cambridge University Press 1909.

HIGGINS, Rosalyn. *The Development of International Law Through the Political Organs of the United Nations*. Oxford University Press, London 1963.

HILL, Martin. *The Economic and Financial Organization of the League of Nations*. Carnegie Endowment for International Peace, Washington, D.C. 1946.

Immunities and Privileges of International Officials, The Experience of the League of Nations, Carnegie Endowment for International Peace, Washington, D.C. 1947.

HINSLEY, F. H. *Power and the Pursuit of Peace*. Cambridge University Press 1963.

Sovereignty. C. A. Watts and Co., London 1966

HOBSON, Arthur. *The International Institute of Agriculture*. University of California Press, Berkeley 1931.

HOHFELD, Wesley Newcomb. *Fundamental Legal Conceptions*. Yale Paperbound Edition, 1963, Yale University Press, New Haven 1919.

HOLBORN, Louise W. *The International Refugee Organization*. Oxford University Press, London 1956.

HOLLAND, T. E. *Studies in International Law*. Oxford University Press 1898.

The Elements of Jurisprudence. 13th edn., Oxford University Press 1924.

HOLLOWAY, Kaye. *Modern Trends in Treaty Law*. Stevens and Sons, London 1967.

HOLMES, Mr. Justice. 'The Path of the Law', *Collected Legal Papers*. Harcourt, Brace and Co., New York 1920.

HORIE, Shigeo. *The International Monetary Fund*. St. Martin's Press, New York 1964.

HOVEY, J. Allen, Jr. *The Super-parliaments*. Frederick A. Praeger, New York 1966.

HOYT, Edwin C. *The Unanimity Rule in the Revision of Treaties: A Re-Examination*. Martinus Nijhoff, The Hague 1959.

HUBER, Max. *Die soziologischen Grundlagen des Völkerrechts*. Grunewald, Verlag Dr. Walther Rothschild, Berlin 1928.

Carnegie Endowment for International Peace, *Perspectives on Peace, 1910–1960*. Frederick A. Praeger, Inc., New York 1960.

HUDSON, Manley O. *International Legislation*. Carnegie Endowment for International Peace, Washington D.C. 1931.

HURST, Sir Cecil. 'A Plea for the Codification of International Law on New Lines' (1946), reprinted in *International Law – The Collected Papers of Sir Cecil J. B. Hurst*. Stevens and Sons, London 1950.

IHERING, Rudolf von. *Law as a Means to an End*. Trans. Hussik, Modern Legal Philosophy Series No. 5, Harvard University Press, Cambridge, Mass. Macmillan, New York 1924.

INTER-AMERICAN INSTITUTE OF INTERNATIONAL LEGAL STUDIES. *The Inter-American Legal System*. Oceana Publications, Dobbs Ferry, New York 1966.

JACOBSON, Harold Karan, and STEIN, Eric. *Diplomats, Scientists and Politicians*. Michigan University Press, Ann Arbor 1966.

JAMES, A. *United Nations Security Forces*. 1968.

JEFFERSON, Thomas. *Manual of Parliamentary Practice*.

JENKS, C. Wilfred. 'The Application of International Labour Conventions by Means of Collective Agreements.' *Festgabe für A. N. Makarov*. W. Kohlhammer Verlag, Stuttgart 1958.

JENKS, C. Wilfred. *The Common Law of Mankind.* Stevens and Sons, London 1958.

'The *Corpus Juris* of Social Justice' in *Law, Freedom and Welfare.* Stevens and Sons, London 1963.

Human Rights and International Labour Standards. Stevens and Sons, London 1960.

'Human Rights, Social Justice and Peace', in Nobel Symposium VII: *The International Protection of Human Rights. Proceedings of the Seventh Nobel Symposium,* Oslo, September 1967, edited by August Schou and Asbjörn Eide, Almqvist and Wilsell, Stockholm 1968.

International Immunities. Stevens and Sons, London 1961.

'The International Protection of Trade Union Rights' in Evan Luard (ed.), *The International Protection of Human Rights.* Thames and Hudson, London 1967.

The International Protection of Trade Union Freedom. Stevens and Sons, London 1957.

Law, Freedom and Welfare. Stevens and Sons, London 1963.

Law in the World Community. Longmans, London 1967.

Liber Amicorum J. P. A. François. 1959.

The Prospects of International Adjudication. Stevens and Sons, London 1964.

The Proper Law of International Organisations. Stevens and Sons, London 1962.

'Some Comments on the Dumbarton Oaks, Proposals' 1945, quoted in *The Proper Law of International Organisations.* Stevens and Sons, London 1962.

Space Law. Stevens and Sons, London 1965.

'Space Law Becomes a Reality', in British Institute of International and Comparative Law, *Current Problems in Space Law: A Symposium.* London 1965.

'Unanimity, the Veto, Weighted Voting, Special and Simple Majorities and Consensus as Modes of Decision in International Organisations' in *Cambridge Essays in International Law: Essays in Honour of Lord McNair.* Stevens and Sons, London 1965.

'The United Nations Covenants Come to Life', in Recueil *d'Etudes de Droit international en hommage à Paul Guggenheim,* Geneva 1968.

The World Beyond the Charter, George Allen and Unwin, London 1968.

JENKS, Edward. *A Short History of English Law.* 4th edn., Methuen and Co., London 1934.

JENNINGS, R. Y. *The Acquisition of Territory in International Law.* Manchester University Press 1963.

JESSUP, Philip C. *The Law of Territorial Waters and Maritime Jurisdiction.* G. A. Jennings Co., New York 1927.

Transnational Law. Yale University Press, New Haven 1956.

The Use of International Law. University of Michigan Law School, Ann Arbor 1959.

JESSUP, Philip C., and TAUBENFELD, Howard J. *Controls for Outer Space and the Antarctic Analogy.* Columbia University Press, New York 1959.

JOLOWICZ, H. F. *Lectures on Jurisprudence,* The Athlone Press, London 1963.

JUSTINIAN. *Institutes.* (*Corpus Juris Civiles*) trans. Clarendon Press, Oxford 1913.

KAHN, Herman. *On Escalation.* Frederich A. Praeger, New York 1965.

KAHN-FREUND, O. *Comparative Law as an Academic Subject.* Oxford, Clarendon Press 1965.

KAPLAN, Morton A., and KATZENBACH, Nicholas de B. *The Political Foundations of International Law.* John Wiley and Sons, New York 1961.

KAZANTZAKIS, Nikos. *Zorba the Greek.* Bruno Cassirer, Oxford 1959.

KELSEN, Hans. *General Theory of Law and the State.* 20th Century Legal Philosophy Series, Harvard University Press, Cambridge, Mass. 1945.

The Law of the United Nations. Stevens and Sons, London 1950.

Principles of International Law, 2nd edn. by Robert W. Tucker, Holt, Rhinehart and Winston Inc., New York 1966.

What is Justice? University of California Press, Berkeley and Los Angeles 1960.

KENNAN, George. *Realities of American Foreign Policy.* Princeton University Press 1954.

KENNEDY, W. P. M. *Statutes, Treaties and Documents of the Canadian Constitution 1713–1929.* 2nd edn. Oxford University Press, Toronto, 1930.

KEYNES, J. M. 'Economic Possibilities for our Grandchildren' in *Essays in Persuasion.* The Norton Library, New York 1963.

KISS, Alexandre-Charles. *Répertoire Français de Droit International Public.* Conseil National de la Recherche Scientifique, Paris 1962–1965. 4 vols. published.

Répertoire de la Pratique Française en Matière de Droit International Public. Centre National de la Recherche Scientifique 1962–1966. 4 vols. published.

KOESTLER, Arthur. *The Art of Creation.* The Macmillan Company, New York 1964.

KRANENBURG, J. L. 'The Consultative Inter-parliamentary Benelux Council', in Kenneth Lindsay, *European Assemblies – The Experimental Period.* Stevens and Sons, London 1960.

KUTNER, Luis. *World Habeas Corpus.* Oceana Publications, Dobbs Ferry, New York 1962.

LADAS, Stephen P. *The International Protection of Industrial Property.* Harvard University Press, Cambridge, Mass. 1930.

LANDY, E. A. *The Effectiveness of International Supervision: Thirty Years of I.L.O. Experience.* Stevens and Sons, London 1966.

LARSON, JENKS and OTHERS. *Sovereignty Within the Law.* Oceana, New York 1965.

LARSON, Arthur (ed.). *A Warless World.* McGraw-Hill Book Company, New York 1963, reproducing a symposium from *International Affairs*, Foreign Languages Publishing House, Moscow, July 1962.

LASSWELL, Harold. *World Politics and Personal Insecurity.* The Free Press, New York 1965 (Paperback ed.).

LAUTERPACHT, Eli. *British Practice in International Law.* British Institute of International and Comparative Law.

LAUTERPACHT, Sir Hersch. 'Brierly's Contribution to International Law', in J. L. Brierly, *The Basis of Obligation in International Law.* Oxford, Clarendon Press 1958.

The Development of International Law by the International Court. Stevens and Sons, London 1958.

The Function of Law in the International Community. Oxford, Clarendon Press 1933.

The Law of War on Land. Her Majesty's Stationery Office, London 1958. (Part III of the War Office Manual of Military Law.)

International Law and Human Rights. Stevens and Sons, London 1950.

Private Law Sources and Analogies of International Law. Longmans, Green and Co., London 1927.

Recognition in International Law. Cambridge University Press 1947.

LAVES, Walter H. C., and THOMSON, Charles A. *Unesco – Purpose – Progress – Prospects.* Indiana University Press, Bloomington 1957.

LEE, Luke T. *Vienna Convention on Consular Relations.* A. W. Sitjhoff, Leiden 1966.

LINDSAY, Kenneth. *European Assemblies – The Experimental Period.* Stevens and Sons, London 1960.

Towards a European Parliament. Council of Europe, Strasbourg 1958.

LLEWELLYN, Karl N. *Jurisprudence – Realism in Theory and Practice.* Chicago University Press 1962.

LLOYD, Dennis. *The Idea of Law.* Penguin Books, Harmondsworth, Middlesex, England 1964.

LØCHAN, Einar. 'The Nordic Council', in Lindsay, *European Assemblies – The Experimental Period.* Stevens and Sons, London 1960.

LORIMER, James. *The Institutes of the Law of Nations.* William Blackwood and Sons, Edinburgh 1884.

LOWES, John Livingston. *The Road to Xanadu.* Houghton Mifflin Co., Boston 1927.

LUARD, Evan (ed.). *The International Protection of Human Rights.* Thames and Hudson, London 1967.

MACDONALD, R. A. J. *The Arctic Frontier.* University of Toronto Press 1966.

McDOUGAL, Myres S., and ASSOCIATES. *Studies in World Public Order.* Yale University Press, New Haven 1960.

McDOUGAL, Myres S., and BURKE, William T. *The Public Order of the Oceans.* Yale University Press 1962.

McDOUGAL, Myres S., LASSWELL, Harold D., and MILLER, James C. *The Interpretation of Agreements and World Public Order.* Yale University Press, New Haven, Conn. 1967.

McDOUGAL, Myres S., LASSWELL, Harold D., and VLASIC, Ivan A. *Law and Public Order in Space.* Yale University Press, New Haven, Conn. 1963.

McILWAIN, Charles Howard. *Constitutionalism: Ancient and Modern.* Revised Edition, Great Seal Books, Ithaca, New York 1958.

McIVER, R. M. *The Modern State.* Oxford Paperbacks 1964.

MACKENZIE, Norman A. M., and LAING, Lionel H. *Canada and the Law of Nations.* 1938. Carnegie Endowment for International Peace.

McNAIR, Lord. 21 *British Year Book of International Law.* Oxford University Press, London 1944.

International Law Opinions. Cambridge University Press 1956. 3 vols.

Law of the Air. 3rd edn. by M. R. E. Kerr and A. H. M. Evans, Stevens and Sons, London 1964.

The Law of Treaties, Oxford University Press 1961.

McNAIR, Lord, and WATTS, A. D. *The Legal Effects of War.* 4th edn., Cambridge University Press, London 1966.

International Legal Materials. The American Society of International Law, Washington D.C.

McWHINNEY, Edward. *International Law and World Revolution.* Canadian Broadcasting Corporation, Toronto 1967.

DE MADARIAGA, Salvador. *Disarmament.* Oxford University Press 1929.

MAHALKOV, A. *The Mystery of the Earth's Mantle.* Moscow 1966.

MAINE, Sir Henry. *Lectures on the Early History of Institutions*. John Murray, London 1874.

International Law. John Murray, London 1888.

MAITLAND, F. W. *Collected Papers*. Cambridge University Press 1911.

Memoranda de Parliamento, reprinted in *Selected Essays*, edited by H. D. Hazeltine, G. Lapsley, P. H. Winfield. Cambridge University Press 1936.

MANNING, C. A. W. *The Nature of International Society*. G. Beel and Sons, London 1962.

MARTIN, Andrew. *The Legal Aspects of Disarmament*. The British Institute of International and Comparative Law, London 1963.

MARX, Daniel, Jr. *International Shipping Cartels*. Princeton University Press 1953.

MASON, Edward S. *Foreign Aid and Foreign Policy*. Harper and Row for the Council on Foreign Relations, New York 1964.

MATEESCO, Nicolas. *La Coutume dans les cycles juridiques internationaux*. Editions A. Pedone, Paris 1937.

MAY, Erskine. *A Treatise on the Law, Privileges, Proceedings and Usage of Parliament*. 16th ed. Butterworth, London 1967.

MELLANBY, Kenneth. *Pesticides and Pollution*. Collins, London 1967.

MEIJERS, H. *The Nationality of Ships*. Martinus Nijhoff, The Hague 1967.

MERILLAT, H. C. L. (ed.). *Legal Advisers and Foreign Affairs*. Oceana Publications for the American Society of International Law, Dobbs Ferry, New York 1964.

Legal Advisers and International Organizations. Oceana Publications for the American Society of International Law, Dobbs Ferry, New York 1966.

MILLER, David Hunter. *The Peace Pact of Paris*. Putnam, New York 1928.

MILLS, C. Wright. *The Sociological Imagination*. New York, Oxford University Press 1959.

MONNET, Jean. *Perspectives on Peace, 1910–1960*. Carnegie Endowment for International Peace. Frederick A. Praeger Inc., New York 1960.

MOORE, John Bassett. *A Digest of International Law*. Government Printing Office, Washington D.C. 1906. 8 vols.

International Law and Some Current Illusions. Macmillan, New York 1924.

MORRISON, Philip and Emily (eds.). *Charles Babbage and His Calculating Engines*. Dover Publications, New York 1961.

MUHAMMAD, V. A. Seyid. *The Legal Framework of World Trade*. Stevens and Sons, London 1958.

DE NAUROIS, Louis. *Les Traités devant les Juridictions Nationales.* Recueil Sirey, Paris 1934.

NOEL-BAKER, Philip J. *The Arms Race.* Stevens and Sons, London 1958.
Disarmament. The Hogarth Press, London 1926.

NEUMANN, Franz. *The Democratic and the Authoritarian State.* Free Press Paperback, New York 1964.

NEWMAN, Ralph. *Equity and Law: A Comparative Study.* Oceana Publications, New York 1961.

NICHOLAS, Calvin J. *Financing the United Nations: Problems and Prospects.* M.I.T. Center for International Studies, Cambridge, Mass. 1961.

NORGAAD, Carl Aage. *The Position of the Individual in International Law.* Manksgaard, Copenhagen 1962.

O'CONNELL, D. P. (ed.). *International Law in Australia.* Stevens and Sons, London 1965.
State Succession in Municipal Law and International Relations. Cambridge University Press 1967. 2 vols.

OPPENHEIM, L. F. *International Law,* 1st edn., Longmans, London 1905. Vol. 1.

PARRY, Clive. *A British Digest of International Law 1965–1967.* 5 vols. Published 1965–1967. Stevens and Sons, London.
The Sources of Evidence in International Law. Manchester University Press 1965.

PASCAL, Blaise. *Pensées de Pascal.*

PASQUET, D. *The Origins of the House of Commons.* Trans. by R. G. D. Laffan, Cambridge University Press 1925.

PATTERSON, Edwin W. *Law in a Scientific Age.* Columbia University Press, New York 1963.

PHELAN, Edward J. *Yes and Albert Thomas.* Cresset Press, London 1936.

PHILLIMORE, Sir Robert. *Commentaries upon International Law.* Vol. II, 3rd edn., Butterworths, London 1879.

PIGGOTT, F. T. *The Freedom of the Seas, Historically Considered.* London 1929.

POLITIS, Nicolas. *La Morale Internationale.* Editions de la Baconnière, Neuchatel 1943.

POLLOCK, Sir Frederick. *A First Book of Jurisprudence.* Macmillan and Company, London 1896.
An Introduction to the History of the Science of Politics. Beacon Paperback, Boston 1960.
Jurisprudence and Legal Essays. Selected and Introduced by A. L. Goodhart, Macmillan, London 1961.
The League of Nations. 2nd edn., Stevens and Sons, London 1922.

POLLOCK, Sir Frederick. *The Law of Torts*. 13th edn. Stevens and Sons, London 1929.

POUND, Roscoe. *The Formative Era of American Law*. Little, Brown and Company, Boston 1938.

An Introduction to the Philosophy of Law. Yale University Press, New Haven 1922.

Jurisprudence. 5 vols. 1959.

Law and Morals. University of North Carolina Press, Chapel Hill, N.C. 1924.

Social Control Through Law. Yale University Press, New Haven 1942.

The Spirit of Common Law. Marshall Jones Company, Francestown, New Hampshire 1921.

QUAL, Lino di. *Les Effets des Résolutions des Nations Unies*. Librairie Générale de Droit et de Jurisprudence, Paris 1967.

RADIN, Max. *Law as Logic and Experience*. Storrs Lectures, Yale University Press, New Haven 1940.

RAJAN, M. S. *United Nations and Domestic Jurisdiction*. Orient Longmans, Bombay 1958. 2nd edn. 1961.

REIFF, Henry. *The United States and the Treaty Law of the Sea*. University of Minnesota Press 1959.

RENNER, Karl. *The Institutions of Private Law and their Social Functions*. Routledge and Kegan Paul, London 1949.

ROBERTSON, A. H. *European Institutions*. Stevens and Sons, London 1959.

Human Rights in Europe. Manchester University Press 1963.

RÖLING, B. V. A. *International Law in an Expanded World*. Djambatan, Amsterdam 1960.

ROOSA, Robert V. *Monetary Reform for the World Economy*. Harper and Row, New York 1963.

ROPER, Albert. *La Convention internationale du 13 octobre 1919 portant règlement de la navigation aérienne*. Recueil Sirey, Paris 1930.

ROSENAU, James N. *International Aspects of Civil Strife*. Princeton University Press 1964.

ROSENNE, Shabtai. *The Law and Practice of the International Court*. A. W. Sijthoff, Leiden 1965. 2 vols.

ROSNER, Gabriella. *The United Nations Emergency Force*. Columbia University Press, New York 1963.

ROSS, Alf. *On Law and Justice*. Stevens and Sons, London 1958.

ROSTOW, Eugene V. *Planning for Freedom*. Yale University Press, New Haven 1959.

The Sovereign Prerogatives: The Supreme Court and the Quest for Law. Yale University Press, New Haven 1962.

ROSTOW, W. W. *The Stages of Economic Growth.* Cambridge University Press 1960.

ROUX, J. M. *Les Pavillons de Complaisance.* Librairie Générale de Droit et Jurisprudence, Paris 1961.

ROUYER-HAMERAY, Bernard. *Les Compétences Implicites des Organisations Internationales.* Librairie Générale de Droit et de Jurisprudence, Paris 1962.

ROWAT, Donald C. *The Ombudsman.* George Allen and Unwin Ltd., London 1965.

ROWE, J. W. F. *Primary Commodities in International Trade.* Cambridge University Press 1965.

ROYAL INSTITUTE OF INTERNATIONAL AFFAIRS. *International Sanctions.* Oxford University Press, London 1937.

ROXBURGH, Ronald F. *International Conventions and Third States.* Longmans, London 1917.

RUBIN, Seymour J. *The Conscience of the Rich Nations.* Harper and Row for the Council on Foreign Activities, New York 1966.

SALMON, Jean. *Le Rôle des Organisations Internationales en Matière de Prêts de d'Emprunts.* Stevens and Sons, London 1958.

SALTER, Sir Arthur. *Recovery – The Second Effort.* G. Bell and Sons, London 1932.

SANKEY, Lord Chancellor. *In Re Piracy Jure Gentium.* 1934, A.C. 586.

SAWYER, Geoffrey. *Law in Society.* Oxford, Clarendon Press 1965.

SCAMMELL, W. M. *International Monetary Policy.* 2nd edn., St. Martin's Press, New York 1964.

SCELLE, Georges. *Précis de Droit des Gens.* Recueil Sirey, Paris 1932–34. 2 vols.

Théorie Juridique de la Révision des Traités. Recueil Sirey, Paris 1936.

SCHENKMAN, Jacob. *International Civil Aviation Organization.* E. Droz, Geneva 1955.

SCHWELB, Egon. *Human Rights and the International Community.* Quadrangle Books, Chicago 1964.

SCOTT, J. B. (ed.). *Reports to The Hague Conferences of 1899 and 1907.* Oxford University Press 1917.

SEYERSTED, Finn. *United Nations Forces in the Law of Peace and War.* A. W. Sijthoff, Leiden 1966.

SHIRRAS, G. F. *Federal Finance in Peace and War.* Macmillan, London 1944.

SHKLAR, Judith. *Legalism.* Harvard University Press 1964.

SHOTWELL, James T. *War as an Instrument of National Policy.* Harcourt, Brace and Co., New York 1929.

SIDGWICK, Henry. *The Elements of Politics.* Macmillan and Co., London 1891.

SIMPSON, Sir John Hope. *The Refugee Problem – Report of a Survey.* London 1939.

SIMPSON, J. L., and FOX, Hazel. *International Arbitration: Law and Practice.* Stevens and Sons, London 1959.

SINGER, J. David. *Financing International Organisations.* Martinus Nijhoff, The Hague 1961.

SINGH, Nagendra. *International Conventions of Merchant Shipping.* Stevens and Sons, London 1963.

Nuclear Weapons and International Law. Stevens and Sons, London 1959.

SINGH, Nagendra. *Termination of Membership of International Organisations.* Stevens and Sons, London 1958.

SMEDAL, Gustav. *De l'Acquisition de Souveraineté sur les Territoires Polaires.* Librairie Arthur Rosseau, Paris 1932.

SMITH, H. A. *The Crisis in the Law of Nations.* Stevens and Sons, London 1947.

The Law and Custom of the Sea. 3rd edn., Stevens and Sons, London 1959.

SØRENSEN, Max. *Jurisprudence and Legal Essays*, selected and introduced by A. L. Goodhart. Macmillan, London 1961.

Les Sources du Droit International. Copenhagen 1947.

SPIROPOULOS, Jean. *Die allgemeine Rechtsgüindsätze in Völkerrecht*, Kiel 1928; *Théorie générale du droit international*, Librairie Générale de Droit et de Jurisprudence, Paris 1930.

STAMP, L. D. *Man and the Land.* Collins, London 1955.

STOESSINGER, John G., and ASSOCIATES. *Financing the United Nations System.* Brookings Institution, Washington D.C. 1964.

STONE, Julius. *Aggression and World Order.* Stevens and Sons, London 1958.

Quest for Survival. Harvard University Press 1961.

STREIT, Clarence K. *Union Now.* Jonathan Cape, London 1939.

SZULC, Tad. *The Bombs of Palomares.* Victor Gollancz, London 1967.

TARACOUZIO, T. A. *Soviets in the Arctic.* Macmillan, New York 1938.

TAWNEY, R. H. *The Acquisitive Society.* G. Bell and Sons Ltd., London 1921.

TEMPERLEY, A. C. *The Whispering Gallery of Europe.* London 1938.

THOMAS, W. J. (ed.). *Man's Role in Changing the Face of the Earth.* University of Chicago Press 1955.

TIMBERG, Sigmund (Friedmann, Wolfgang, ed.). *Anti-Trust Laws.* Stevens and Sons, London 1956.

TRIEPEL, H. *Völkerrecht und Landesrecht*. Leipzig 1899.

TRIFFIN, Robert. *Gold and Dollar Crisis*. Yale University Press, New Haven 1961.

TRISKA, Jan F., and SLUSSER, Robert M. *The Theory, Law and Policy of Soviet Treaties*. Stanford University Press 1962.

TOBIN, Harold J. *The Termination of Multipartite Treaties*. Columbia University Press, New York 1933.

TUCKER, Robert W. *The Law of War and Neutrality at Sea*. Naval War College, International War Studies, Government Printing Office, Washington D.C. 1957.

TUNKIN, Grigori. *Droit International public – Problèmes théoriques*. Editions A. Pedone, Paris 1965.

VAN DER POST, Laurens. *Journey into Russia*. Penguin Books, Harmondsworth, Middlesex 1965.

VANDERPOL, A. *La doctrine scolastique du droit de la guerre*. Pedone, Paris 1919.

VATTEL, E. de. *Le Droit des Gens ou Principes de la Loi Naturelle. Classics of International Law*. Carnegie Institution of Washington 1916.

DEL VECCHIO, Giorgio. *La Guistizia*. 4th edn., Edit Studium, Rome 1951.

Philosophy of Law, translated by Thomas Owen Martin, The Catholic University of America Press, Washington D.C. 1953.

VELAS, Pierre. *Introduction en Droit International Economique et Social*. Tome I, 'Droit International Agricole'. Librairie Sirey, Paris 1965.

VERNANT, Jacques. *The Refugee in the Post War Period*. London 1953.

VINOGRADOFF, Paul. *Collected Papers*. Oxford, Clarendon Press 1928. Vol. I.

WALKER, Patrick Gordon. *The Commonwealth*. Secker and Warburg, London 1962.

WAMBAUGH, Sarah. *A Monograph on Plebiscites*. Oxford University Press, New York 1920.

Plebiscites Since the World War. Carnegie Endowment for International Peace, Washington 1933.

WEBSTER, Sir Charles. 'The Council of Europe in the Nineteenth Century' in *The Art and Practice of Diplomacy*. Chatto and Windus, London 1960.

WEIZBERG, Guenther. *The International Status of the United Nations*. Stevens and Sons, London 1961.

WESTLAKE, John. *International Law*, Part I, Peace. 2nd edn., Cambridge University Press 1910.

International Law. 2nd edn., Cambridge University Press 1913.

WHEARE, K. C. *Federal Government*. Oxford University Press, London 1946.

WHITEMAN, Marjorie. *Digest of International Law.* Government Printing Office, Washington D.C. 1963–1967. 8 vols. published.

WHITTON, John B., and LARSON, Arthur. *Propaganda.* Oceana Publications, Dobbs Ferry, New York 1964.

WIENER, Norbert. *Cybernetics.* 2nd edn., M.I.T. Press, Cambridge, Mass. 1961.

WILCOX, Clair. *A Charter for World Trade.* Macmillan, New York 1949.

WILCOX, Francis O. *The Ratification of International Conventions.* George Allen and Unwin, London 1935.

WILD, Payson S. *Sanctions and Treaty Enforcement.* Harvard University Press, Cambridge, Mass. 1934.

WOLFKE, Karol. *Custom in Present International Law.* Wroclaw Scientific Society, Wroclaw, Poland 1964.

WOODBRIDGE, George. *The History of UNRRA.* Columbia University Press, New York 1950.

WRIGHT, Sir Michael. *Disarm and Verify.* Chatto and Windus, London 1964.

WRIGHT, Quincy. *A Study of War*, 2 vols., Chicago University Press 1944.

WYZANSKI, Charles E., Jr. *Whereas – A Judge's Premises.* Atlantic – Little, Brown and Company, Boston 1965.

YOUNGER, Kenneth. *Changing Perspectives in British Foreign Policy*, Oxford University Press for Royal Institute of International Affairs, London 1964.

Journals

American Journal of International Law, 49, Washington 1955.

American Journal of International Law, No. 2, April 1967.

Annuaire de l'Insuitut de Droit International, 1957.

BROCHES, Aaron. 'International Legal Aspects of the Operations of the World Bank', *Recueil des Cours de l'Académie de Droit International*, 98, 1959 III.

Bulletin of the World Health Organization, 1948 and 1949. 2 vols.

BURNET, Sir Macfarlane. 'Men or Molecules?', *The Lancet*, London, Saturday, 1 January, 1966.

CHAYES, Abram. 'A Common Lawyer Looks at International Law', *Harvard Law Review*, 78, No. 7, May 1965.

DE VISSCHER, Charles. 'Coutume et traité en droit international public', *Revue générale de droit international public*, 3, Paris, 1955.

DOLLOT, René. 'Le droit international des espaces polaires', in *Recueil de l'Académie de Droit International*, 75, 1949 II.

ENGEL, Salo. 'Les clauses de révision dans les traités multilateraux internationaux de l'après guerre', *Revue de droit international et de législation comparée*, 1939.

FAWCETT, J. E. S. 'The International Monetary Fund and International Law', *British Year Book of International Law*, 40, 1964.

FITZMAURICE, Sir Gerald. *British Year Book of International Law*, 30, 1953.

GUGGENHEIM, Paul. 'Duguit et le Droit International Publique', in *Revue Juridique et Economique du Sud Ouest*, Série Juridique, No. 34, 1959.

HAMMARSKJÖLD, Åke. 'Les immunités des personnes investées de fonctions internationales', *Recueil des Cours de l'Académie de Droit International*, 56, 1936 II.

JENKS, C. Wilfred. 'Co-ordination: A New Problem of International Organisation', *Recueil des Cours de l'Académie de Droit International*, 77, 1950 II.

'The Conflict of Law-Making Treaties', *British Year Book of International Law*, 30, 1953.

'The Constitutional Capacity of the International Labour Organisation to Undertake Operational Tasks and Sponsor Executive Agreements between Governments: Memorandum by the Legal Adviser of the International Labour Office (Jenks)', *Official Bulletin of the International Labour Office*, XXXI, No. 3, 31 December 1948.

'Co-ordination in International Organisation: An Introductory Survey', *British Year Book of International Law*, 28, 1951.

'Fischer Williams: The Practitioner as Reformer', 40 *British Year Book of International Law*, 1964.

'The Future Development of the Constitution and Constitutional Practice of the International Labour Organisation: Memorandum by the Legal Adviser of the International Labour Office (Jenks)', *Official Bulletin of the International Labour Office*, XXVII, No. 2, 10 December 1945.

'Hersch Lauterpacht – The Scholar as Prophet', *British Year Book of International Law*, 1960.

'Les Instruments Internationaux à Caractère Collectif', *Recueil des Cours de l'Académie de Droit International*, 69, 1939 III.

'The Legal Personality of International Organisations', in *British Year Book of International Law*, 22, 1945.

'Liability for Ultra-Hazardous Activities in International Law' in *Recueil des Cours de l'Académie de Droit International*, 117, 1966 I.

'The Need for an International Legislative Drafting Bureau', *American Journal of International Law*, 39, 1945.

'The New Science and the Law of Nations' in *International and Comparative Law Quarterly*, Vol. 17, Part 2, April 1968.

'Some Constitutional Problems of International Organisations', *British Year Book of International Law*, 22, 1945.

'Some Legal Problems of the Financing of International Institutions', *Transactions of the Grotius Society*, 28, 1942.

'Some Problems of an International Civil Service', *Public Administration Review*, Vol. III, No. 2, Spring 1943.

JESSUP, Philip C. 'Parliamentary Diplomacy: An Examination of the Legal Quality of the Rules of Procedure of Organs of the United Nations', *Recueil des Cours de l'Académie de Droit International*, Vol. 89, 1956 I.

JOHNSON, D. H. N. 'The Conclusions of International Conferences', in *British Year Book of International Law*, 35, 1959.

'The Effect of Resolutions of the General Assembly of the United Nations', *British Year Book of International Law*, 32, 1955–1956.

Kansas Law Review, 13, 1965.

KELSEN, H. 'Théorie du droit international, coutumier', *Revue internationale de la théorie du droit*, vols. 1–3, 1939.

KOPELMANAS, Lazare. 'Custom as a Means of the Creation of International Law', *British Year Book of International Law*, 1937.

KOSTERS, Jan. 'Les fondements du droit des gens', 4 *Bibliotheca Visseriana*, Leyden, 1925.

KUNZ, Josef J. 'The Nature of Custom in International Law', 47 *American Journal of International Law*, 1953.

LACHS, Manfred. 'Space Law', *Recueil de l'Académie de Droit International*, 113, 1964 III.

LAUTERPACHT, Sir Hersch. 'Codification and Development of International Law', in *American Journal of International Law*, 49, No. 1, January 1955.

'Decisions of Municipal Courts as a Source of International Law', 10, *British Year Book of International Law*, 1929.

'The Grotian Tradition in International Law', in 23 *British Year Book of International Law*, 1946.

MACGIBBON, Ian O. 'Customary International Law and Acquiesence', *British Year Book of International Law*, 1957.

MCNAIR, Lord. 'The Functions and Differing Legal Character of Treaties', 11 *British Year Book of International Law*, 1930, reprinted in *The Law of Treaties*, Oxford, Clarendon Press 1961.

'International Legislation', *Iowa Law Review*, 19, No. 2, 1934, reprinted in *The Law of Treaties*, Oxford, Clarendon Press 1961.

MEADE, James. 'A Plea for Flexible Exchange Rates', *The Guardian*, 3 January 1961.

MOUTON, M. W. 'The International Regime of the Polar Regions', *Recueil des Cours de l'Académie de Droit International*, 107, 1962 II.

PEP. 'The Parliament of the European Communities', *Planning*, XXX, No. 478, 9 March 1964.

PINTO, Roger. 'Les règles du droit international concernant la guerre civile' in *Recueil des Cours de l'Académie de Droit International*, 114, 1965 (I).

POLITIS, Nicolas. 'L'influence de la doctrine de Léon Duguit sur le développement du droit international' in *Archives de philosophie de droit et de philosophie juridique* t. II, 1932.

RIPERT, Georges. 'Les règles du droit civil applicables aux rapports internationaux', *Recueil des Cours de l'Académie de Droit International*, 44, 1933.

ROSENNE, Shabtai. 'United Nations Treaty Practice', *Recueil des Cours de l'Académie de Droit International*, 86, 1954 III.

RUSK, Dean. 'The Control of Force in International Relations', *The Department of State Bulletin*, LII, No. 1350, 1965.

SABA, Hanna. 'L'Activité Quasi-Legislative des Institutions Spécialisées des Nations Unis' in *Recueil des Cours de l'Académie de Droit International*, Vol. 113, 1964 I.

SCELLE, Georges. 'La doctrine de Léon Duguit et le fondement du droit des gens' in *Archives de philosophie et droit et de philosophie juridique* II, 1932.

SCHNYDER, F. 'Les aspects juridiques actuels du problème des réfugiés', *Recueil des Cours de l'Académie de Droit International*, 114, 1965.

SCHACHTER, Oscar. 'The Relation of Law, Politics and Action in the United Nations', *Recueil des Cours de l'Académie de Droit International*, Leiden, 1963 (I).

'The Quasi-Juridical Role of the Security Council and the General Assembly', *American Journal of International Law*, 58, No. 4, October 1964.

SLOANE, F. Blaine. 'The Binding Force of a "Recommendation" of the General Assembly of the United Nations', 25 *British Year Book of International Law*, 1948.

TAMMES, A. I. R. 'Decisions of International Organs as a Source of International Law', *Recueil des Cours de l'Académie de Droit International*, 94, 1958 II.

VALLAT, F. A. 'The Competence of the United Nations' General Assembly', *Recueil des Cours de l'Académie de Droit International*, 97, 1959 II.

VALTICOS, N. 'Un Systeme de Controle Internationale: La Mise en Oeuvre des Conventions Internationales du Travail', *Recueil des Cours de l'Académie de Droit International*, Vol. 123, 1968.

von VERDROSS, Alfred. 'Les principes généraux du droit dans la jurisprudence internationale', *Recueil des Cours de l'Académie de Droit International*, 52, 1935, II.

WOLF, Francis. 'L'Interdependence des Conventions Internationales du Travail' in *Recueil des Cours de l'Académie de Droit International*, Vol. 121, 1967 II.

Index

Acheson–Lilienthal–Baruch Plan, 1946, 11
Acton, Lord, 227
Adarkar, B. P., 252
African Development Bank, 71
agriculture, 82–4
Alabama Arbitration, 1872, 153
Algeçiras Conference on Morocco, 1905, 214
Allen, Sir Carleton (C. K.), 129, 138
Alliance for Progress, 57
Alvarez, Alejandro, 243
American War of Independence, 32
Amerisinghe, C. F., 118
Amundsen, Roald, 93
Antarctic Treaty, 1 December 1959, 90, 101–2, 103, 112, 114, 167
Anzilotti, Judge Dionisio, 132
Arab Common Market, 84
arbitrary force, immorality of, 294–5
Arctic Treaty, an, 101–2
Aristotle, 57, 129
armament, 32–6
Asamoah, Obed Y., 201, 204, 205
Asher, Robert E., 234
Asian Development Bank, 71
Assembly of the League of Nations. *See* League of Nations
Assyria, 7
Astronauts, agreement on rescue and return, 19 December 1967, 96
Asylum Case, 286
Auboin, Roger, 59
Aufricht, Hans, 59
Austin, John, 125, 126, 131

Bank for International Settlements, 59, 61, 256
Barker, Ernest, 129
Barnet, Richard J., 35
Basdevant, Jules, 142–3
Basdevant, Suzanne (Mme Bastid) 249
Beard, Charles A., 276
Bebr, Gerhard, 66, 242
Bechhoefer, B. G., 34
Becker, Carl L., 103
Beckett, Sir Eric, 263
Bedjaoui, Mohammed, 249
Benelux Assembly, 215
Bentham, Jeremy, 272
Berlin Conference on Africa 1884–1885, 214
Berlin Congress, 1878, 214
Black, Eugene R., 75
Black Book of the Admiralty, 79
Blackstone, William, 138
Blix, Hans, 168
Blomfield, Lincoln P., 35
Bloustein, Edward J., 93
Bluntschli, Johann Caspar, 162
Boczek, Boleslaw Adam, 80
Bodin, Jean, 131
Borchard, Edwin, 70, 85
Bowen, Catherine Drinker, 21
Bowett, D. W., 29, 36, 99
Bracton, Henry de, 132
Brandeis, Louis D., 21, 66, 271
Braun, Werner, von, 96
Bretton Woods, 59
Brierly, J. L., 15, 125, 131, 132, 162, 174
Briggs, Herbert, 163
Broches, Aaron, 71, 197
Brownlie, Ian, 28
Bryce, James, 125, 132, 135, 137
Burke, William T., 99, 141
Burnet, Sir Macfarlane, 112
Bury, J. B., 9
business practices, restrictive, 68–70

Cairns, Huntington, 279

Callières, 296
Campbell, Alan, 70
Cardozo, Benjamin, 19, 95, 271, 279, 280, 284, 285
Caribbean Free Trade Association, 65, 85
Carson, Rachel, 104
Castel, J. G., 117
Castrén, Erik, 31
Casto, Josué de, 82
Central African Economic and Customs Union, 65, 85
Central American Common Market, 65, 85
Central American Court of Justice, 149
Centre of the Earth Treaty, a, 102–3
Certain Expenses of the United Nations Case, 37, 233, 252, 254
Chailley, Pierre, 168
Chamberlain, Neil W., 36
Chaput, Roland Aimée, 34
Charter of the United Nations. *See* United Nations
Chaumont, Charles, 95
Chayes, Abram, 19
Cheng, Bin, 149, 194
China, People's Republic of, 194
Christol, Carl Q., 95
civil liberties, 47–52
Clark, Grenville, 217
Cobbett, Pitt, 140
Codding, G. A., Jr., 93, 195
codification, 162–5, 207–8
Cohen, Felix, 287
Cohen, Morris Raphael, 25
Coke, Lord, 21, 51, 132, 138, 271
collective security, 39–42
Colombos, C. John, 79, 99, 195
commodity policy, 67–8
Commonwealth Parliamentary Association, 215
Conan, A. R., 62
concept of law, 124–30
Concert of Europe, 214
Conditions of Admission of a State to Membership in the United Case, 222
Congo Basin Treaties, 9
Congress of Vienna, 1815, 214
Connally Amendment, 157–8
consensus,
  possible contribution to international legislative procedure, 205–11
  as element in processes of community decision, 247–8
Consolato del Mare, 79
Constantinides-Megret, C., 66
Convention on the Continental Shelf, 163
Convention on Discrimination in Education, 190
Convention on Fishing and Conservation of Living Resources of the High Seas, 163
Convention for Protection of Cultural Property in Event of Armed Conflict, 190
Conventions and Protocols on Nationality Questions, 164
Convention on Regulation of Aerial Navigation, 1919, 193
Convention on Settlement of Investment Disputes between States and Nationals of Other States, 74–5
Convention on Territorial Sea and the Contiguous Zone, 163
Corbett, Percy E., 17, 185
Corwin, Edward S., 168
Council of Europe, 45, 46
  Committee of Ministers, 45, 214
  Consultative Assembly, 214, 215
Council of the League of Nations. *See* League of Nations
Covenant of the League of Nations. *See* League of Nations
Convention on the Privileges and Immunities of the Specialised Agencies, 260, 261, 263
Convention on the Privileges and Immunities of the United Nations, 260
Cowen, D. V., 133
Crandall, Samuel B., 168
creative effort, goals of, 26–119
creative scholarship and the law, 268–300
creative spirit, 22–4

Creighton, Mandell, 277
crusades, 299
Curzon, George N., 200
custom, 137–48
  collective, 144
  continued vitality of, 138–9
  formation of, 139–41
  proof of, 146–7
  role of General Assembly in formation of, 146
  Soviet view of, 141–3
  specialised custom, 144–5
  spontaneous custom, 143–4
Customs Union Case, 132
cybernetics, 108–11

Darwin, Charles, 274
De Visscher, Charles, 15, 140, 142–3, 259, 274, 279
De Visscher, Paul, 168
Declaration on Elimination of Discrimination against Women, 204
Declaration on Elimination of All Forms of Racial Discrimination, 204
Declaration on Elimination of all Forms of Religious Intolerance, 204
Declaration of General Principles dedicating Science and Technology to the Service of Man, a, 114, 115–16
Declaration on Granting of Independence to Colonial Countries and Peoples, 204
Declaration on Permanent Sovereignty over Natural Wealth and Resources, 204
Declaration of Legal Principles Governing the Activities of States in the Exploration and Use of Outer Space, 13 December 1963, 11, 96, 115, 116, 146, 204, 210
Declaration of the Presidents of America of Intention to establish a Latin American Common Market, 14 April 1967, . . . 85
Declaration on Prohibition of the Use of Nuclear and Thermo-Nuclear Weapons, 204
Declaration of Punta del Este, 57
Declaration on the Right of Asylum, 204
Declaration on Rights of the Child, 204
Dehousse, Fernand, 168
De Lima v *Bidwell*, 209
Detter, Ingrid, 177, 178, 186, 195
  development aid, 75–8
Devlin, Lord (Patrick), 291
Dicey, A. V., 125, 131, 135
Dickinson, Edwin D., 15, 139
dignity of man, 43–57
disarmament, 33–6
Disarmament Negotiations, Joint Statement of Agreed Principles for, 20 September 1961, 34
disarmament organisation. *See* International Disarmament Organisation
disputes, settlement of, 42, 156–62
Dollot, René, 101
Domke, Martin, 66
Draft Convention on Protection of Foreign Property, 73–4
due process and orderly procedure, 244–7
Duguit, Léon, 125, 131, 280

East African Common Market, 65, 85
East African Community, 65, 85
East India Company, 32
Economic Community of Eastern Africa, 65
Economic Community of West Africa, 65
  Articles of Association for the Establishment of, 4 May 1967, 85
Economic and Social Council of the United Nations. *See* United Nations
economic stability and growth, 58–91
Edwards, R. W., 104
Effect of Awards of Compensation Made by the United Nations Administrative Tribunal Case, 232, 286
Egypt, 7

Ehrlich, Eugen, 274
Eide, Asbjörn, 53, 54, 189
Einstein, Albert, 274
electronics, 108–11
Engel, Salo, 178
environmental changes, 103–4
equity, 153–5
escalation, 30
Eshag, Eprime, 62
Eurocontrol, 112–13
European Atomic Energy Community (Euratom), 95, 214, 256
  Commission, 214
  Treaty, 256
  See also European Communities
European Charter of Social Rights, 45–6
European Civil Aviation Conference, Standard Clauses (Strasbourg Standard Clauses), 194
European Coal and Steel Community (E.C.S.C.), 70, 256
  High Authority, 214
  See also European Communities
European Commission of Human Rights, 45, 46, 49
European Communities, 65, 70, 214, 256
  Court of Justice, 159, 242
  Parliamentary Assembly, 214
European Company for Chemical Processing of Irradiated Fuels, 113
European Convention for Protection of Human Rights and Fundamental Freedoms, 45, 46, 49
European Court of Human Rights, 45, 46, 242
European Economic Commission, 214
European Economic Community (E.E.C.), 70, 84, 85, 256
  European Economic Commission, 214
  European Investment Bank, 71
  See also European Communities
European Free Trade Association (E.F.T.A.), 65, 85
European Launcher Development Organisation, 113
European Molecular Biology Laboratory, 113
European Nuclear Energy Agency, 95
European Organisation for Nuclear Research (C.E.R.N.), 111, 113
European Space Research Organisation, 113
Evans, A. H. M., 194

fair play, 296–7
Falk, Richard A., 15–16, 20, 31, 35
Fawcett, J. E. S., 59, 196
Feller, A. H., 230
Feuer, G., 78
Field, David Dudley, 161
Fifoot, C. H. S., 21
Fiore, Pasquale, 162
First World War, 87, 143, 176
Fischer Williams, Sir John, 15, 27, 117, 125–6, 132, 140, 174, 290
Fitzmaurice, Sir Gerald, 149, 157
Food and Agriculture Organisation (FAO), 189–90, 234
  Conference, 190
  Constitution, 82–3, 189–90, 250
  Council, 190
food production and distribution, 82–4
force, threat or use of, 28–9
Fortescue, Sir John, 132
Fox, Hazel, 245
France, 223
Frank, Jerome, 287
freedom of the mind, 54–6
freedom, political, 46–7
French Foreign Legion, 32
Freud, Sigmund, 274
Freund, Ernst, 272
Friedmann, Wolfgang, 16, 68, 70, 72, 204
Frye, W. R., 36
Fulbright, Senator J. William, 76
Fuller, Lon, 292
fullness of opportunity, 56–7
Fulton, T. W., 98

Garner, J. W., 33
General Agreement on Tariffs and Trade (GATT), 59, 62–4, 66, 67, 69, 90, 167, 200, 234

General Assembly of the United Nations. *See* United Nations
general principles of law, 148–53
General Treaty for Central American Economic Integration, 85
General Treaty for the Renunciation of War, 1928, 27, 44, 167
Geneva Convention on High Seas, 29 April 1958, 80, 105, 163, 208
Gentili, Alberico, 139, 272
Gentlemen's Agreement of 1907–1908 between the United States and Japan, 84
Gény, François, 130, 280
Ghiselin, Brewster, 283
Gianni, G., 140
Gidel, G., 99
Gihl, Torsten, 180
Gill, Crispin, 106
Ginestet, Pierre, 214
Ginsberg, Morris, 128, 129
Gladstone, William Ewart, 9
Global Commercial Communications Satellite System, 96, 111, 112
Gold, Joseph, 59, 61
good faith, 296
Goodhart, A. L., 137, 144
Goodman, G. T., 104
Goodrich, Leland M., 27, 234
Gotlieb, Allan, 34
Grain and Chemical Products Agreements, 200
Great Britain, 34, 266
Greater East Asia Co-Prosperity Sphere, 7
Greenspan, Morris, 33
Griswold, A. Whitney, 84
Griswold v *State of Connecticut*, 89
Grotius, Hugo, 17, 18, 99, 124–5, 272, 275
Guggenheim, Paul, 125, 140, 143
Gurvitch, Georges, 280
Gutenberg, B., 102

Habeas Corpus Act, 1679, 51
Hackworth, Green Haywood, 117, 145
Hague Codification Conference, 1930, 162
Hague Conventions on Peaceful Settlement of International Disputes, 1899 and 1907, 164, 245
Hague Peace Conference, 1899, 33, 164, 215
Haley, Andrew G., 95
Hall, William Edward, 14–15
Hallam, Henry, 51
Hambidge, Gove, 83
Hambro, Edvard, 27
Hammarskjöld, Åke, 259
Hammarskjöld, Dag, 236, 250–1
Hamilton, Alexander, 262, 271
Hapsburg Empire, 7
Hardy, M., 118
Harrod, R. F., 60, 62
Hart, Herbert L. A., 126, 291, 293, 298
Harvard Research in International Law, 162
Havana Charter for an International Trade Organization, 1948, 69, 203
Hawkins, C. H., 62
Hazeltine, H. D., 216
Hegel, G. W. F., 131
Heidelberg, Franz C., 214
Henkin, Louis, 16, 35
Hexner, Ervin, 69
Higgins, A. Pearce, 33
Higgins, Rosalyn, 19, 200, 222, 230
Hill, Martin, 59, 258
Hinsley, F. H., 17, 131
Hiroshima, 10
Hitler, Adolf, 294
Hobbes, Thomas, 131
Hobson, Arthur, 82
Hoffman, Paul G., 258
Hohfeld, Wesley Newcomb, 282
Holborn, Louise W., 86
Holland, T. E., 13, 138
Holloway, Kaye, 168, 177
Holmes, Mr. Justice, 134, 227, 271, 273, 280, 283, 285, 287, 299
Horie, Shigeo, 59
Horowitz Plan, 77
Hovey, J. Allen, Jr., 215
Hoyt, Edwin C., 178
Huber, Max, 15, 133, 279, 293
Hudson, Manley O., 15, 142, 176

Hudson Bay Company, 209
Human dignity, 43–57, 298–9
Human rights, 43–57
Human Rights, a High Commissioner of, 52
Human Rights Committee, 48–9
Hurst, Sir Cecil, 116, 162, 259

Ihering, Rudolf von, 130, 280
Ilbert, Courtenay, 272
implied powers, 231–33
industrial development, 79
Institute of International Law, 52, 81, 105
Insular Cases, the, 1900, 209
insurance, 81–2
Inter-American Development Bank, 71
Inter-Governmental Maritime Consultative Organisation (IMCO), 194–5, 234
  Assembly, 194–5
  Convention of 1948, 80
  Council, 195
  International Code of Signals (revised), 195
  Maritime Safety Committee, 195
internal war, 30
International Atomic Energy Agency (IAEA), 95, 196, 198–200, 234, 256
  Basic Safety Standards for Radiation Protection, 94, 199
  Board of Governors, 199
  Convention on Civil Liability for Nuclear Damage, 95
  Convention on Liability of Operators of Nuclear Ships, 95
  Draft Convention concerning Disposal of Radioactive Waste into the Sea, 105
  Regulations for Safe Transport of Radioactive Material, 199
  Statute, 94, 198–9, 256
International Bank for Reconstruction and Development. *See* World Bank
International Centre for Settlement of Investment Disputes, 74
International Civil Aviation Conference, Chicago, 1944, International Civil Aviation Convention, 112, 193–4
International Civil Aviation Organization (ICAO), 93, 192–4, 234
  Assembly, 194
  Council, 193
International Code of Signals, 195
International Commission for Air Navigation, 193
International Convention for the Prevention of the Pollution of the Sea by Oil, 12 May 1956, 105
International Convention for the Protection of Industrial Property, 1958, 261
International Court of Habeas Corpus, an, 50
International Court of Justice
  application of general principles of law, 149–53
  and *Certain Expenses of a United Nations Case*, 254
  Re *Conditions of Admission of a State to Membership of the United Nations Case*, 222
  and custom, 146–8
  duty to apply law, 123
  and flags of convenience States, 80
  jurisdiction, 160
  opinions of, in *Reparation for Injuries Suffered in the Service of the United Nations* and *Certain Expenses of the United Nations* cases, 37, 260
  and precedent, 286
  and principle of implied powers, 231–3
  procedure, 245
  and regional courts, 242
  and *South-West Africa Cases*, 159
  and sovereignty, 135–6
  and the sovereign State, 17
  and a world writ of Habeas Corpus, 50
  Rules of Court, 160, 245
  Statute, 149, 152, 154, 160, 167, 201, 202, 245
  See also Permanent Court of International Justice

International Development Association, 71, 76–7, 198, 234
International Disarmament Organisation, an, 34
International Finance Corporation, 71, 198, 234
International Institute of Agriculture, 82
international jurisprudence, ultimate values of, 299–300
International Labour Organisation (ILO)
as executing agency of UN, 54, 234
Constitution and Procedure, 53, 57, 90–1, 167, 186–9, 227–30, 257–8
conventions on agricultural labour, 83
Declaration of Philadelphia, 1944, 57, 58
Director-General of International Labour Office, 187, 188, 228, 251
Fact-Finding and Conciliation Commission on Freedom of Association, 228–9
financial procedure 257–8
Governing Body of International Labour Office, 188, 228–9, 257–8
Governing Body Committee on Freedom of Association, 229
International Labour Conference, 184, 186–9, 257
international status and immunities, 259, 261–2
Manual of Industrial Radiation Protection, 94
Migration for Employment Convention (Revised), 1949, 85–6
population policies, 89
Radiation Protection Convention, 1960, 94
International Law Association, 27, 81, 105
International Law Commission of the United Nations. *See* United Nations
international legislation, 166, 218
International Legislative Drafting Bureau, an, 184–5
International Meteorological Organization, 196
International Military Tribunals at Nuremburg and Tokyo,
Charters, 29, 291
See also Nuremburg Judgment
International Monetary Fund, 59, 60–2, 196–7, 234, 250, 256
Articles of Agreement, 59, 61, 62, 64, 77, 90, 167, 196
Board of Governors, 196
Executive Directors, 196
General Arrangements to Borrow, 5 January 1962, 60, 197
International Plant Protection Convention, 190
international public policy, 155–6
International Regulations for Preventing Collisions at Sea, 195
International Sanitary Convention, 1926, 191
International Sanitary Convention for Aerial Navigation, 1933, 191
International Sanitary Regulations, 1951, 191–2
International Telecommunication Convention, 112, 195
International Telecommunication Union (ITU), 92–3, 97, 192, 195–6, 234, 256
International Trade Law Commission. *See* United Nations
interparliamentary approach, the, 214–17
interparliamentary assemblies, 214–16
Inter-Parliamentary Union, 215
Interpretation of the Treaty of Lausanne Case, 223
intuition and public policy, 284–5
investment, 70–5
Islam, 298

Jacobson, Harold Karan, 33
James, A., 36
Jefferson, 245
Jenkes, 51
Jenks, Edward, 51
Jennings, R. Y., 118
Jessup, Philip C., 15, 19, 23, 92, 95, 98, 99, 101, 245
Johnson, D. H. N., 204, 205

Joint Institute for Nuclear Research, Moscow, 113
Jolowicz, H. F., 287
Judicial process, 156–62
Justinian, 297

Kahn-Freund, Otto, 152
Kahn, Herman, 31
Kalmanoff, George, 72
Kaplan, Morton A., 15
Katzenbach, Nicolas de B., 15
Kazantzakis, Nikos, 21
Kelsen, Hans, 15, 27, 125, 129, 132, 135, 139, 140, 273
Kennan, George, 17
Kennedy, W. P. M., 209
Kennedy Round, 63
Kerr, M. R. E., 194
Keynes, John Maynard, 60, 276
Kiss, Alexandre-Charles, 117, 145
know-how, 78–9
Koestler, Arthur, 274
Kopelmanas, Lazare, 140
Korea, 36
Korovin, E. A., 35
Kosters, Jan, 140
Kotschnig, Walter M., 234
Krabbe, 132
Kranenburg, J. L., 215
Kunz, Josef, J., 140
Kutner, Luis, 50

Lachs, Manfred, 95
Ladas, Stephen P., 78
Laffan, R. G. D., 216
Laing, Lionel H., 117
Lambert, J. M., 104
Landy, E. A., 189
de Lapradelle, A. de G., 125
Lapsley, G., 216
Larson, Arthur, 18, 35, 56, 132
Lasswell, Harold, 6, 95, 108, 110, 167
Latin American Common Market, 65, 85
Latin American Free Trade Association, 65, 85
Lauterpacht, Eli, 117
Lauterpacht, Sir Hersch, 13, 15, 33, 42, 44, 117, 118, 125, 140, 148–9, 154, 163, 176, 289
Laves, Walter H. C., 55
law,
  concept of, 124–30
  general principles of, 148–53
  in motion, 123–267
  and institutional development, 265–67
  and other studies, 273–81
law of treaties, 168–75
  agreements with subjects of international law other than States, 171
  amendment and modification of treaties, 173
  conclusion of treaties, 172–3
  invalidity, termination and suspension of the operation of treaties, 173–4
  invalidity of treaties procured by the threat or use of force, 169
  jus cogens, 169–70
  reservations, 173
  treaties adopted within international organisations, 171–2
  treaties and other rules of international law, 170
law-making treaties, 175–86
  concept and development of, 175–6
  defective technique of, 176–9
  modification of, 181–4
  termination of, 179–81
League of Nations
  allegiance of officials, 249–50
  Assembly, 250, 252
  attitude to restrictive business practices, 68–9
  budget and funds, 252–3, 255
  Council, 223
  Covenant, 8, 27, 28, 40, 203, 225, 258–9
  financial organisation, 58–9
  legal status and immunity, 258–9
  modus vivendi with Switzerland, 259
  protection of refugees, 86
  report on nutrition, 82
  World Economic Conference, 1927, 68

League of Nations Codification Conference, 1930, 164
Lee, Luke T., 118
legal régime of world services, 258–64
legal scholarship, challenge to, 13–20
legislation as a creative force, 166–8
Leibniz, Gottfried Wilhelm, 217
Lenormand, Sergei, 104
liberties, civil, 47–52
Lincoln, Abraham, 226
Linde, Hans A., 35
Lindsay, Kenneth, 214, 215
Littleton, Sir Thomas, 138
living law, 123–4
Llewellyn, Karl N., 287
Lloyd, Dennis, 126
Løchan, Einar, 215
Locke, 131
logic and experience, 282–4
London Conference on the Balkans, 1912–1913, 214
London Conference on Belgium, 1830–1832 and 1838–1839, 214
Long-Term Cotton Textiles Arrangement, 200
Lorimer, James, 166, 217
Lowes, John Livingston, 271
Luard, Evan, 47, 53, 189, 229, 246
Lycurgus, 88

McCulloch v *Maryland*, 231
Macdonald, R. A. J., 101
Macdonald, Robert W., 65
McDougal, Myres, S., xi, 15, 95, 99, 126, 141, 167, 275
Macgibbon, Ian O., 140
McIlwain, Charles Howard, 226
McIver, R. M., 13
Mackenzie King, prime minister, 259
Mackenzie, Norman A. M., 117
McNair, Arnold (Lord), 15, 40, 117, 119, 144, 168, 174, 175–6, 177, 194
McWhinney, Edward, 16
Machiavelli, Niccolo, 291
Madariaga, Salvador de, 34, 294
Mahalkov, A., 102
Maine, Sir Henry, 131, 148, 166, 272
Maitland, F. W., 14, 125, 130, 216, 271, 272
Malthus, Robert, 88
Mann, F. A., 118
Manning, C. A. W., 117
Mansfield, Lord, 21, 271
Marlowe, Christopher, 219
Marshall, Chief Justice, 227, 231, 262, 271
Martin, Andrew, 34
Martin, Thomas Owen, 134
Marx, Daniel, Jr., 80
Marxism, 295
Mason, Edward S., 76
Mateesco, Nicolas, 140
May, Erskine, 245
Meade, J. E., 60
Meijers, H., 80
Mellanby, Kenneth, 104
Mercenaries, 31–2
Merillat, H. C. L., 185
migration, 84–7
Miller, David Hunter, 27
Miller, James C., 167
Mills, C. Wright, 280
mind control, 111–12
molecular biology, 111–12
Monaco, Riccardo, 81
monetary policy, 58–62
Monnet, Jean, 19
Moore, John Bassett, 33, 117, 118, 145
Morrison, Emily, 108
Morrison, Philip, 108
Moscow Treaty, 5 August 1963. *See* Nuclear Test Ban Treaty
Mouton, M. W., 101
Muhammad, V. A. Seyid, 62
mutability, 287–90
mutual aid, 64

Nansen, Fridtjof, 93
Napoleon I, 294
Naurois, Louis de, 168
Neumann, Franz, 277
Newman, Ralph, 291
Newton, Isaac, 274–5
Nicholas, Calvin J., 252
Nicolas II, His Imperial Majesty, Tsar of All the Russias, 33

Noel-Baker, Philip J., 34
noise, 106–8
non-alignment, 39–42
Nordic Council, 215
  Assembly, 215
Norgaad, Carl Aage, 177
North Atlantic Treaty Organisation (NATO), 36, 215
  Parliamentarians' Conference, 215
Nottingham, Lord, 51, 271
nuclear energy, 93–5
Nuclear Test Ban Treaty, 33, 90, 93–4, 103, 167, 172
Nuremburg judgment, 56, 153

ocean depths, 98–101
ocean depths treaty, an, 100
O'Connell, D. P., 117, 118
Oppenheim, L. F., 93, 125, 175, 260
opportunity, fullness of, 56–7
Ordwaz, Frederick I, III, 96
Organisation of African Unity, 32, 46
Organization of American States, 57
  Charter, 57
Organization for Economic Co-operation and Development (OECD), 59, 73–4, 95
  Development Assistance Committee, 76, 90
orthodoxy and vision, 271–2
Ottoman Empire 7

parliament of man, 166–218
Parry, Clive, 117, 145
Partial Nuclear Test Ban Treaty. *See* Nuclear Test Ban Treaty
Pascal, Blaise, 277
Pasquet, D., 216
Patterson, Edwin W., 92
peace,
  with justice, 27–42
  sinews of, 251–8
peace and security fund, a, 258
Peace of Westphalia, 9
peacekeeping forces, 36–9
Peary, Robert, 93
Penn, William, 217
Permanent Court of Arbitration, 149
Permanent Court of International Justice, 58, 83, 144, 149, 223, 227, 232, 252
  Statute, 142, 149
  See also International Court of Justice
Pescatore, Pierre, 66
Phillimore, Lord, 142, 260
Piggott, F. T., 98
Pinto, Roger, 31
Plato, 14, 57, 88, 129
Phelan, E. J., 251
Politis, Nicolas, 15, 125, 132, 298
polar regions, 101–2
political freedom, 46–7
Pollak, Louis, xi
Pollock, Sir Frederick, 27, 125, 131, 137, 138, 143–4, 297
pollution, 104–6
pollution treaty, a world, 106
Pope Paul VI, 300
population, 87–90
Portugal, 237
Pound, Roscoe, 22, 50, 118, 124, 126, 274, 280
precedent and inventiveness, 285–6
public policy, 284–5
  international, 155–6
public service of mankind, 249–51
Pufendorf, Samuel, 139

Qual, Lino di, 201

Radin, Max, 72–3
Rajan, M. S., 135, 230
Read, John, 259
reason and morality, 291–9
refugees, 84–7
Regulus, 296
Reiff, Henry, 99
Renner, Karl, 276
Reparation for Injuries Suffered in the Service of the United Nations Case, 37, 231, 232, 260
restrictive business practices, 68–70
Rhodian Sea Law, 79
Ripert, Georges, 149
Robertson, A. H., 46, 215, 242
Robertson, Norman A., 259
Rolin, Henri, 15
Röling, B. V. A., 16

Rolls of Oleron, 79
Roosa, Robert V., 60
Roosevelt, Franklin D., 7
Root, Elihu, 142
Roper, Albert, 193
Rosenau, James N., 31
Rosenne, Shabtai, 177, 245
Rosner, Gabriella, 36
Ross, Alf, 129, 137, 139
Rostow, Eugene V., xi, 25, 276
Rostow, W. W., 82
Rousseau, Jean-Jacques, 131
Roux, J. M., 80
Rouyer-Hameray, Bernard, 233
Roxburgh, Ronald F., 177
Rowat, Donald C., 51
Rowe, J. W. F., 67, 68
Rubin, Seymour J., 76
Rupert's Land, 209
rural development, 82–4
Rusk, Dean, 18, 88, 236

Saba, Hanna, 190
St. Paul, 299
Salter, Lord (Sir Arthur), 68, 69
Salmon, Jean, 71
Sankey, Lord Chancellor, 283–4
San Francisco Conference, 1945, 224–5, 240, 249–50
Sawyer, Geoffrey, 129–30, 280
Scammell, W. M., 59
Scelle, Georges, 15, 125, 174, 279
Schachter, Oscar, 16, 78, 212
Schenkman, Jacob, 93, 194
Schnyder, F., 86
Schou, August, 53, 54, 189
Schweitzer, Pierre-Paul, 61
Schwelb, Egon, 204
science in the service of man, 113–19
science and technological progress, 92–119
Science Treaty, a World, 116
Scott, James Brown, 33
Scott, Robert F., 93
Second World War, 9, 10, 15, 71, 152–3, 176, 252
Secretary-General of the United Nations. *See* United Nations
Security Council of the United Nations. *See* United Nations
self-defence, 29–30
settlement of disputes, 42, 156–62
Seyersted, Finn, 36
Shanghai Municipal Council, 36
Shelley, Percy Bysshe, 287
Sherman Act, 1890, 68
shipping, 79–81
Shklar, Judith, 17
Shirras, G. F., 252
Shotwell, James T., 27
Sidgwick, Henry, 131–2, 135
Simpson, J. L., 245
Simpson, Sir John Hope, 86
sinews of peace, 251–8
Singer, J. David, 252
Singh, Nagendra, 33, 80, 221
Skelton, O. D., 259
Sloane, F. Blaine, 201
Slusser, Robert M., 168
Smedal, Gustav, 101
Smith, H. A., 17, 99
social justice, 53–4
Socrates, 14
Sohn, Louis, 217
sonic boom, 106–8
Soper, Tony, 106
Sørensen, Max, 140, 143
South Africa, 237, 245
South West Africa Cases, 159
sovereignty, 130–7, 295
  erosion of concept, 131–3
Spaak, Paul-Henri, 231
space, 95–8
Space Treaty. *See* Treaty on Principles Governing the Activities of States in the Exploration and Use of Outer Space, including the Moon and Other Celestial Bodies
Spiropoulos, Jean, 149
Stalinism, 294
Stamp, L. D., 104
Stein, Eric, 33
Stewart, Michael, 300
Stoessinger, John G., 252, 254, 255, 256
Stone, Julius, 17, 28
Stowell, Lord, 271
Story, J., 272
Streit, Clarence K., 217

Suez Canal Clearance Surcharge Scheme, 256
Sully, Duc de, 217
Switzerland, 259
Szulc, Tad, 106

Tammes, A. I. R., 201
Tarracouzio, T. A., 101
Taubenfeld, Howard J., 95, 98, 101
Tawney, R. H., 276
Temperley, A. C., 34
third-party judgment, 295–6
Thomas, Albert, 251
Thomas, W. J., 104
Thompson, Dennis, 70
Thomson, Charles A., 55
threat or use of force, 28–9
  prohibition of, 28–9
Thring, Lord, 272
Timberg, Sigmund, 68
Tobin, Harold J., 178
trade, 62–7
Trail Smelter Award, 105
travel, 84–7
Treaty for East African Co-operation, 6 June 1967, 85
Treaties, law of. *See* Law of treaties
Treaties, law-making. *See* Law-making treaties
Treaty on Non-Proliferation of Nuclear Weapons, 94
Treaty on Principles Governing the Activities of States in the Exploration and Use of Outer Space, including the Moon and Other Celestial Bodies, 27 January 1967,
  general provisions, 96–7, 112, 115
  nuclear weapons, 94
  principle of international interest, 11, 96
  procedure of conclusion, 172
Treaty for Prohibition of Nuclear Weapons in Latin America, 94
Triepel, H., 175
Triffin, Robert, 60
Triska, Jan F., 168
Tucker, Robert W., 33, 125
Tunis-Morocco Nationality Decrees Case, 144
Tunkin, Grigori, 142–3

Ulpian, 138, 297
Uncertainty,
  in the law of nations, 288–90
  in the new jurisprudence, 287–8
Union of Soviet Socialist Republics (USSR), 7, 34, 94, 97, 102, 194, 217, 229
United Kingdom, 216
United Nations,
  Administrative Committee on Co-ordination (ACC), 239
  agencies, 202
  as world organisation, 135–6, 222–6
  Charter, 8, 9, 10, 17, 27–9
    interpretation and consensus, 206–8, 230–1
    principles and purposes
      economic and social, 10, 43, 90–1 299
      independent service, 249–51
      legal, 17
      maintenance of peace, 40–2, 43
      prohibition of force, 27–9, 153, 169, 207, 294
    provisions and procedure
      articles, 201–2, 203
      immunity, 260–4
      membership, 221–6
      peacekeeping forces, 37
      use of regional arrangements, 239–44
  civil liberties, 47–52
  commodity policy, 67–8
  constitutional development, 230
  disarmament negotiations, 34–5
  Economic and Social Council, 48, 52, 54, 69, 239
    Commission on Human Rights, 50, 204–5, 263
  financial arrangements, 253–8
  General Assembly
    Advisory Committee on Administrative and Budgetary Questions, 239
    and custom, 146–8
    and sovereignty, 135

U.N. General Assembly—*cont.*
covenants, 44, 47
legislative potentialities, 200–11
agencies established by, 202–3
declarations, 203–5
legislation by Consensus, 205–11
recommendations, 203
resolutions, 201–2
population programme, 89
proposal of habeas corpus, 50
resolution on ocean depths, 100
See also Space Declaration, Space Treaty, United Nations: constitutional development, financial arrangements, immunity, implied powers
international trade, 64–6
International Trade Law Commission, 66
Joint Inspection Unit, 239
Joint Panel of External Auditors, 239
legislative action, 185–6
measures of enforcement, 161, 264–5
military operations, 36–42, 264
peacekeeping forces, 36–9
nuclear energy, 93–5
refugees, 86–7
Regional Economic Commissions, 234
restrictive business practices, 68–9
Secretariat, 232
Secretary-General, 37, 87, 211, 212, 230, 232, 239, 250
Secretary-General's Regulations, 37
Security Council
legislative potentialities, 211–14
threat to peace, 211–13,
disputes, 213–14
See also United Nations: Charter: membership use of regional arrangements; constitutional development, military operations
space law, 96–7, 209–10
Staff Regulations, 202
structure, 234–9
technical co-operation projects, 78–9
Uniting for Peace Resolution, 1950, 230
United Nations Committee on Human Rights, 50, 204
United Nations Committee on Racial Discrimination, 50
United Nations Conferences on the Law of the Sea, 80, 99, 163, 164
United Nations Conference on the Law of Treaties, 168, 169–75
Draft Articles on the Law of Treaties, 169–75
United Nations Conference on Trade and Development (UNCTAD), 10, 64–5, 66, 77, 90, 203, 234
United Nations Congo Force, 39, 254
United Nations Convention on the Law of Treaties, 175, 179–84
United Nations Convention on Racial Discrimination, 50
United Nations Convention on the Status of Refugees, 25 July 1951, 87
United Nations Covenant on Civil and Political Rights, 8–9, 44–50, 55, 84, 207
See also United Nations Covenants on Human Rights
United Nations Covenant on Economic and Social Rights, 8–9, 44–50, 53–4, 55, 207
See also United Nations Covenants on Human Rights
United Nations Covenants on Human Rights, 44–50, 57, 90, 167, 207
See also United Nations Covenant on Civil and Political Rights *and* United Nations Covenant on Economic, and Social Rights.
United Nations Cyprus Force, 36, 39
United Nations Declaration on Territorial Asylum, 14 December 1967, 86
United Nations Development Programme (UNDP), 78, 202, 234
resident representatives, 239

United Nations Educational, Scientific and Cultural Organization (UNESCO), 55, 89, 190, 234
  Conference, 190
  Constitution, 55, 189–90
United Nations Emergency Force for the Middle East, 37, 254
United Nations High Commissioner for Refugees, 86, 234
United Nations Industrial Development Organisation (UNIDO), 79, 90, 203, 234
United Nations International Children's Emergency Fund (UNICEF), 89, 234
United Nations Model Rules of Arbitral Procedure, 245, 246
United Nations Monetary and Financial Conference, Bretton Woods, 1944, 59
United Nations Ombudsman, a, 51–2
United Nations Operational and Executive Personnel Scheme (OPEX), 78–9
United Nations Population Trust Fund, 89
United Nations Special Fund, 202, 258
United States of America, 102, 209, 288
  Constitution, 17, 136, 231
  See also International Labour Organisation, Space Treaty, United Nations: disarmament negotiations, population programme, restrictive business practices
unity of mankind, the, 293
universal community, the. *See* world community
Universal Copyright Convention, 55, 190, 261
Universal Declaration of Human Rights, 8, 9, 44–9, 53, 55, 57, 87, 90, 167, 204, 207
Universal Postal Convention, 195
Universal Postal Union (UPU), 192, 195–6, 234, 256
  Universal Postal Congress, 195
universal and regional action, 239–44

Vallat, Sir Francis, 201
Valticos, N., 189
van der Post, Laurens, 277
Vanderpol, A., 27
van Vollenhoven, Cornelius, 15
Vattel, E. de, 56, 125
Vecchio, Giorgio del, 129, 134, 137
Velas, Pierre, 83
Vernant, Jacques, 86
Verne, Jules, 93
Vienna Conferences on Diplomatic and Consular Relations, 163
Vienna Convention on Consular Relations, 1963, 163, 164
Vienna Convention on Diplomatic Relations, 1961, 163, 164
Vienna Convention on the Law of Treaties, 163
Vinogradoff, Paul, 130, 138
Vittoria, Francisco de, 9, 272
Vlasic, Ivan A., 95
von Verdross, Alfred, 143, 149

Walker, Patrick Gordon, 215
Wambaugh, Sarah, 47
Watts, A. D., 40
wealth and welfare, 90–1
Webster, Sir Charles, 214
Wehberg, Hans, 15
Weizberg, Guenther, 260
Wells, H. G., 93
Western European Union Assembly, 215
Westlake, John, 27, 93, 218, 272
West Rand Central Gold Mining Co. v *The King*, 142
Wheare, K. C., 252
Whiteman, Marjorie, 117, 145
Whitton, John B., 56
Wiener, Norbert, 108, 109–10
Wilberforce, 9
Wilcox, Clair, 62, 69
Wilcox, Francis O., 176
Wild, Payson S., 178
Wilson, Woodrow, 7
Wimbledon Case, 286
Wolf, Francis, 189
Wolfke, Karol, 141

Woodbridge, George, 86
World Bank, 71, 74–5, 76, 77, 196, 234, 250, 256
  Articles of Agreement, 167, 197
  Bond Regulations, 198
  Loan and Guarantee Agreements, 198
  Loan Regulations, 197–8
World Bank Group, 90, 196, 197–8
world community,
  architecture of, 219–67
  effectiveness of decisions, 264–5
  implied powers of, 231–3
  as organism, 226–31
  processes of decision, 247–9
  universal, 221–6
World Health Organisation (WHO), 89, 190–2, 234
  Constitution, 190–2
Director-General, 191
  International Sanitary Regulations, 1951, 191–2
  Nomenclature Regulations, 1948, and Supplementary Regulations, 1949, 191
  Regulations, 198
  World Health Assembly, 190–2
World Leaders' Declaration on Population, 11 December 1967, 87–8
World Meteorological Organisation (WMO), 97, 195–6, 234
  Congress, 196
  Constitution, 196
  Convention, 196
  world political morality, basic elements of, 292–9
World Pollution Treaty, a, 106
World Science Treaty, a, 116
Wright, Sir Michael, 35
Wright, Quincy, 27
Wyzanski, Charles E., Jr., 24, 124

York–Antwerp Rules of General Average, 198
Younger, Kenneth, 134